CHRISTIAN ETHICS
AND CONTEMPORARY PHILOSOPHY

CHRISTIAN ETHICS AND CONTEMPORARY PHILOSOPHY

edited by

IAN T. RAMSEY

SCM PRESS LTD
BLOOMSBURY STREET LONDON

334 00180 3

First published 1966
by SCM Press Ltd
56 Bloomsbury Street London
Second impression 1973

© SCM Press Ltd 1966

Printed in Great Britain by
Redwood Press Limited
Trowbridge, Wiltshire

CONTENTS

Acknowledgments   7

Editor's Introduction   9

I INTRODUCTORY

1 GODS, BLISS AND MORALITY by Ninian Smart   15
2 GOD AND MORALITY by Graeme de Graaff   31

II MORALITY AND RELIGION

3 AN EMPIRICIST'S VIEW OF THE NATURE OF RELIGIOUS
   BELIEF by R. B. Braithwaite   53
4 DISCUSSION
   1. by J. N. Schofield   74
   2. by D. M. Mackinnon   77
   3. by Ian T. Ramsey   84
   4. by R. B. Braithwaite   88

III DUTY AND GOD'S WILL

5 MORALITY: RELIGIOUS AND SECULAR by P. H. Nowell-
   Smith   95
6 DISCUSSION
   1. by A. Boyce Gibson   113
   2. by J. R. Lucas   126
7 GOD AND OUGHT by Dewi Z. Phillips   133
8 SOME REMARKS ON THE INDEPENDENCE OF MORALITY
   FROM RELIGION by Kai Nielsen   140
9 MORAL JUDGMENTS AND GOD'S COMMANDS by Ian T.
   Ramsey   152
10 THE VOICE OF CONSCIENCE AND THE VOICE OF GOD by
   H. D. Lewis   172

IV MORAL DECISIONS:
THE PLACE OF IDEALS AND PRINCIPLES,
AUTHORITY AND REASON

11 VISION AND CHOICE IN MORALITY
    1. by R. W. Hepburn   181
    2. by Iris Murdoch   195
12 MORAL CHOICE AND DIVINE AUTHORITY by Helen
    Oppenheimer   219
13 MORAL PRINCIPLES by I. M. Crombie   234
14 MORAL DILEMMAS by John Lemmon   262
15 SOCIAL MORALITY AND INDIVIDUAL IDEAL by P. F.
    Strawson   280
16 MORALITY AND THE TWO WORLDS CONCEPT by R. F.
    Holland   299
17 THE CHRISTIAN CONCEPT OF LOVE by Dewi Z. Phillips   314
18 SITUATIONAL ETHICS by George Woods   329

V TOWARDS A CHRISTIAN MORALITY

19 THE FAMILY IN CONTEMPORARY SOCIETY from an
    Anglican Report   340
20 TOWARDS A REHABILITATION OF NATURAL LAW by Ian
    T. Ramsey   382

Index   397

ACKNOWLEDGMENTS

Chapter 1 First published in the *Proceedings* of the Aristotelian Society, vol. lviii (1957–58) and reproduced by courtesy of its Editor.

Chapter 3 First delivered in Oxford as the Eddington Memorial Lecture for 1955, and reproduced by courtesy of the publishers, the Syndics of the Cambridge University Press, and the Eddington Trustees.

Chapter 4 Reproduced from the *Cambridge Review* (issues of 18 and 25 February, 3 and 10 March 1956) by courtesy of its Editor.

Chapter 5 First published in the *Rationalist Annual* (1961) and reproduced by courtesy of the Rationalist Press Association.

Chapter 6 (1) First published in the *Journal of Theological Studies* (1962) and reproduced by courtesy of its Editors.

Chapter 8 First published in *Mind* (1961) and reproduced by courtesy of its Editor.

Chapter 11 First published in the *Proceedings* of the Aristotelian Society, supplementary vol. for 1956, and reproduced by courtesy of its Editor.

Chapter 14 First published in the *Philosophical Review* (1962) and reproduced by courtesy of its Editor.

Chapter 15 First published in *Philosophy* (1961) and reproduced by courtesy of its Editor.

Chapter 16 First published in the *Proceedings* of the Aristotelian Society, vol. lvi (1955–56), and reproduced by courtesy of its Editor.

Chapter 19 Extracts from a report to the Archbishop of Canterbury before the Lambeth Conference of 1958. Reproduced by courtesy of the publishers, SPCK.

All other material is original.

*10. H. D. Lewis is Professor of the History and Philosophy of Religion, King's College, London.

11. R. W. Hepburn is Professor of Philosophy in the University of Edinburgh and Iris Murdoch, the novelist, was formerly a Lecturer in Philosophy in the University of Oxford. Their discussion was first published in the supplementary vol. for 1956 of the *Proceedings* of the Aristotelian Society.

*12. Lady Oppenheimer, a graduate of Lady Margaret Hall, Oxford, is author of *Law and Love, The Character of Christian Morality* and various articles in philosophical journals.

*13. I. M. Crombie is a Fellow of Wadham College and a Lecturer in Philosophy in the University of Oxford.

14. John Lemmon, formerly a Fellow of Trinity College, Oxford, is now a Professor at the Graduate School of Philosophy, Claremont College, California. His chapter was first published in the *Philosophical Review* (1962), and is reproduced by courtesy of its Editor.

15. P. F. Strawson is a Fellow of University College and a Lecturer in Philosophy in the University of Oxford. His chapter was first published in *Philosophy* (1961), and is reproduced by courtesy of its Editor.

16. Roy Holland is a Lecturer in Philosophy in the University College of South Wales, Swansea. His chapter was first published in the *Proceedings* of the Aristotelian Society, vol. lvi (1955-56).

*17. Dewi Z. Phillips.

*18. George Woods is Professor of Divinity in the University of London.

19. *The Family in Contemporary Society* was a report to the Archbishop of Canterbury before the Lambeth Conference of 1958 by a Commission of which the Chairman was Dr M. A. C. Warren and the Secretary was the Rev. G. R. Dunstan. Extracts are reproduced by courtesy of the publishers, the Society for Promoting Christian Knowledge.

*20. The Editor's concluding paper was prepared for a group of which he is Chairman, called together by the Joint Board of Studies, whose parent Boards are the Church Assembly's Boards of Education and of Social Responsibility.

Chapters 1, 10, 11 and 16 from the *Proceedings* of the Aristotelian Society are reprinted by permission of their Editor.

The Editor acknowledges with gratitude the great help he received from the SCM Press, and from the Rev. Michael King in particular, in the preparation of this book, and its index.

EDITOR'S INTRODUCTION

WHEN the deists of the eighteenth century, such as John Toland[1] and Matthew Tindal,[2] were challenging the Christian faith with what in its own day was a much too restricted empiricism and a much too rigid notion of reasonableness, apologists like William Law[3] and Joseph Butler[4] were concerned to broaden men's views alike of experience as of reason. Butler in particular tried to show how attention to morality helps us to understand the point of religious claims and assertions, and probably his most valuable work was to draw out a logical kinship between religious assent and moral conviction by using moral situations to illuminate religious ones.

It is interesting to see a certain parallelism in our own day. The broadening and mellowing which has come to empiricism, so that the arctic breezes of thirty years ago are now largely a memory, first showed itself in relation to the language of morals, and it might well be claimed that it has been because of the patient, thorough and sympathetic analysis of this language, of which Mr R. M. Hare's work provides an outstanding example, that logical empiricism now breathes a much richer air. Certainly the work done in this field has helped to disperse the earlier stifling atmosphere.

The example of Butler, who hoped to take his age from a narrower empiricism by concentrating on the significance of morality, believing that in such a wider empiricism not only could religion but even Christianity be defended, has been somewhat followed in our own day by Professor R. B. Braithwaite, whose Eddington lecture is reprinted in this volume and is followed by a brief discussion of this attempt to assimilate religion and morality. It is interesting to notice that the criticism, often levelled, whatever the justification, against Butler, that such an assimilation does less than justice to distinctively religious claims, is repeated against Braithwaite.

[1] 1670-1722. His *Christianity not Mysterious* was published in 1696.

[2] 1657-1733. His *Christianity as Old as the Creation, or the Gospel a Republication of the Religion of Nature* was published in 1730.

[3] 1686-1761. *A Serious Call to a Devout and Holy Life* (1728) has been spoken of as a 'forceful exhortation to embrace the Christian life in its moral and ascetical fullness'. Cf. also his *Case of Reason* (1732) directed in particular against Tindal.

[4] 1692-1752. Most famous of course for his *Analogy of Religion* (1736) and the sermons he preached in the Rolls Chapel.

A*

But there the parallel ends, even if it was satisfactory before. For it seems to many nowadays that any distinctive association of morality with religion will be disastrous not so much for religion as for morality. Here is a new turn in religious controversy. Far from religion claiming, as in the eighteenth century, to afford new sanction for old duties, far from religion being the acknowledged basis of all true morality, there are many amongst us, and they number amongst them believers as well as unbelievers, who find insuperable, and from a practical point of view disastrous, difficulties in the traditional underpinning of morality by religion.

It is at this point that I may perhaps best refer to the two introductory essays. In the first, Professor Ninian Smart in effect warns us against taking too simple a view of the relation between the moral and religious strands of discourse, showing us the kind of diversity this relation has displayed. He warns us in particular that we must be alert to the complex logic of theological language. We must be on our guard against reading it at its face value. It is a warning that will be reiterated more than once throughout the book. The different ways in which morality and religion have been related is also the theme of the second introductory essay by Mr Graeme de Graaff. Besides this, the essay in a most useful way pegs out a broad area for discussion and points to some practical implications as well. In doing this, it brings us closer to some of the crucial problems with which the book is concerned. Chief amongst these crucial problems, and the one which not surprisingly Mr Graeme de Graaff puts first, is the problem of relating Duty to the Will of God, moral obligation to religious belief. Many people, as we know, would speak of doing their duty because it is God's will, and of religion in this way providing a basis for morality.

Professor Nowell-Smith, whose article from the *Rationalist Annual* opens our third section, is amongst those who, from many different points of view, are critical of such a theologically based morality. Even someone as sympathetic to Christian claims as Mr R. M. Hare has remarked, in his first series of Wilde lectures at Oxford,[5] that 'once people realize that they can have a rational morality without the orthodox God, and cannot have one with him, one of his chief props—indeed, perhaps, his only surviving prop that had any strength—will have disappeared. And it is this situation for which Christians ought to be preparing.'

Again, we may recall that a Christian like Professor Maclagan,

[5] At present unpublished.

whose views are discussed in a later chapter, has written: [6] 'What of those to whom religion as they understand it, and as it is so often presented to them, makes no appeal, and for whom, as for all of us, the self-restraint required by any conception of a moral standard is irksome? Is it sufficiently recognized that the formula "no morality without religion", proclaimed though it is with the design of bringing them to religion, may instead have the effect of divorcing them from morality, seeming to license and encourage them, in view of their unbelief, to abandon all serious moral concern? No doubt some self-deception would also have to be at work; but then it is at work all the time. Men were self-deceivers ever. The danger of the formula is that it makes easier this all too welcome self-deception.' So his own view is that 'what is needed is a continuing conviction of morality's independence of religion save in the sense in which religion is just the fully moral attitude itself'.[7]

It is with the problem of a theologically-based morality that the third section of the book is concerned; and besides a discussion of Professor Nowell-Smith's article from various standpoints, there are also some independent contributions relevant to the general theme.

My colleague, Mr Richard Robinson, who has some hard things to say about religion in a recent book *An Atheist's Values*,[8] remarks that 'great harm is done to morality by its authoritarian connexions, by the notion that the parson is the depository of it, by the habit of turning to the parson when the question is what is morally right. The average parson is a worse judge of right and wrong than the average layman, and that is simply because he takes his moral laws on authority.'[9] Mr Robinson's main criticism of religion as he pictures it is that 'it is a fundamental rejection of the ideas of truth and reason'.[10] Mr Robinson also believes that 'the truly moral world is essentially anarchical in that to be a really moral agent a man must judge and choose for himself'.[11]

It is perhaps therefore specially topical that the next section of this book is concerned with problems which cluster around the topics of moral authority and the character of reasoning in ethics, on the status of moral principles, and the sense in which a person is characteristically involved in decision-making.

The papers all stress the diversity of what are commonly called 'moral situations', and show *inter alia* that these are far from being

[6] *The Theological Frontier of Ethics*, Allen and Unwin, and Macmillan, New York, 1961, p. 186. See ch. 9, esp. pp. 152–6.
[7] *Op. cit.*, p. 188.   [8] O.U.P. 1964.   [9] *Op. cit.*, p. 133.
[10] *Ibid.*, p. 130.   [11] *Ibid.*, p. 133.

uniformly homogeneous and 'rule determined'. We see the kind of
personal involvement which a moral decision demands, yet how
there can arise 'good' and 'bad' 'objective reasons' for making that
decision. The papers also help us to see better the character of moral
disagreements, and what is implied in men possessing different
moral 'standpoints'; and they also remind us that morality is not
only of individual but also of social significance. The papers in this
section provide us with a discussion which is all the more challenging for the differences they reveal here and there, and the later
papers, in providing examples of philosophizing about moral problems which arise in religious or quasi-religious contexts, raise what
for some traditional ethical discussions are novel difficulties.

In this way the fourth section prepares us for a final section whose
topics are slanted in the direction of Christian ethics. For Christian
ethics at the present time displays a turmoil of its own. Not only, as
we have seen, are the most diverse people critical on philosophical
grounds of underpinning morality by theology; many would despair
about Christian ethics anyway. What are we to make of an appeal to
Bible and Church in the light of biblical and historical scholarship?
Can Christian ethics resolve the tensions it tries to embrace between
'fixity and freedom', 'law and love', 'authority and experience'?—
to use expressions which form the chapter headings of Dr John
Robinson's *Christian Morals Today*.[12] The present book of essays
does not set out to examine these specifically Christian questions in
any sort of theological detail: its main concern is with problems
that arise principally in a philosophical context. But it is concerned
with issues which lie behind the present bewilderment in Christian
morality. In a recent speech in the Church Assembly[13] the Bishop
of Exeter, Dr R. C. Mortimer, complaining about the present position, criticized at least the Church of England for what he considered to be 'its neglect of, and even contempt for, moral theology
during the last two or three hundred years'. He continued: 'The
great work of the schoolmen in reformulating the concept of the
natural law as they found it in Aristotle, and the making of it a
basis and a support for the New Testament revealed ethic, has been
far too long ignored in Anglican circles. The result is that we have
almost nobody within the ranks of Anglican theologians who is able
to set out clearly and forcibly the concept of the natural law upon
which, in fact, both Gospel ethics and ordinary sexual morality rest.
What is urgently needed throughout the whole of Christendom is a

12 SCM Press 1964.   13 4th July, 1963.

reformulation in modern terms of the concept of natural law, taking into full account the assured conclusions of modern psychology.'

But what is left nowadays of the concept of Natural Law? Has it not been altogether eroded by developments in anthropology, psychology and philosophy? Will it ever be possible again to have a theory of morality which links both natural law theory and Christian ethics? Can the Bishop's hopes in principle be fulfilled?

There are questions faced in the last section of the book, which also includes an extract (slightly rearranged) from *The Family in Contemporary Society* which was a report prepared by a group of scholars convened at the behest of the Archbishop of Canterbury in relation to the Lambeth Conference of 1958. The extract is concerned with the problems and possibilities of theological reasoning about social problems, and includes a concrete example of the different ways in which, faced with a specific problem like contraception, even Anglicans with all their diversity, and in the present turmoil, can reason not unhelpfully about its morality. What becomes quite evident however—and it has a plain bearing on the earlier discussions in the book—is that Christian morality is no morality of rules, no morality of mere obedience to commands.

The contributors to this volume include unbelievers, agnostics and Christians, and amongst the Christians there is a typical diversity. If the reader shares Mr Robinson's view of parsons, and is inclined to take as one of his moral rules 'Never go to church to learn how to behave unless the sermon is preached by a layman',[14] he may be further encouraged to know that of the Christians the laymen heavily outnumber the parsons. Not that the book in any event is a collection of sermons. It is rather a dialogue in which Christians have attempted to take up points and problems which must be faced sympathetically, patiently and honestly if there is to be a Christian morality which deserves both the noun and the adjective. How far the attempt is successful the reader must judge for himself, but it is hoped that at any rate he will be encouraged to continue the dialogue—on either side. Meanwhile, I hope the book will at least be evidence that Christians are concerned both with the moral challenge of the present situation, and with reasoning reliably about it.

[14] *Op. cit.*, p. 133.

I · INTRODUCTORY

I

GODS, BLISS AND MORALITY

Ninian Smart

I WISH here to review rather generally the relations between religious and moral discourse. At first sight, such an enterprise might seem odd or objectionable on a number of counts. First, some might think that there is no real distinction between the two; for is not such a commandment as 'Love thy neighbour as thyself' an integral part of spiritual discourse? Yet it is at least doubtful whether any moral principles or rules are entailed by specifically religious doctrines, except trivially (e.g., where we have 'God's Will is . . .' and 'One ought to conform to God's Will': therefore 'One ought to . . .'). One does not require religious insight to see that lying or stealing is wrong; or, to put it a little more formally, one can justify such pronouncements without asserting anything which refers to a religious entity, etc. It is therefore convenient to make a rough distinction between specifically religious utterances and those which are specifically moral: thus 'God created the world' would fall into the former class, 'Adultery is wrong' into the latter. Perhaps, however, it will be questioned whether there is any clearly discernible field of discourse to be described as 'moral language'. For though moral philosophers have traditionally addressed themselves to such problems as the justification of social rules and the nature of (so-called) moral judgment, it is by no means clear which practical affairs are to count as falling under the aegis of morality and which judgments about people are to count as 'moral'. Is to commend someone as gay to make a moral pronouncement? And while most folk would say that the Wolfenden report is about morals, what pigeon-hole would a report on pensions fit into? Nevertheless, though it is unclear what the limits of morality are, and though

within the area there is great variegation in kinds of assertion, a
rough indication of the sort of discourse which we can call moral is
possible: those assertions, etc., which concern the dispositions and
conduct to be cultivated by individuals so that their and their
neighbours' lives will benefit or at least not avoidably suffer—these
would hold a pretty central place in this sphere of language. Next,
some may complain on the other side: 'It is foolish to talk about
religious language—there is Christian, there is Buddhist, there is
Hindu—very different sorts.' True; and it is grossly mistaken for
philosophers (as they have so frequently done) to pretend to discuss
something called 'religion' when they have merely been speaking
about Christianity or Judaism.[1] Nevertheless, there is at least a
family resemblance between religions, and phenomenologists of
religion have not been utterly frustrated in their attempts to adduce
similarities: thus one does not always have to speak with incurable
particularity. And though in this paper I shall confine attention
largely to examples drawn from Western religions, some of the
remarks will have a wider relevance. Finally—and this is the most
powerful objection to my project: since both fields display much
subtlety and variety, it would seem shockingly crude, in so short a
space, to try to characterize the relations between the two. But I
think that it does no harm to try to present a rather general picture,
which can function as a kind of plan if one wishes to deal with
individual and knotty problems in this area. Thus the intention of
this paper is to provide certain preliminaries to the investigation in
more detail of problems (e.g., those clustering about *grace* and
analogous concepts) which arise on the boundary between ethics
and the philosophy of religion. As such, I wish to give something
like a *description* of the relation between religious and moral concepts: I shall not therefore be indulging in philosophical *arguments*. These, perhaps, come later.

My task requires the exposition of certain points about religion
which I shall have to state somewhat dogmatically. To this I now
proceed.

A

A striking aspect of spiritual discourse is its variegation. However
hard it may be to translate into a foreign tongue common words for

---

[1] A possible reply: Philosophers do not base their enlightened comments (on the nature
of scientific explanation, etc.) upon discredited theories, though they may use these as a
warning; why should not the philosopher similarly concentrate on examining the true
religion? But criteria of truth here are so misty that it is presumptuous to pay exclusive
attention to one faith.

colours, shapes, objects, feelings, etc., the difficulty is small in comparison with that which besets attempts to give the meaning of key expressions occurring in the discourse of an alien faith. This is mainly because each religion has a doctrinal system—or *scheme*, a word I prefer because it is less rigour-suggesting—and the propositions thereof have, so to speak, a mutual effect, such that not merely does one have to understand a proposition by reference to its neighbours, but the comprehension of a key expression requires the exposition of a number of central propositions at least. But further, even within a faith, the language is far from homogeneous. For example, in Christianity certain assertions are made about a Creator God who is, so to say, beyond or behind the visible world; while others concern a divine human being who lived within the world. Again, some propositions in Buddhism concern *nirvāna*, which is neither God nor man nor both. Already, therefore, we have three types of doctrinal proposition: those dealing with invisible and mysterious objects of worship, those concerning incarnate deities and those which deal with a mystical path and goal. These types of propositions (and it is sufficient for our purposes here to consider these three varieties) I propose to call respectively the *numinous*, the *incarnation* and the *mystical* strands of spiritual discourse.[2] And some doctrinal schemes are woven together from different strands and so are in a special way complex. But further, not all propositions in a strand are of the same logical sort: e.g., those about *nirvāna* are sometimes expressions of its joys, sometimes recommendations on how to attain it, and so forth.

An illustration of the weaving together of strands into a complex doctrinal scheme is to be found in Brahmanism. Here two disparate concepts are identified: Brahman, the Sacred Power lying behind the visible world, and the Ātman or Self, lying within man and attainable through mystical endeavour. Again, in Christianity, Jesus, the sinless human Teacher, is identified with the Father in heaven. These points prompt such questions as: Why should the mystical goal and the object of worship be one? Why should a certain human be one with the Creator?

The first of these questions may be put in a sharper way by asking why the Christian mystic should consider his *nirvāna*-like state to be union with God while the agnostic Buddhist does not so speak?[3] An

---

[2] As in some cases and respects an incarnate deity is a limiting form of the saintly prophet, the range of propositions of this strand is wider than here indicated; but it is convenient to focus attention on the extreme cases.

[3] It is not just that each has been brought up in a certain doctrinal tradition, so that

account which covers both the similarity between some of the
things said by Buddhist and by Christian contemplatives and their
doctrinal differences is this: that there are certain loose resemblances between the mystical state and the object of worship—both
are timeless, glorious, transcendent, liberating and imperceptible.[4]
Again an incarnate deity may have likenesses to the Creator—he
has the power to save (by teaching and performatively through self-
sacrifice); is miracle-working (a sign of omnipotence); has deep
spiritual insight (a sign of omniscience); is good—and so forth. The
moral here is that the similarities justifying identifications in religion are looser than those criteria which would justify a mundane
claim that A and B are identical (consequently, while there may be
a case for asserting a given identity in religion, it is not absurd to
deny it). And, briefly, a complex doctrinal scheme has a certain
artistic composition, so to speak, which makes the disparate elements hang together.

This point is relevant to the way moral propositions are incorporated into the fabric of spiritual discourse. That is, moral discourse, in the context of religion, functions like one of the strands
of specifically religious discourse mentioned above. Thus (i) the
justification for integrating moral and religious discourse lies in a
somewhat loose agreement between certain moral concepts and
certain specifically religious ones, an agreement which I wish to
illustrate here; and (ii) the moral strand and the others have, as do
the latter reciprocally, an effect on each other: crudely, the moral
attitudes, etc., of the religious man differ in flavour from those of the
secular, while religion itself is moralized. It may be thought that the
first of these points is hardly relevant to a descriptive project such as
this; but it is often hard to penetrate to the meaning of an utterance
without considering the sort of backing it would have. Actually,
however, I shall be dealing not so much with the explicit justifica-
tions ordinary men might give for such claims as that morality in
some sense presupposes religious doctrine,[5] as with the reasons why

---

the Christian mystic for instance 'reads into' his experience Christian doctrines: there
appears to be an inner plausibility in the theistic account of these matters—though I
do not wish to imply by this that it is correct (nor by *this* that it is *incorrect*).

[4] These predicates are applicable in often peculiar and diverse senses: e.g., the mystical
attainment is timeless and banishes the fear of death, while God is immortal; it is transcendent because it is unworldly, while God is in another world, etc. A proper exposition
of these important and interesting points is, however, impossible here.

[5] These are often confused, and in any case may be formulated in language where the
integration of morality and religion is already taken for granted. Further, in some circles
only the ghost of an argument would be permitted—where there is fundamentalist appeal

the integration has such convincingness as it may possess; though it is not to be thought that the considerations I shall describe have no place in explicit religious arguments. (Unfortunately, religious language itself is .bedevilled in at least two ways: first, through having been mixed up with philosophical metaphysics; and secondly, because the logical status of religious concepts has been far from clear even to their employers—so that, for instance, certain spiritual doctrines have been inappropriately taken as straightforward empirical pronouncements.)

B

A central activity for one who is the adherent of a numinous faith is worship. For a God is by definition to be worshipped.[6] That is, the recognition of X as a God is a recognition that X is to be worshipped. An object of worship is holy and the adherent conversely unclean and sinful; and he expresses this profanity of his in awe-struck abasement, which is given ritual shape in formal worship. However, we discover that the notion of worship is considerably extended, so that the service of God in everyday life, through being virtuous and charitable, counts as a kind of worship. Thus it is written:

> Pure religion and undefiled before God and the Father is this, to visit the fatherless and widows in their affliction, and to keep himself unspotted from the world.[7]

And in a somewhat similar vein:

> Take my life, and let it be
> Consecrated, Lord, to Thee.
> Take my moments and my days,
> Let them flow in ceaseless praise.[8]

But this kind of worship can only count as such if there is worship in the primary sense (i.e., the religious ritual): otherwise we cannot know what it means to say that it is actions performed *in the right spirit* that count as worship, It may be objected that even if·we had lost the notion and institution of ritual worship, there might still be a use for the word 'worship'—as in, e.g., 'the worship of the State'.

---

to the authority of the scriptures, for example (and this is not quite like someone's being irrational in purely non-religious matters).

[6] Though there are queer cases: e.g., what are we to make of the attitude of Ivan in *The Brothers Karamazov*? or of devil worship?

[7] James 1.27.

[8] Hymn 512, *Church Hymnary*.

But the important example here is: suppose we still spoke of 'worshipping God', but all that would count as this would be visiting the fatherless, etc. It seems to me extremely doubtful whether we could understand this as a religious concept, nor could we easily comprehend the sense of the word 'God' as used here. It would doubtless have the same status as 'ether' in such locutions as 'The programme came over the ether'—a mere element in a stereotyped phrase: and so 'Visiting the fatherless is a way of worshipping God' would be equivalent in import to 'Visiting the fatherless is a way of doing good'. But it would hardly have the same sense as it would in a *serious* religious context.

But though the existence of formal worship would be a necessary condition for counting daily conduct seriously as a form of worship, it is hardly a sufficient one. What would make the extension of the concept plausible?

(i) In any case, the concept *worship* is extended within the sphere of the specifically religious, so that more than a public ritual performance counts as worship. Private devotions of a certain pattern—these count as a kind of worship: it being seen that the so-called 'external' performances without proper humility before God are useless, even though this humility is taught in part *through* the rituals. But further, in a monotheistic faith, God is given the most exalted value, is infinitely to be praised—so that it is insufficient to worship him on fixed occasions (more will be said below on this).

(ii) More vitally, humility is an important moral disposition, since the common tendency among humans towards pride is liable to issue in conflict and suffering, while conversely humility involves a comparatively high prizing of others and so brings greater interest in their welfare. Personal abasement, then, before the All-Holy fits in with the disposition of humility which is important in moral conduct. The solidarity between the two is enhanced in monotheistic faiths by the above-mentioned infinite praiseworthiness of God. His utter transcendence is expressed by saying: We never sufficiently praise him. But at least we can increase the quantity and intensity of our praise when daily actions performed in the right spirit count as worship. In speaking of 'quantity' and 'intensity' here I am formulating crudely two aspects of expressive speech. For in the non-expressive giving of plain information, for example, repetition only has a marginal use—to drum facts into the obtuse or hard of hearing, say; and intensity of manner and verbal expression has no obvious function here. On the other hand, in the expressing of gratitude, for instance, repetition and intensity do count for something: to repeat one's thanks is not otiose, and to say seriously and sincerely 'My *immense* gratitude' is to express more, *ceteris paribus*, than is done by 'My gratitude'. A further point: *sincerity* is what may be termed a 'pattern concept', for though it may be applied to particular actions (etc.), the criteria for its application spread over a much wider area; and to say that an action is sincere is to imply (roughly) that it fits consistently into a pattern of actions. Consequently, once the notion of worship is extended to cover daily actions performed in the right spirit, the idea of intensity in worship is affected: fervent praise will not be thought to be truly so if it fails to fit into a pattern of worshipful behaviour.

The performance of duties and services in a humble spirit can, then, be presented as a form of worship. By consequence, moral blemishes and inadequacies are to be regarded not merely as failings, but as sins. The latter notion is, indeed, incomplete without reference to some numinous entity. Thus the Psalmist can say:

> Wash me throughly from mine iniquity, and cleanse me from my sin. For I acknowledge my transgressions; and my sin is ever before me. Against thee, thee only, have I sinned.[9]

Sin, then, is here moralized, inasmuch as it is not merely the uncleanness of a profane creature before the All-Holy, but covers his moral wickedness (and this becomes a sort of uncleanness). Both *worship* and *sin* are thus given extended scope, beyond their specifically religious applications.

Another example of the way in which religious concepts (in the numinous strand) and moral ones exhibit a certain solidarity is as follows. Sacrifice is a religious ritual which is fairly closely linked, for a number of reasons, with worship. But, like other rituals, it can become mechanical and indelicate; so that, by way of protest, it is said:

> The sacrifices of God are a broken spirit.[10]

Here already there is a wide extension of the concept beyond its specifically religious use, leading to the notion that good conduct, or at least the dispositions leading thereto, are a kind of sacrifice. Now although sacrifices have often been offered to the gods in order to buy them off, much as one might give presents to the powerful to sweeten them, the deeper spiritual point of sacrifice is that it is a

[9] Psalm 51.   [10] Psalm 51.

gesture of expiation, and the object sacrificed a token. (In speaking of a deeper spiritual point, I am aware that herein lies a value-judgment, and there are many objections to using valuations when one is engaged on a descriptive task; but the deeper point mentioned does exist, and it is not entirely unphilosophical to be charitable in matters of interpretation.) Sacrifice is a gesture of expiation, for words alone are not sufficient to express properly man's abasement before the numinous and the sincerity of his worship. This idea of something's 'going beyond mere words' is interesting to investigate, and is connected with what was said above about repetition and intensity. For whereas it might well be deemed absurd to speak of some factual matter as inexpressible, as eluding description —since language defines, so to speak, the realm of the possible[11]— when we come to expressive (and some other) modes of speech, it is by no means suspect. For here the notion of something's being 'too much to express' has a use, for already we are in an area where quantitative expressions have (in a peculiar way) application. Nor, since here speech is often in a narrower sense a way of doing something, is it absurd to speak of non-linguistic performances as transcending speech. Thus a gesture, for instance, is a manner of transcending language when there is, say, a felt necessity to render a situation morally tolerable. If A saves the life of B's child, B can only make the situation tolerable by performing a gesture as a pledge of his continuing and overwhelming gratitude: for instance, he can invite A's children on a long summer holiday. But what counts as an appropriate gesture is governed by the most delicate rules—many such gestures seem gross and unfeeling, as with the rich man who repays kindnesses by gifts of money.[12] Hence indeed the Psalmist's protest. For though by giving up a prized possession —a ram or a bullock—one performs a gesture of expiation, it may not be a good one. But a broken spirit? How is this a sacrifice? What plausibility is there in holding that a moral disposition counts as an expiatory gesture?

Nothing is a sacrifice unless something is being given up; and

---

[11] Though: (a) certain things may be very hard to describe, e.g., a complicated piece of machinery; for the uninitiate it is too complex and unfamiliar to describe. This is contingent indescribability. (b) There may be 'facts' no one can describe, because science has not yet given us the conceptual framework.

[12] There are of course other uses of 'gesture' besides cases where the balance between two or more people is upset: e.g., the Hungarian who shakes his fist at a Soviet tank—a gesture of defiance (not, however, entirely unconnected in type from the unbalance cases). Also obviously, the behavioural sense. Incidentally, speech-transcending actions are clearly relevant to a discussion of religious ineffability.

holy conduct is a sort of giving up for the following reasons: (i) There are many occasions on which the performance of duty conflicts with self-interest. Indeed, if it were not so there would hardly be a practical use for the word 'duty' and its cousins—a point which is probably responsible for the idea that nothing counts as a duty *unless* it so conflicts. (Though also this idea is in line with the ascetic outlook of Puritanism: on asceticism, see below.) And failing to attain one's interests is a sort of loss, even if not always of the sort we call 'tangible'. (One might draw a distinction between tangible and intangible sacrifices: and compare visible and invisible exports—the latter need not be 'ex-' and cannot be ported, but it is still useful to have the word.) (ii) Ascetic training—the giving up of certain pleasures—is sometimes thought to conduce to virtue, inasmuch as dispositions are created which facilitate the correct decision in the event of a conflict of interest and duty. Although asceticism plays a more prominent spiritual role in mystical rather than numinous religion, it has a part to play in the latter, both as a way of atoning for sins and as a method of directing our thoughts and inclinations away from the world towards the things of God. (iii) Self-indulgence, it is often thought, leads to unhappiness, both first- and second-order, i.e., the unhappiness directly occasioned by indulgence and that which accrues upon recognition of one's own wickedness and weakness. In such ways, then, moral conduct aimed at the production of others' and one's own happiness is considered to involve some degree of giving up. Thus is the path open for an extension of the notion of sacrifice so that a man's life or stream of conduct can count as a holy and living sacrifice to the Lord. And so he can do something to expiate his sinfulness and moral unworthiness. (Note that even in the quotation with which we started, which might be used out of context to show that religion is simply or mainly a matter of doing good, there is the requirement not merely that we should visit the fatherless and widows but also that we should 'keep ourselves unspotted from the world'.)

I have given two instances of the superimposition of religious upon other concepts. The effects are often subtle and difficult briefly to explicate. But one point worth mentioning is that, though there is an independent application for the notion of happiness, the major goal of life is thought to be salvation. (Here, by the way, the conflation of morality and numinous religion results in disputes about faith versus works as being necessary or sufficient or both conditions for salvation.) Further, specifically religious duties remain, so to speak, at the centre of life; and in themselves constitute the chief difference in content between secular and religious morality. Often, by consequence, a believer's path will diverge widely from that of the non-believer—as when a man dies for his faith. Another effect is that since a supremely holy entity is regarded as being the source, in some way, of all that is holy, holy conduct has as its source God, who is held to grant grace to his devotees. And it is not just that God is supposed to have the power to release the worshipper from his religious uncleanness, but given that sin comprises moral un-worthiness as well, God can give him grace to do good and avoid evil. (And it is a good indication of the difficulties besetting analysis of this notion that grace is connected with a numinous object of worship, whose status, so to speak, is already obscure.) Two further points. (i) The superimposition of religious upon moral concepts as illustrated above gives the latter a different flavour: (*a*) because a moral action will have a double significance (not mere kindness, but consecrated kindness; not mere self-control, but a sacrifice, etc.); (*b*) because the solemnity of moral utterances becomes considerably increased: it is not merely that murder is wrong, but that life is *sacred*; a bad action is *sinful* and *impious*; discrimination against black folk in South Africa is not merely a great injustice, but it is (to quote a churchman's recent pronouncement) *blasphemy*; marriage is more than a fine institution, it is a *sacrament*. (ii) The presenta-tion of morality as part of numinous religion involves it in the con-servatism of the latter (which is due to two main factors: first, the inexcogitability of revelation means that the ordinary man is dis-couraged from formulating his own beliefs and so must take doc-trines on authority; and secondly, there are social causes for the entrenchment of religious organizations). Hence, although there are ways and means of reforming the moral teaching of a faith in accordance with scientific, technical and social changes, there is much greater difficulty here than where moral beliefs are thought not to have divine sanction.

Finally, two general remarks on the preceding. First, it might be objected that when one 'does all to the glory of God' one is perform-ing many actions which lie outside the area of morals—for instance, in doing one's daily work 'to the glory of God' one is not performing works of charity, etc. Are not discussions of humility and asceticism beside the point here? A brief answer: roughly, we tend to regard the spirit of what we do (of whatever sort this is) as falling within the purview of moral judgment and training. Thus, we praise a man for playing a game fairly and enthusiastically, and this is a kind of moral praise: though the rules of the game could not be thought to be *moral* rules, and success in the game is not thought to be, in normal circumstances, morally praiseworthy.[13] Second, the foregoing illustrations of the extension of religious concepts should not lead one to suppose that the performance of duties, etc., in the right spirit is simply to be justified as being religious acts. The good is not good because it is the Will of God, but because it is good. On the other hand, the good is not the Will of God just because it is good, but because it has divine qualities. Much of the structure of independent moral discourse remains, even though morality is integrated with religion; just as much of the characteristic language of mysticism remains even when it is woven into discourse about God.

C

Because of its convenience and familiarity I shall use the Christion doctrine of the Incarnation to illustrate briefly the relation which this sort of belief bears to morality. (i) The doctrine involves a deepening of the points already made about humility and sacrifice. For the teaching here is that only the self-sacrifice of God could be enough to expiate the enormous weight of sin upon mankind and to bring about atonement.[14] But God could only achieve this in a state of solidarity with mankind; hence the obstinate rejection by the Church of any form of docetism—it must insist on the humanity of Christ as well as on his divinity. This seeming paradox that Christ is both God and man[15] brings new light to the religious demand for humility. Christ himself seems to exhibit the most profound humility; and he is, because divine (and uniquely so among humans) the central model for imitation. We too must take up our Cross. (ii) The abasement and suffering of Christ is on behalf of mankind: our most luminous evidence that God is Love (a point foreshadowed in doctrines of grace; and one which finds some, though ambiguous, backing in the claim that God is Creator). Hence there accrues a

---

[13] As a commemorative plaque in the Wanderers Ground in Johannesburg has it: 'And when the one great Scorer comes to write against your name, He writes not how you won or lost, but how you played the game.'

[14] Christ is not a sacrifice the way a lamb might be or the way Isaac was intended, in that his death on the Cross was voluntary. He was not offered by others as a sacrifice, nor is God wicked in providing a human sacrifice.

[15] It is doubtful whether the God-manhood of Christ is a strict contradiction, e.g., Christ was for a time in Galilee while God is from eternity in Heaven, and Christ is God: does this constitute a contradiction? Only if Heaven and Galilee are both places in the same sense of 'place'.

tighter knitting together of the moral demand 'Love thy neighbour as thyself' and the spiritual one 'Love God'. (iii) As mentioned above, the belief that a human is divine, and uniquely so, implies that there is one supreme life to model our conduct on (models are one main method of inculcating moral insight). This, incidentally, has both an advantage and a defect: for while it harnesses the re- sources of worship and meditation to the task of self-improvement, a single main model is likely to be hard to apply to the varied circum- stances of many lives. Note also that the life to be imitated is a religious one (though the religion of Christ might be thought to differ in certain particulars from that expected of the ordinary ad- herent) and this serves to cement the moral and religious require- ments in the faith. (iv) The Teacher founded a Church, member- ship of which is thought necessary or conducive to salvation: this creates special loyalties and obligations for the faithful. These are given supernatural expression in such notions as 'fellowship in Christ'. (v) Finally, certain concepts concerning Christ are given application to individual lives. Thus:

> Like as Christ was raised up from the dead by the glory of the Father, so we also should walk in newness of life.[16]

Christ's resurrection, though claimed to be a physical fact, has a significance beyond the marvel of a man's rising from the dead. It is a demonstration that Christ has overcome death, though this is a peculiar sort of victory (and a peculiar sense of 'death'). For the victory is so described partly at least because Christ has saved mankind. But this saving is only hypothetical: if such-and-such conditions are fulfilled you will be saved (not: you are saved in any case). And one of the conditions is a change of heart: you must repent and believe. This conversion is a 'new birth'. What might at first glance appear a merely metaphorical use of a phrase can hardly be considered as such in view of the ramified nexus of analogical expressions connected with this one (the converted die unto sin; this also through grace, wherefore Christ is life—which is borne out, so it is said, in the spiritual life: for me to live is Christ).[17] Again:

> And they that are Christ's have crucified the flesh.[18]

[16] Romans 6.4.
[17] Unfortunately it is hard to see any dividing line between analogical uses of expres- sions in religion (i.e., non-literal but indispensable ones) and mere metaphors and alle- gories, etc. But one rough test is to consider how closely related a locution is to central doctrines. Some expressions in religious discourse are not, of course, non-literally used e.g., 'god'.
[18] Gal. 5.24.

The notion 'crucifixion of the flesh' is applicable to expiatory asceticism in virtue of the extension of the concept *sacrifice* as explicated above and of the history of the divine model's career.

In such ways, then, certain spiritual concepts prominently instantiated in Christ's life are applied also to individual lives.

Briefly, then, while the main point of Christ's career is his specifically religious role as Saviour of men, his words and conduct illustrate in a profound manner the way numinous religion and morality hang together.

D

Mysticism is usually or always associated with some degree of ascetic training. Through such endeavour (known variously as 'the Path', 'the Way', etc.) one attains a blissful goal (in this life). The purest form of this goal—inasmuch as there is no theistic complication of doctrine—is the Buddhist aim of *nirvāṇa*. This is given such epithets as 'The Other Shore', 'Peace', 'The Immortal', 'The Unshakeable', etc. For in gaining bliss we go beyond the impermanent and painful world, attain calm and detachment, lose the fear of death, etc. These epithets serve to indicate, perhaps, that there is (as claimed earlier) a pattern of loose resemblances between *nirvāṇa* and an object of worship; but it is not of course a God. It is this principally that makes agnostic Buddhism so unlike Christianity, Judaism and Islam—the faiths we have the greatest acquaintance with in the West. And even the traditional gods of Indian religion are assigned the status merely of somewhat remarkable items in the furniture of the impermanent universe. These facts account for the disinclination felt by some to calling Buddhism a religion. Nevertheless, the mystical quest occurs also in theistic faiths, and there are certain other resemblances we can point to; and so we are justified in giving it the title of a spiritual system. There are two aspects of agnostic Buddhism which I wish to draw attention to, since they throw light on two general points about mystical religion.

First: the *anicca* doctrine, that all things are impermanent, is a mild form of those idealistic doctrines commonly associated with mysticism in which the world is declared to be unreal or not fully real.[19] At first sight, we might wish to dismiss such doctrines as being, metaphysics-wise, vacuous through lack of contrast (all life, surely, cannot be a dream, for the concept *dream* gains its force from the contrast of dreaming and waking). But such criticism would pass

[19] The use of 'fully' and other such adverbs is significant here.

the mystic by, for there is, so to speak, an *inner* life which is real. The world is illusory or impermanent: but not the Ātman, not *nirvāṇa*. And a sense can be given to 'inner' here (whether or not a sense can be given to the rather different philosophical inner-outer distinction enshrined in such phrases as 'the external world'), because a method of training is laid down as conducive to spiritual well-being, and this involves the rejection of ordinary interests and pleasures: it is, roughly, this range of enjoyments that delimits the 'external world'. This mystical ascetic training has, incidentally, a likeness to the abnegation practised by worshippers to atone for their sins, and is peripherally one of the considerations making the identification of the numinous object with the mystical goal convincing. It may be mentioned also that a full-blown mystical idealism fits easily into the theistic picture: the inner state is outside the web of unreality, and so is God—the one on the hither, the other on the farther side, so to speak; and this may help to explain the moderate idealism of early Buddhism, for indeed the extreme Mahāyānist idealists paved the way for theistic forms of the faith. Briefly then, the idealistic beliefs function as a picture advertising the mystical quest. Normally, therefore, since many moral issues concern the so-called outer world, a mystical faith will tend to pay little attention to these, and will be quietistic. On the other hand, this tendency is mitigated by three factors: (*a*) idealistic doctrines are not likely to affect the content of ordinary moral rules to any great degree, since practical affairs nearly all fall within the orbit of the illusory world, and there is no special reason to abandon ordinary moral distinctions within that sphere—any more than there is to abandon colour-contrasts. (And certain mystical theologians make a contrast between higher and lower knowledge: thus Śaṅkara distinguishes between the two in a manner which corresponds with his distinction between the higher and lower Brahman—the former being without attributes [*nirguṅam*], the latter with attributes [*saguṅam*]; the latter is the Lord and object of worship, and the performance of moral duties goes with the ceremonial worship, etc., due to him: in such ways characteristically theistic doctrines and practices have a place even though 'in the highest truth' the world is illusory.) (*b*) Belief in rebirth takes an edge off the rigorous demands of mystical religion, since the ordinary adherent who does not tread the monk's path can hope to raise himself in a future existence to within striking distance of the supreme spiritual goal. (*c*) It is generally considered that no one can attain the goal who is not morally good: the cultivation of benevolent dispositions and others is part of the spiritual training. This indeed is the second aspect of agnostic Buddhism I wished to draw attention to: that moral training is built into the Noble Eightfold Path.[20] This is understandable in two ways. First, the mystical goal is, after all, merely a very peculiar *summum bonum*: herein, it is claimed, lies the highest joy, and therefore the truly wise man will tread the Path. So a moral code containing a recommendation of this as the right aim would not differ in structure, one would expect, from that with more mundane goals: one aims at happiness (of whatever quality) in accordance with virtue. Secondly, the dispositions to be cultivated as morally important are in line with the ascetic requirements of the mystic, though the latter involve more rigour (hence the difference in rules laid down for the layman and the *bhikku* respectively in Buddhism). In addition, detachment from worldly interests is assisted by the cultivation of impartiality.[21] Finally, the picture of the saintly *arhat* who has attained *nirvāṇa* is that of one who has undergone a transfiguration of character, and the calm and radiant peacefulness of such a man is presented as a glorious example to follow.[22]

E

The outline that I have given will, I hope, help to throw light on the peculiarities of such passages as the following (written by a theistic mystic):

> You must understand that, as St Gregory says, there are two ways of life in Holy Church through which Christians may reach salvation; one is called active and the other contemplative. The active life consists in love and charity shown outwardly in good works, in obedience to God's Commandments, and performing the seven corporal and spiritual works of mercy for the benefit of our fellow-Christians. . . . Another requirement of the active life is the disciplining of our bodies through fasting, vigils and other severe forms of penance. For the body must be chastised with discretion to atone for our past misdoings, to restrain its desires and inclinations to sin, and to render it obedient to obey the spirit. Provided that they are used with dis-

---

[20] The third, fourth and fifth stages are: right speech, right conduct and right mode of livelihood.

[21] An important segment of Buddhist spiritual exercises is concerned with the cultivation of dispositions such as universal compassion (*Visuddhimagga*, ch. iv).

[22] Though the picture lost much of its appeal: one of the main motives in the development of Mahāyāna Buddhism was the feeling that the Hīnayāna aim was too self-centred.

cretion, these practices, although active in form, greatly assist and dispose a person in the early stages of the spiritual life to approach the contemplative life.[23]

Gestures of atonement, the cultivation of good character and mystical asceticism can plausibly be thought to hang together. Probably it is the convincingness of the pattern of doctrine and moral teaching that would tend to justify those who loosely assert that morality presupposes religion, rather than any dry arguments about the objectivity of ethics or the evolution of conscience. In any case I hope to have given enough description to have shown (what is perhaps obvious) that an analysis of religious moral language requires an investigation of such concepts as *atonement, worship, sacrifice, sin, grace, holiness,* and so on: it is not just that religious people, while sharing principles, have different factual or metaphysical beliefs. There may, however, be those who would be indifferent to such investigations because of a prior rejection of religious beliefs. Yet these enquiries ought to have some interest even for them. For instance, if my cursory attempt at sketching some of the relations between spiritual and moral concepts is in any degree accurate, it may help to show the kind of absurdity which (on their view) characterizes religious morality.

[23] William Hilton, *The Ladder of Perfection,* trans. L. Sherley-Price, London (1957).

2

GOD AND MORALITY

Graeme de Graaff

WHAT has God to do with morality? A great deal, it would seem, if one gives ear to common belief. The presumption that there is some sort of connection between morality and God seems even to be shared by those who, for one reason or another, want to secularize morality. And of course it is obvious that those who want God back in morality presume that there is a place there for him.

The nature of the supposed connection between God and morality is not nearly so obvious. In what ways is it possible to link God and morality? I set down here a few of the more obvious views. None of them is original—that is not the point. All of them I have come across, but seldom clearly stated. I have tried to separate them from each other. Some appear to be mutually incompatible, even to be of a different logical order from each other. It is part of my purpose to try and say what sort of view each is—to say how they could be assessed—rather than to declare any choice between them.

I have spoken of 'God', not of 'religion'. The question as to what is the connection between morality and religion may be the same question as that with which I started. But it leaves room for extra confusion. Buddhism and Confucianism, for instance, are 'religions' and each with a respectably old and serious connection with morality. I want to ignore them and their like. To use the word 'God' as it is used by the Jews and the Christians is one way to severely prune the branch. I am interested to discover what people brought up within earshot of the Jewish and Christian idea of God have contended for, when they have believed that they could not get far in morality without God.

I

Surely the most common belief in this whole matter is that what God has to do with morality is to issue the orders. Morality is a matter of what men should not do and, occasionally, of what they should do. It is God who tells them what they should and should not do. When it is said, 'You ought not to commit adultery' this is taken to mean, really, that God commands, 'Do not commit adultery.' Moral imperatives are orders addressed to moral agents by God, the moral law-giver.

In its purest form this view seems to go the whole way with the model of the sergeant-major. What he says is binding, no matter what it is. In its less pure form the view makes a concession to the reasonableness, even goodness, of God. His role in morality is still to give the instructions, but the list of possible instructions is restricted to those found morally acceptable—by God knows what standard.

This is the primitive way of tying up one's God with one's conduct. It is primitive not only in the sense that we find it early in the piece (I obviously have in mind an attitude to the Decalogue) but also in that it is rather obvious. Given the notions of God as a super, if invisible, Person, the creator of us and our world, omniscient and omnipotent; and of morality as a deadly serious business (and what primitive people have not thought this?)—then linking God with morality in this way would seem almost inevitable. One is inclined to say that it is so obvious that we will be able finally to overthrow it only at some peril somewhere to our morality, or to our belief in God.

This is a view which has nevertheless been criticized clearly and convincingly.[1] It starts with the assumption that it is as easy to know what God is commanding as it is to know what order the sergeant-major is giving his men. (Though a twist of the argument later is in casting doubt on the source of the order via the immorality of that order.) The trouble is that we can imagine God issuing commands which it would be downright immoral for us, or for any human beings, to obey. Now this had better be stated carefully, for since we are allegedly talking of 'God' and not of any old god, it is by no means so clear as has sometimes been suggested that we can imagine God issuing morally berserk commands.

[1] See, for example, K. M. Baier, *The Moral Point of View*, Cornell Univ. Press 1958, ch. 1. [See also Section II of the present volume. *Editor*.]

Let us take it first at a purely logical level, to bring out the mechanics of the point, and then later see whether it can be allowed to stand in connection with the 'God' of Abraham, Isaiah and Paul. God may command a man to sacrifice his son as a burnt offering following the end of a drought. If what ought to be done is what God commands, then the morally right thing is for that man to sacrifice his son. He is morally blameworthy if his feelings get the better of him and he substitutes a dummy figure or an animal.

There are very few people who would now maintain that it could ever be other than morally wicked to sacrifice a human being under these conditions. But what can 'morally wicked' mean? For remember that it is being supposed to mean: failing to do what God commands. It would seem that we cannot make it take that meaning. Since it is possible to imagine God commanding something about which we have absolutely no doubt but that it would be wicked for us to perform it, we must be locating our criterion for moral right and wrong somewhere other than in the notion 'commanded by God'. The case is an instance of the 'naturalistic fallacy'. 'Good' cannot mean 'commanded by God', because it makes sense to ask: 'But is what God commands really good?' Sometimes it will even make sense to answer this question in the negative.

However, can it really make sense to ask of what our 'God' commands whether it is really good? We know that 'God' is the Being who could not give wicked commands. Someone could imagine that God was commanding him to strangle his possessive wife and go off and preach to the Esquimaux, but the hideousness of the proposed action is such to make us quite confident in our assertion that the command does not come from God. God is not only all-powerful and all-seeing. He is also all-good. It is outside his nature to command evil things. It would have been logically possible for Winston Churchill to have secretly sold out the Allies to Hitler for the price of a German generalship. But that does not make the suggestion that he might have done so any less fantastic.

Alternatively, we might ask where we have learnt what is morally wicked. If we are speaking of the God of the Jews and Christians then many people would seriously claim that our concepts of what is right and wrong have been, culturally, built up together with and as a result of our community acceptance of the revelation of the nature of God in both Testaments. Neither the 'truth' nor the reasonableness of this claim are here at issue. What is important is that the claim is both made, understood and heavily relied on by a school of contemporary theologians. What follows from it is that while 'morally good' may not *mean* 'what is commanded by God', God's role in morality remains that of the issuer of the moral commands, and that this is possible because we cannot imagine God having given any other than the commands which he did give.

There is still a difficulty, however, and one which arises after the attempt has been made to rescue the view from naturalism by referring to what God is taken to have actually willed or be capable of willing. That is that as a matter of history God has been taken to have commanded what we now believe to be pretty terrible things. He did renegue on the sacrifice of Isaac in time. But the command of God has been appealed to in defence of slavery, apartheid and no birth control, to mention only three issues. Opinions may still differ about the morality of the latter two issues, but there is no disagreement about the first. We now know that we must have been wrong in thinking that God commanded us to keep brothers in bondage. Did God change his mind or do we listen more carefully than did, say, the American Baptists? It seems more sensible to say that the 'God's commands' view of morality is unsatisfactory. It does and must make religious sense to speak of God's people coming to understand his will for them better. But that does nothing for the command theory.

The trouble with the view is neither God nor our understanding of God. It lies with the notion of 'command' and the attempt to tie this on to morality. There is no room in morality for commands, whether they are the father's, the schoolmaster's or the priest's. There is still no room for them when they are God's commands. A moral agent is only in very special circumstances permitted to shelter behind the excuse, 'I was ordered to do it.' In morality we are responsible for our own actions and responsible even for those actions which are responses to commands. We are responsible for obeying a command. Some commands given by some people ought not be obeyed. It would be wicked to obey them.

Of course we can and do introduce a sort of command talk into morality. I can command myself to tell the truth—I steel myself to do so. My conscience can order me to keep the promise—I determine not to let my weaker self get away with it. I am commanded by the Moral Law to pay the debt—I declare my conviction that paying the debt is the solution to the problem to which I will always return. Commands are permissible in morality only if they are so unlike ordinary commands that they would be better not thought of as commands at all. The use of the notion of God's commands is particularly misleading because in this case the bindingness of moral obligation is caught at the expense of our being seriously misled into thinking that a sort of boss really has given a sort of order.

This way of connecting God and morality would seem, then, to involve us in bad ethics and bad theology. Morality has no need of God the commander because morality has no place for commands given by one person to a moral agent. God comes dangerously near to being reduced to a Big Brother—something less than the Christian conception of him. God may require moral conduct of his followers. But he is unable to require them to substitute obedience to orders for morality while still calling it morality.[2]

II

There is more than a suspicion of the Old Testament in the notion of God as the moral commander. If New Testament love is the flowering of Old Testament law then our next move is surely in the direction of seeing morality as the result of God's love and man's attempt to love. If we can conveniently ignore most of the Christian sects, then we have this next ethical position exemplified in the Christian move from law to the fulfilment of the law. God does not command, 'Do this . . . Do that . . . Do not do this . . . or sin.' God is taken to invite men to live, or to attempt to live, a certain sort of life. Better still, to live life in a certain sort of way which (following Braithwaite)[3] can be called the way of agapeism. To be moral on this view is not to obey a set of commands. Nor is it necessarily to conform to a precise list of actions. It is to do whatever is done from a particular point of view, some things being not even possible to do from that point of view. It is to have the 'proper intention' in whatever one does. It is not what a man does which makes him morally good or bad. It is what he was attempting to achieve, in doing whatever it was that he did do, which makes him good or bad.

It is not that God is taken to command, 'Attempt always to live agapeistically, or else . . .'. There would be nothing logically odd about such a command to approach problems of conduct agapeistically, as there would certainly be something odd in anyone instructing me to *like* Jones. I either like, dislike or am neutral about Jones

---

[2] [For a further discussion of points raised here see III below, especially 5, 6, 8 and 9. *Editor.*]
[3] [See ch. 3 below. *Editor.*]

and that is that. My feelings about him cannot be changed—at least, not by an order. But I *can* be instructed to love someone, in the sense of *agape*, even someone whom I do not like. The position, however, is not that God commands us to live a life of love. He shows us what such a life amounts to and then invites us to have a shot at it. The difference is like that between the sergeant-major bellowing an order and a preacher sermonizing (when he is not misguidedly mimicking the sergeant-major).

The relation here between God and morality is very different from that in our previous section, and it can take two forms:

First, it has been suggested[4] that to be moral is simply to live agapeistically, and to live agapeistically *is* to believe in God. Few people seem to be prepared to make this latter claim, but a whole school of theologians would be making it if they were to philosophize their theology. On this identity-theory it is impossible to separate God from morality. The mention of God is redundant— but that is precisely because God himself is now inseparable from morality. Further, the good if not noble pagan is well in the picture. A man is believing in God, if not whenever he acts 'lovingly', then whenever he deliberately adopts a policy of living lovingly, though only an occasional bishop will be quick enough to cross the t's and dot the i's for him.

On the other hand, God's connection with morality through agapeism can be seen quite differently—in a way which entails the non-identity of God and the moral life. Thus, it is said that there are two respects in which agapeism is dependent on God. First, the revelation or declaration of the nature of *agape*, of its possibility and of its possibilities is revealed by God in Christ. Second, the invitation to live agapeistically (the demand, not the command, that one should) comes from God. As a matter of history it is taken to have come from God,[5] and it could only come from God—the absurdity of the demand would laugh it out of court were it not divinely sanctioned. Thus morality is very different from God. But unless there were a God and unless he had acted in Christ, there would be no 'morality'.

Not altogether different from this, at least in its conception of 'morality', is the account which Professors Maclagan[6] and Boyce

---

[4] R. B. Braithwaite, *An Empiricist's View of the Nature of Religious Belief*, C.U.P. 1955. [Reprinted below, pp. 153 ff. *Editor*.]

[5] The rule-proving exceptions like Gandhi have to be explained in terms of, e.g., his contact with Christians in South Africa.

[6] W. G. Maclagan, *The Theological Frontier of Ethics*.

Gibson give in terms of what could be called 'disinterestedness'. They appear to see this feature as the core of morality and in their hands it turns out to be a very similar notion to that of *agape*. God and morality are connected through this notion. Disinterestedness begins in science—you cannot make the world around you conform to your egocentric preconceptions. It flourishes in genuine morality —you cannot be moral if you see everyone else only as potential servers of your own ends. It ends in the worship of God—where obsessive concern for oneself disappears in adoration of the divine. The difference between this and the former account is not that here no identity between the moral life and 'God' is sought. We have seen already that that is not necessary in agapeism anyway. The difference is that where in agapeism God is the source of morality, here he is the culmination of it.

What sort of accounts are these of the relationship between God and morality? What can we make of them? As an informal account of 'what the Christian Church has done for morality'—the sort of thing which occurs in parish magazines which rely on black and white categories (the Christian West and primitive heathen)—it ties in quite nicely. If one indulges in world-history then it is reasonable to assert that agapeism was introduced into our world through the Christian Church, grew with the Church and spread with the Church. And we would still have to say this even after the obvious retort that the Church has been incredibly slow to learn the lessons she herself was teaching. The critics of the Church, morally speaking, can be assured of a field day whenever they take down their guns. Sinful human beings continue to guarantee that the process of learning to love, morally, is slow and subject to appalling lapses. Yet something seems to have come out of the Sermon on the Mount. The critics are in the wretched position of taking their standards from the Gospel, even if they are unacknowledged. They are doomed to be critical of the achievement, not of the ideal.

Even if the claim is true that morality as agapeism was born in the Christian Church, God's status is far from being secured. That he did (if he did) reveal what morality really is, does not entail that we could never have discovered the truth for ourselves by other means or that other people actually did not do so. On this account God may be no more essential to morality than is the telephonist who telephones through my telegram. As it happens I hear the news first from her. I will receive it on a printed form from the telegraph boy half an hour later. The choice appears, then, to be between a 'weak'

claim—'We believe that agapeism did come from God', and a
daring claim—'It could only have come from God.' To the latter I
would not know what to say. It is presumably backed up by reference to the nature of God, and of his world. And that is where one
tends to get lost (is perhaps intended to get lost) in definitions and
inferences from definitions.

In its identity-theory form the account looks exciting. As I have
mentioned, it would seem to harbour an elegant little proof of God's
existence. If to live agapeistically, provided only that one is *committed* to living agapeistically, is all there is at the heart of Christianity, then for these Christians the question, Does God exist? can
only mean: Is it possible to commit oneself to agapeism? Some
people find that the answer is 'Yes'. What is more, they find that
with the adoption of agapeism come accompanying forms of the
traditional religious phenomena. For them, the existence of God is
proved, not simply experientially, but in logic. Agapeism exists,
therefore God exists.

Perhaps even the exponents of agapeism would not over-stress
their proof. They are more likely to stress a consequence of their
view which puts in order one of the really embarrassing features
with which any attempt to tie morality to God is faced, the problem
of the good atheist. From the point of view of agapeism, even in its
milder form, there is little difficulty in fitting nature's saint into
the picture. He is really a worshipper of God, a believer in God,
even though he does not recite the dogma or engage in the 'usual'
performances of worship. To live the morally good life *is* to believe
and to worship. For people like Kant it is the prime thing about the
Christian religion. All dogma and all forms of devotion are excus-
able only in so far as they promote the agapeistic life. Of course one
may be inclined to believe that this way of accommodating the
naturally good man is so effective that the account which makes it
possible must be tautologically true. That would be a comment on
the *worth* of the project. The point remains that it does follow from
agapeism that God is connected with morality even for the man
who never mentions his name, never thinks about him—who perhaps even vocally abuses him, or the institutions built around him.
And that is quite an achievement.

However, it is not clear that God does not (morally) turn out to be
unnecessary, even at the last theoretical level. God comes into
morality because we have him to thank for the revelation of it all.
That entails that we could, logically, have arrived at agapeism with-

out the aid of God, or, if we hold that this is impossible, that our reference to God is the same thing as our affirmation of agapeism. That is, God is either contingently the source of agapeism, which is religiously unsatisfactory, or God is necessarily the source of morality, which will be true only by definition. Can we take God seriously if we believe either? One sympathizes with Kant's exhortation that we should get on with the business of being moral.

The most appealing thing about this position has yet to be mentioned. That is the fact that whatever other difficulties it may get itself into it is a view which commits itself to a specific account of what 'morality' is and that this account is extraordinarily difficult to challenge from a moral point of view.

The point can be brought out by contrast with the position discussed in Section I. It made sense there, we remember, to suggest imaginatively that God's commands might go awry from a point of view which, by overwhelming agreement among good men, would be called 'moral'. God's commands 'could be' commands to do things which good men would know that they ought not to do. God 'could' command immorally. By contrast, God could not reveal agapeism other than agapeistically. While God's *commands* can be moral or immoral, agapeism *is* morality in anybody's book, however secular the book may be. Now that is, perhaps, a very bold claim— a definition of morality free from the definitional fallacy! This is not the place to set out to defend it. It will have to be sufficient to point out that no alternative to agapeism could rate as a 'morality' except in the sense of that expression in which it is used as a label for *any* set of customs or *mores*. Commands can go in any direction, but agapeism can go only in the direction of morality—the direction in which most 'moralities' have tended and which, at this time of day, we insist is morality proper. Some principles are not simply bad moral principles, they are not moral principles at all. Thus, 'Treat other people as means for your own purposes', 'Act in such a way that you could not want anybody else ever to act in the same way towards you', 'Promote the greatest possible degree of misery for as many human beings as often as you possibly can'—these principles, as basic principles, are not moral principles at all but the antitheses of moral principles. They are all antitheses of agapeism too. If this is true, then the big difference between the accounts of the link between God and morality discussed in Sections I and II is that while the first account must fail to keep in the picture a God who is taken seriously, the second account keeps God well in things, but so much so that we now feel a little embarrassed at his too all-prevading presence.

A view which tends to get entwined with the one which I have just discussed, but which is in reality different from it, is the view that God in the person of Jesus is the moral model—the exemplar of the Moral Man. If Jesus Christ is God, then Jesus' way of behaving, in a world of sinful men, is God's way of behaving. If Jesus Christ is also Man, then Jesus' way of behaving is the way which good men would adopt. To be moral is to live as near as is humanly possible to the way in which Jesus lived, or—since circumstances will keep changing—to live as nearly as we can to the way in which we imaginatively believe that Jesus would act if he were in our shoes now. To fail to try to do this is to be immoral. It follows of course that the majority of the world's population is immoral.

The virtue, from a logical point of view, of this position is that it is ruthless. It is true that it does condemn many moral men to the invidious position of not even being starters on the moral race track, but it does prevent any version of the definitional criticism taking root against it. It does this by what we might call sheer obstinacy. The acts of Jesus Christ are *deliberately* taken as the model for what is good, right and obligatory. It is nonsense then to ask, But what if what Jesus does or says is immoral? As Basil Mitchell says[7] of Kant's suggestion that even the Holy One of the Gospel must get his diploma from secular morality, the suggestion is absurd because the standard of secular morality, if it is worth worrying about, has been taken from the Holy One of the Gospel anyway. That is, Kant's point could only be a logical one which had no instance in fact. There is little point in telling people that they are making their position true by definition when their position is that their position is true by definition. God's connection with morality is that he makes it possible by showing us, in Christ, what it is.

In another respect, however, this view is less radical and less exclusivist than is that of Section II. The adoption of, and adherence to, one model is not incompatible with there being other models or with the recognition of this by an adherent of the first model. From this it follows that morality itself must be thought of as something other than the commitment to any model. Otherwise it would be impossible either to assert that one's own model was

---

[7] *Sophia* I 2.

morally superior to another or to defend one's adoption of a model. A feature of this view, however, is the belief that something can be said for the adoption of Jesus rather than anybody or anything else as the model, a belief which is expressed in the notion of Jesus being the culmination of the Law and the Prophets. Even those purists who would argue that Jesus carries his own credentials—strikes us speechless in our tracks by his very purity—still need a criterion for the credentials. So, while he may persist sincerely in adhering to his chosen model (or the model which, as it would be fashionable to say, has chosen him), the moralist on this view is at the same time bound to admit the possibility of alternative models.

An interesting consequence of this liberalism is that it is impossible to criticize this link between God and morality along the lines by which the view of Section I is criticized, but for the opposite reason. It is pointless to ask, But what if Jesus did (or would have done/would do) that which is 'clearly immoral'?—e.g. in a fit of anger taken a whip to moneylenders who had set up their stalls in a place he did not like. If God *commands* 'Whip those who make you angry', we reject his command on the grounds of its immorality. But here, this is what God *does*. We have committed ourselves to trying to follow in his steps. We thus have to come to see that the whipping is right—contrary to what were our over-sentimentalized feelings and prejudices. Again, it is not that whatever God does cannot be immoral—as it *was* that whatever is agapeistic cannot be immoral. It is that it cannot be immoral *for us,* once we have committed ourselves to the view in question. Therein lies the logical strength and the moral danger of the view. The danger is clearer to us when we see what can happen to people bound by themselves to follow in the way Confucius, say, has taught than it is when we are so near to home. There is no difference between the follower of Confucius and this sort of Christian in the logic of their adherence to a model. Each has said, with regard to morality, 'Here I take my stand.' It is always dangerous to settle every moral issue in principle before one has come to it. But if this is the relation between God and morality which is being proferred then it can be shaken only by conversion to a most rigorous objectivism. As I see it, it would only be the conviction that if something is 'right' then it is right for everybody, everywhere and at all times—believers in God or not— that could persuade someone devoted to the idea of God as his model for morality that there was anything problematical about his view.

B*

The view of Section II holds God to be the revealer of the nature, or of the essence of morality. God displays what morality is all about but does not give us the details of moral performance. The Law prescribed right conduct in detail, but Love does away with minute prescription and seeks the essential meaning which the Law should have conveyed but ended by confusing. The view of this section (as I have represented it—there is also a version of it which is 'essentialist') returns to God as the revealer of the content of morality. It is a different type of content from Section I. It bears the marks of the retreat from legalism undergone by its related view. But the critic of the view will be entitled, if not required, to criticize it on the grounds that the morality which is produced by this sort of attachment to God is shown to be an inferior product, if it is, by a standard which has more universal appeal (and which may even be that of Section II).

IV

I now move to a view which concerns the part of the will in the moral life, rather than the role of the understanding. God is connected with morality, on this view, as the sustainer of moral effort. The view is that of the mystic and the devotional believer rather than of the theologian or the philosopher. I do not remember seeing any reference to it in philosophical writings, and when I have come across it in theological writing the category is devotional rather than systematic. The view is an expression of religious faith and a testimony to the believer's experience in the life of faith. It entails, none the less, an account of what God has to do with morality.

'Without God I could not have done it.' 'I did not do it; God did it through me.' There are many variations. All of them make one point (which can be seen as pious modesty and left at that). They insist, after a man has done his duty on an occasion when it was particularly difficult or unpleasant, or after a man has done the right thing, or been good, in circumstances when, as we say, we would not blame even a saint for giving in, that the strength of will for the performance was granted by God.

Without the knowledge of God, as the supreme Being who has redeemed his world and watches what I do now, I could not have risen to the occasion. Nor could I have done so without the experience of his power in my life. More generally—I could not be moral (i.e. act other than in what I take to be my own interest) even so far as I am, without the help of God. It is only by his grace.

The importance of God to the moral agent who takes this view of the relationship between God and morality cannot be doubted. It would be characteristic of such a person, of course, that he would object to that way of putting the matter—as though God had a use, like a pill to give one the will-power to stop smoking. He is claiming that, but for God, he could not be as good a moral agent as he in fact is.

It will be equally clear that the agent's claim about himself need carry no implication about other men. The claim is not made, nor need it in consistency be made, that anyone who achieves any moral purpose does so only with the aid of God nor that every act of the agent's is thus really God's. There would be nothing remarkable about my having told the truth this time *with the help of God* if every time I (or anybody) do anything worth doing it is done with the help of God.

Were one to claim that the acknowledgment of God's help is irrelevant to the question of whether or not God did help, or to whether the act could have been performed without his help, because all our actions depend on God's help (some people acknowledging this, others not), the view would similarly end in vacuity. The difficulty with it would be closely parallel to, if not an aspect of, the worries which theologians have about how to talk of God's grace operating without having to grant that it characterizes the whole performance.

The most interesting thing about the view is its utter untestability and the way in which this is taken to be utterly irrelevant to its meaningfulness. 'But for God I could not have done it.' It is like the remark of the famous European singer who was applauded for his performance of some Mahler songs, 'Had I not read Kant at the University I could not sing them like that.' What on earth can Kant have to do with singing Mahler? The singer claims that the moving performance which we hear comes only from his intellectual encounter earlier in his life. But does it? I do not mean: How do we know that the man is not lying? There may be no question of it, we may be completely certain that he is not, just as we are usually confident that whatever else the moral mystic may be up to, he is not lying. One does not know what to do with the claim.

The testifier, his critic and the interested observer all know the peculiarity of the claim which is being made. It is made on the basis of an experience—but the experience (it would be said) seems to be highly subjective. The claim is made often in the face of what would

appear to be the facts. The moral agent who claims on one occasion
to have been sustained by God might well be known to have done
just as well on other occasions on which he had neither felt nor
claimed that God had got him through. He joins the rest in knowing that other people are better moral performers than he is—and
they never acknowledge or believe even that they should acknowledge God's help. Some explicitly belittle the whole notion, perhaps
not even believing that there is a God. And the man who does
acknowledge God's help on a particular occasion is very likely to be
the sort of man who, while being grateful for having been able to do
as well as he did do, believes nevertheless that he alone *could be* a
much better performer than he is. In short the claim is untestable
and is known to be untestable. The critic may become exasperated
with this sort of God-acknowledging moralist—may think that he
would in fact do much better, would be capable of greater effort, if
only he would approach moral problems as though he were entirely
on his own. But he can do nothing about it. 'Without God I could
not have done it' may be as true of a mediocre performance as it is of
a winning performance. The only thing we can do is be sure that it
is said sincerely. Thereafter many things, including no doubt a
man's moral character, will go to affect our assessment of what has
been said. But we can never penetrate the mystery. As he who
'knows that his Redeemer liveth' knows that he can only 'know' this
in a special sense—and would not be satisfied unless that were so—
so he who couldn't have done right except for God is not talking
about what he could nor could not have done in the ordinary sense
of the expression.

I have discussed the view as though it were always made in reference to a feeling of dependence on a particular occasion or occasions.
One hears also expressions of dependence on God for the whole
moral endeavour—as a reforming criminal might say to his proba-
tion officer, 'I could not keep it up but for you.' I believe that many
more believers would be prepared to subscribe here than at the level
of help in particular problems. A number of people do believe that
they manage their moral lives only because of God. I am convinced
that the logic of their belief is no different from that of the view I
have discussed. It is not for philosophers, certainly, to say anything
to them, and I think I have said of them all that is philosophically
interesting.

V

From the extreme of intimacy between God and the moral agent I move to the extreme of remoteness between the two. The view which I am about to consider would seem to put as much distance between God and moral beings as it is possible to have while yet maintaining that the one has something to do with the other. This is the view that as God is the creator of the physical universe so too is he the creator of the moral order. His creatorship in the second case as in the first bears almost no relationship to creatorship in the non-religious sense; it is as profoundly important in terms of 'metaphysical' consequences, and as inconsequential in terms of morality. It is part of the background to the moral life, not part of its daily bread and butter.

The view is this. This is God's world, and he has made it of a particular regular nature. It is not haphazard. Whether or not it is the best world he possibly could have made is quite beside the point. It is the sort of world in which, at a physical level, things behave in a law-like manner. If I throw an egg from an upper window it always hits the pavement (unless someone catches it, or it is *interfered with* in some other way). It does not sometimes fall, sometimes float, and sometimes remain in mid-air. God has created the moral order for free human beings in a parallel way. There are certain things which human beings ought to do, or there are certain basic attitudes which men ought to have.[8] While they do not come to physical grief if they do not do them, as they do bring physical injury on themselves if they 'break' the laws of the material universe, they do come to moral grief if they fail to keep the moral laws. As there is a limit to the amount of battering a physical body can take, so there is a limit, it is said, to the amount of moral battering a soul can withstand. There is a way to live uprightly. The penalty for failing to do so is guilt, despair and disintegration.

Human beings are free to break the moral laws. They are free, not just to try but actually to live their lives on their own terms, in their own way. Were they not free they could not be counted as moral agents; there is never the suggestion that moral wrong-doing is finally impossible. The view parallels physical and moral laws, it does not identify them with each other. But men find, according to this view, that it is morally disastrous to live out of tune with the moral order, morally rewarding to try to keep the laws. Moral

[8] The view is amenable to either a moral-law or a moral-attitude interpretation.

disaster must not apparently be thought of as quite so disastrous as physical disaster. Anyone who *courts* physical disaster is either a suicide or a lunatic. But some wicked men know that they are court-ing 'moral disaster'.

In short, the moral laws (or morality as such) are thought of as God's way for the free human world to work. While we are free to have a shot at making it work differently, and even free to pursue the alternative schemes throughout not just one life but an entire civilization, no alternative way of life works as well as 'the moral life'. God's relationship to morality is that of the Creator and sus-tainer of the moral order.

God himself need never, of course, be acknowledged even by a morally impeccable agent. It is possible never to break the law of the road without having the faintest idea whence it emanated. It is possible to keep the law without knowing even that it is the law. Similarly with the moral law—a man may be a good man in the sense that he always does what we think he ought to do (assuming that 'we' operate on an understanding of what 'the moral law' is) without his acknowledging or even caring that he acts in accordance with what we believe is the moral order. He may even say that he does not believe it—or that if he *did* believe that *God* had created the world in such a way that only by keeping promises could one avoid the psychiatrist's couch, then he would break all his promises by way of protest.

That is, God comes into the picture on this showing at the theoretical not the practical level. If this is God's connection with morality then God has more to do with moral philosophy than he has to do with morality. He is a theoretical entity which is popped into place to complete the jig-saw puzzle which pictures man in his world. To be moral demands no religious commitment. It demands only living by the tried ways of the moralists. To give an account of *why* one should bother with morality, would take the arguer to God. But such an account lies outside morality itself.

While no commitment to God is required, on this view, for a man to be a moral man, this account of the relationship of God to moral-ity is only likely from a man whose experience *of morality* happens to fit this by being of the 'natural law' variety. And this is perhaps the moment to remark that analogous remarks have to be made for each of the accounts I have mentioned. That such would be the case should have been obvious, as also should be what follows from this, namely, that it is useless to ask for *the* relationship between *God* and *morality* since both the terms to be related are plastic. *One* of the ways of discovering what sort of notion a man has of God, as well as what sort of philosophy of morals he holds, is to ask him what God has to do with morality!

It is better that this theory should remain at the purely theoretical level. If it is thought that it makes a difference to a man who is asking himself and his moral advisers, 'What ought I to do now?' that he should know that the right thing for him to do will be that which is in line with the way God has built the world, then moral disaster may lie not far away. If it is thought that the man has any other job on his hands than finding out what he ought to do (or if it is thought that he can find out what he ought to by finding out, there and then, how God meant this bit of the universe to work right now), then his attention may be being directed away from the moral issue. A solution to a moral problem is being sought by non-moral means. The case here is similar to that in Section I. What is right is (always) what is in accordance with God's way and can be re-phrased: we find out what is right by finding out what God's way is. If it is 'fed-back' into morality—as though he who subscribes to this view of the relationship of God to morality is at some sort of advantage in the business of finding out what is right—there is a danger that moral mis-sight will be attributed to God. And if there is one thing worse than a straight-cut moral blunder, it is a moral blunder for which the agent claims that God is in it with him. It is awful, not simply because it encourages us to feel that we know better than God in this instance, but because the agent will have to be shaken much longer before he sees moral sense. *Some* atrocities would never have been perpetrated but for God's name.

If the view is not fed-back into morality then it remains, of course, practically useless. But not tautologically so. It is a view, a meaningful view, which is perhaps best seen as expression of faith in God. Via a sort of teleological argument it could even become an argument for the existence of a Creator. If it is true that the moral order is orderly it bespeaks an orderly Creator. The more typical form of a moral argument for God's existence is different. I am about to discuss it in its more usual form. Let me note here that it can be put in different ways, one of which is to speak as here of the whole moral order rather than, as in Section I, of moral *laws* or commands.

Undoubtedly the most exciting way of relating God and morality is the traditional moral argument for the existence of God. This view of the relationship between God and morality is invigoratingly clear of any suggestion that God is a necessary prop for morality. It is *necessarily* clear of any such suggestion. The panic policy which is currently aired (teach religion in the secular schools and stop the moral disintegration of our society) could not arise if we took the moral argument for God's existence seriously.

I have said '*the* moral argument', but in truth there are many. In this concluding section I will look at Kant's best-known version of the argument, not to assess its worth, as though that could be done in such short space, but to see what it amounts to in terms of an account of the relationship that holds between God and morality. The version of the argument I will look at it is concisely stated by Kant in both the *Critique of Practical Reason* and the *Critique of Judgment*. It occurs elsewhere in Kant too, but so do other slightly different moral arguments for the existence of God. Very similar indeed to the former argument is John Baillie's moral argument in *Invitation to Pilgrimage*.

The argument goes like this. When I am morally obliged to do something I am faced by a categorical imperative. Although I remain physically free to do evil, I have no choice *but* to do what I am morally obliged to do. To be obliged to do something is not to want to do it, to be inclined to do it, to believe that it would be a good thing if one were to do it—it is to be (morally) 'compelled' to do it. It is *as though* I am *commanded* to do it. Kant says that the Moral Law itself bids me. Baillie says that he, in his childhood, was bound to do what he was told he ought to do by his parents. As he grew up he realized that their instructions were not haphazard, but referred to a moral law greater even than them and for which they were merely the mouthpiece. But the authority which he early interpreted as their authority remained, indeed increased, even when he discovered that in moral matters his parents were fallible.

I learn about moral imperatives, it is said, by learning that there are some things which I am bound to do. I discover that as a matter of fact there is no human agency (either person or institution) binding me. But this discovery does *not* incline me to believe that I am not, after all, bound. On the contrary, the subjective certainty of being under a law withstands the discovery that there is, in the

ordinary sense, no law. What the human reason then sets about
doing is to find a satisfying, if abstract, explanation of these phenomena. The explanation—the only possible one, according to Baillie,
the most satisfying one according to Kant—is that God stands to the
moral law as the legislator stands to ordinary law, that God stands to
the adult who is confronted with the requirement to, say, tell the
truth as a young child's parents stand to it. The inescapability of a
truly moral imperative argues an authority in which the imperative
originates. But there is no such authority, indeed Kant clearly sees,
none such is possible if the purity of the moral imperative is to be
preserved. (I have to be compelled by a moral imperative for *moral*
reasons—not because a big stick is being held over me.) We are then
left with the *demand* for an author of the moral law and, while we
remain within the area of the human understanding, with a vacuum
at just this point. God, the divine commander, is required to complete the picture.

It is an *argument*, not a proof. For Kant a proof is theoretical,
involving either regulative or constitutive concepts. It is well known
that by the time he wrote the first *Critique* he was convinced that no
such proof of God's existence was possible. The moral argument
does not establish that 'God' is a necessary notion, except in the
sense of 'necessary' which means that until we get around to this
notion we are left with an irritating gap in our picture of morality.

We should be clear about the nature of this gap. It is not such as
to delay the operation of morality until Reason fills it in. On the
contrary, morality has no need of God. Kant reiterates this beyond
all possibility of misunderstanding. Natural religion needs morality
(the moral argument for the existence of God is the only argument
there is); and the religious life *par excellence* for Kant *is* the moral
life (with a few fundamentally unnecessary acrostics and mnemonics
thrown in). But the nature of morality is such to demand God once
we start reflecting on what is implied by our way of life when we are
living morally. Unless we take the jig-saw completing step to God
then Ethics remains, as Kant technically put it, merely an 'Idea'.
This does not mean that morality remains mind-bound; that it cannot get on to the ground and have something to do with practice.
On the contrary, it means that ethics can have no (pseudo-) theoretical justification until God is brought into the picture. Here we all
are feeling bound by our moral obligations as though we were children with our father standing over us, with no explanation of why
we should feel like that. God is the explanation.

If one can be (completely) moral without making the reference to God, so also one's morality is unaffected if and when one does go on to make the reference. That one has acknowledged that the moral imperative 'keep your promise' is also God's command, does not help one to be any clearer about the fact that one ought to keep one's promise. One had to be as clear as one possibly could be about *that* before one admitted that it was a *moral* imperative. Nor does it make one more inclined to do the right thing—it was only because one was already feeling that the moral obligation was totally binding that one was able to make the move to God. If this is the connection which God has with morality then it follows, in other words, that God is needed only for theoretical completeness. He *can* be of no aid to the moral man. Certain devotional practices can aid him, but these in the same way as certain psychological practices might. Morality has to come first in point of time, for the argument even to appear. And morality has to come first, in order of importance, for the argument to be sustained.

An interesting facet of this view appears when we ask not whether you can be moral without God, but whether you can believe in God without being moral. Usually the answer here is a (somewhat vague) assertion that you *can* believe in God and be immoral. (Kant in one of his common 'anti-Jesuitical' passages makes the point that some forms of belief in some aspects of God actually *encourage* immorality by offering the escape-hatch of an unconfirmed death-bed repentance.) Kant makes it clear that the only possible form of belief in a God which could be held by an immoral man is a purely metaphysical or magical belief. *Natural* religion for Kant is the antithesis of theoretical or metaphysical dogma. It is moral practice, pure and almost simple. One cannot then believe there is God without being moral. One can believe in some metaphysical system, without being moral, but that is not to believe in God.

The difficulty which is likely to arise in this argument for God's existence brings out the peculiar nature of the view of the relationship between God and morality which it embodies. The difficulty is that a number of philosophers, who are not guilty simply of not having thought about the point, do not believe that the moral imperative is an absolutely binding imperative at all. There *are* ethical subjectivists abroad and for them the essential premise of Kant's argument is non-existent. And of those philosophers who do take the view that an 'I ought' (if not a 'you ought') is binding, some will give such an account of the nature of this bindingness as to, again, forestall a moral argument for God's existence. Thus it is possible to believe that when someone has said, 'I ought to tell the truth now' there is absolutely nothing more to be said: that that is final. But the finality need not be attributed to the law-like binding-ness of the obligation which necessitates the postulated God. It may be attributed to the fact that the agent has, by the stage of saying 'I ought', declared that he has made up his mind. People do not, *having made up their minds*, proceed to unmake and remake them —unless new facets come to light between the thought or the act, or unless they are chronic ditherers. A declaration that one has *decided* on one's course of action explains why one feels bound to act in that way (if one can give no reason for changing one's mind). No embar-rassing gap is left requiring, apparently, God to save Ethics from remaining only an Idea.

There are less extreme accounts of why an imperative is taken to be binding which similarly require no God. The point here is not which of them is the correct account (on which there is *no* agree-ment) but the consequence of their existence as candidates. It en-tails that the Kantian premise itself requires defence (which Kant himself of course gave it in full measure). This view of the relation between morality and ethics depends on holding first that a moral obligation is absolutely binding, and second that the nature of this bindingness is *external*—both of which are views which have been subjected to serious challenge in the history of the subject. The view depends, as did that of Section I, on believing that moral impera-tives are commands. But commands given to oneself, or decisions, entail the presence of no commander other than oneself.

There are undoubtedly further ways of connecting, in the arm-chair, God and morality. As I said at the beginning, I have not tried to provide an exhaustive list of the possibilities. Neither have I tried to defend my choice from among them. I do not believe that one has to choose. I have been concerned to show that there are at least these possibilities.

The matter is of more than academic interest. Disputes such as that which occurred in the columns of the *Listener* after Margaret Knight's discussion of moral education in a secular community are important disputes and perennial, though their *form* may give the impression that they are the temporary product of a particular stage in community development. Such disputes can generate only heat if the question of whether there can or cannot be morality without

belief in God is tackled as though God's part in morality were clear
to everybody and agreed on by all. Clearly there can be morality, of
a sort, even if there is no Jesus to reveal agapeism to a learning
world. There can be morality, and not just of a sort, if God never
issues any commands from within a burning bush. Yet even so far,
where we have agreement, the sense of *morality* is different, and the
sense in which there *could be* morality is also different in each case.
How much worse the confusion when the 'defender' of holding God
and morality together is someone impressed by the 'moral argument
for God's existence'. He may find himself saddled with 'religious
education' in secular schools. Not because he wants it or thinks it
can do anything for either religion or the schools, but because he has
been told that moral standards are slipping and that he himself
believes that God and morality go together. So he does—but, if he
only knew it, he does not then have to believe that it is useful to
drag in God to save the discarded *mores* of the community.

II · MORALITY AND RELIGION

3

AN EMPIRICIST'S VIEW OF THE NATURE OF RELIGIOUS BELIEF

R. B. Braithwaite

'T H E meaning of a scientific statement is to be ascertained by reference to the steps which would be taken to verify it.' Eddington wrote this in 1939. Unlike his heterodox views of the *a priori* and epistemological character of the ultimate laws of physics, this principle is in complete accord with contemporary philosophy of science; indeed it was Eddington's use of it in his expositions of relativity theory in the early 1920's that largely contributed to its becoming the orthodoxy. Eddington continued his passage by saying: 'This [principle] will be recognised as a tenet of logical positivism—only it is there extended to all statements.'[1] Just as the tone was set to the empiricist tradition in British philosophy—the tradition running from Locke through Berkeley, Hume, Mill to Russell in our own time—by Locke's close association with the scientific work of Boyle and the early Royal Society, so the contemporary development of empiricism popularly known as logical positivism has been greatly influenced by the revolutionary changes this century in physical theory and by the philosophy of science which physicists concerned with these changes—Einstein and Heisenberg as well as Eddington—have thought most consonant with relativity and quantum physics. It is therefore, I think, proper for me to take the verificational principle of meaning, and a natural adaptation of it, as that aspect of contemporary scientific thought whose bearing upon the philosophy of religion I shall discuss this afternoon. Eddington, in the passage from which I have quoted, applied the verificational principle to the meaning of scientific statements only.

[1] A. S. Eddington, *The Philosophy of Physical Science* (1939), p. 189.

But we shall see that it will be necessary, and concordant with an empiricist way of thinking, to modify the principle by allowing *use* as well as *verifiability* to be a criterion for meaning; so I believe that all I shall say will be in the spirit of a remark with which Eddington concluded an article published in 1925: 'The scientist and the religious teacher may well be content to agree that the *value* of any hypothesis extends just so far as it is verified by actual experience.'[2]

I will start with the verificational principle in the form in which it was originally propounded by logical positivists—that the meaning of any statement is given by its method of verification.[3]

The implication of this general principle for the problem of religious belief is that the primary question becomes, not whether a religious statement such as that a personal God created the world is true or is false, but how it could be known either to be true or to be false. Unless this latter question can be answered, the religious statement has no ascertainable meaning and there is nothing expressed by it to be either true or false. Moreover a religious statement cannot be believed without being understood, and it can only be understood by an understanding of the circumstances which would verify or falsify it. Meaning is not logically prior to the possibility of verification: we do not first learn the meaning of a statement, and afterwards consider what would make us call it true or false; the two understandings are one and indivisible.

It would not be correct to say that discussions of religious belief before this present century have always ignored the problem of meaning, but until recently the emphasis has been upon the question of the truth or the reasonableness of religious beliefs rather than upon the logically prior question as to the meaning of the statements expressing the beliefs. The argument usually proceeded as if we all knew what was meant by the statement that a personal God created the world; the point at issue was whether or not this statement was true, or whether there were good reasons for believing it. But if the meaning of a religious statement has to be found by discovering the steps which must be taken to ascertain its truth-value, an examination of the methods for testing the statement for truth-value is an essential preliminary to any discussion as to which of the truth-values—truth or falsity—holds of the statement.

[2] *Science, Religion and Reality*, ed. by J. Needham (1925), p. 218 (my italics).
[3] The principle was first explicitly stated by F. Waismann, in *Erkenntnis*, vol. 1 (1930), p. 229.

There are three classes of statement whose method of truth-value testing is in general outline clear: statements about particular matters of empirical fact, scientific hypotheses and other general empirical statements, and the logically necessary statements of logic and mathematics (and their contradictories). Do religious statements fall into any of these three classes? If they do, the problem of their meaningfulness will be solved: their truth-values will be testable by the methods appropriate to empirical statements, particular or general, or to mathematical statements. It seems to me clear that religious statements, as they are normally used, have no place in this trichotomy. I shall give my reasons very briefly, since I have little to add here to what other empiricist philosophers have said.

1. Statements about particular empirical facts are testable by direct observation. The only facts that can be directly known by observation are that the things observed have certain observable properties or stand in certain observable relations to one another. If it is maintained that the *existence* of God is known by observation, for example, in the 'self-authenticating' experience of 'meeting God', the term 'God' is being used merely as part of the description of that particular experience. Any interesting theological proposition, e.g. that God is personal, will attribute a property to God which is not an observable one and so cannot be known by direct observation. Comparison with our knowledge of other people is an unreal comparison. I can get to know things about an intimate friend at a glance, but this knowledge is not self-authenticating; it is based upon a great deal of previous knowledge about the connection between facial and bodily expressions and states of mind.

2. The view that would class religious statements with scientific hypotheses must be taken much more seriously. It would be very unplausible if a Baconian methodology of science had to be employed, and scientific hypotheses taken as simple generalizations from particular instances, for then there could be no understanding of a general theological proposition unless particular instances of it could be directly observed. But an advanced science has progressed far beyond its natural history stage; it makes use in its explanatory hypotheses of concepts of a high degree of abstractness and at a far remove from experience. These theoretical concepts are given a meaning by the place they occupy in a deductive system consisting of hypotheses of different degrees of generality in which the least general hypotheses, deducible from the more general ones, are

generalizations of observable facts. So it is no valid criticism of the view that would treat God as an empirical concept entering into an explanatory hypothesis to say that God is not directly observable. No more is an electric field of force or a Schrödinger wave-function. There is no *prima facie* objection to regarding such a proposition as that there is a God who created and sustains the world as an explanatory scientific hypothesis.

But if a set of theological propositions are to be regarded as scientific explanations of facts in the empirical world, they must be refutable by experience. We must be willing to abandon them if the facts prove different from what we think they are. A hypothesis which is consistent with every possible empirical fact is not an empirical one. And though the theoretical concepts in a hypothesis need not be explicitly definable in terms of direct observation—indeed they must not be if the system is to be applicable to novel situations—yet they must be related to some and not to all of the possible facts in the world in order to have a non-vacuous significance. If there is a personal God, how would the world be different if there were not? Unless this question can be answered God's existence cannot be given an empirical meaning.

At earlier times in the history of religion God's personal existence has been treated as a scientific hypothesis subjectable to empirical test. Elijah's contest with the prophets of Baal was an experiment to test the hypothesis that Jehovah and not Baal controlled the physical world. But most educated believers at the present time do not think of God as being detectable in this sort of way, and hence do not think of theological propositions as explanations of facts in the world of nature in the way in which established scientific hypotheses are.

It may be maintained, however, that theological propositions explain facts about the world in another way. Not perhaps the physical world, for physical science has been so successful with its own explanations; but the facts of biological and psychological development. Now it is certainly the case that a great deal of traditional Christian language—phrases such as 'original sin', 'the old Adam', 'the new man', 'growth in holiness'—can be given meanings within statements expressing general hypotheses about human personality. Indeed it is hardly too much to say that almost all statements about God as immanent, as an indwelling spirit, can be interpreted as asserting psychological facts in metaphorical language. But would those interpreting religious statements in this way be prepared to abandon them if the empirical facts were found to be different? Or would they rather re-interpret them to fit the new facts? In the latter case the possibility of interpreting them to fit experience is not enough to give an empirical meaning to the statements. Mere consistency with experience without the possibility of inconsistency does not determine meaning. And a metaphorical description is not in itself an explanation. This criticism also holds against attempts to interpret theism as an explanation of the course of history, unless it is admitted (which few theists would be willing to admit) that, had the course of history been different in some specific way, God would not have existed.

Philosophers of religion who wish to make empirical facts relevant to the meaning of religious statements but at the same time desire to hold on to these statements whatever the empirical facts may be are indulging, I believe, in a sort of 'double-think' attitude: they want to hold that religious statements both are about the actual world (i.e. are empirical statements) and also are not refutable in any possible world, the characteristic of statements which are logically necessary.

3. The view that statements of natural theology resemble the propositions of logic and mathematics in being logically necessary would have as a consequence that they make no assertion of existence. Whatever exactly be the status of logically necessary propositions, Hume and Kant have conclusively shown that they are essentionally hypothetical. $2 + 3 = 5$ makes no assertion about there being any things in the world; what it says is that, *if* there is a class of five things in the world, *then* this class is the union of two mutually exclusive sub-classes one comprising two and the other comprising three things. The logical-positivist thesis, due to Wittgenstein, that the truth of this hypothetical proposition is verified not by any logical fact about the world but by the way in which we use numerical symbols in our thinking goes further than Kant did in displacing logic and mathematics from the world of reality. But it is not necessary to accept this more radical thesis in order to agree with Kant that no logically necessary proposition can assert existence; and this excludes the possibility of regarding theological propositions as logically necessary in the way in which the hypothetical propositions of mathematics and logic are necessary.

The traditional arguments for a Necessary God—the ontological and the cosmological—were elaborated by Anselm and the scholastic philosophers before the concurrent and inter-related development of natural science and of mathematics had enabled necessity

and contingency to be clearly distinguished. The necessity attributed by these arguments to the being of God may perhaps be
different from the logical necessity of mathematical truths; but, if
so, no method has been provided for testing the truth-value of the
statement that God is necessary being, and consequently no way
given for assigning meaning to the terms 'necessary being' and
'God'.

If religious statements cannot be held to fall into any of these
three classes, their method of verification cannot be any of the
standard methods applicable to statements falling in these classes.
Does this imply that religious statements are not verifiable, with the
corollary, according to the verificational principle, that they have
no meaning and, though they purport to say something, are in fact
nonsensical sentences? The earlier logical positivists thought so:
they would have echoed the demand of their precursor Hume that a
volume ('of divinity or school metaphysics') which contains neither
'any abstract reasoning concerning quantity or number' nor 'any
experimental reasoning concerning matter of fact and existence'
should be committed to the flames; though their justification for
the holocaust would be even more cogent than Hume's. The volume
would not contain even 'sophistry and illusion': it would contain
nothing but meaningless marks of printer's ink.

Religious statements, however, are not the only statements which
are unverifiable by standard methods; moral statements have the
same peculiarity. A moral principle, like the utilitarian principle
that a man ought to act so as to maximize happiness, does not seem
to be either a logically necessary or a logically impossible proposition. But neither does it seem to be an empirical proposition, all
the attempts of ethical empiricists to give naturalistic analyses having failed. Though a tough-minded logical positivist might be
prepared to say that all religious statements are sound and fury,
signifying nothing, he can hardly say that of all moral statements.
For moral statements have a use in guiding conduct; and if they
have a use they surely have a meaning—in some sense of meaning.
So the verificational principle of meaning in the hands of empiricist
philosophers in the 1930's became modified either by a glossing of
the term 'verification' or by a change of the verification principle
into the use principle: the meaning of any statement is given by the
way in which it is used.[4]

    [4] See L. Wittgenstein, *Philosophical Investigations* (1953), especially §§ 340, 353, 559, 560.

Since I wish to continue to employ verification in the restricted sense of ascertaining truth-value, I shall take the principle of meaning in this new form in which the word 'verification' has disappeared. But in removing this term from the statement of the principle, there is no desertion from the spirit of empiricism. The older verificational principle is subsumed under the new use principle: the use of an empirical statement derives from the fact that the statement is empirically verifiable, and the logical-positivist thesis of the 'linguistic' character of logical and mathematical statements can be equally well, if not better, expressed in terms of their use than of their method of verification. Moreover the only way of discovering how a statement is used is by an empirical enquiry; a statement need not itself be empirically verifiable, but that it is used in a particular way is always a straightforwardly empirical proposition.

The meaning of any statement, then, will be taken as being given by the way it is used. The kernel for an empiricist of the problem of the nature of religious belief is to explain, in empirical terms, how a religious statement is used by a man who asserts it in order to express his religious conviction.

Since I shall argue that the primary element in this use is that the religious assertion is used as a moral assertion, I must first consider how moral assertions are used. According to the view developed by various moral philosophers since the impossibility of regarding moral statements as verifiable propositions was recognized, a moral assertion is used to express an *attitude* of the man making the assertion. It is not used to assert the proposition that he has the attitude —a verifiable psychological proposition; it is used to show forth or evince his attitude. The attitude is concerned with the action which he asserts to be right or to be his duty, or the state of affairs which he asserts to be good; it is a highly complex state, and contains elements to which various degrees of importance have been attached by moral philosophers who have tried to work out an 'ethics without propositions'. One element in the attitude is a feeling of approval towards the action; this element was taken as the fundamental one in the first attempts, and views of ethics without propositions are frequently lumped together as 'emotive' theories of ethics. But discussion of the subject during the last twenty years has made it clear, I think, that no emotion or feeling of approval is fundamental to the use of moral assertions; it may be the case that the moral asserter has some specific feeling directed on to the course of action said to be right, but this is not the most important element in his 'pro-attitude' towards the course of action: what is primary is his intention to perform the action when the occasion for it arises.

The form of ethics without propositions which I shall adopt is therefore a conative rather than an emotive theory: it makes the primary use of a moral assertion that of expressing the intention of the asserter to act in a particular sort of way specified in the assertion. A utilitarian, for example, in asserting that he ought to act so as to maximize happiness, is thereby declaring his intention to act, to the best of his ability, in accordance with the policy of utilitarianism: he is not asserting any proposition, or necessarily evincing any feeling of approval; he is subscribing to a policy of action. There will doubtless be empirical propositions which he may give as reasons for his adherence to the policy (e.g. that happiness is what all, or what most people, desire), and his having the intention will include his understanding what is meant by pursuing the policy, another empirically verifiable proposition. But there will be no specifically moral proposition which he will be asserting when he declares his intention to pursue the policy. This account is fully in accord with the spirit of empiricism, for whether or not a man has the intention of pursuing a particular behaviour policy can be empirically tested, both by observing what he does and by hearing what he replies when he is questioned about his intentions.

Not all expressions of intentions will be moral assertions: for the notion of morality to be applicable it is necessary either that the policy of action intended by the asserter should be a general policy (e.g. the policy of utilitarianism) or that it should be subsumable under a general policy which the asserter intends to follow and which he would give as the reason for his more specific intention. There are difficulties and vaguenesses in the notion of a general policy of action, but these need not concern us here. All that we require is that, when a man asserts that he ought to do so-and-so, he is using the assertion to declare that he resolves, to the best of his ability, to do so-and-so. And he will not necessarily be insincere in his assertion if he suspects, at the time of making it, that he will not have the strength of character to carry out his resolution.

The advantage this account of moral assertions has over all others, emotive non-propositional ones as well as cognitive propositional ones, is that it alone enables a satisfactory answer to be given to the question: What is the reason for my doing what I think I ought to do? The answer it gives is that, since my thinking that I ought to do the action is my intention to do it if possible, the reason why I do the action is simply that I intend to do it, if possible. On every other ethical view there will be a mysterious gap to be filled somehow between the moral judgment and the intention to act in accordance with it: there is no such gap if the primary use of a moral assertion is to declare such an intention.

Let us now consider what light this way of regarding moral assertions throws upon assertions of religious conviction. The idealist philosopher McTaggart described religion as 'an emotion resting on a conviction of a harmony between ourselves and the universe at large',[5] and many educated people at the present time would agree with him. If religion is essentially concerned with emotion, it is natural to explain the use of religious assertions on the lines of the original emotive theory of ethics and to regard them as primarily evincing religious feelings or emotions. The assertion, for example, that God is our Heavenly Father will be taken to express the asserter's feeling secure in the same way as he would feel secure in his father's presence. But explanations of religion in terms of feeling, and of religious assertions as expressions of such feelings, are usually propounded by people who stand outside any religious system; they rarely satisfy those who speak from inside. Few religious men would be prepared to admit that their religion was a matter merely of feeling: feelings—of joy, of consolation, of being at one with the universe—may enter into their religion, but to evince such feelings is certainly not the primary use of their religious assertions.

This objection, however, does not seem to me to apply to treating religious assertions in the conative way in which recent moral philosophers have treated moral statements—as being primarily declarations of adherence to a policy of action, declarations of commitment to a way of life. That the way of life led by the believer is highly relevant to the sincerity of his religious conviction has been insisted upon by all the moral religions, above all, perhaps, by Christianity. 'By their fruits ye shall know them.' The view which I put forward for your consideration is that the intention of a Christian to follow a Christian way of life is not only the criterion for the sincerity of his belief in the assertions of Christianity; it is the criterion for the meaningfulness of his assertions. Just as the meaning of a moral assertion is given by its use in expressing the asserter's intention to act, so far as in him lies, in accordance with the moral principle involved, so the meaning of a religious assertion is given by its use in

<hr>

[5] J. M. E. McTaggart, *Some Dogmas of Religion* (1906), p. 3.

expressing the asserter's intention to follow a specified policy of behaviour. To say that it is belief in the dogmas of religion which is the cause of the believer's intending to behave as he does is to put the cart before the horse: it is the intention to behave which constitutes what is known as religious conviction.

But this assimilation of religious to moral assertions lays itself open to an immediate objection. When a moral assertion is taken as declaring the intention of following a policy, the form of the assertion itself makes it clear what the policy is with which the assertion is concerned. For a man to assert that a certain policy ought to be pursued, which on this view is for him to declare his intention of pursuing the policy, presupposes his understanding what it would be like for him to pursue the policy in question. I cannot resolve not to tell a lie without knowing what a lie is. But if a religious assertion is the declaration of an intention to carry out a certain policy, what policy does it specify? The religious statement itself will not explicitly refer to a policy, as does a moral statement; how then can the asserter of the statement know what is the policy concerned, and how can he intend to carry out a policy if he does not know what the policy is? I cannot intend to do something I know not what.

The reply to this criticism is that, if a religious assertion is regarded as representative of a large number of assertions of the same religious system, the body of assertions of which the particular one is a representative specimen is taken by the asserter as implicitly specifying a particular way of life. It is no more necessary for an empiricist philosopher to explain the use of a religious statement taken in isolation from other religious statements than it is for him to give a meaning to a scientific hypothesis in isolation from other scientific hypotheses. We understand scientific hypotheses, and the terms that occur in them, by virtue of the relation of the whole system of hypotheses to empirically observable facts; and it is the whole system of hypotheses, not one hypothesis in isolation, that is tested for its truth-value against experience. So there are good precedents, in the empiricist way of thinking, for considering a system of religious assertions as a whole, and for examining the way in which the whole system is used.

If we do this the fact that a system of religious assertions has a moral function can hardly be denied. For to deny it would require any passage from the assertion of a religious system to a policy of action to be mediated by a moral assertion. I cannot pass from asserting a fact, of whatever sort, to intending to perform an action, without having the hypothetical intention to intend to do the action if I assert the fact. This holds however widely fact is understood—whether as an empirical fact or as a non-empirical fact about goodness or reality. Just as the intention-to-act view of moral assertions is the only view that requires no reason for my doing what I assert to be my duty, so the similar view of religious assertions is the only one which connects them to ways of life without requiring an additional premise. Unless a Christian's assertion that God is love (*agape*)—which I take to epitomize the assertions of the Christian religion—be taken to declare his intention to follow an agapeistic way of life, he could be asked what is the connection between the assertion and the intention, between Christian belief and Christian practice. And this question can always be asked if religious assertions are separated from conduct. Unless religious principles are moral principles, it makes no sense to speak of putting them into practice.

The way to find out what are the intentions embodied in a set of religious assertions, and hence what is the meaning of the assertions, is by discovering what principles of conduct the asserter takes the assertions to involve. These may be ascertained both by asking him questions and by seeing how he behaves, each test being supplemental to the other. If what is wanted is not the meaning of the religious assertions made by a particular man but what the set of assertions would mean were they to be made by anyone of the same religion (which I will call their *typical* meaning), all that can be done is to specify the form of behaviour which is in accordance with what one takes to be the fundamental moral principles of the religion in question. Since different people will take different views as to what these fundamental moral principles are, the typical meaning of religious assertions will be different for different people. I myself take the typical meaning of the body of Christian assertions as being given by their proclaiming intentions to follow an agapeistic way of life, and for a description of this way of life—a description in general and metaphorical terms, but an empirical description nevertheless—I should quote most of the Thirteenth Chapter of I Corinthians. Others may think that the Christian way of life should be described somewhat differently, and will therefore take the typical meaning of the assertions of Christianity to correspond to their different view of its fundamental moral teaching.

My contention then is that the primary use of religious assertions is to announce allegiance to a set of moral principles: without such allegiance there is no 'true religion'. This is borne out by all the accounts of what happens when an unbeliever becomes converted to a religion. The conversion is not only a change in the propositions believed—indeed there may be no specifically intellectual change at all; it is a change in the state of will. An excellent instance is C. S. Lewis's recently published account of his conversion from an idealist metaphysic—' a religion [as he says] that cost nothing'—to a theism where he faced (and he quotes George MacDonald's phrase) 'something to be neither more nor less nor other than *done*'. There was no intellectual change, for (as he says) 'there had long been an ethic (theoretically) attached to my Idealism'; it was the recognition that he had to do something about it, that 'an attempt at complete virtue must be made'.[6] His conversion was a re-orientation of the will.

In assimilating religious assertions to moral assertions I do not wish to deny that there are any important differences. One is the fact already noticed that usually the behaviour policy intended is not specified by one religious assertion in isolation. Another difference is that the fundamental moral teaching of the religion is frequently given, not in abstract terms, but by means of concrete examples—of how to behave, for instance, if one meets a man set upon by thieves on the road to Jericho. A resolution to behave like the good Samaritan does not, in itself, specify the behaviour to be resolved upon in quite different circumstances. However, absence of explicitly recognized general principles does not prevent a man from acting in accordance with such principles; it only makes it more difficult for a questioner to discover upon what principles he is acting. And the difficulty is not only one way round. If moral principles are stated in the most general form, as most moral philosophers have wished to state them, they tend to become so far removed from particular courses of conduct that it is difficult, if not impossible, to give them any precise content. It may be hard to find out what exactly is involved in the imitation of Christ; but it is not very easy to discover what exactly is meant by the pursuit of Aristotle's *eudaemonia* or of Mill's *happiness*. The tests for what it is to live agapeistically are as empirical as are those for living in quest of happiness; but in each case the tests can best be expounded in terms of examples of particular situations.

A more important difference between religious and purely moral principles is that, in the higher religions at least, the conduct

[6] C. S. Lewis, *Surprised by Joy* (1955), pp. 198, 212-13.

preached by the religion concerns not only external but also internal behaviour. The conversion involved in accepting a religion is a conversion, not only of the will, but of the heart. Christianity requires not only that you should behave towards your neighbour as if you loved him as yourself: it requires that you should love him as yourself. And though I have no doubt that the Christian concept of *agape* refers partly to external behaviour—the agapeistic behaviour for which there are external criteria—yet being filled with *agape* includes more than behaving agapeistically externally: it also includes an agapeistic frame of mind. I have said that I cannot regard the expression of a feeling of any sort as the primary element in religious assertion; but this does not imply that intention to feel in a certain way is not a primary element, nor that it cannot be used to discriminate religious declarations of policy from declarations which are merely moral. Those who say that Confucianism is a code of morals and not, properly speaking, a religion are, I think, making this discrimination.

The resolution proclaimed by a religious assertion may then be taken as referring to inner life as well as to outward conduct. And the superiority of religious conviction over the mere adoption of a moral code in securing conformity to the code arises from a religious conviction changing what the religious man wants. It may be hard enough to love your enemy, but once you have succeeded in doing so it is easy to behave lovingly towards him. But if you continue to hate him, it requires a heroic perseverance continually to behave as if you loved him. Resolutions to feel, even if they are only partly fulfilled, are powerful reinforcements of resolutions to act.

But though these qualifications may be adequate for distinguishing religious assertions from purely moral ones, they are not sufficient to discriminate between assertions belonging to one religious system and those belonging to another system in the case in which the behaviour policies, both of inner life and of outward conduct, inculcated by the two systems are identical. For instance, I have said that I take the fundamental moral teaching of Christianity to be the preaching of an agapeistic way of life. But a Jew or a Buddhist may, with considerable plausibility, maintain that the fundamental moral teaching of his religion is to recommend exactly the same way of life. How then can religious assertions be distinguished into those which are Christian, those which are Jewish, those which are Buddhist, by the policies of life which they respectively recommend if, on examination, these policies turn out to be the same?

Many Christians will, no doubt, behave in a specifically Christian manner in that they will follow ritual practices which are Christian and neither Jewish nor Buddhist. But though following certain practices may well be the proper test for membership of a particular religious society, a church, not even the most ecclesiastically-minded Christian will regard participation in a ritual as the fundamental characteristic of a Christian way of life. There must be some more important difference between an agapeistically policied Christian and an agapeistically policied Jew than that the former attends a church and the latter a synagogue.

The really important difference, I think, is to be found in the fact that the intentions to pursue the behaviour policies, which may be the same for different religions, are associated with thinking of different *stories* (or sets of stories). By a story I shall here mean a proposition or set of propositions which are straightforwardly empirical propositions capable of empirical test and which are thought of by the religious man in connection with his resolution to follow the way of life advocated by his religion. On the assumption that the ways of life advocated by Christianity and by Buddhism are essentially the same, it will be the fact that the intention to follow this way of life is associated in the mind of a Christian with thinking of one set of stories (the Christian stories) while it is associated in the mind of a Buddhist with thinking of another set of stories (the Buddhist stories) which enables a Christian assertion to be distinguished from a Buddhist one.

A religious assertion will, therefore, have a propositional element which is lacking in a purely moral assertion, in that it will refer to a story as well as to an intention. The reference to the story is not an assertion of the story taken as a matter of empirical fact: it is a telling of the story, or an alluding to the story, in the way in which one can tell, or allude to, the story of a novel with which one is acquainted. To assert the whole set of assertions of the Christian religion is both to tell the Christian doctrinal story and to confess allegiance to the Christian way of life.

The story, I have said, is a set of empirical propositions, and the language expressing the story is given a meaning by the standard method of understanding how the story-statements can be verified. The empirical story-statements will vary from Christian to Christian; the doctrines of Christianity are capable of different empirical interpretations, and Christians will differ in the interpretations they put upon the doctrines. But the interpretations will all be in terms of empirical propositions. Take, for example, the doctrine of Justification by means of the Atonement. Matthew Arnold imagined it in terms of

> . . . a sort of infinitely magnified and improved Lord Shaftesbury, with a race of vile offenders to deal with, whom his natural goodness would incline him to let off, only his sense of justice will not allow it; then a younger Lord Shaftesbury, on the scale of his father and very dear to him, who might live in grandeur and splendour if he liked, but who prefers to leave his home, to go and live among the race of offenders, and to be put to an ignominious death, on condition that his merits shall be counted against their demerits, and that his father's goodness shall be restrained no longer from taking effect, but any offender shall be admitted to the benefit of it on simply pleading the satisfaction made by the son;—and then, finally, a third Lord Shaftesbury, still on the same high scale, who keeps very much in the background, and works in a very occult manner, but very efficaciously nevertheless, and who is busy in applying everywhere the benefits of the son's satisfaction and the father's goodness.[7]

Arnold's 'parable of the three Lord Shaftesburys' got him into a lot of trouble: he was 'indignantly censured' (as he says) for wounding 'the feelings of the religious community by turning into ridicule an august doctrine, the object of their solemn faith'.[8] But there is no other account of the Anselmian doctrine of the Atonement that I have read which puts it in so morally favourable a light. Be that as it may, the only way in which the doctrine can be understood verificationally is in terms of human beings—mythological beings, it may be, who never existed, but who nevertheless would have been empirically observable had they existed.

For it is not necessary, on my view, for the asserter of a religious assertion to believe in the truth of the story involved in the assertions: what is necessary is that the story should be entertained in thought, i.e. that the statement of the story should be understood as having a meaning. I have secured this by requiring that the story should consist of empirical propositions. Educated Christians of the present day who attach importance to the doctrine of the Atonement certainly do not believe an empirically testable story in Matthew Arnold's or any other form. But it is the fact that entertainment in thought of this and other Christian stories forms the context in which Christian resolutions are made which serves to

---

[7] Matthew Arnold, *Literature and Dogma* (1873), pp. 306-7.
[8] Matthew Arnold, *God and the Bible* (1875), pp. 18-19.

distinguish Christian assertions from those made by adherents of another religion, or of no religion.

What I am calling a *story* Matthew Arnold called a *parable* and a *fairy-tale*. Other terms which might be used are *allegory, fable, tale, myth*. I have chosen the word 'story' as being the most neutral term, implying neither that the story is believed nor that it is disbelieved. The Christian stories include straightforward historical statements about the life and death of Jesus of Nazareth; a Christian (unless he accepts the unplausible Christ-myth theory) will naturally believe some or all of these. Stories about the beginning of the world and of the Last Judgment as facts of past or of future history are believed by many unsophisticated Christians. But my contention is that belief in the truth of the Christian stories is not the proper criterion for deciding whether or not an assertion is a Christian one. A man is not, I think, a professing Christian unless he both proposes to live according to Christian moral principles and associates his intention with thinking of Christian stories; but he need not believe that the empirical propositions presented by the stories correspond to empirical fact.

But if the religious stories need not be believed, what function do they fulfil in the complex state of mind and behaviour known as having a religious belief? How is entertaining the story related to resolving to pursue a certain way of life? My answer is that the relation is a psychological and causal one. It is an empirical psychological fact that many people find it easier to resolve upon and to carry through a course of action which is contrary to their natural inclinations if this policy is associated in their minds with certain stories. And in many people the psychological link is not appreciably weakened by the fact that the story associated with the behaviour policy is not believed. Next to the Bible and the Prayer Book the most influential work in English Christian religious life has been a book whose stories are frankly recognized as fictitious— Bunyan's *Pilgrim's Progress*; and some of the most influential works in setting the moral tone of my generation were the novels of Dostoevsky. It is completely untrue, as a matter of psychological fact, to think that the only intellectual considerations which affect action are beliefs: it is *all* the thoughts of a man that determine his behaviour; and these include his phantasies, imaginations, ideas of what he would wish to be and do, as well as the propositions which he believes to be true.

This important psychological fact, a commonplace to all students of the influence of literature upon life, has not been given sufficient weight by theologians and philosophers of religion. It has not been altogether ignored; for instance, the report of the official Commission on Doctrine in the Church of England, published in 1938, in a section entitled 'On the application to the Creeds of the conception of symbolic truth' says: 'Statements affirming particular facts may be found to have value as pictorial expressions of spiritual truths, even though the supposed facts themselves did not actually happen. . . . It is not therefore of necessity illegitimate to accept and affirm particular clauses of the Creeds while understanding them in this symbolic sense.'[9] But the patron saint whom I claim for my way of thinking is that great but neglected Christian thinker Matthew Arnold, whose parable of the three Lord Shaftesburys is a perfect example of what I take a religious story to be. Arnold's philosophy of religion has suffered from his striking remarks being lifted from their context: his description of religion as *morality touched by emotion* does not adequately express his view of the part played by imagination in religion. Arnold's main purpose in his religious writings was that of 'cementing the alliance between the imagination and conduct'[10] by regarding the propositional element in Christianity as 'literature' rather than as 'dogma'. Arnold was not prepared to carry through his programme completely; he regarded *the Eternal not ourselves that makes for righteousness* more dogmatically than fictionally. But his keen insight into the imaginative and poetic element in religious belief as well as his insistence that religion is primarily concerned with guiding conduct make him a profound philosopher of religion as well as a Christian teacher full of the 'sweet reasonableness' he attributed to Christ.

> *God's wisdom and God's goodness!*—Ay, but fools
> Mis-define these till God knows them no more.
> *Wisdom and goodness, they are God!*—what schools
> Have yet so much as heard this simpler lore?[11]

To return to our philosophizing. My contention that the propositional element in religious assertions consists of stories interpreted as straightforwardly empirical propositions which are not, generally speaking, believed to be true has the great advantage of imposing no restriction whatever upon the empirical interpretation which can

---

[9] *Doctrine in the Church of England* (1938), pp. 37-8.
[10] Matthew Arnold, *God and the Bible* (1875), p. xiii.
[11] From Matthew Arnold's sonnet 'The Divinity' (1867).

be put upon the stories. The religious man may interpret the stories in the way which assists him best in carrying out the behaviour policies of his religion. He can, for example, think of the three persons of the Trinity in visual terms, as did the great Christian painters, or as talking to one another, as in the poems of St John of the Cross. And since he need not believe the stories he can interpret them in ways which are not consistent with one another. It is disastrous for anyone to try to believe empirical propositions which are mutually inconsistent, for the courses of action appropriate to inconsistent beliefs are not compatible. The needs of practical life require that the body of believed propositions should be purged of inconsistency. But there is no action which is appropriate to thinking of a proposition without believing it; thinking of it may, as I have said, produce a state of mind in which it is easier to carry out a particular course of action, but the connection is causal: there is no intrinsic connection between the thought and the action. Indeed a story may provide better support for a long-range policy of action if it contains inconsistencies. The Christian set of stories, for example, contains both a pantheistic sub-set of stories in which everything is a part of God and a dualistic Manichaean sub-set of stories well represented by St Ignatius Loyola's allegory of a conflict between the forces of righteousness under the banner of Christ and the forces of darkness under Lucifer's banner. And the Marxist religion's set of stories contains both stories about an inevitable perfect society and stories about a class war. In the case of both religions the first sub-set of stories provides confidence, the second spurs to action.

There is one story common to all the moral theistic religions which has proved of great psychological value in enabling religious men to persevere in carrying out their religious behaviour policies —the story that in so doing they are doing the will of God. And here it may look as if there is an intrinsic connection between the story and the policy of conduct. But even when the story is literally believed, when it is believed that there is a magnified Lord Shaftesbury who commands or desires the carrying out of the behaviour policy, that in itself is no reason for carrying out the policy: it is necessary also to have the intention of doing what the magnified Lord Shaftesbury commands or desires. But the intention to do what a person commands or desires, irrespective of what this command or desire may be, is no part of a higher religion; it is when the religious man finds that what the magnified Lord Shaftesbury commands or desires accords with his own moral judgment that he decides to obey or to accede to it. But this is no new decision, for his own moral judgment is a decision to carry out a behaviour policy; all that is happening is that he is describing his old decision in a new way. In religious conviction the resolution to follow a way of life is primary; it is not derived from believing, still less from thinking of, any empirical story. The story may psychologically support the resolution, but it does not logically justify it.

In this lecture I have been sparing in my use of the term 'religious belief' (although it occurs in the title), preferring instead to speak of religious assertions and of religious conviction. This was because for me the fundamental problem is that of the meaning of statements used to make religious assertions, and I have accordingly taken my task to be that of explaining the use of such assertions, in accordance with the principle that meaning is to be found by ascertaining use. In disentangling the elements of this use I have discovered nothing which can be called 'belief' in the senses of this word applicable either to an empirical or to a logically necessary proposition. A religious assertion, for me, is the assertion of an intention to carry out a certain behaviour policy, subsumable under a sufficiently general principle to be a moral one, together with the implicit or explicit statement, but not the assertion, of certain stories. Neither the assertion of the intention nor the reference to the stories includes belief in its ordinary senses. But in avoiding the term 'belief' I have had to widen the term 'assertion', since I do not pretend that either the behaviour policy intended or the stories entertained are adequately specified by the sentences used in making isolated religious assertions. So assertion has been extended to include elements not explicitly expressed in the verbal form of the assertion. If we drop the linguistic expression of the assertion altogether the remainder is what may be called religious belief. Like moral belief, it is not a species of ordinary belief, of belief in a proposition. A moral belief is an intention to behave in a certain way: a religious belief is an intention to behave in a certain way (a moral belief) together with the entertainment of certain stories associated with the intention in the mind of the believer. This solution of the problem of religious belief seems to me to do justice both to the empiricist's demand that meaning must be tied to empirical use and to the religious man's claim for his religious beliefs to be taken seriously.

Seriously, it will be retorted, but not objectively. If a man's religion is all a matter of following the way of life he sets before himself and of strengthening his determination to follow it by imagining exemplary fairy-tales, it is purely subjective: his religion is all in terms of his own private ideals and of his own private imaginations. How can he even try to convert others to his religion if there is nothing objective to convert them to? How can he argue in its defence if there is no religious proposition which he believes, nothing which he takes to be the fundamental truth about the universe? And is it of any public interest what mental techniques he uses to bolster up his will? Discussion about religion must be more than the exchange of autobiographies.

But we are all social animals; we are all members one of another. What is profitable to one man in helping him to persevere in the way of life he has decided upon may well be profitable to another man who is trying to follow a similar way of life; and to pass on information that might prove useful would be approved by almost every morality. The autobiography of one man may well have an influence upon the life of another, if their basic wants are similar.

But suppose that these are dissimilar, and that the two men propose to conduct their lives on quite different fundamental principles. Can there be any reasonable discussion between them? This is the problem that has faced the many moral philosophers recently who have been forced, by their examination of the nature of thinking, into holding non-propositional theories of ethics. All I will here say is that to hold that the adoption of a set of moral principles is a matter of the personal decision to live according to these principles does not imply that beliefs as to what are the practical consequences of following such principles are not relevant to the decision. An intention, it is true, cannot be logically based upon anything except another intention. But in considering what conduct to intend to practise, it is highly relevant whether or not the consequences of practising that conduct are such as one would intend to secure. As R. M. Hare has well said, an ultimate decision to accept a way of life, 'far from being arbitrary . . . would be the most well-founded of decisions, because it would be based upon a consideration of everything upon which it could possibly be founded'.[12] And in this consideration there is a place for every kind of rational argument.

Whatever may be the case with other religions Christianity has always been a personal religion demanding personal commitment to a personal way of life. In the words of another Oxford philo-

[12] R. M. Hare, *The Language of Morals* (1952), p. 69.

sopher, 'the questions "What shall I do?" and "What moral principles should I adopt?" must be answered by each man for himself'.[13] Nowell-Smith takes this as part of the meaning of morality:
whether or not this is so, I am certain that it is of the very essence of
the Christian religion.

[13] P. H. Nowell-Smith, *Ethics* (1954), p. 320.

4

DISCUSSION

1. *J. N. Schofield*

IN this ninth Eddington Memorial Lecture[1] Professor Braithwaite argues that, on the basis of the logical positivist proposition that the meaning of any statement is given by its method of verification, religious statements have no meaning because they do not fall into any of the three classes of statements whose truth-value can be thus tested. Then he puts religious statements into the same category as moral statements, and applies to them the empiricist proposition that the meaning of a statement is given by the way in which it is used; in his view a religious, like a moral, assertion is used to express an intention and can be tested by resultant action. He finally attempts to differentiate between moral and religious assertions, and between assertions made by adherents to different religions.

It is surprising that an empiricist should almost completely ignore the existence and verifiable truth-value of Christian experience. There are observable facts in the large body of spiritual experiences known from the past and from our own life, and it is these facts which belong to his first class as testable by direct observation. He puts the *existence* of God into this class, where obviously it cannot belong because it is a theological proposition derived from experience; it belongs to his second class. To put it in the first class is as wrong as to put the theory of relativity into this class, and to argue that scientific statements cannot be tested because this theory cannot be known from direct observation. He goes further and will not allow that such theological propositions have a place in his second class, that of scientific hypotheses, because we are not 'willing to

[1] *An Empiricist's View of the Nature of Religious Belief:* the preceding contribution in this book.

abandon them if the facts prove different from what we think they are'. But does the scientist, similarly placed, 'abandon his hypothesis', or 'reinterpret his statements' to fit the new facts? If originally there was sufficient factual evidence to justify the hypothesis, he would *modify* not abandon it. Of course the new contrary facts must be relevant. No physicist abandons the theory of relativity because he cannot answer the question, How would the spiritual world or personal life be different if it were not true? The lecturer suggests that the Christian may have to abandon the hypothesis of a personal God if he cannot answer the question, How would the physical world be different if it were not true? The theory of relativity is tenable in relation to the space-time-matter group of experiences, the existence of God is tenable in relation to a different group—that of spiritual experiences. The physicist believes in the reality of the physical quantities with which he deals and he may be convinced that, could he handle sufficiently complex equations, he could show an all-embracing unity of space-time-matter; the Christian believes in the reality of the concepts he deals with, and he may be convinced that there is sufficient evidence to warrant the hypothesis that the personal God controls the physical and spiritual worlds: the story of Elijah's contest and many of the stories of Jesus show this conviction, and it is a pity if 'most educated believers' ignore the religious experiences of those who believe that they have 'detected God in this way'. Certainly the prophets of Israel believed that the course of history would have been different without a personal God, and even that it could be altered by man's repentance.

A more careful attention to the religious experiences related in the Bible—Prophetic books, Gospels, Epistles—would have prevented the lecturer from stating that 'the primary use of religious assertions is to announce allegiance to a set of moral principles' and 'this is borne out by all accounts of what happens when an unbeliever becomes converted'. He would have been reminded that there are conversions more typical of Christian experience than the one he quotes. The primary use of Christian assertions is to announce allegiance to a living God knowable through the stories of Jesus and the records of Christian experience: an allegiance which releases into the convert's life spiritual power enabling him to form an intention and act on it. In humility such a convert as Paul asks what God will have him do, and tells us that whereas before he could not do the good he knew and wanted to do, now he says, Thanks be to God who gives us the victory through our Lord Jesus

Christ. No theological proposition, not even 'God is love', 'epito-mizes the assertions of the Christian religion', but the personal experience of a loving power outside ourselves transforming our lives as we respond to it.

The entire lack of this concept from the lecture is its most serious blemish for the Christian. Even the form of the quotation chosen from Matthew Arnold is the dogmatic 'the Eternal not-ourselves that makes for righteousness', rather than the more widely-known form which shows what Arnold meant by 'the Eternal'—'the en-during power' or 'the Eternal power'. Arnold's 'insistence that religion is primarily concerned with guiding conduct' sprang from a more profound philosophy of religion than one which equates religious and moral assertions, and believes man can pass unaided from moral judgments to intentions and thence to action. The aid offered by Professor Braithwaite to Christians in 'their behaviour policies' and in the 'intention to follow an agapeistic way of life' is firstly 'thinking of Christian stories' (although it is not necessary to believe in the truth of the story, which may be allegory, fable, fairy-tale, or myth), and secondly the 'great psychological value' of the most important 'story', namely, that they are doing the will of God (this story or lie, too, need not be believed, because it is just a new way of describing the Christian's own previous moral judgment).

The reason why the lecturer qualifies his acceptance of the Chris-tian stories appears to be his fear lest he be expected to accept as true the stories of creation and the last judgment 'believed by many unsophisticated Christians'; so, although he concedes that a Chris-tian will naturally believe some or all of the straightforward his-torical statements about Jesus, he puts the Christian stories along-side *Pilgrim's Progress* and the novels of Dostoevsky. By so doing he fails to value aright the Gospels. Communication between story-writer and reader is bound up with recognizing the writer's inten-tion; the intention of the Gospel-writers was not to entertain, nor cause temporary willing suspension of disbelief, nor to gain a moral decision, but by giving accurate knowledge about Jesus to win readers to allegiance to him and instruct believers. The stories are important as providing an empirical basis for doctrine, and it is wrong to say that 'Educated Christians of the present day who attach importance to the doctrine of the Atonement certainly do not be-lieve an empirically testable story'.

The lecturer is right to fear the 'tough-minded logical positivist' when propounding a view of the nature of religious belief which makes Christianity either a ritual game or a great pretence. A fundamentalist may refuse to let us look at the fundamentals, but this lecture advocates a worse obscurantism that refuses to abandon theological propositions refuted by experience. For the lecturer the primary element in religion is the resolve to follow a way of life, but he does not regard himself as insincere if he suspects that he will not have the strength of character to carry out his resolution—he resolves to love his enemy, continues to hate him, and makes the heroic perseverance of continually behaving as though he loved him.

For a Christian, the nature of religious belief must be much more closely related to the statements of the first Christians recorded in the New Testament. They were convinced that man is spirit as well as flesh; that there is an external invariant force acting on the spirit of man which can be called the power of God, the spirit of God or the living, risen Christ, whose action is described by the analogy of the love and care of a Father for his children, and whose nature was revealed in the life and death of Jesus. They believed that the power that raised Jesus from the dead was active to change their lives. The change in the life of Christians needs the hypothesis of the existence of such a force to explain it.

The lecturer has done good service to religion by attempting to speak to logical positivists from a discipline that is not theological, and to search for common ground. He can take courage from the experience of countless Christians who have found in life not a hard, lonely, laudible struggle to keep resolutions, but forgiveness, peace, guidance, and strength. The Christian's Lord fulfils his promise, Lo I am with you always.

2. *D. M. Mackinnon*

Professor Braithwaite's Eddington Lecture is an interesting contribution to the philosophy of religion. It is clearly and vigorously written and attempts to answer a question of first-order importance, namely what view of religious belief is compatible with acceptance of a thorough-going logical empiricism.

Braithwaite begins with an outline of the different types of meaningful statement he is prepared to allow, viz. every-day experiential statements, the necessary propositions of logic and mathematics, scientific theories. Of all such he claims we can describe the use in intelligible terms; although their functions are different, their roles can be recognized and their relations one to another made plain. He includes, in this section of his lecture, a sharp reminder to supporters of a prevalent fashion in religious philosophy that the problem of assigning sense to such a proposition as 'God is personal' is not solved by appeal to a supposedly self-authenticating experience of 'meeting God' (p. 55). It is one of the many merits of Braithwaite's approach that it puts a clear question-mark against the value of the widely-diffused language of 'encounter', 'meeting' and the rest and shows how the facile indulgence in such jargon has compelled neglect of the real problems of the philosophy of religion.

On page 59, he defines 'the kernel for an empiricist of the problem of the nature of religious belief' of explaining, in empirical terms, how a religious statement is used by the man who asserts it to express his religious convictions. In slightly different terms, it is the problem of locating religious expressions on the language-map. Braithwaite's own account of their use and place involves him in a brief summary of his views concerning ethical statements. These are for him declarations of intention, to the best of one's ability, to live in a certain way. Thus if a person says (speaking deliberately in general terms) that we ought to promote the greatest happiness of the greatest number, he is by his use of the word 'ought' in that sentence deliberately committing himself to a utilitarian policy of life. He may fail almost completely to live up to his profession (p. 60); but by his chosen form of words he has shown that he is confessing his ethical faith. Similarly where, e.g., Christian religious belief is concerned, we are dealing with a man's declaration of his intention to live in a particular way. Thus a Christian policy of life is not one which follows on (whether in a temporal or a logical sense) conviction of the truth of certain empirical and meta-empirical propositions; that is putting the cart before the horse; it is the intention to behave which constitutes characteristically Christian religious conviction, and provides the context within which the language the believer uses concerning, for instance, the historical life of Jesus and his relation to the Father has its place. Braithwaite would clearly like, as far as possible, to analyse belief in the truth of any religious or theological statement in terms of a manifested habit of behaviour; thus to believe that God is love on his view should consist in behaving, or in trying to behave, in a particular way.

He realizes that he must differentiate characteristically religious from ethical professions of faith; and he does this by saying that the former are always associated, in the mind of the believer, with the entertainment of a particular story. Using the language of Matthew Arnold, he speaks of such entertainment as 'cementing the alliance between the imagination and conduct'; letting the mind dwell on the concrete details of the life of Jesus may be causally efficacious in strengthening the individual's resolve to follow the agapeistic way of life; whether, as a matter of fact, it is so is as much a matter of observation as the resolution itself. But there is considerable inductive evidence for assigning such efficacy to such an exercise; indeed Professor Braithwaite implies that the power is there quite independent of the historical truth of even those parts of the story of Jesus which the most radical criticism would allow us. The synoptic portrait of Christ may be completely on all fours with a novel of Dostoevsky, or Bunyan's *Pilgrim's Progress*; the significance of all alike for religion lies in their power to concentrate attention, and direct the will through discipline of imagination, in pursuit of a particular style of life.

For all his obvious sympathy with behaviourism, Braithwaite emphatically includes reference 'to inner life as well as to outward conduct' (p. 65) in the resolution proclaimed by a religious assertion. If he insists that the reality of religious conviction shall be found not in theory but in practice, he does not confine that practice to matters of public observation; it is obvious that he is not prepared to treat the spiritual life of the individual as a 'logical construction' out of his overt behaviour. Indeed, the sort of fortification of resolve by meditation on the traditional Christian story, of which he judges Matthew Arnold to have given so illuminating an account, is something inherently private to the individual. If the efficacy of mental prayer is to be judged by the way an individual acts, the thing itself remains his own; the colloquies, imaginings, wonderings, resolvings, etc., in which it is expressed are in a true sense private.

Braithwaite makes much of the notion of the Christian *story*, and it is a definite weakness in his argument on e.g. pp. 66 and 68 that he does not distinguish two different senses of the notion. Thus there are certainly a number of historical statements concerning Jesus of Nazareth which Christians believe as they believe other similar historic statements about other individuals. They may be more, or less, certain; thus the statement that Jesus was put to death by crucifixion is more certain than e.g. the precise nature of the charges for which he was condemned before the sanhedrin, or of the meal which he ate with his disciples before his arrest. The situation where these statements are concerned is precisely on all fours with that in respect to the murder of Julius Caesar; we are more more certain that Caesar was murdered on the Ides of March than we are, e.g., concerning his precise intentions for his own future, had he lived longer, and for that of Rome. On all these matters there is historical work to be done. Braithwaite would not deny this; but he leaves it uncertain how important he judges that work to be. On page 68 he comes very near asserting that it would not matter whether or not there was such a person as Jesus of Nazareth, provided that the entertainment of the story about him retained its causal efficacy. Here it is impossible to agree with Braithwaite; for as a matter of fact, the efficacy for cementing the alliance between will and imagination that men have found in meditation upon the life and death of Jesus of Nazareth has been bound up with their belief that some at least of the events about which they are thinking actually happened. Of course this is a matter of fact; it is logically possible that the causal efficacy of meditation upon these events should survive the establishment as certain that they never happened. But few will seriously suppose that as a matter of fact such efficacy would remain, if the record of the Synoptic Gospels were shown to be entirely fictitious, or to use a word with a frankly pejorative nuance, fraudulent. And that such a word would be used inevitably is clear from the fact that the authors of the Gospels, including the Fourth Gospel itself, are at such pains to distinguish, in what they write, what they are doing from what is being done by a writer of fiction. No doubt works of fiction that pretend to be no more than they are, novels and allegories alike, do have the causal efficacy of which Professor Braithwaite speaks. But that cannot reasonably be expected to be the case with works which claim in some way to describe what actually happened, and are then shown to be free imaginative compositions.

But, of course, when Braithwaite uses the word *story*, he is not thinking simply of statements which purport to be records of observable fact; as his quotation from Arnold's *Literature and Dogma* makes very clear, he is thinking rather of such phrases in the creed as 'He came down from Heaven', 'was crucified *for us* under Pontius Pilate', etc. These sentences do in some sense refer to historical events; thus it would be very hard to see how any one could speak of Jesus having come down from heaven who did not believe that as a matter of fact a man of that name at one time lived; but it is equally clear that the sentence is doing very much more than simply stating that fact. Again we cannot speak of Christ as crucified *for us*, unless he was actually put to death in that particular way; but it is again clear that the two words 'for us' do transform the character of what is being said. When Braithwaite speaks of the causal efficacy of the Christian story, it is of the power of such phrases as these that he is really thinking, phrases that are at once historical and meta-historical in import. He is sufficiently convinced of the impossibility of attaching any sort of sense to these statements along the tradi-tional ways of metaphysical theology to be prepared to treat them simply (the word here is my own) as incantations which may deepen an individual's dedication to the agapeistic path of life. To see them in this way liberates the individual from the stress and strain in-volved in doing more with them than Matthew Arnold by his 'parable of the three Lord Shaftesburys' succeeded in doing with what Professor Braithwaite calls (it must be said quite inaccurately) the Anselmian doctrine of the Atonement.

It is certainly very important to have emphasized as strongly as Professor Braithwaite has done the primacy of *agape* or love in the Christian life; the way of love does provide the context from which the individual must attack the problems of faith, and of hope; for it is the 'greatest of the three'. But it may be asked whether Braith-waite has altogether measured up either to what the present re-viewer can only call the ascetic theology of faith, or to the character of the agapeistic way of life which he emphasizes, in *all* its aspects. It was noticed earlier that he was prepared to allow to the prayer life of the individual, however secret and private to himself, an intrinsic dignity and validity; why should not that life include as part of its discipline a deliberate engagement with the tremendous, even impenetrable mysteries of faith, as they are conveyed by the creeds? After all, St John of the Cross says somewhere that in the 'dark night of the soul' the most familiar and foundational items of belief of the catholic, like the hypostatic union and the presence in the eucharist, acquire a new sort of incomprehensibility. Of course those for whom John was writing were men and women who did not know the sort of difficulties, e.g. Hume's and Kant's criticisms of the notions of cause and substance, that any one as serious as Professor Braithwaite must experience in the presence of onto-logical divinity; men who have felt the sharpness of those criticisms have their own special difficulties, even their own special 'dark night' to undergo. But may it not be better in the long run to acknowledge this than to dodge the issue by a conception of faith which in the end robs it of any sort of intellectual content? Of course what we are

really looking for is a means of understanding what is beyond understanding, of coming at least to the outskirts of the incomprehensible; it was something which schoolmen like Cajetan believed they
possessed in their method of analogy. But because we do not share
their 'intuition of being', we cannot avail ourselves of that particular instrument; yet it may be that by remembering what they did,
or tried to do, we can see something at least of what has to be done.

It is also possible that in these matters philosophers have something to learn from the method pursued in dogmatic theology by
Dr Karl Barth, a method which, in the judgment of some of the
students of his massive and still unfinished *Dogmatik*, he is still
perfecting; this is sometimes described as the method of 'Christological analogy', and partly takes the form of subordinating logically
all other Christian theological utterances to Christology. Barth extends this procedure to the interpretation of even the most seemingly general and abstract statements concerning God's being and
attributes, and the relation of the world to him. In carrying out his
enterprise he displays an extraordinary intellectual virtuosity, and
whatever else should be said, it must be admitted that he does throw
into the clearest possible relief the actual role in the intellectual
structure of theology played by those statements in which we notice,
as in the ones mentioned and discussed above, an interplay of the
historical and the meta-historical. He does bring out the cruciality
of their status in characteristically Christian theology, and by doing
so, even if he does not directly advance the solution of the problem
of their intelligibility, does bring out something important about
their peculiar 'logic'. A study of some part at least of Barth's work
might have its place in the total *askesis* of faith to which the believer, by his Credo, commits himself.

But Braithwaite, in spite of his wise and gentle counsels of respect
for the individual person on the last pages of his lecture, raises a
doubt whether he has faced up to the problems of the agapeistic
way of life in all its aspects; he sometimes comes near identifying it
with something not unlike that universal benevolence, which
Butler argued we could not regard as the whole of virtue. It is
surely impossible to ignore the age-old questions of the opposition
between love and justice, and between pity and resentment (to raise
another profound discussion of Butler's). Certainly Braithwaite is
right to insist on the sovereignty of love; but the character of that
love of which he speaks is surely obscured rather than revealed if,
for instance, the gravity of the consequences of the things which

men do, and the choices which they make, is somehow slurred over. To develop this line of thought in full would involve an effort to bring out in a new way the underlying grounds of the dispute in ethics between 'intuitionists' and utilitarians; if it is Braithwaite's virtue to emphasize the supremacy of love, it is perhaps in part a source of weakness to him in his philosophy of religion, that in his ethics he has too uncritical a sympathy with utilitarian policies of life as complete recipes for moral living.

It is, however, always among his strengths in this lecture to prefer concrete to abstract methods of treatment, and therefore in conclusion it might be well to refer to an episode in the gospel story peculiarly relevant to the present argument; namely, the anointing of Jesus before his sufferings (recorded by Mark and Matthew). The motives of the woman's extravagant act remain obscure; but the tensions and disturbance provoked by her action are on record. It is perhaps illuminating to remark the response of Jesus; he finds a context for what the woman has done in the preparation of his body for burial. He gives a certain significance to her action; his words to her may be called, in modern jargon, *performatory*, or in more archaic style, creative. The background of their creative force is what lies immediately before him in the way of endurance; in the language of theologians, that endurance is the supremely creative act. In the reference made to it in his words to the woman, Jesus reveals it, indirectly but certainly, as the deed through whose utter purity, and selflessness of intention, the fragile acts of love performed by others are freed from the corroding taint of their own corruption, and given a firmness and permanence, which, if received from without, is still properly predicated of them in themselves.

If this language is partly metaphorical, that is perhaps inevitable; but at least it may serve to bring out a problem which both Professor Braithwaite's emphasis on *agape*, and his treatment of the role of religious stories and symbols in life, makes peculiarly acute. Is it not possible that a failure on his part fully to measure up to the question how *agape* as a way of life is practically possible has led him to misunderstand radically the character and the role of e.g. Christological affirmation? Were he to revise his views in the manner indicated, he would still have to face most serious difficulties, for instance the sense of the word creative (a word of most subtle and perplexing logic) when the life of Christ is spoken of as creative of the very possibility of love in others. His fully justified edginess in the presence of ontological theology would come back here in full force. But perhaps such an approach would succeed in pin-pointing the real focus of difficulty more effectively than, for instance, Matthew Arnold, for all his insight and grace of style, has succeeded in doing.

Yet it remains true that Professor Braithwaite in this lecture has made a most stimulating contribution to his subject, for whose vigour and honesty no reader can fail to be grateful.

3. *Ian T. Ramsey*

While sympathizing with Professor Braithwaite's aim 'to do justice both to the empiricist's demand that meaning must be tied to empirical use, and to the religious man's claim for his religious beliefs to be taken seriously', my difficulties with his treatment of religious belief in the Eddington lecture are broadly two-fold:

(*a*) While he is willing to admit as 'empirical' something far beyond what the first naïve formulations of the 'verification principle' would have allowed, has he even now gone far enough? Are there not even odder empirical facts than the lecture allows? Compared with the empirical austerity of twenty years ago, Professor Braithwaite is extravagant, but is he extravagant enough?

(*b*) Does the lecture take seriously enough *all* that the religious man—and in particular the Christian—claims in his religious beliefs?

Let me develop these difficulties in four points.

1. Professor Braithwaite urges that the 'primary use' of Christian assertions is to declare the Christian's commitment to an 'agapeistic way of life': now what is involved in a commitment to 'a way of life'?

For instance, there is no doubt a 'Pentonville way of life'—where that phrase describes some recognizable behaviour, whose behaviour 'policy' is determined by H.M. Commissioners for Prisons. Now two prisoners for whatever reason may well declare their intention to make this particular behaviour policy their own. But the one, as Professor Braithwaite says of the Confucianist, might merely obey the rules, while the other, devoting himself single-eyed to the prison, displays Pentonville commitment. The prisoners might then be distinguished by saying of the one that he wasn't a 'genuine' Pen-

tonville man—his heart wasn't in the place, he hadn't a Pentonville 'frame of mind', whereas the other had all these characteristics. Would the second prisoner then be a religious man? I take it
that Professor Braithwaite would say 'yes', at any rate if the
prisoner kept his enthusiasm warm, and stimulated his devotion
by reference to a Pentonville folk-lore; and it must be allowed to
Professor Braithwaite that many of those who talk in a similar kind
of way of the 'Democratic way of life' are sometimes said to make a
'religion' of it. But unless there were something more to be said,
religious people would rather call it 'idolatry'. For while it would
resemble religious devotion in being the loyalty of one's whole life,
it would differ from religious devotion in being a response to no
more than a straightforwardly empirical claim, viz. the Pentonville
pattern of living which in principle could be given an exhaustive
spatio-temporal description. Now Professor Braithwaite says that
I Cor. 13 contains 'an empirical description' of the agapeistic way
of life. But if it only contains an 'empirical description' even in the
full Pentonville sense demanding reference to 'hearts' and 'frames
of mind', it would lead to no more than agapeistic idolatry: as
much idolatry as devotion to a block of wood or stone.

2. Is there then another sense in which I Cor. 13 contains an
'empirical description' of an 'agapeistic way of life'? Fortunately,
yes, but we do not find it by supposing that *agape* is something quite
straightforwardly empirical—a life of endurance, long-suffering
kindness, and so on—because we read, 'Love beareth all things,
believeth all things, hopeth all things, endureth all things'. If that
is our conclusion, we shall certainly have misread the logical gram-
mar of this verse. 'Love beareth all things' is *not* equivalent to 'Love
is notably persevering', whereupon an agapeistic way of life might
be *observationally verified* by the stiff upper lip and the set chin,
which persevere through all kinds of misunderstandings and
jealousies. What we have rather to do to discover *agape*, and what
I Cor. 13 intends, is to tell a story which begins with a model situation of 'bearing', 'believing', 'hoping', or 'enduring'. Thereafter,
this situation is developed in the way that such a qualifying phrase
as 'all things' suggests: in other words, we start on an infinite development to which there is no necessary end. The story must be
able to go on for ever. With what hope, then, do we pursue and
develop it? Until somehow or other a characteristically different
situation is evoked, when the light dawns, the penny drops. We
pursue the story until in Bradley's sense we are 'satisfied'. At that

point *agape* is disclosed, and we respond with an agapeistic way of life. Here is a commitment empirically odder than Pentonville commitment, and not only in its psychological origin but (as could be shown) in its ontological character as well. Further it might be pointed out that it is with reference to such a situation as this, reached and evoked by developing 'model situations' in particular ways, that the word 'God' is posited and given an empirical anchorage. No doubt part of what is claimed by 'God is *agape*' is just such logical kinship between 'God' and '*agape*'.

At the same time, if there were no more to say than is said by the story above, would we be *necessarily* theists? Rather have we said in relation to such a situation as has been evoked: '*Agape* be thou my God'. 'God is *agape*' may have been read '*Agape* is God'. We are rather Agapeists than theists. Now is this Professor Braithwaite's position? Does he wish to suggest that all that is worthwhile in the Christian claim, all that is worthwhile in Christian assertions, could be retained and a good many embarrassments, not to mention crudities, avoided if, recognizing this logical kinship between *agape* and God, we opted rather for *agape*, using the Christian stories to this end? Plainly we have come a long way from agapeistic idolatry. But have we given an adequate account of Christian belief as Christians have professed it? True, the Christian would say, once the light dawned, 'Love so amazing, so divine, demands my soul, my life, my all'—and he could call this *agape* commitment; but if he did, he would be claiming that I Cor. 13 is fulfilled in what is evoked by the gospel narratives, in relation to which the Epistle must be taken, and which it echoes. In other words, when the Christian asserts, 'God is love', he declares *primarily not* his commitment to *agape* or to an agapeistic way of life, but his commitment to certain 'facts' somehow or other described in the Gospels: 'When I survey the wondrous Cross'.

3. Now Professor Braithwaite, of course, is keen to recognize that the Christian claim stems from certain stories; indeed, in its stories, he could agree, lies its distinctiveness. He points out, what none of us would deny, that such stories are causally and psychologically related to the agapeistic way of life. But, he says, it is sufficient that the stories be entertained; they need not be believed.

Let us agree forthwith that we do not do justice to the Christian stories if we only 'believe' them in an ordinary sense; if we assert their 'truth' in an ordinary sense. 'Virgin Birth' and 'biological parthenogenesis'; 'Cross' and 'Crucifixion'; 'Resurrection' and 'Resuscitation'—these are no equivalents. For we *might* believe of Jesus of Nazareth all that the second words in each pair stand for without being Christian; how far we could be Christian while disbelieving what they stand for is a matter on which Christians differ. But the fact that we have *not* logical synonyms is the important point in the present discussion, for it does emphasize that the logic of Christian stories is nothing if not odd. Now Professor Braithwaite may have come to the conclusion he does from noticing this fact. But has he done justice to the oddness by calling the stories 'allegory, fable, tale or myth' or 'parables' or 'fairy-tales'?—all of which in his sense might then presumably be called 'fictional'. Is this to be the logical alternative to 'straightforwardly empirical'? Matthew Arnold may have known no other alternative, but do we not benefit by the logical waters that have flowed under bridges on the Cam and Isis, not to mention the Danube, since his day?

4. The Christian appeals then to certain situations centring around the empirical Jesus of Nazareth, which he describes in such language as 'God so loved the world that he gave his only begotten Son . . .' and if and when we respond to the claim which these situations portray, we say, 'we love because he first loved us'. Christians thus display an agapeistic way of life in response to a challenge which is centred on and is disclosed around the empirical facts of the life, death and resurrection of Jesus of Nazareth. There is no short cut as to what this challenge is. All we can say is that it is embodied in the whole structure of Christian life, worship and faith, which has developed from Jesus and which has, for its public expression, something suitably peculiar and certainly complex; bristling with odd claims and running over with improprieties. If we wanted to portray the challenge to a non-Christian we might begin by telling the Lord Shaftesbury story, but this would not be the 'perfect example' of a *Christian* story, because the Christian wants to speak of a 'pre-existent' Son. So is this story, like any other story, complicated—qualified—until it tells the tale the Christian wishes. When it has done that, the whole range of Christian doctrine—the Christian stories and models together with rules for their manipulation—and the Christian challenge come together, and our response is what the Christian would mean by an agapeistic way of life. It may be by their 'fruits', it is certainly by their qualifiers, that Christians are known; and though many religions might use the same parables, they would differ in the logical qualifiers they gave to them, and so in the 'facts' on which they were based.

What I have tried to do then has been to develop some puzzles which arise from Professor Braithwaite's attempt to assimilate 'religious assertions' to 'moral assertions', though I warmly agree that such an assimilation can do much to illuminate the 'nature of religious belief'. My main difficulty is that *Christian* assertions at any rate are meant to declare that 'something happened' in response to which what is called an 'agapeistic way of life' occurs. It is in their endeavour to portray this 'something' that Christian stories become 'odd'; but while odd, they are not fictional. They have a logic of their own, suited to the odd fact for which they are currency. Professor Braithwaite has given us a part, and an important part, of 'the nature of religious belief' and it is a part which has sometimes been overlooked—has not Professor Braithwaite himself condemned some evangelism for just this omission? But has he himself given us the whole story? Does the Eddington lecture give a meaning to Christian assertions which accounts for all Christians have said and done? People might die for a parable which led to an agapeistic way of life—but would we call it Christian martyrdom? The question as to whether it would be better or worse, more or less reasonable, than Christian martyrdom does not here arise. For, like Professor Braithwaite in his lecture, I have not at all in this article been concerned with the truth or falsity of Christianity: only its meaning.

4. *R. B. Braithwaite*

The preceding articles discussing my recent Eddington Memorial Lecture have raised so many interesting points that I shall only be able to comment here on the most important of them. Before doing so I want to say that in my lecture I deliberately 'stuck my neck out' by propounding a definite and positive view of the way in which an empiricist can take religious assertions. I did so because the *via negativa*, whatever function it may have for a theologian discussing the attributes of God, has no place in the philosophy of religion. It is no profit to be told what religious belief is *not*, unless some indication can be given of what it *is*. I have never for a moment thought that the positive account I gave in the lecture is the whole truth about religious belief—nothing, for instance, is said about the relation of 'mystical experience' to 'looking at the world in a new way' —but I thought that the views expressed in the lecture contained

an important enough part of the truth to be worth putting forward
for discussion. The lecture was concerned with the philosophy of
any religious belief, not with Christian belief only. This was taken
as the principal example, both because Christianity is the only
religion of which I can speak with any knowledge, and because it
would have been disingenuous of me to conceal the fact that, according to the view of religious belief given in the lecture, I count myself
a Christian.

Mr Schofield takes me to task for a defective empiricism. He says
that I 'almost completely ignore the existence and verifiable truth-
value of Christian experience', and that 'a more careful attention
to the religious experiences related in the Bible' would have prevented me from accounting for religious assertions primarily in
moral terms. He suggests, in fact, that I don't know what the biblical writers were talking about. But I can assure Mr Schofield that
I do at least know what *he* is talking about: I know something of
what he means when he says that 'the primary use of Christian assertions is to announce allegiance to a living God . . . an allegiance
which releases into the convert's life spiritual power enabling him
to form an intention and act on it'. My difference from Schofield is
that, *qua* philosopher of religion, I should give a different account
of what is involved in such allegiance. But a point upon which he
lays great emphasis makes me doubt whether he has realized what I
was driving at in my lecture, which is the problem presented to a
contemporary empiricist by religious statements. He says that I fail
'to value aright the Gospels', because 'communication between
story-writer and reader is bound up with recognizing the writer's
intention', and the Gospel-writers' intention was 'by giving accurate
knowledge about Jesus to win readers to allegiance to him and
instruct believers'. But if one has a reasonable knowledge of the
historical background (and some historical imagination), one can
'recognize' a writer's intention without sharing his presuppositions.
How is it relevant to an attempt to philosophize about religion today that the writers who have provided some of the data for this
philosophizing were themselves either not philosophizing or were
philosophizing in a manner which is now impossible for us, heirs of
Galileo and Kant as well as of the Christian tradition, to practise
with sincerity? When a physicist reports that he *sees* electrons moving in a Wilson cloud-chamber, surely this does not settle once and
for all the semantic status of the term 'electron'.

Mr Schofield agrees with me that the existence of God—a theological proposition—is not directly observable (by omitting an 'if' in citing a remark of mine he makes it appear as if we disagree). But he sees fewer difficulties than I do in treating theological propositions as scientific hypotheses, difficulties which have been discussed so extensively in recent philosophical writings (e.g. in several of the *New Essays in Philosophical Theology*, ed. Flew and MacIntyre) that I devoted only three pages to them. Schofield is right in thinking that scientists frequently speak of *modifying* rather than of *abandoning* a hypothesis which has been empirically confirmed by many sorts of fact if it does not fit facts of a new sort. The 'modify' language is used in order to emphasize the continuity of scientific advance and to prevent the unscientific public from supposing that, when Einstein proposed a better explanation of gravitation than Newton's, he thereby showed Newton to have been a fool. But the propriety, in certain cases, of the 'modify' or 're-interpret' language in science does not alter the fact that the meaning of the terms entering into a set of scientifically explanatory hypotheses is given by answering the question, How would the world be different if the hypotheses were not all true? (I carefully did not limit the world to 'the physical world', as Schofield reads me as doing: I employed this expression only in connection with Elijah's experiment, using elsewhere such phrases as 'the world of nature', 'the empirical world', 'the empirical facts'.)

Mr Schofield says that my philosophy of religion 'believes man can pass unaided from moral judgments to intentions and thence to action'. My lecture identified moral judgments with intentions (of certain sorts), so there is no question of passing from the former to the latter. And I did not discuss the conditions under which an intention does or does not pass into action, conditions which require to be elucidated by a psychological study of weakness of will (Aristotle's *akrasia*) and which Schofield would describe in terms of 'an external invariant force acting on the spirit of man which can be called the power of God'. Certainly the unknown cause-factor may be *called* this—just as it may also be called 'the ego-ideal'; but, until its method of operation can be empirically explained, neither term is more than a something I know not what which sometimes enables me to carry out my resolutions.

Professors Mackinnon and Ramsey realize that my lecture was concerned with philosophy of religion and was an essay neither in theology nor in Christian apologetic. Mackinnon's two main criticisms, however, refer to the application of my general view to

Christianity. His first criticism (which I accept) is that my 'Christian set of stories' is a portmanteau term, and that I ought to have distinguished between stories of different types. It appears to me that there are four types of stories in the Christian set (all exemplified in the Apostles' Creed). (1) Mackinnon's 'historical statements' for which Christians and non-Christians would consider exactly the same empirical evidence to be relevant, e.g. that Jesus was 'crucified, dead, and buried'; (2) Historical statements where some Christians would consider non-empirical considerations also relevant, e.g. that Jesus was 'born of the Virgin Mary' (in the 'biological parthenogenesis' sense of Professor Ramsey); (3) Mackinnon's statements employing 'phrases that are at once historical and meta-historical in import', e.g. that Jesus was 'conceived by the Holy Ghost'; (4) Purely non-empirical statements, e.g. that 'God [is] Maker of heaven and earth'. There is no trouble about the understanding of statements of types (1) and (2); and I agree with Mackinnon that the efficacy of the Christian set of stories in promoting a Christian way of life has in the past depended, and will doubtless continue to depend, upon many of the type (1) statements being believed on reasonable grounds to be true. The case is somewhat different in the case of type (2) statements. A Christian may well think that the historical evidence for the story of the Virgin Birth is inadequate, and base his belief or disbelief in it on extra-historical considerations as to how well the story coheres with the body of type (3) and type (4) stories involved in the religious assertions he makes. Mackinnon is right in supposing that it was statements of these two types (3 and 4) which I had principally in mind when I said that, for an empiricist, they must be taken as telling stories which were empirical propositions but whose efficacy for a Christian did not depend upon their being believed to be true, i.e. to correspond to empirical fact. I must protest, however, against Mackinnon's suggestion that I would regard these stories as 'incantations'— unless, indeed, he would also apply this derogatory word to the representations of God on the roof of the Sistine Chapel or in the engravings of Blake.

The reason why I have to take the 'meta-historical' Christian statements in this pictorial way is that, as a conscientious empiricist, *ich kan nicht anders*. Professor Mackinnon agrees that this method of taking them 'liberates the individual from the stress and strain' involved in doing more with them; but he thinks that what I might call *ontological Angst* should be part of the Christian *aske-*

sis, at least for an intellectual like myself. 'Why should not [the prayer life of the individual] include as part of its discipline a deliberate engagement with the tremendous, even impenetrable, mysteries of faith, as they are conveyed by the creeds?' Now it is part of the philosophical *askesis* always to be puzzled about something, just as it is the empiricist's burden to hold all his beliefs as subject to future correction. But is it the duty of a philosopher, even of a philosopher of religion, to focus his vocational anguish on to, for example, the hypostatic union rather than on to the relationships between language, thought, action? Here, surely, are 'mysteries' enough (and not, perhaps, completely 'impenetrable') to satisfy the most ascetic of philosophers on the path to perfection.

Professor Mackinnon's second criticism concerns my description of the agapeistic way of life, which, he thinks, does not give sufficient weight to the notion of justice. My remarks about *agape* were *obiter dicta* made so as to give a content to my general philosophical thesis, which is in no way affected if the Christian way of life were to be described in some more adequate manner. But Mackinnon is wrong in thinking that I would wish to identify *agape* with 'universal benevolence' or to recommend choosing between behaviour policies purely by regard to consequences. The more I study ethics the more convinced I become that the traditional distinction between a 'teleological ethics' basing the rightness of an action upon its consequences and a 'deontological ethics' which makes the rightness of an action depend upon the nature of the action itself is a false one: teleologists have emphasized certain features, and deontologists certain other features, in the total universes associated with alternative actions, and both features are always relevant in choosing between the alternatives. In the context of Christian ethics, a Christian does not love his neighbour *only* to secure joy, peace, the *visio Dei*, but neither does he do so *only* to obey a Kantian imperative: he does so in order to become a member of the Kingdom of Heaven; that is, he opts for one total universe rather than for another.

Professor Ramsey's article is concerned, as was my lecture, with the meaning of Christian assertions, not with their truth or falsity. He suggests that my empiricism is too rigid and my logic not subtle enough: there are 'odder' empirical facts than I allow for, and I have not 'done justice to the oddness [of] the logic of Christian stories'. I cannot agree that I ignore any facts: the Bradleyan 'satisfaction' obtainable by pursuing the agapeistic policy is one of the facts relevant to choosing that policy. Ramsey quotes I Cor. 13.7 to make the point that it is 'all things' that *agape* beareth, believeth, hopeth, endureth; and takes this 'qualifying phrase' to imply that 'we start on an infinite development to which there is no necessary end'. Now it is perfectly true that one does not know what is involved in, or will come out of, pursuing the agapeistic policy until one has embarked on it. But this is also the case in pursuing any general policy whatever, even that of the purest egoism. A 'characteristically different situation is evoked' when the pure egoist attains bliss as a heroin addict. Every general policy for living has an 'open structure'. As I said in my lecture (p. 64), Aristotle's *eudaemonia* or Mill's *happiness* can only be given content by examples: experiments in trying to live agapeistically may lead to more unexpected results than experiments in questing happiness; but is this difference a difference in kind?

Professor Ramsey sometimes uses the words 'empirical' and 'fact' in contexts which surprise (I would almost say shock) me. He speaks of a 'straightforwardly empirical claim', of a 'commitment empirically odder than Pentonville commitment', of a Christian declaring his 'commitment to certain "facts" somehow or other described in the Gospels'. Use of these expressions makes it look as if Ramsey were committing the gravest of all category mistakes—that of supposing that an *ought* can follow from an *is*. How can one commit oneself to an empirical fact? How can a fact have a claim upon one? If all that Ramsey means by his phrases is what he in other places expresses by speaking of the Christian way of life as being a *response* to certain empirical facts (e.g. about the life of Jesus), there is very little that separates our two positions.[2]

I suspect, however, that the inverted commas which Ramsey sometimes puts round his *facts* indicate that these can only be referred to by statements whose 'logic' is 'odd' in that it includes the use of special 'logical qualifiers'. But what is this odd logic? I should understand what was meant were someone to say to me that the logic of scientific thinking is odder than deductive logic (though I should protest against his way of putting it). But that is because I know what scientific thinking is, and know how to teach it to someone who is ignorant of it. (I should, of course, get him to perform experiments as well as talking about results of experiments.) But how would Professor Ramsey (or indeed Professor Mackinnon, who similarly speaks of a 'peculiar "logic"' and of a 'most subtle and

---

[2] [I hope the reader will find that ch. 9 furthers this discussion and elucidates some of the points raised in this paragraph. *Editor*.]

perplexing logic') set about teaching this 'logic' (or these 'logics') to a non-Christian? Until Christian philosophers can explain how this may be done, a characterization of Christian belief in terms of knowledge of an inexplicable way of thinking will only save an 'intellectual content' for Christianity at the price of making of it a secret doctrine open only to the Elect.

5

MORALITY: RELIGIOUS AND SECULAR

P. H. Nowell-Smith

I

THE central thesis of this paper is that religious morality is infantile. I am well aware that this will sound absurd. To suggest that Aquinas and Kant—to say nothing of millions of Christians of lesser genius—never grew up is surely to put oneself out of court as a philosopher to be taken seriously. My thesis is not so crude as that; I shall try to show that, in the moralities of adult Christians, there are elements which can be set apart from the rest and are, indeed, inconsistent with them, that these elements can properly be called 'religious' and that just these elements are infantile.

I shall start by making some assumptions that I take to be common ground between Christians and secular humanists. I propose to say almost nothing about the *content* of morality; that love, sympathy, loyalty, and consideration are virtues, and that their opposites, malice, cruelty, treachery, and callousness, are vices, are propositions that I shall assume without proof. One can't do everything at the same time, and my job now is not to refute Thrasymachus. Secondly, I propose to occupy, as common ground, some much more debatable territory; I shall assume in broad outline the metaphysical view of the nature of man that we have inherited from Plato and Aristotle. The basis of this tradition is that there is something called 'Eudaimonia' or 'The Good Life', that this consists in fulfilling to the highest possible degree the nature of Man, and that the nature of Man is to be a rational, social animal. Love, I shall assume, is the supreme virtue because the life of love is, in the end, the only life that is fully rational and fully social. My

concern will be, not with the content of morality, but with its form
or structure, with the ways in which the manifold concepts and
affirmations of which a moral system is composed hang together;
not with rival views of what conduct is moral and what is immoral,
but with rival views of what morality *is*.

This contrast between form and content is not difficult to grasp,
but experience has taught me that it is often ignored. When they
discover that I have moral views but no religious beliefs, people
often ask me this question: 'Where do you get your moral ideas
from?' Faced with this question, my habit is to take it literally and
to answer it truthfully. 'From my father and mother,' I say, 'from
the companions of my boyhood and manhood, from teachers and
from books, from my own reflections on the experience I have had
of the sayings and doings of myself and others, an experience
similar in countless ways to that of other people born of middle-
class English parents some forty-five years ago, but in its totality
unique.' This boring and autobiographical answer never satisfies
the questioner; for, though it is the right answer to the question he
actually asked, it is not, as I very well knew, the answer to the
question he really had in mind. He did not want to know *from
whom* I learnt my moral views; he wanted to know what *authority*
I have for holding them. But why, if this is what he wanted to
know, did he not ask me? He has confused two different questions;
and it is natural enough that he should have confused them, since
it is often the case that to point to the source of an opinion or
claim is to show the authority on which it is based. We appeal to
the dictionary to vindicate an assertion about the spelling of a
word, and the policeman's production of a warrant signed by a
magistrate is a necessary and sufficient condition of his authority to
enter my house. But even a dictionary can make mistakes, and one
may doubt whether one *ought* to admit the policeman even after
his legal title to enter has been satisfactorily made out. 'He certainly
has a legal right,' one might say, 'but even so, things being as they
are, ought I to admit him?'

Those who put this question to me have made an assumption
that they have not examined because they have not reflected sufficiently on the form of morality. They have simply assumed that
just as the legal propriety of an action is established by showing it
to emanate from an authoritative source, so also the moral propriety
of an action must be established in the same way; that legal rightness has the same form as moral rightness, and may therefore be

used to shed light on it. This assumption made, they naturally suppose that, even when I agree with them—for example, about the immorality of murder—I have no right to hold this impeccable view unless I can show that I have received it from an authoritative source. My autobiographical answer clearly fails to do this. My parents may have had a right to my obedience, but no right to make the moral law. Morality, on this view, is an affair of being commanded to behave in certain ways by some person who has a right to issue such commands; and, once this premise is granted, it is said with some reason that only God has such a right. Morality must be based on religion, and a morality not so based, or one based on the wrong religion, lacks all validity.

It is this premise, that being moral consists in obedience to commands, that I deny. There is an argument, familiar to philosophers but of which the force is not always appreciated, which shows that this premise cannot be right. Suppose that I have satisfied myself that God has commanded me to do this or that thing—in itself a large supposition, but I will waive objections on this score in order to come quickly to the main point—it still makes *sense* for me to ask whether or not I *ought* to do it. God, let us say, is an omnipotent, omniscient creator of the universe. Such a creator might have evil intentions and might command me to do wrong; and if that were the case, though it would be imprudent to disobey, it would not be wrong. There is nothing in the idea of an omnipotent, omniscient creator which, by itself, entails his goodness or his right to command, unless we are prepared to assent to Hobbes' phrase, 'God, who by right, *that is by irresistible power*, commandeth all things'. Unless we accept Hobbes' consistent but repugnant equation of God's right with his might, we must be persuaded *independently* of his goodness before we admit his right to command. We must judge for ourselves whether the Bible is the inspired word of a just and benevolent God or a curious amalgam of profound wisdom and gross superstition. To judge this is to make a moral decision, so that in the end, so far from morality being based on religion, religion is based on morality.

Before passing to my main theme, I must add two cautions about what this argument does *not* prove. It does not prove that we should in no case take authority as a guide. Suppose that a man's aim is to make money on the Stock Exchange. He decides that it would be most profitable to invest his money in company A; but his broker prefers company B. He will usually be well advised to

accept the verdict of his broker, even if the broker is, as they often
are, inarticulate in giving his reasons. He might decide to put all
his financial affairs in the hands of a broker, and to do nothing but
what the broker tells him to do. But *this* decision, even if it is the
only financial decision he ever makes in his life, is still his own.
In much the same way, a man might decide to put his conscience
wholly into the hands of a priest or a Church, to make no moral
decisions of his own but always to do what the priest tells him. Even
he, though he makes but one moral decision in his life, must make
and continually renew that one. Those who accept the authority
of a priest or a Church on what to do are, in accepting that
authority, deciding for themselves. They may not fully comprehend
that this is so; but that is another matter.

Secondly, to deny that morality need or can have an external
non-moral basis on which to stand is by no means to deny that it
can have an internal basis, in the sense of one or a few moral
beliefs that are fundamental to the other beliefs of the system. A
man's views on gambling or sex or business ethics may (though
they need not) form a coherent system in which some views are
held *because* certain others views are held. Utilitarianism is an
example of such a system in which all moral rules are to be judged
by their tendency to promote human happiness. A moral system
of this kind is like a system of geometry in which some propositions
appear as axioms, others as theorems owing their place in the
system to their derivability from the axioms. Few of us are so
rationalistic as to hold all our moral beliefs in this way, but to move
towards this goal is to begin to think seriously about morals.

II

In any system of morality we can distinguish between its content
and its form. By its 'content' I mean the actual commands and
prohibitions it contains, the characteristics it lists as virtues and as
vices; by its 'form' I mean the sort of propositions it contains and
the ways in which these are thought of as connected with each
other. The basic distinction here is between a teleological morality
in which moral rules are considered to be subordinate to ends, to
be rules *for* achieving ends and consequently to be judged by their
tendency to promote those ends, and a deontological system in
which moral rules are thought of as absolute, as categorical imperatives in no way depending for their validity on the good or
bad consequences of obedience, and in which moral goodness is

thought to lie in conformity to these rules for their own sake. The first of these ways of looking at morality as a whole derives from the Greeks, so I shall call it the Greek view of morality; it can be summed up in the slogan 'the Sabbath was made for man, not man for the Sabbath'. The second, deriving mainly from Jewish sources, I shall call the Hebrew view. This involves a serious over-simplification, since we find deontological elements in the Greek New Testament and teleological elements in the Hebrew Old Testament; but, taken broadly, the contrast between the deontological character of the Old and the teleological character of the New Testaments is as striking as the difference of language. I shall also indulge in another serious over-simplification in speaking of Christianity as a morality of the Hebrew type while it is, of course, an amalgam of both with different elements predominating in different versions. This over-simplification would be quite unjustifiable if my task were to give an account of Christian morality; but it is legitimate here because my task is to contrast those elements in the Christian tradition which secular humanists accept with those which they reject, and these are broadly coterminous with the Greek and the Hebrew elements in Christianity respectively.

How there can be these two radically different ways of looking at morality, one which sees it as a set of recipes to be followed for the achievement of ends, the other which sees it as a set of commands to be obeyed, can best be understood if we consider the way in which we learn what it is to be moral. For a man's morality is a set of habits of choice, of characteristic responses to his environment, in particular to his social environment, the people among whom he lives; and habits are learnt in childhood. Growing up morally is learning to cope with the world into which we find ourselves pitched, and especially to cope with our relations with other human beings. In the course of living we learn to reflect on our responses, to find in some of them sources of satisfaction, in others sources of regret, and 'coping with the world' means coping with it in a manner ultimately satisfactory to ourselves. Philosophers such as Aristotle and Hobbes who boldly and crudely identified 'good' with 'object of desire' may have made a technical mistake; but they were certainly on the right lines. If men had no desires and aversions, if they felt no joy and no remorse, if they were totally indifferent to everything in the universe, there would be no such thing as choice and we should have no concept of morality, of good and evil.

The baby is born with some desires, not many; others it acquires as time goes on. Learning to cope with the world is learning how to satisfy and to modify these desires in a world that is partly propitious and partly hostile. For the world does not leap to gratify my desires like an assiduous flunkey; I do not get fed by being hungry. My desires are incompatible with each other and they come into conflict with those of other people. We have to learn both to bend the world to our wills and to bend our wills to the world. A man's morality is the way in which, in important matters, he does this.

Men are by nature rational and social animals, but only potentially so; they become actually rational and social only in a suitable environment, an environment in which they learn to speak a language. Learning how to cope with one's environment goes on side by side with learning to talk. The child's concepts, the meanings which, at every stage, words have for him, change as his horizon becomes wider, as he learns to grasp ideas that are more and more complicated, more and more remote from the primitive actions and passions that initially constitute his entire conscious life. It is not therefore surprising that the *form* of his morality, the meanings which moral words have and the ways in which they hang together, reflect at each stage the kind of experience he has. To babies who cannot yet talk we cannot, without serious error, attribute any thoughts at all; but though they cannot think, they can certainly feel, experience pleasure and pain, satisfaction and frustration. It is in these pre-verbal experiences that the origin of the ideas of 'good' and 'bad', even of 'right' and 'wrong', must be found; for their later development I turn to Piaget. My case for saying that religious morality is infantile cannot be conclusively made out without a much more detailed study of Piaget's researches than I have space for; I shall concentrate on a few points that seem to me to bear directly on the issue between the religious morality of law and the secular morality of purpose.

Piaget made a detailed study of the attitudes of children of different ages to the game of marbles, and he found three distinct stages. A very small child handles the marbles and throws them about as his humour takes him; he is playing, but not playing a *game*; for there are no rules governing his actions, no question of anything being done right or wrong. Towards the end of this stage he will, to some extent, be playing according to rules; for he will imitate older children who are playing a rule-governed game. But the child himself is not conscious of obeying rules; he has not yet grasped the concept of a 'rule', of what a rule *is*. We may call this the pre-moral attitude to rules.

The second type of attitude is exhibited by children from five to nine. During this stage, says Piaget, 'the rules are regarded as sacred and inviolable, emanating from adults and lasting for ever. Every suggested alteration in the rules strikes the child as a transgression.' Piaget calls this attitude to rules 'heteronomous' to mark the fact that the children regard the rules as coming, as indeed they do, from the outside, as being imposed on them by others. We might also call this the 'deontological stage', to mark the fact that the rules are not questioned; they just *are* the rules of marbles, and that's that. At this stage the child has the concept of a rule, he knows what a rule is; but he has not yet asked what a rule is *for*. This deontological character is obviously connected with the unchangeability of the rules. Like laws in a primitive society, they are thought of as having been handed down from time immemorial, as much a part of the natural order of things as sunrise and sunset. The child may chafe at obedience and may sometimes disobey; but he does not question the authority of the rules.

Finally, at the third stage, the child begins to learn what the rules are for, what the point of having any rules is, and why it is better to have this rule rather than that. 'The rule', says Piaget, 'is now looked upon as a law due to mutual consent, which you must respect if you want to be loyal, but which it is permissible to alter on condition of enlisting the general opinion on your side.' He calls this type of attitude 'autonomous' to mark the fact that the children now regard themselves, collectively, as the authors of the rules. This is not to say that they falsely suppose themselves to have invented them; they know well enough that they received them from older children. But they are the authors in the sense of being the final authorities; what tradition gave them they can change; from 'this is how we learnt to play' they no longer pass unquestioningly to 'this is how we ought to play'. We might also call this stage 'teleological' to mark the fact that the rules are no longer regarded as sacred, as worthy of obedience simply because they are what they are, but as serving a purpose, as rules for playing a game that they want to play. Rules there must certainly be; and in one sense they are sacred enough. Every player must abide by them; he cannot pick and choose. But in another sense there is nothing sacred about them; they are, and are known to be, a *mere* device, to be moulded and adapted in the light of the purpose which they are understood by all the players to serve.

To illustrate the transition between the second and the third stages I should like to refer to a case from my own experience. Last summer I was with one other adult and four children on a picnic, and the children wanted to play rounders. We had to play according to the rules they had learnt at school because those just were the rules of rounders. This involved having two teams, and you can well imagine that, with only three players in each team, the game quickly ran on the rocks. When I suggested adapting the rules to our circumstances all the children were scandalized at first. But the two older children soon came round to the idea that, situated as we were, we should have to change the rules or not play at all and to the idea that it would not be wicked to change the rules. The two younger children were troubled, one might say, in their consciences about the idea of changing the rules. In Piaget's words, they thought of an alteration of rules as a transgression against them, having as yet no grasp of the distinction between an alteration of the rules by common consent to achieve a common purpose and the unilateral breach or defiance of them. In the eyes of these younger children we were not proposing to play a slightly different game, one better adapted to our situation; we were proposing to play the old game, but to play it wrong, almost dishonestly.

In another of Piaget's researches, this time directly concerned with moral attitudes, he told the children pairs of stories in each of which a child does something in some sense 'bad' and asked which of the children was naughtier, which deserved most punishment. In one such story a child accidently breaks fifteen cups while opening a door, and in the companion story a child breaks one cup while stealing jam. The replies of the very young children are mixed, some saying that the first child was naughtier; older children are unanimous in calling the second child naughtier. They have got beyond the primitive level of assessing moral guilt by the extent of the damage done.

Some of the youngest children do not recognize an act as wrong unless it is actually found out and punished, and we may call these last two points taken together 'moral realism', because they display an attitude of mind that makes questions of morality questions of external fact. The inner state of the culprit—his motives and intentions—have nothing to do with it. To break crockery is wrong; therefore to break more crockery is more wrong. Moral laws are like laws of Nature, and Nature gives no marks for good or bad intentions and accepts no excuses. The fire will burn you if you touch it, however careful you were to avoid it. But if you are careless and, by good luck, avoid it, you will not be burnt; for Nature gives no bad marks for carelessness either. In the same way, if you lie and are punished, that is bad; but if you lie and are not punished, that is not bad at all. The fact that retribution did not follow *shows* that the lie was not, in this case, wrong.

III

I want now to compare the religious with the secular attitude towards the moral system which, in its content, both Christians and Humanists accept. I shall try to show that the religious attitude retains these characteristics of deontology, heteronomy and realism which are proper and indeed necessary in the development of a child, but not proper to an adult. But I must repeat the caution with which I began. The views which I called 'moral realism', which make intentions irrelevant, were expressed by very young children. No doubt many of these children were Christians and I do not wish to suggest that they never grew up, that they never adopted a more mature and enlightened attitude. This would be absurd. My thesis is rather that these childish attitudes survive in the moral attitudes of adult Christians—and of some secular moralists—as an alien element, like an outcrop of igneous rock in an alluvial plain. When Freud says of someone that he is fixated at the oral stage of sexuality he does not mean that he still sucks his thumb; he means rather that some of his characteristic attitudes and behaviour-patterns can be seen as an adult substitute for thumb-sucking. In the same way, I suggest that some elements characteristic of Christian morality are substitutes for childish attitudes. In the course of this comparison I shall try to show how these infantile attitudes belong to a stage that is a *necessary* stage on the way to the fully adult, a stage which we must have passed through in order to reach maturity.

It needs little reflection to see that deontology and heteronomy are strongly marked features of all religious moralities. First for deontology. For some Christians the fundamental sin, the fount and origin of all sin, is disobedience to God. It is not the nature of the act of murder or of perjury that makes it wrong; it is the fact that such acts are transgressions of God's commands. On the other hand, good acts are not good in themselves, good in their own nature, but good only *as* acts of obedience to God. 'I give no alms only to satisfy the hunger of my brother, but to accomplish the will and command of my God; I draw not my purse for his sake that demands it, but his that enjoined it' (Sir Thomas Browne, *Religio Medici* II, 2). Here charity itself is held to be good *only because* God has told us to be charitable. It is difficult not to see in this a reflection of the small child's attitude towards his parents and the other authorities from whom he learns what it is right to do. In the first instance little Tommy learns that it is wrong to pull his sister's hair, not because it hurts her, but because Mummy forbids it.

The idea of heteronomy is also strongly marked in Christian morality. 'Not as I will, but as thou wilt.' The demand made by Christianity is that of surrendering self, not in the ordinary sense of being unselfish, of loving our neighbour and even our enemy. It is the total surrender of the *will* that is required; Abraham must be prepared to sacrifice Isaac at God's command, and I take this to mean that we must be prepared to sacrifice our most deeply felt moral concerns if God should require us to do so. If we dare to ask why, the only answer is 'Have faith'; and faith is an essentially heteronomous idea; for it is not a reasoned trust in someone in whom we have good grounds for reposing trust; it is blind faith, utter submission of our own reason and will.

Now, to the small child morality is necessarily deontological and heteronomous in form; he must learn *that* certain actions are right and others wrong before he can begin to ask *why* they are, and he learns this from other people. The child has his own spontaneous springs of action; there are things he wants to do off his own bat; morality is a curb, at first nothing but a curb on his own volition. He comes up against parental discipline, even if only in the form of the giving and withdrawing of love, long before he can have any compassion, long before he has any conception of others as sentient beings. When he begins to learn language, words like 'bad' must mean simply 'what hurts me; what I don't like'; through the mechanism of parental discipline they come to mean 'what adults forbid and punish me for'. It is only because actions which cause suffering to others figure so largely among parental prohibitions that the child learns to connect the word 'bad' with them at all.

If we consider the foundations of Christian ethics in more detail we shall find in them moral realism as well. Christianity makes much of charity and the love of our neighbour; but it does not say, as the Greeks did, that this is good because it is what befits the social animal, Man. We ought to be charitable because this is laid on us as a duty and because this state of the soul is the proper state for it during its transient mortal life. We must be charitable because (we are told) only so can we arrive at the soul's goal, the right relation to God. This fundamental isolation of the individual soul with God seems clearly to reflect what one supposes must be the state of mind of the small baby for whom, at the dawn of consciousness, there is only himself on the one side and the collective world of adults, represented largely by his parents, on the other, for whom the idea of others as individuals, as beings like himself, does not yet exist.

This impression is increased when we consider some accounts of what this right relationship between the soul and God is. Granted that to achieve this is the object of right living, just *what* relationship is it that we are to try to achieve? The terms of the relation are an omnipotent creator and his impotent creature, and between such terms the only relation possible is one of utter one-sided dependence, in which the only attitude proper to the creature must be one of adoration, a blend of love and fear. Surely this is just how the world must appear to the young child; for he really *is* impotent, wholly dependent on beings whose ways he cannot understand, beings sometimes loving, sometimes angry, but always omnipotent, always capricious—in short, gods. 'As for Dr Wulicke himself personally, he had all the awful mystery, duplicity, obstinacy, and jealousy of the Old Testament God. He was as frightful in his smiles as in his anger.'[1]

Consider in this connection the ideas of original sin and grace. Every son of Adam is, of his own nature, utterly corrupt, redeemable only by divine grace. Once more, the conditions in which the child learns morality provide an obvious source for this remarkable conception. Parents are not only omniscient and omnipotent; they are also necessarily and always morally in the right. This must be so, since they are, as the child sees it, the authors of the moral law. Morality, the idea of something being right or wrong, enters the horizon of the child only at those points at which he has, so to speak, a dispute with authority, only on those occasions on which

[1] Thomas Mann, *Buddenbrooks*, referring to the headmaster whom Hanno and Kai nicknamed 'The Lord God'. The whole chapter, Part XI, ch. 2, illustrates this point.

he is told or made to do something that he does not spontaneously want to do. From these premises that, at the time when the meanings of 'right' and 'wrong' are being learnt, the child must disagree with its parents and that they must be right he naturally passes to the conclusion that he must always be wrong. To have the sense of actual sin is to have the sense that one has, on this occasion, done wrong; to have the sense of original sin is simply to feel that one must be always and inevitably wrong. This sense of sin has often been deliberately and cruelly fostered; John Bunyan is not the only man to have left on record the agony of his childhood; but the point I wish to make is that the infantile counterpart of the sense of sin is a necessity at a certain stage of moral development, the stage at which moral words are being learnt and moral rules accepted as necessarily what parents say they are.

On the other side of the picture there is the doctrine of grace. Each individual soul is either saved or damned; but its fate, at least according to some versions, is wholly out of its own control. In these extreme versions, grace is absolutely necessary and wholly sufficient for salvation; and grace is the *free* gift of God. As far as the creature is concerned, there is absolutely nothing that he can do or even try to do either to merit or to obtain it.[2] From his point of view the giving or withholding of the means of salvation must be wholly capricious.

Once more, this is how parental discipline must seem to the child who cannot yet understand its aims and motives. Consider, for example, how even the most careful and consistent parents react towards what they call the clumsiness of a child. He knocks things over; he fumbles with his buttons. Though most parents do not think of themselves as punishing a child for such things, their behaviour is, from the child's point of view, indistinguishable from punishment. They display more irritation when the child knocks over a valuable vase than when he knocks over a cheap cup, when the button-fumbling happens to occur at a moment when they are in a hurry than when it does not. If a father takes from a small child something that is dangerous to play with or stops him hurting himself by a movement necessarily rough, that to the child is indistinguishable from punishment; it is a thwarting of his inclination for no reason that he can see. Children often say things that

---

[2] This is, I know, heretical; yet I cannot see in the subtle palliatives offered by Catholic theologians anything but evasions, vain attempts to graft a more enlightened moral outlook on to a theological tree which will not bear them. The reformers seem to me to have been right in the sense that they were restoring the original doctrine of the Church.

they know to be untrue; sometimes they are reprimanded for lying, sometimes complimented on their imagination. How can the child know under which heading, the good or the bad, a piece of invention will come, except by observing whether it is punished or rewarded? The child, by this time, is beginning to make efforts to try to please his parents, to do what, in his childish mind, he thinks right. The parents, not being expert child-psychologists, will often fail to notice this; more often they will disregard it. To the child, therefore, there is little correlation between his own intentions and the reactions he evokes from the adult world. Salvation in the form of parental smiles and damnation in the form of parental frowns will come to him, like grace, in a manner that both seems and is wholly unconnected with any inwardly felt guilt. The mystery of God's ways to Man is the mystery of a father's ways to his children.

This characterization of religious morality as essentially infantile may seem to be unnecessary; for do not Christians themselves liken their relationship to God as that of child to father? In so doing they do not seem to me always to realize how incompatible this father–child relationship is with the Greek conception of the good life which they recognize as one of the sources of their moral doctrine. Aristotle says that children, like animals, have no share in the good life (a remark which always sounds so odd when people translate it as 'children have no share in happiness'), and the reason he gives is that children do not *act*. This is a deep furrow to begin to plough at this stage—what is meant by 'action'; but briefly it is motion that is self-initiated and responsible. The prime difference between the adult and the child is that the adult has freedom to choose for himself and has, what goes with freedom, responsibility for his actions. In the life of a child there is always, in the last resort, the parent or some substitute for a parent to turn to. The father is responsible at law for the actions of his child; he will undo what harm the child has done; he will put things right, will save the child from the consequences of his mistakes. To pass from childhood into adulthood is essentially to pass from dependence into freedom, and the price we pay is responsibility. As adults we make our own choices and must accept their consequences; the shield that in our childish petulance we once thought so irksome is no longer there to protect us. To many of us this is a matter of life-long regret, and we search endlessly for a father-substitute. Surely 'they' will get us out of the mess; there ought to be a law; why doesn't somebody . . . These, in this godless age, are the

common secular substitutes; religion, when it is not a patent substitute, is only a more profound, a more insinuating one.

I V

The postulation of a god as the author of the moral law solves no
more problems in ethics than the postulation of a god as first cause
solves problems in metaphysics. Nor need we base morality, as I
have done, on the metaphysical conception of Man as a rational,
social animal, though we shall do so if we care to maintain the link
with the old meaning of the word 'humanist'. To me, as a philosopher, some systematic view of the whole of my experience, some
metaphysic, is essential, and this conception of the nature of Man
makes more sense of my experience than any other I know. But I
certainly should not argue that *because* the species Man has such
and such a nature, *therefore* each and every man ought to act in
such and such ways. In trying to sketch a humanist morality I shall
start simply with the idea that a morality is a set of habits of choice
ultimately determined by the question 'What life is most satisfactory to me as a whole?', and I start with this because I simply do
not *understand* the suggestion that I ought to do anything that does
not fit into this conception. Outside this context the word 'ought'
has for me no meaning; and here at least I should expect Christians
to agree with me.

If we start in this way, inquiries into my own nature and into
the nature of Man at once become relevant. For my nature is such
that there are some things that are impossible for me to do. Some
hopes must be illusory, and nothing but frustration could come of
indulging them. I could not, for example, become an operatic tenor
or a test cricketer. Inquiries into the nature of Man are relevant
in two ways; first, because I have to live as a man among men,
secondly, because all men are to some degree alike and some of my
limitations are common to us all. None of us can fly or witness
past events. It is only in so far as men are alike that we can even
begin to lay down rules as to how they should (all) behave; for it is
only in so far as they are alike that they will find satisfaction and
frustration in the same things. Prominent among the similarities
among men are the animal appetites, the desire for the love and
companionship of their own species, and the ability to think; and it
is these three similarities that make us all 'moral' beings. Morality
consists largely, if not quite wholly, in the attempt to realize these
common elements in our nature in a coherent way, and we have

found that this cannot be done without adopting moral rules and codes of law. Humanism does not imply the rejection of all moral rules, but it does imply the rejection of a deontological attitude towards them. Even Piaget's older children could not have played marbles without rules; but they treated them as adaptable, as subservient to the purpose of playing a game, which is what they wanted to do. They treated the rules as a wise man treats his motor car, not as an object of veneration but as a convenience.

This, I suggest, is how we, as adults, should regard moral rules. They are necessary, in the first place, because one man's aim in life often conflicts with the aims of others and because most of our aims involve the co-operation of others, so that, even for purely selfish reasons, we must conform to rules to which others also conform. Most moral rules, from that prohibiting murder to that enjoining punctuality, exist for this purpose. But morality is not wholly an affair of regulating our dealings with others; each man has within himself desires of many different kinds which cannot all be fully satisfied; he must establish an order of priorities. Here I think almost all moralists, from Plato to D. H. Lawrence, have gone astray; for they have over-emphasized the extent to which men are like each other and consequently been led to embrace the illusory concept of a 'best life' that is the same for all of us. Plato thought this was a life dominated by the pursuit of knowledge, Lawrence one dominated by the pursuit of sensual experience and animal activity. I do not happen to enjoy lying naked on the grass; but I should not wish to force my preference for intellectual endeavour on anyone who did. Why should we not, within the framework of uniformity required for any life to be satisfactory to anyone at all, seek satisfaction in our own different ways?

The word 'morality' is usually understood in a sense narrower than that in which I have been using it, to refer to just this necessary framework, to the rules to which we must all conform in order to make our aims, however diverse, realizable in a world which we all have to share. In Hobbes' words, the sphere of morality is limited to 'those qualities of mankind that concern their living together in peace and unity' (*Leviathan*, ch. xi). If this is the purpose of moral rules, we must be willing to keep them under review and to discard or modify those that, in the light of experience, we find unnecessary or obstructive. But they must retain a certain inflexibility, since, in our casual contacts, it is important that people should be reliable, should conform so closely to a publicly agreed code that, even if we do not know them as individuals, we know what to expect of them. 'That men perform their covenants made' is an adequate summary of morality in this limited sense.

But, though morality in this sense is necessary, it is not all. Rules belong to the superficial periphery of life. Like the multiplication table and other thought-saving dodges, they exist to free us for more important activities. It is beyond the power of any man to regulate all his dealings with all the people with whom he comes in casual contact by love; for love requires a depth of understanding that cannot be achieved except in close intimacy. Rules have no place in marriage or in friendship. This does not mean that a man must keep his word in business but may break promises made to his wife or to a friend; it is rather that the notion of keeping a promise made to a wife or friend from a sense of duty is utterly out of place, utterly foreign to the spirit of their mutual relationship. For what the sense of duty requires of us is always the commission or omission of specific acts.

That friends should be loyal to one another I take for granted; but we cannot set out a list of acts that they should avoid as disloyal with the sort of precision (itself none too great) with which we could list the things a man should not do in business. Too much will depend on the particular circumstances and the particular natures of the people concerned. Rules must, of their very nature, be general; that is their virtue and their defect. They lay down what is to be done or not done in *all* situations of a certain general kind, and they do this because their function is to ensure reliability in the absence of personal knowledge. But however large we make the book of rules, however detailed we try to make its provisions, its complexity cannot reach to that of a close personal relationship. Here what matters is not the commission or omission of specific acts but the spirit of the relationship as a whole. A man thinks, not of what his obligation to his wife or his friend requires of him, but of what it is best for his wife or his friend that he should do. A personal relationship does indeed consist of specific acts; the spirit that exists between husband and wife or between friends is nothing over and above the specific things they do together. But each specific act, like each brush-stroke in a picture or each note in a symphony, is good or bad only as it affects the quality of the relationship as a whole. The life of love is, like a work of art, not a means to an end, but an end in itself. For this reason in all close human relationships there should be a flexibility in our attitude to rules characteristic to the expert artist, craftsman or games player.

The expert moves quickly, deftly, and, to the untutored eye, even carelessly. It takes me hours to prune an apple tree, and I have to do it book in hand; the expert goes over the tree in a few minutes, snipping here and slashing there, with the abandonment of a small boy who has neither knowledge of pruning nor intention to prune. Indeed, to someone who does not know what he is about, his movements must seem more like those of Piaget's youngest children who just threw the marbles about. But the similarity is superficial. For one thing, the master-craftsman's movements do mostly follow the book for all that he never refers to it; and for another he does know what he is about and it is just this knowledge that entitles him to flout the rules when it is suitable to do so. No apple tree is exactly like the drawing in the book, and expertise lies in knowing when and how to deviate from its instructions.

This analogy must not be pressed too far. The conduct of life is more complicated and more difficult than any such task as pruning a tree and few of us could claim, without improper pride, the master-craftsman's licence. But I should like to press it some way, to suggest that, in all important matters, our chief consideration should be, not to conform to any code of rules, but simply how we can produce the best results; that we should so act that we can say in retrospect, not 'I did right', but 'I did what befitted the pattern of life I have set myself as a goal'.

As a philosopher, I cannot but speak in abstract generalities, and it is central to my thesis that at this point the philosopher must give way to the novelist. Tolstoy, Thomas Mann, and Forster have given us many examples of the contrast between the rule-bound and the teleological attitudes to life. But I should like to end by descending one level, not to the particular, but to the relatively specific, and to consider as an example one moral rule, the prohibition of adultery.

By 'adultery' I understand the act of sexual intercourse with someone other than one's spouse. It is expressly forbidden in the Bible, absolutely and without regard to circumstances; it is a crime in some countries and many would make it a crime in this. Until very recently it was almost the only ground for civil divorce. A marriage is supposed to be a life-long union. It could be entirely devoid of love—some married couples have not spoken to each other for years, communicating by means of a blackboard; yet no grounds for divorce existed. Or the husband might insist on sexual intercourse with his wife against her will and yet commit no sin. But let him once go out, get drunk, and have a prostitute and the whole scene changes. He has sinned; his wife has a legal remedy and, in the eyes of many who are not Christians but have been brought up in a vaguely Christian tradition, he has now done a serious wrong. This is a rule-and-act morality according to which what is wrong is a specific act; and it is wrong in all circumstances even, for example, if the wife is devoid of jealousy or so devoid of love that she would rather have her husband lie in any bed but hers.

If we look at this rule against adultery from a teleological stand-point it must appear wholly different. A humanist may, of course, reject the whole conception of monogamy; but if, like myself, he retains it, he will do so only because he believes that the life-long union of a man and a woman in the intimacy of marriage is a supreme form of love. Copulation has its part to play in such a union; but, for the species Man, it cannot be its essence. If someone who holds this view still thinks adultery is wrong, he will do so because it appears to him to be an act of disloyalty, an act likely to break the union which he values. Two consequences follow from this. The first is that if a marriage is, for whatever reason, devoid of love, there is now no union to break; so neither adultery nor any other act can break it. The second is that since adultery is now held to be wrong, not in itself, but only *as* an act of disloyalty, it will not *be* wrong when it is *not* an act of disloyalty. An adultery committed with the full knowledge and consent of the spouse will not be wrong at all. A so-called 'platonic' friendship, even too assiduous an attendance at the local pub or sewing-circle, anything that tends to weaken the bonds of love between the partners will be far more damaging to the marriage and consequently far more deeply immoral. Just *what* specific acts are immoral must, on this view, depend on the particular circumstances and the particular people concerned. Christians also insist on the uniqueness of individual people; but since law is, of its nature, general, this insistence seems wholly incompatible with the morality of law to which they are also committed.

6

DISCUSSION

1. *A. Boyce Gibson*

HAVING used Professor Nowell-Smith's work on *Ethics* for four years as a textbook for Honours students, I know perhaps better than most how difficult he is to argue with. There is a flexibility, an open-mindedness, one might almost say a Janus-quality about him, which ensures that any criticism one wishes to direct to him has been forestalled in the text. This quality, evident in his book, is bountifully exhibited also in this recent article, 'Morality: Religious and Secular'. His main theme, which he bases on the findings of Piaget and his own observations of parent–child behaviour, is that 'religious morality is infantile'. Yet for the most part he does not question the content of Christian morality, and even quotes, in the act of expelling religion from morals, 'the Sabbath was made for man, not man for the Sabbath'. This time, however, the scale is small enough to permit of detailed dissection, and the prejudices show out strongly enough to be understood for what they are. I am therefore emboldened to attempt a Christian reply.

I

As we have noticed, Nowell-Smith carefully distinguishes between the form and the content of religious morality. The content, however, he regards as not specifically religious, being the property of humanists also. What he objects to, and finds specifically religious, and treats as a form of infantilism, is the *formal* aspect of Christian behaviour, and by that he means primarily (though, as we shall see, not exclusively) its reliance on rules. And this view of the matter I find extraordinary. It is not that I wish to question his views on the place of rules in the good life: by the time (p. 109) that he has had time for his accustomed qualifications, the sharp edge of his distinction between rule and end is considerably blunted, and the result is one which a Christian would not wish to challenge. No: what is extraordinary is what Nowell-Smith believes Christians to believe. For if there ever was a religion which challenged the morality of rules, it was Christianity. Right from the beginning, Christ preached that the 'rules' of the Jewish law were not enough: 'Except your righteousness shall exceed the righteousness of the scribes and Pharisees, ye shall in no case enter into the kingdom of heaven.' It is the character of rules to apply impartially: it is the character of Christian morality to do more than any rule could demand, in a spirit of love and service. 'The wind bloweth where it listeth: so is every one that is born of the Spirit.' Could Nowell-Smith demand a looser texture than that? 'He maketh his sun to rise on the evil and on the good, and sendeth rain on the just and on the unjust.' By all the canons of rules-morality this is grossly unfair, and many justice-fans have said so, and given it as a moral reason for being atheists. And what about that ex-rules-moralist, the apostle Paul? 'But now the righteousness of God without the law is manifested.' 'That no man is justified by the law in the sight of God, it is evident; for the just shall live by faith.' These texts are indeed the scaffolding of Christian history. The Gospel has confronted and confounded Roman rules, Nordic rules, Shinto rules, Confucian rules, and not least Greek rules; and the common charge against Christians among responsible Eastern conservatives today is that by breaking down rules they produce anarchy and pave the way to communism—a charge more disconcerting, because better grounded, than Nowell-Smith's. Only twice has Christianity been philosophically entangled with rules: once when it was infiltrated by the Stoic doctrine (a Greek doctrine) of natural law, and once again when, in the time of the Calvinist ascendancy, it lapsed into Old-Testament primitivism. Certainly the basic Christian texts are as hostile to mere rules as Nowell-Smith himself. If Christian behaviour has impressed him otherwise, that is not because it is Christian, but because it is not Christian enough.

There is, of course, a place for rules in Christian behaviour: as may be seen if we complete some of the passages quoted above. 'Think not I am come to destroy the law, or the prophets: I am not come to destroy, but to fulfil . . . Till heaven and earth pass, one jot or one tittle shall in no wise pass from the law, till all be fulfilled.' 'The righteousness of God without the law is manifested, being witnessed by the law and the prophets.' 'The law was our schoolmaster to bring us unto Christ, that we might be justified by faith.' These are the passages which should prevent Christians from running off into antinomianism; but each one of them represents the law as a stage on the journey and not as a destination. And this is exactly what Nowell-Smith wants. He understands the part played by rules in the education of children; he merely protests that they should not continue to play the same part in adult life. Paul's analogy of the schoolmaster should surely suit him admirably. For Paul's schoolmaster (the law) knows that when his pupils are fully grown they will freely confront their future in his spirit, but in their own new way.

There is, it is true, a foot-hold for misunderstanding, and Nowell-Smith has built it up into a platform. As he says, in the more intimate and affectionate relations such as marriage and friendship, one does not stop behind with the rules; and this is the reason why these relations are so much more central than those which require of us only justice. But even here, and elsewhere much more, sitting loose to the rules can be a perilous adventure for the unprepared; it so often means not rising above them, but sinking below them. We are not all of us all the time moral aristocrats like Aristotle (who, by the way, did not pretend to be moralizing for the vulgar). We are constantly pricked by desire or enraged by opposition; and the best thing we can do is to sit on ourselves till we come round. To that end rules are a great stand-by, and they are most serviceable when most inflexible: otherwise we shall make exceptions in our own favour. If Nowell-Smith has never felt like that, he is to be congratulated, but he is not in a position to speak to the multitude. However, as a matter of fact, he consents to 'certain inflexibilities', mainly for the social ground that people must know what they may expect from each other. This is an urbane common-room commutation for 'what I would, that I do not, but what I hate, that I do'; but at least it provides some sort of frame for his open-texture weaving. Nowell-Smith proposes to treat rules as a wise man treats his car, 'not as an object of veneration but as a convenience'. 'Convenience' is an understatement resulting from his under-playing of evil (one *can* do without a car); but substitute 'necessary second best' and there is nothing to distinguish him from a Gospel Christian. I hope he will not be disappointed.

As much of the nursery lore which is the mainspring of his paper is introduced to show how the morality of rules is a prolongation of childhood, there is no need to examine it in detail. We can be sure that Piaget saw straight and that Nowell-Smith is a faithful reporter. The trouble is that the whole episode supports the specifically Christian and religious element in Christian morality against the Pharisee, the Roman, and the modern rationalist pagan.[1] On the subject of rules orthodox Christianity is, from Nowell-Smith's point of view, on the side of the angels; and we may pass to another issue.

II

There are, however, other matters, also pointing back to the nursery, on which Nowell-Smith dissents from 'religious' morality. Though he gives far less space to these considerations than he mistakenly gives to rules, I shall develop them at greater length, for it is in canvassing them that he shows the real cause of his irritation.

The first is his subordination of deontology to teleology. On this I shall only observe that he assumes that attention to duty means attention to rules. Against it I should urge that attention to duty can never be attention to rules only, because what is in question, whenever one does one's duty, is what one ought to do in a particular case, and every particular case is a meeting-place of rules at least potentially in conflict. For duty, as for Nowell-Smith's alternative, 'coping with the world in a manner satisfactory to ourselves', rules are in the category of ways and means. In another context, I should press this point, because the association between duty and universalizability seems to have been far too easily accepted. Here I pass it by, because duty is not the end-product of a Christian life, any more than it is for Nowell-Smith's eudaemonists: and I proceed to the alleged infantilism of the concepts of faith and grace. It is at this point that the collision occurs: though even here the main cause is Nowell-Smith's teen-age (I will not say infantile) translation of these cardinal theological concepts.

The subject is introduced by a discussion of heteronomy, by which Nowell-Smith, following Kant for once, means the determination of the will by reference to some external authority. It is clear that this does happen in the nursery, and also that the answer 'Because I tell you' may be unreasonably perpetuated beyond its

[1] One has only to think of the ferocious justice of French atheists like Clemenceau, so self-standing and self-sufficient that he left instructions that he should be buried upright—clearly it does not take a Christian to be implacable, though it does take a Christian to deactivate the more far-reaching implacabilities.

proper age-limit. Nowell-Smith calls heteronomy infantile because
it means that in adult life we defer to authority instead of deciding
for ourselves. The authority which he is concerned to challenge is
the will of God. ('Not as I will, but as thou wilt', he quotes with
disparagement—forgetting not only the divine compassion of it
but also the agonizing effort of a human decision.) There are many
other authorities which he might have challenged, especially the
political mass-movements which have been in the past most effectively withstood by men who appealed to the will of God. However,
it is the most liberating authority which most disturbs him, so let
us follow where he leads.

To appeal to the will of God, then, even against tyrants, is to
submit oneself *and not to decide*. If that assertion is mistaken, the
whole argument breaks down. I propose to argue that this view of
the matter is both untenable and bad theology.

The first qualm induced in the reader is set in motion, in his
usual Janus-fashion, by Nowell-Smith himself. He observes that
'those who accept the authority of a priest or a church on what they
are to do, are, in accepting that authority, deciding for themselves'.
This is surely true, and it shows that authority and deciding are not
incompatible. And if it is true of a priest or a church, *a fortiori* it is
true of the decision to follow God's will. It is indeed a decision, not
a mere slide from one allegiance to another. Many of us have taken
it without the advantage of a religious training, and maintain it
despite the pressure of a pagan environment, e.g. in universities. It
is not at all a natural or easy continuation of obedience to parents.

It might be replied that it is a decision, but a decision to end
decisions; but Nowell-Smith sees that this account will not do. He
realizes that the decision has constantly to be reaffirmed. His objection must therefore be either to the content of the decision, or to
the reasons for the decision. But he has already conceded that the
content is common ground between himself and his opponents. It
must be the reasons for the decision which he finds fault with. But,
supposing he were right on this issue, it would still be wrong to
confuse it with the quite different issue, whether doing the will of
God entails the total obliteration of decision.

The objection which Nowell-Smith takes to the will of God as a
reason for moral action is that it is not a reason. The decision is
taken on the strength of an unsocial and unsharable intimation. It
is not even based on 'a reasoned trust in someone in whom we have
good grounds for reposing trust'; it is 'blind faith, utter submission

of our own reason and will' (p. 104). And one effect of this attitude is to cut away all the good social reasons even for such of our actions as the will of God also commends to us, substituting for them the sole requirement of 'the right relation to God'.

We may begin with the corollary because it illustrates graphically the underlying misrepresentation. Nowell-Smith quotes Sir Thomas Browne, *Religio Medici* II, 2, as saying: 'I give no alms only to satisfy the hunger of my brother, but to accomplish the will and command of my God: I draw not my purse for his sake that demands it, but his that enjoined it.' He interprets this to mean that 'charity itself is held to be good *only because* God has enjoined us to be charitable' (p. 104). He has certainly misinterpreted Browne by displacing the word 'only': he has made it appear that in Browne's view reference to the will of God *excludes* reference to the man's hunger, whereas all Browne said was that the expressed will of God is a further reason for relieving it. The man's hunger is one of the things the will of God is about. This tendency to depict religion as a set of dichotomies is persistent in Nowell-Smith. If Browne had meant what Nowell-Smith thinks he meant, he would have been much to blame, but he would not have been talking Christianity. I remember vividly how the first Lord Lindsay of Birker, speaking as a Christian, used to declaim against that Victorian classic for children, *The Fairchild Family*, in which the author takes exactly the point of view ascribed to Browne by Nowell-Smith. '"He that giveth to the poor lendeth to the Lord, and shall be repaid", said Mrs Fairchild, hastily slipping a shilling into the poor woman's hand.' Here the poor woman *is* treated heteronomously, and without Christian charity: it is just that sort of thing which launched the word 'charity' on its downward path. The heteronomy, it may be remarked, though hardly Christian, is not the worst thing about this utterance: what is really evil in it is the teleological tag. To obey God without regarding one's neighbour is only half of the Christian vocation; to obey God with an eye to one's own advantage is to subtract the other half as well. Some teleological arguments, it would seem, are worse than any sort of deontology.

Let us, however, admit that to appeal to the will of God as *opposed to* the welfare of one's neighbour is morally insensitive, and that when the quality of religion declines this is the way the issue is apt to be presented. It is still not what the Christian is expected to do. Love of God and love of neighbour are presented as complementary and collateral, but not as cause and consequence. Text for text, it would actually be possible to argue the other way round. 'If a man loveth not the brother whom he hath seen, how shall he love the God whom he hath not seen?' 'Blessed are the pure in heart, for they shall see God'—not vice versa. The Christian God cannot be loved by high-minded self-centred people, and this is why Jesus kept up the barrage against the Pharisees. In doing what we can for others, we are *ipso facto* doing it for God; God is not so other than others, that we can serve them without serving him. It is the will of God that we should love our neighbour *because he is our neighbour*; only so do we do it for his greater glory.

Thus Christian heteronomy is always qualified. Obedience to the will of God is never pure and simple. It is always in respect of some act or kind of act specifiable in other terms. It is always to be rendered but not to arbitrary command. It is true that Christian morality is through and through religious, and is not primarily concerned with 'what befits the social animal, Man' (p. 105). But it is concerned with what befits *men* (not man), as children of one Father. If we sometimes think the will of God commands us to do to others what does not befit children of God, we can be sure we have got it wrong: as Abraham discovered in the nick of time, and as Jephthah tragically forgot. The tradition of the Church, as well as human affections, warns us to be on our guard against diabolical simulations of the will of God; and if it is wholly heteronomous there is no way of telling the one from the other. So far from disagreeing with Nowell-Smith on this point, I entirely endorse him. But whatever it is he is attacking—I should call it popular Calvinism desiccating into deism—it is not, as he seems to think, Christian morality.

It may be replied that in that case the will of God is being subjected to the demands of human nature and will thus fade away into a ghostly double. But that is to forget two of the main features of a distinctively Christian philosophy: creation and incarnation. As a creature, man is made, and as God's creature, he is made in God's image. His demands are therefore at the same time God's demands on him. Further, the will of God was made manifest on earth in specific form and under specific conditions, and it was actually exhibited in human form as a human will. Philosophers may find this belief incredible, though it brought life (and sense) into the bloodless abstractions of later Greek philosophy, and

wherever it has gone has dispersed a whole cloud of local super-
stitions. But they should not write about some highest-common-
factor God-in-general and expect Christians to understand them.
If incarnation is taken seriously, the whole contrast between
autonomy and heteronomy in respect of God goes by the board.
The will of man is all the more autonomous for a heteronomy
which, flowing up from inside it, in no way constrains it from
without. The distinction is between an autonomy thus continually
reinforced and the humanist autonomy which locks itself up and
declines reinforcement.

But, to return to the immediate issue, once again Nowell-Smith's
charge of infantilism—of maintaining in adult life attitudes proper
to the early learning-process—rests on a wrong diagnosis. All religion celebrates the process of growing up—from aboriginal initia-
tion ceremonies to confirmation services and experiences of conversion—and the Christian religion certainly follows the course of
nature in celebrating and emphasizing the passage from childhood
to maturity. Moreover, being an incarnational religion it is not
immaterialist and assigns a proper value to the humanist enter-
prises of personal and social improvement. It includes everything
that Nowell-Smith wants to include, but in a richer and more
resonant context. The reason he misses the point is that he mistakes
incarnational Christians for Cathari or Manichees, and plants upon
them, in place of an ordered hierarchy, an implacable and un-
reasonable Either/Or.

III

I have devoted some time to the theme of Christianity and
heteronomy, because it is the source of other mistakes, notably with
regard to sin and grace. Nowell-Smith points out, justly enough,
that from the child's point of view 'right' and 'wrong' must seem to
be arbitrary expressions of parental approval or disapproval, and
that the alternation of smiles and frowns must seem inexplicable
and fortuitous. He goes on to say that the experience of sin and
grace in adult life perpetrates this incomprehension and perplexity
of childhood. 'The mystery of God's ways to man is the mystery of
a father's ways with his children' (p. 107).

In setting out the comparison, Nowell-Smith states the classical
doctrine of sin and grace in what he admits to be an extreme form:
'grace is the *free* gift of God, and . . . there is absolutely nothing
that (the creature) can do, or even try to do, either to merit or to

obtain it'. This Calvinist deviation is, however, presented deliberately as the model on the ground that it is the original doctrine of
the Church, and that 'the subtle palliatives offered by Catholic
theologians' are nothing but 'evasions'. This could be disputed, and
not only by Catholics: Arminians, Methodists and Quakers, and
individuals from other communions, would also insist on the
'subtleties', and their effect on the doctrine of God and man. If I
do not stress them here, it is because Nowell-Smith is correct in
thinking that they are not the main point at issue.

The point of his analogy between the grace of God and the
favours of a father is that both are inexplicable and both are substitutes for human effort. In the extreme form of the doctrine, this
is obvious. In its moderate forms, for example, when it is stated
that 'sufficient grace' is given to us to improve ourselves by our own
efforts, and that if they are successful they are crowned by the
'efficacious grace' which has power to save, a limited field of opera-
tions is left for human effort, and the sense of sheer arbitrariness
is alleviated; but the fact remains that the first and the final moves
rest entirely in God's hands. Even if (as I think we should) we
accumulate the subtleties and alleviations, we are still not re-
assured about human effort. There is (it will be said) less of it than
there would be if people rejected the whole conception of grace,
and with it the alternative secular father-substitutes: 'they', 'the
law', or the Welfare State.

But traditionally too much emphasis has been placed on the
mechanism of grace and too little on its effects. What matters is
that grace *saves*: it does not keep men dangling for the sake of
ensuring their dependence. It sets them on their own feet and
keeps them there. '*Stand fast* in the liberty wherein Christ has
made us free, and be not entangled again in the yoke of bondage.'
The effect of grace is exactly like the effect of those parents whom
Nowell-Smith approves. It intervenes to foster independence. It
meets every creature in his own style: the radicals by subverting
and reconstructing them, the gradualists by building them up and
luring them on. The end of it all is that they all grow up; grace is
the perfecting of our nature, not its destruction: *naturam non
tollit gratia sed perficit*, as Thomas Aquinas so admirably observed;
and our decisions grow in grace along with the rest of us. The
descent of grace upon us is known by the presence of grace in us.
By grace we are stronger, more resolute, more creative and imaginative, than we could possibly be without it. This we *know*—especially

those of us to whom it comes as a wholly unexpected glory and not as part of our system of expectations.

Once again, Nowell-Smith has taken an external view of the operation of God on man; and he has failed to note the difference brought about in one's experience of God by the traditional but (among philosophers) neglected doctrines of the Incarnation and the Holy Spirit. And, once again, the objection is not to his theories of education but to his backwoods rendering of Christian belief.

In assessing Nowell-Smith's central passages on the will and the grace of God, I hope it will not seem flippant, and believe that it is consonant with his own attitude, to suggest that coming of age should be celebrated by a ceremonial parricide.

Anthropologists relate that fathers in some communities are ceremonially slaughtered, with every appearance of genuine regret, at about the age of forty-five. The reasons are economic; but that may be the work of a Freudian censor. It could be (and here I simply speculate) that the younger generation feels it cannot grow up until the elder has been finally disposed of. If that is so, we should have an exact parallel to Nowell-Smith's account of the religious and secular elements in morality. As long as anyone has a filial feeling for a father-substitute, as long as he attempts to direct his actions in accordance with his will, he is playing truant from his manhood. At least, so the argument demands: though, as we have seen, it is sometimes quite proper to take authority as a guide in our personal decisions. But this open-minded back door is an escape-hatch for the religious moralist. He has only to say that he *chooses* to abide by the will of God and the thing is done. Family analogies would even point to that conclusion. Adult sons *do* go to their fathers for advice. True, they need not and often do not take it; but then men often do not take it from God, even those who consult him. It would be safer for Nowell-Smith's argument if he closed the escape-hatch. But if he does, he will have to say, in an authoritarian tone of voice, Thou shalt not consult authorities: which is neither his intention, nor good sense. And if he does not, he must allow the moral adult the adult option of doing the will of the Father which is in Heaven.

I trust that I have not essentially misrepresented Nowell-Smith's argument, though I have hardly done justice to his numerous qualifications. Of these I can only say in general that they reassure me about Nowell-Smith but do not save the argument. And I trust I have shown where the error lies: in presenting a picture of God and man in which there is no mention of incarnation. According to the view attacked by Nowell-Smith God is on one side of the line and man (collectively) is on the other; the will of God is something outside us, to be conformed to; the grace of God descends upon us and does not grow up in us. According to Christian morality God is on both sides of the line; the will of God works *in* the wills of those who love him; and the grace of God is made known in the ability to love him. Once more we are reminded of the observation in Dostoevsky's *Idiot* that 'the atheist is always talking about something else'.

IV

It would be neater and more satisfactory to conclude at this point. It would, however, be evasive. Nowell-Smith, in his conclusion (pp. 111-112) discusses a practical moral problem; and it is right than anyone joining issue with him should do the same.

Nowell-Smith takes as his special case the moral rule prohibiting adultery. It is in fact a trump card. Adultery is the only kind of activity with specific and overt characteristics which the Sermon on the Mount condemns without exception or qualification. And he attacks the rule, *qua* rule, as he attacks rules in general, on the ground (p. 112) that 'just *what* specific acts are immoral must depend on the particular circumstances and the particular people concerned'. Now we have argued that Christianity is not a religion of rules; I have rejected on that account his imputation of 'infantilism'. But here it would seem that we have as bleak and categorical a rule as ever existed. No wonder it is this example that Nowell-Smith has kept for his final throw.

Nowell-Smith proposes to look at the rule against adultery from a 'teleological standpoint', as opposed to the 'rule-and-act' morality of the traditionalists. Now to give consequences as a reason for a rule does not destroy the working efficacy of a rule: it destroys only its absoluteness. Nowell-Smith's teleological morality condemns adultery, because he thinks highly of loyalty as a principle of action and accepts 'life-long union in the intimacy of marriage' as 'a supreme form of love'. Now this means that adultery is to be avoided only because it conduces to the breakdown of loyalties. In that case, where adultery is consented to by the other party, or where there is no love left in the partnership, the rule against it no longer applies.

The question for a Christian who has offered the defence that

Christianity is not a religion of rules is how he can avoid Nowell-Smith's conclusion; or, if he insists on unqualified condemnation of adultery, how he can avoid Nowell-Smith's premise, i.e. that Christianity *is* a religion of rules.

1. The first oddity in the argument is the tie-up between 'teleology' and 'loyalty'. Loyalty in itself is not in any sense a matter of consequences. It may be one consideration in a predicament in which consequences have also to be taken into account; but *in so far* as they are done from loyalty actions are not motivated by consequences at all. One is tempted to suggest that Nowell-Smith has conflated two types whose only point in common is that they do not live by rules. If that *is* so, there will be confusion as soon as rules cease to be the centre of discussion, e.g. as soon as Christianity appears on the scene. If it is *not* so, Nowell-Smith must be saying that not committing adultery is praiseworthy if it leads, instrumentally, to the maintenance of loyalties (which is normally the case); but ceases to be of moral importance if there are no loyalties to maintain. This second alternative is more in line with his general position.

2. The second oddity in the argument is the extremely subjective interpretation of 'loyalty'. It is read off as 'feeling loyal', and not as 'having loyalties'. But it is a part of the morals of loyalty that one *has* loyalties whether one *feels* loyal or not—and the overruling of disloyal feelings is not a reversion to the morality of rules. Loyalty is mainly a matter of status and certainly not only a matter of contract. It far transcends the mere promise which can be set aside by agreement. Even if neither party feels like observing it, they owe it to their families, their neighbours, their country, and themselves to work themselves back into wanting to observe it. An overt breach such as adultery makes the task harder. And if we are talking about consequences, it is necessary to consider the effect of adultery by consent on unilateral adultery, which stands condemned as cheating on Nowell-Smith's own formula. Human nature being what it is, i.e. rather more fascinated by wickedness than Nowell-Smith thinks it is, it is to be suspected that the effect would be considerable.

3. It begins to be apparent that loyalties are nearly as exacting as rules; but they have the great advantage of being owed to persons and not to principles. If Nowell-Smith takes his stand on loyalties, he may have to go farther than he intends. And he makes it quite clear that he does want to stand on loyalties. He thinks it a good

thing that there should be loyalties (and therefore no adultery) even if he sees nothing wrong about adultery in the absence of loyalties. But loyalties don't just happen: they have to be sustained by example and environment. They are hardly encouraged by a mutual agreement that they need not be observed.

4. It is now clear why adultery has no place in the Christian life. The Christian *agape* is a liberal and flexible kind of loyalty, not restricted to the demands of justice, willing to take the initiative in reconciliation, and centred, not on society, but on people's relation with each other. If this attitude is displayed by the parties to a marriage, adultery will be inconceivable. This is not the result of external rules (the breach of which is only too easily conceivable), but the internal and necessary expression of a way of life. And if it be asked why, then, the prohibition? the answer is that the way of life is practised by men who in its despite sometimes relapse into unsanctified imaginings; and then it is surely appropriate that they should be snapped out of them by a stiff injunction. The injunction, however, is not the reason for their loyalties, but merely the measure of their failure. If that is what Nowell-Smith finds distasteful in the New Testament, in view of his evident concern about loyalties, I cannot see why.

5. It may be thought that I have been pressing too hard Nowell-Smith's incidental reference to loyalties, and have taken too little note of his official profession of teleology. The fact remains, however, that he uses no other test than that of loyalties to distinguish humanist believers in monogamy like himself from other humanists who reject monogamy; and the critic is entitled to explore the implications of his criterion. If it is taken seriously, it is not consistent with adultery by mutual consent: loyalty is shown by what people do, and even if they agree to do what is disloyal, it is disloyal all the same.

I agree, of course, that adultery is not the only offence against married loyalties; I agree even that some unstigmatized offences may well be deadlier. And I do not believe that the ordinary ban on adultery is simply a taboo or arbitrary rule. But it does not follow that it is merely 'one of a set of recipes' 'for the achievement of an end'—even though it is admitted to be a good recipe, and the end the generally laudable end of maximum and integral satisfaction. The fact is that Nowell-Smith accepts too easily the fashionable dichotomy between rule and end, and, rightly understanding that the ban on adultery is not merely a matter of rules, presents in the guise of teleology an alternative theory which being outside the ordinary categories of means and end is far from teleological. It is because his epilogue on adultery forces him to recognize a third possibility which his official theory does not allow for that it has more than an epilogue's significance.

In conclusion, we may summarize as follows:

1. Christian morality is not a set of rules.

2. The will of God is not an external agency, but works on men from within.

3. The grace of God is not arbitrarily bestowed, and in any case, when it has been bestowed, it produces independence of character.

4. The suggestion that the religious element in morality is 'infantile' rests on the view that those who appeal to it are perpetuating the attitude of dependence which is inevitable in childhood but should be outgrown. This is just not the case with Christian morality.

5. Nowell-Smith propounds, instead, a goal of integral human satisfaction. As a counter-proposal to a morality of rules, this has its attractions. But teleological morality does not have to be humanistic (Aquinas is as teleological as Nowell-Smith); and Nowell-Smith's detailed discussion of a moral issue does not rest on his teleology. The concept of loyalties, so unexpectedly introduced, would bear further investigation.

For the rest, Nowell-Smith may be assured that his kind of morality is one that Christians can feel at home with, much more so than with Kant or Nietzsche or Sartre; he is a consoling and comfortable fellow citizen. But he misunderstands the autonomy which we both value, because he overlooks what is specifically Christian in Christian theology. Only in the enjoyment of God's love are we finally autonomous; and that is why, on his own criterion, no one is adult but the saints.

2. *J. R. Lucas*

Professor Nowell-Smith claims that religious morality is infantile, that is, that many elements of our morality, especially those peculiarly associated with religion, are hangovers from our childish experience before the age of five, and between the ages of five and nine. I do not want so much to controvert Professor Nowell-Smith's thesis as to complement it. Most of what he says is true, and needs to be far more widely known by Christians than at present. My aim, as a Christian, is, rather, to make some further points about the Christian understanding of man and morality, so as to show that Professor Nowell-Smith's thesis, instead of being against Christian morality, is essentially consonant with it.

Professor Nowell-Smith criticizes the rule-bound character of many religious codes. Quite rightly. But Christ and St Paul made the same criticisms long before. The very slogan that Professor Nowell-Smith chooses to fight under—'the Sabbath was made for man, not man for the Sabbath' (p. 99)—was first uttered by Christ (Mark 2.27). Christ it was who, holding the same high ideal of monogamy as that put forward by Professor Nowell-Smith (p. 112), nevertheless refused to condemn, as Professor Nowell-Smith would refuse to condemn, the woman taken in adultery (John 8.11). Christ is much harder than Professor Nowell-Smith on the conventional morality of the conventionally religious; he does not merely deprecate them as infantile or immature, but damns them as dead— whited sepulchres (Matt. 23.27). St Paul is more concerned with the Law, and has more of a theory about it, than what has come down to us of our Lord's sayings; but from the multiplicity of his utterances, one thing at least is clear: he is not a deontologist in Professor Nowell-Smith's sense. 'The Letter killeth, the Spirit maketh alive' (II Cor. 3.6).

It would be too easy a triumph to point out that Christian morality is not at all what Professor Nowell-Smith says it is, and is as much concerned to controvert what he is trying to controvert as he himself is. For it is a sad truth that most professing Christians are in fact practising Pharisees, all Christ's own teaching to the contrary notwithstanding. Moreover, not everything Christ said would meet with Professor Nowell-Smith's approval: 'Except your righteousness exceed the righteousness of the Pharisees, ye shall in no wise enter into the Kingdom of Heaven' (Matt. 5.20). Christian morality, as Professor Nowell-Smith concedes (p. 99), is a fusion between Greek and Hebrew types of morality, and the New Testament Christian does not reject the Old Testament in the way a modern humanist thinks he should. I shall try to explain why.

The Old Testament is not simply a set of commandments and laws, though Judaism became largely just this: its primary theme is the growing sense of the inexorability of God, a greater and greater awareness of a reality other than oneself, making for good.

The peculiar tone of religious morality stems from this sense of the objectivity of values. Just as my believing something does not make it true, so my choosing something does not make it good: and just as I find myself under a relentless pressure to discover what the truth is, so equally I feel an unremitting urge to seek out and perform whatever it is that I ought to do. Some humanists believe in the objectivity of values too, but they take exception to the uncompromising stringency of the demands which the believer believes God to make on him.

The Christian differs from the humanist not only in believing in God, but in disbelieving in man. The Christian holds that men are always imperfect: that though their aspirations may be infinite, their achievements are always limited. The Kantian ideal of the entirely autonomous man is only an ideal. Being the mere mortal clay that we are, we never do have and never shall have Holy Wills. The Christian is deeply imbued with a sense of his own fallibility. Although each of us is autonomous in the sense that only he can make up his own mind, it does not follow from a man's having made a decision, that he has made it rightly. And our decisions not only may be wrong, but quite often are. Autonomy for the humanist is a standard of adult behaviour which most men do, or can, attain: the Christian does not believe that men can attain an adequate standard. We may—some men do —grow better with the passage of time; but to the end of our lives we remain something of the child in moral matters; still growing, perhaps, but never grown up; capable often, perhaps, of acting rightly, but always capable of being wrong. For the humanist 'adult' and 'infantile' are polar terms, and 'adult' is clearly a *pro-word*, and 'infantile' a *con-word*: the Christian does not regard 'child-like' as pejorative word. 'Unless ye turn and become as little children, ye can in no wise enter into the kingdom of heaven' (Matt. 17.3). By comparison with the Kantian ideal of autonomy, we are none of us fully adult: and though we should aspire towards being as adult as may be, we ought always to recognize that we have not reached in moral matters a level of complete adult-hood.

The Old Testament element in Christian morality reflects also the fact of man's being imperfect. We need the Moral Law, St Paul can be roughly rendered (Gal. 3.23), because we are not adult enough to take our own decisions correctly. But when, and if, we come to a full knowledge of God's love, then we shall be emancipated from the shackles of the Law, and shall be able to enter into the full freedom of the Christian who takes all his decisions for himself, and being filled with the spirit of love takes them all correctly. St Paul sometimes talk of complete emancipation coming at a man's conversion to Christianity; but occasionally speaks as if even converted Christians see through a glass darkly, and only in the next world face to face. I think the latter view is right. It is not in the nature of finite man to know as he is known.

If we only know in part, then our decisions, being based on partial knowledge, are not fully rational. Often the father lets the child go its own way, and learn by its mistakes, but sometimes he lays down a ruling, the reason for which is beyond the comprehension of child, but which the child is nevertheless required to obey. To me it seems obvious that one's attitude to an omniscient and loving being should be the same. The Christian, just turned twenty-one, is enjoined to follow the Christian teaching on, say, to take the most unpopular example, sexual morality in the same spirit of blind obedience as that in which, at an earlier stage, he followed his mother's injunctions about washing behind the ears. It is not, as Professor Nowell-Smith suggests, the arbitrary edict of a capricious being, but rather the wise instructions of an infinitely far-sighted one. Many men come in the end to believe with Professor Nowell-Smith that monogamy is the best and happiest form of life: and not a few will testify that chastity supports and supplements monogamy. But few adolescents really believe them, nor every adult; even among the middle-aged there are some who are tempted to break up their marriages, and will regret it if they do. The Christian code is clear and firm on this point. Of course it is not enough, as Professor Nowell-Smith points out, to secure the happiness of a marriage; nor would it be necessary to lay it down at all if we were all the time fully apprised of the pattern of life we wished to live and the means required to secure its realization. But for men, such as we actually are, often inconsiderate, often lustful, often impatient, the seventh commandment is a helpful instruction.

The basic objection Professor Nowell-Smith has to Old Testament morality is the element of blind obedience in it. The Christian is prepared to do things for no other reason than that God tells him to do them; whereas the humanist believes that the only acceptable moral actions are those whose rationale is transparent, those which can be seen to befit a pattern of life accepted as a goal (p. 111). This objection can be largely met by a consideration of a disposition Professor Nowell-Smith does approve of, loyalty (p. 110). For, though I cannot set out a precise list of acts that constitute loyalty or disloyalty, it seems to me to be the essence of loyalty that one trusts the person one is loyal to *beyond* the limits of one's own knowledge. I show my loyalty to someone when I do a thing which he wants me to do and which I would *not* have done on my own account, when I believe in him and accept his judgment without being able to justify it in the particular case under consideration. To believe one's friend when one can see for oneself that what he says is true is not to show any loyalty towards him: one would do that much for anyone, friend or foe alike. Loyalty, like faith, is an essentially heteronous idea. It involves being ready to say 'Not as I will, but as thou wilt' (Matt. 26.39) (p. 104). Churchill showed his faith in, and loyalty to Roosevelt when in 1940 he made a sacrificial sale of Courtauld's American assets to the United States Government (*Second World War* II, *Their Finest Hour*, p. 506). It was certainly not something he would have done if he had been acting according to his own judgment nor something for which he could see any justification at the time of the request. This I would offer as a paradigm case of loyalty in place of that of Abraham and Isaac. The story of Abraham and Isaac confuses the issue because it was originally told to a people who had not yet realized that human sacrifice was wrong, who had not yet been told that they should not offer the fruit of their body for the sin of their soul. It is the sacrifice of Abraham's affections, not of his scruples, that the story is meant to illustrate. How far one should be prepared to sacrifice one's scruples out of loyalty is a difficult question—if an inquisitor had done violence to his conscience, and had allowed a heretic to escape the flames out of deference to divine commands, I am not sure that we could be categorical in our disapproval—but this is a question I do not want to discuss. I only want to make two points: first, that some degree of loyalty, faith, obedience, trust, is a necessary virtue for non-omniscient, finite, fallible beings, such as we ourselves are, if we are to have any relations with other beings, and are not to be utterly autarkic and sufficient in ourselves. And secondly, that the obedience demanded of a Christian, although blind in the particular instance, is not without a general justification. The Christian is told to be chaste, to be long-suffering, not to impute bad motives to other people, irrespective of whether he can see how

these characteristics fit into a desirable pattern of life, or are justified
in any other way. But his obedience and loyalty to God are themselves justified by his belief that God loves him. Much has to be
taken on trust, so much that some people's faith in God is severely
strained. But the obedience demanded of the Christian is not
utterly blind. Faith is not (*pace* many Protestant theologians)
arbitrary. Although we are told not to expect God to justify his
ways to us to our own satisfaction, we have a fair token of his
general good will towards us in his willingness to undergo the
agonies of death upon the cross. The non-Christian will reject that
this actually happened, but that does not affect the *logic* of the
Christian's position. The Christian's loyalty, although complete
and unswerving, is not groundless or arbitrary. He has his reasons
for believing in God and in God's goodness towards us, though he
is not in a position to constitute himself a supreme court to adjudi-
cate the moral worth of God's every edict and action.

The great merit of rules and commands is that they are fairly
precise. I know how to keep the rules and obey commands long
before I am able to carry out the agapeistical policy of loving God
and doing what I like, and whereas there may be many disputes
about what the best pattern of life is, or wherein the greatest good
of the community lies, there is little room for dispute on whether
one has committed adultery or whether one has broken the speed
limit. And therefore we make use of rules, in spite of all their
many disadvantages noted by Professor Nowell-Smith, both for
propaedeutic purposes and in promulgating legal and social codes.
In so far as the Christian Church is a corporate body with social
organization of its own, it has rules and regulations, just as any
other community does; and because Christians regard their moral
and spiritual education as never complete, they never claim that
Christian teaching can be dispensed with. There are dangers in
making use of rules. What was intended to be a signpost can
become a straitjacket, and men are all too ready to regard the
observance of rules as a sufficient condition, instead of merely a
necessary condition, of trying to live according to a certain ideal in
common with other men. Many churchmen have been deplorably
rule-bound. What gives Professor Nowell-Smith's paper its point
is that what he is attacking corresponds so often with the actual
practice of Christians: but not the practice of Christ nor the
teaching of the Christian Church. And though Christ and the
saints go much further than Professor Nowell-Smith would ap-

prove in accepting the necessity of rules and in regarding obedience as a virtue, it is far from clear that in this he is right and they are wrong.

It is difficult to pinpoint the Christian's disagreement with Professor Nowell-Smith. So much of what he says can be found in Christ's sayings and St Paul's writings, that it is tempting to claim him for an unwitting believer instead of a convinced adversary of the Christian faith. Yet to do this would be to do scant service to the truth, and I want to end by attempting to summarize the heads of agreement and disagreement between Christians and humanists. There is substantial agreement on the content of morality, 'that love, sympathy, loyalty and consideration are virtues . . .' (p. 95), though Christians lay greater stress on loyalty and humility than would Professor Nowell-Smith. Christian teaching is as insistent upon the dangers of mere rule-observance as Professor Nowell-Smith could want, though many Christians are heedless of the warning, and are as infantile in their religious outlook as Professor Nowell-Smith maintains. Christians are, however, a good deal readier to recognize the necessity of having rules than Professor Nowell-Smith would be himself. This is because Christians take a very much lower view of themselves than do humanists. They do not think that because they choose to do something, therefore it is right. On the contrary, the Christian believes that most of his unaided choices would have been likely to land him in chaos. The Christian differs from the humanist, therefore, in having a much livelier sense of the difficulty of leading the good life or of coming to the knowledge of the truth. He differs also from some humanists at least, and all sceptics, in having an overpowering conviction that, incompetent though he is, there is a truth to be discovered and a good life to be lived; and these for him are based on his belief in God, and therefore are an absolute 'must'.

7

GOD AND OUGHT[1]

Dewi Z. Phillips

WHY should I obey God's commands? Many philosophers suggest
that I should do so only if I have judged that *this* command of
God's is good or that *all* God's commands are good. In other words,
an acceptance of God's commands must depend on my moral judgment. I want to deny this. I am not denying that one can understand certain moralities without understanding religion or that
God is sometimes the object of moral judgment. What I am denying
is that the relation between God and what I ought to do is *necessarily* parasitic on moral judgment. On the contrary, for believers,
'good' means 'whatever God wills'.

But is it not obvious that what I have just said cannot be the
case? If 'good' means 'whatever God wills', the question 'Is what
God wills good?' ought to be redundant. Clearly, the question is
perfectly meaningful. Must we not admit then that *we* are the
ones to decide whether what God wills is good or not? I do not
think so. Often in the theses of philosophers who argue in this
way, 'good' is a blanket term under which all its complexities and
variations slumber unnoticed. I want to suggest that such arguments cannot account for moral situations with which we are all
perfectly familiar, and that this failure to account for moral
situations applies equally to religious phenomena. Let us examine
these two shortcomings.

[1] [Though this paper was not written with special reference to Professor Nowell-Smith's
discussion, its very different use of considerations about children and fathers, as well as its
very different contextualization of the will of God make it very appropriate to place here.
It further leads naturally to the crucial question of the propriety of talking about Duty
in terms of God's will and so to the particular problems with which Professor Nielsen and
subsequent writers are concerned. *Editor.*]

We are often asked in philosophical discussions on morality and religion to distinguish between descriptive statements and evaluative statements. One cannot argue from a descriptive statement about God to the assertion of an obligation to God. Because God is our Father it does not follow that his name should be hallowed. To think otherwise, these philosophers would have us believe, is to confuse the moral and the non-moral; to attempt to derive an 'ought' from an 'is'. But if the Heavenly Father has fared so ill at their hands, would the earthly fathers fare any better? The problem of the nature of the connection between the matter-of-fact status of being a father and the obligations children have to their parents has been treated by A. I. Melden in *Rights and Right Conduct* (Blackwell 1959). Readers will no doubt recognize many of his arguments in the following remarks.

Melden stresses the need to take account of the institution of the family in any explanation of parental rights and the obligations of children to their parents. The only weakness of an otherwise illuminating analysis is what I take to be an over-emphasis on what Melden calls 'the role' of the father. He concentrates too much on what the father does, and too little on who he is, namely the father of his children. But then Melden speaks sometimes as if this distinction is non-existent; as if what a father is can be explained in terms of what he does. This is especially the case when he talks of the father as forfeiting his rights. The child says to his father, 'You have never been a father to me.' If one fails to play the role of father, one sacrifices one's rights as a father. It must be admitted that there are occasions when we should say that a man is no longer fit to be a father, and we would not blame the child for disowning him. ('He drove my mother to her grave.') The trouble with Melden's way of talking, however, is that it makes it look as if being a father is a role that *anyone* can play. He points out, for instance, that the child may come to regard someone other than his natural father as his 'father'. But there is a difference between a natural father and a 'father' nevertheless. It is the ignoring of the connection between fatherhood and nature which constitutes an important gap in Melden's account. So many problems concerning the child-parent relationship cannot be understood unless this connection is recognized. So many of the obligations I have to my father do not depend on whether he has done things for me or even on whether he loves me. It is certainly not a case of tit-for-tat. ('If my father hits me, why shouldn't I hit him back?') I do not want to deny that imperfections in the father may lead to his being rejected by the child. On the other hand, many people would say that the rejection of the father is an imperfection in the child; that the child who loves his father only as long as he is a good father has an imperfect love of his father. ('You should not leave your father destitute in his old age.'—'But he never went out of his way to help me.'—'That doesn't matter.'—'He never tried to understand me.'—'That's not the point.'—'What is the point then?'—'That he is your father.')

'Because he *is* your father': what does this mean? Surely it refers to the fact that this is the man who begat you; this is the man to whom you owe your existence. There is only *one* such man. The sadness of those who never knew their fathers cannot normally be explained in terms of what the father has done. Neither can the restless desire to find a lost father one has never known be explained in this way. These sentiments together with the situations discussed above cannot be understood unless one takes into account, not simply what the father does for his children, but who the father is, namely, the man to whom the children owe their existence.[2] (Is not this the root of the analogy with 'God the Father' —One to whom I owe my existence?)

No doubt I shall be accused by some philosophers of having moved my argument from descriptive to evaluative statements. Evaluative statements are said to depend on my preferences or pro-attitudes. But one cannot understand my obligations to my father in terms of my decision that to obey my father is good. When did I *decide* that I have obligations to my father? Surely, the most natural explanation of my considerate conduct is, 'Because he is my father.' Melden is correct when he says that my father's rights and my obligations to him cannot be understood in isolation from the institution of the family in which these rights and obligations flourish. The distinction between descriptive and evaluative statements in this context is confused and misleading. Outside the institution of the family the fact that this is the man who begat me would not have the moral significance that it has within the family. As Melden points out, the embryological facts about a male parent do not yield the concept 'father' at all. We appreciate the force of a reminder of our obligations when someone says, 'Remember, he is your father.' He does not have to add, 'And you ought to give

---

[2] The distortions which result from ignoring this aspect of fatherhood were pointed out to me in discussion by Mr Rush Rhees.

special consideration to your father,' since to understand what is meant by calling someone your father is to understand that one has certain obligations towards him.

It seems, then, that the status of being a father entails certain rights which the children of the father have obligations to satisfy. It is possible to argue from 'He is my father' to 'I ought not to leave him destitute' for example, since the understanding of the latter statement is involved in the understanding of the former. But here the dissenting philosophers could ask, If 'He is my father' means 'I ought to give him special consideration' why is it that I can come to a moral decision on a given occasion not to satisfy my father's rights? But the fact that I decide sometimes not to satisfy my father's rights does not imply that my father only has rights when I decide to satisfy them! Melden exposes the confusion between actions which meet obligations and obligatory actions. I can meet my obligations to my father in a variety of ways. Melden calls these actions 'obligation-meeting' actions. But obligation-meeting actions are not always obligatory. Rights compete for satisfaction. Sometimes I decide that I ought not to give moral satisfaction to my father's rights. If obligation-meeting actions were always obligatory, Melden points out, many familiar moral situations would be distorted or unintelligible. For example, it would be moral depravity to waive one's rights, whereas in fact we often praise people for doing so. Again, moral perpexity over competing rights would not be a practical problem but a logical absurdity. The question, 'What ought I to do?' does not make the right any less a right, for what one is questioning is not the right, but whether the right is a sufficient reason for action favourable to it in a given situation. The fact that we must decide sometimes what our duty is does not imply that there are no competing rights; it is these rights which make the decision difficult. Otherwise, what is moral tragedy, where, whatever one does, one is going to hurt someone?

Although Melden seems to contrast his account of moral rights with a religious account of morality, I see no reason why the lesson he teaches in moral philosophy cannot be applied to the philosophy of religion.

To understand what it means to call someone a father is to understand why his children act towards him in certain distinctive ways. To understand what it means to believe in God is to understand why God must be obeyed. Certain actions can only be understood in the light of the child–parent relationship. For example, the fact that I do not hit a man who has hit me is given new significance if I tell you that the man who hit me is my father. Other actions cannot be understood unless one understands that they are responses to God's will, as for example, the sacrifice of financial betterment in the vocation to the ministry. As in morality, in religion too, there are reminders of duty in face of laxity: 'Remember the Lord your God.' The prophets said this time and time again to the Children of Israel. There was no need for them to add, 'You ought to obey God.' They *knew* that because they knew *him*.

But what of the so-called trump card in the argument? If 'good' means 'the commands of God', the question, 'Is the will of God good?' ought to be redundant. But why should the question be redundant? God's will does not cease to mean what it does simply because it is questioned. We saw that moral rights compete for satisfaction, but here, the competition is not between rights *within* the same moral community, but between the claims of morality and religion as such. The believer who is not troubled by doubts and to whom life has been kind, does not ask, 'Is what God wills good?' When the question is asked, morality has invaded the realm of religion and the fight is on. The struggle begins simply because the will of God is questioned. It is important to notice, however, that the fight is not confined to one camp. If belief has doubts, so has unbelief: if morality invades religion, religion invades morality. For example, the believer may begin to doubt the goodness of God because of the death of a loved one. On the other hand, the unbeliever may, through the moral experience of his own inadequacy as a person, begin to wonder whether there is something important after all in the idea of divine forgiveness and salvation. The fact that the will of God is questioned does not destroy the internal connection between the will of God and what one ought to do, since when someone is torn between morality and religion what decides the issue is to be found not, as many philosophers think, in an independent moral judgment,[3] but in the nature of the decision; that is, in the relevant moral or religious considerations which win the day.

The religious concept of duty cannot be understood if it is treated as a moral concept. When the believer talks of doing his duty, what he refers to is doing the will of God. In making a decision, what is important for the believer is that it should be in

[3] What would this *independent* judgment be?

accordance with the will of God. To a Christian, to do one's duty *is* to do the will of God. There is indeed no difficulty in envisaging the 'ethical' as the obstacle to 'duty' in this context. For example, a man may, because of what he takes to be his moral obligations towards his family, refuse to give up his job in response to what he believes is God's call to enter the ministry. The Christian would then say with Kierkegaard, 'Here there can be no question of ethics in the sense of morality. . . . Ordinarily speaking, a temptation is something which tries to stop a man from doing his duty, but in this case it is ethics itself which tries to prevent him from doing God's will. But what then is duty? Duty is quite simply the expression of the will of God' (*Fear and Trembling*, O.U.P. 1939, pp. 84–85).

At this point, I must warn the reader that despite my remarks hitherto, I am not arguing for a sharp separation between religious discourse and moral discourse. I cannot accept the account offered by some theologians which makes religion appear to be a technical language, cut off, alien and foreign to the language spoken by everyone else in the community. This picture is false and misleading. It cannot account even for religious phenomena such as the traffic between unbelief and belief. But more important is the fact that it fails to see the importance of calling religion a language or a way of life. Such accounts make religion look like a technique. But a technique in itself could never be a language nor a way of life. Religious doctrines, worship, ritual, etc., would not have the importance they do were they not connected with practices other than those which are specifically religious. When a man prays to God for forgiveness, for example, his prayer would be worthless did it not arise from problems in his relationship with other people. These problems can be appreciated by the religious and the non-religious alike. Because of such connections between religious and non-religious activity it is possible to convey the meaning of religious language to someone unfamiliar with it, even if all one achieves is to stop him from talking nonsense. But one hopes for more than that. By the use of analogies, contrasts and comparisons with which we can journey so far, but must then discard in favour of others, one hopes to convey something of the meaning and force of religious language. It is not my purpose here to discuss which analogies can best be employed for this task. What I do want to stress is that despite the existence of connections between religious and non-religious discourse, the criteria of sense and nonsense in the former are to be found *within* religion. It is this religious meaning which the analogies, contrasts and comparisons try to explain. Just as Melden insists on the basic role to be played by the institution of the family in an explanation of the moral concepts he is dealing with, so I am insisting on a reference to the institution of religion whenever one wants to understand what religious people are saying.

One can be faced with conflicting obligations. Some of these may be obligations to God. Unlike morality, which recognizes that sometimes it is not wrong to decide against one's obligations to one's father, religion recognizes no circumstances in which one is justified in deciding against one's obligations to God. This is because in rejecting God's will, one is not rejecting *one* claim among many within an institution such as the family; one is rejecting the foundation of an institution. To reject God's claim is not to reject one of many competing claims in a way of life; it is to reject a way of life as such.

Many philosophers think that moral judgment is necessarily prior to religious assent. Nothing could be further from the truth, for as Camus says, 'When man submits God to moral judgment, he kills him in his own heart.'

8

SOME REMARKS ON THE INDEPENDENCE OF MORALITY FROM RELIGION[1]

Kai Nielsen

UNTIL recently most analytic philosophers, as well as many other philosophers, have assented to the claim, as old as the *Euthyphro*, that morality and religion are logically independent and that it is impossible in principle to base a morality (any morality) on religion. But of late some Oxford-oriented linguistic philosophers have seriously challenged this claim.[2] While I am completely in sympathy with their overall methodological approach and with their attempt to make detailed and careful explications of the actual functions of religious discourse, I do not find their arguments convincing on this point. It seems to me that the essential logical point that both rationalist and empiricist philosophers, from Plato to Russell, have tried to enforce is sound.[3] I shall try here to vindicate this belief of mine.

The traditional argument may be put as follows. No information about the nature of reality, or knowledge that there is a God and that he issues commands, will by itself tell us what is good or

---

[1] [The reader might care to know also of another paper by Kai Nielsen, 'God and the Good: does morality need religion?' (*Theology Today* 21, April 1964, pp. 47-58), which in some ways is complementary to the present article. *Editor.*]

[2] See, for example, D. A. Rees, 'The Ethics of Divine Commands', *Aristotelian Society Proceedings* (1956-57); G. E. M. Anscombe, 'Modern Moral Philosophy', *Philosophy* (1957); R. N. Smart, 'Gods, Bliss and Morality', *Aristotelian Society Proceedings* (1957-58). [Reprinted above, pp. 15 ff.]

[3] The traditional argument for independence of morality from religion has recently been briefly and ably stated by W. D. Falk, 'Moral Perplexity' *Ethics* 66 (January 1956), 125-129 and by William R. Dennes, 'Knowledge and Values' in *Symbols and Values: An Initial Study*, ed. Lyman Bryson *et al.*, 1952: Cooper 1964, pp. 604-606.

what we ought to do. The statement, 'God wills x', is not a moral pronouncement. Before we know whether we ought to do x, we must know that what God wills is good. And in order to know that what God wills is good, we should have to judge independently that it is good. That something is good is not entailed by God's willing it, for otherwise it would be redundant to ask, 'Is what God wills good?' But this question is not redundant. 'God wills x' or 'God commands x' is not equivalent to 'x is good', as 'x is a male parent' is equivalent to 'x is a father'. 'God wills it but is it good?' is not a senseless self-answering question like 'Fred is a male parent, but is he a father?'. The moral agent must independently decide that whatever God wills or commands is good.

Here it is natural for the believer to say, 'Well, it isn't just God's saying so or ordering it that makes an action obligatory or good. True enough we moral agents must freely choose or decide what to do. God in his wisdom gives us this choice. Otherwise we would be automata, doing what we do simply on authority. Barth and Brunner are of course right in saying we owe God unconditional obedience, but we owe this to God because he is supremely good and supremely loving. When we reflect on what he must be like, as a Being worthy of worship, we realize he ought unconditionally to be obeyed.'

But to say this is really to give Plato and Russell their point. We, as moral agents, form moral convictions and decide that such a Being must be good and his commandments must be followed. But this is so *not* because he *utters* them but because God, being God, is good. But we have here used our own moral awareness and sensitivity to decide that God is *good* and that God *ought* to be obeyed. We have not derived our moral convictions just from discovering what are the commands of God. No command, God's or anyone else's, can simply, as a command, serve as our ultimate standard; and that this is so is purely a matter of logic and not just a result of 'sinful, prideful rebellion' against God's law.

One might, however, attempt to show that religion and morality are not independent by arguing in the following way. 'When Brunner says "the Good consists in always doing what God wills at any particular moment" he does not mean to be giving an analysis of the ordinary uses of "good" at all.' The plain man is too caught up in sin, too confused and prideful to know his true condition. Only the man who has known sickness unto death, who has despaired of the world, who has been willing to die to the world uses 'good' in its deepest, fullest, most correct sense. It is to him I will turn when I wish to come to define 'good' in any adequate way. He, as a man of faith, knows God; through his despair and then faith he has finally come to hear God and thus to perceive the good. My definition does not aim to report, and thus enshrine, the inevitable selfishness and aggression of the plain man embodied in the plain man's use of 'good'; rather it reports the use of the word by the man of faith and stipulates a new use for the man who would really know the good. Like a really consistent hedonist who would argue that 'Pleasure is good' really means just 'Pleasure is pleasure' or 'Pleasure is pleasant,' I shall say that I will take 'good' when used in a fundamental moral sense, to mean just what God wills. 'X is good' is stipulated to be equivalent to 'X is willed by God' or 'X is a command of God'. On this *stipulated use* 'X is commanded by God but is X good?' becomes a self-answering question in the same way 'X is a rectangle but does X really have four sides?' is a self-answering question. I admit that in ordinary language my question is not self-answering but I am not talking about confused ordinary language but about the more adequate language of the man who really knows the good.

Now neither the consistent hedonist nor the Christian moralist can be shown to have committed a *fallacy* if he takes this tack. But it can be shown that both have begged the issue in a complicated way and trivialized their own position in a way in which it is doubtful that any hedonist or Christian moralist would wish to do. And, more importantly, it has not been shown by such a move how, in any ordinary senses of the words 'good', 'right', 'obligatory', etc., moral judgments can be derived from non-moral religious claims. If we continue to use moral language, as in fact we— Christians and non-Christians—do, such a derivation has not been made. The subject has only been changed. The man in moral perplexity wants to know whether in the sense in which the terms are generally used, he can discover what is good by discovering what God wishes him to do. To do this he must be able literally to derive moral judgments from non-moral religious assertions. To be told that in some specially stipulated sense of 'good' he can do so will not relieve his perplexity, and to be told that this stipulated definition is justified because the man of faith knows, as much as any man can know, what is really good begs just the question that is at issue. That we know what we ought to do when we have found out (assuming that in some sense we can 'find out') what God really wishes us to do, is just the point in question. Thus, when God says, 'Depart from me, ye cursed, into everlasting fire' it is, on the Christian's more adequate use, really senseless to ask if this command of God is good. We are told we ought to accept this stipulated definition because it really enshrines a more adequate conception of good. But does it really? In ordinary language it is not senseless to ask if this command of God's is really good. A believer cannot answer this question in the *negative* and remain a believer; but people like Mill, McTaggart and Russell have rejected a belief in Christianity on issues like this.[4] And it has provided torment for many of the great believers. Is it really possible to show Mill, McTaggart and Russell to be wrong by definitional fiat? We can stipulate a new use for the mark (token, sign-vehicle) 'good'. But what do we prove by this move? Isn't the old question back again in only a thinly veiled linguistic disguise? Would we not ask, 'Is this really a better—a morally more adequate—use of "good"?' How else could we answer this but by an appeal to *our own* admittedly fallible moral understanding? We cannot stipulate our way out of this question, for when we say our stipulative definition is more adequate or better or reflects a more heightened moral awareness than the ordinary uses of 'good', we still have appealed to 'more adequate', 'better' or 'a more heightened moral awareness' in the ordinary non-stipulated senses of these terms.

There is another and more plausible way of attacking the claim that morality is independent of religion. D. A. Rees has correctly argued that 'it is not possible within a framework of theistic belief such as we are familiar with, to say, "God commands me to do X but I ought not to do it".'[5] The Judaeo-Christian tradition does not countenance this move. It is a mistake to treat *divine* commands as if they were of the same logical type as political, technical or practical commands. But 'God commands me to do X' is not equivalent to 'I ought to do X'. It is true enough that 'I ought to do X' can be understood without any reference to the commands of God at all. Yet since we would not call God good unless he is regarded as *worthy* of obedience, it is not possible to fully understand 'God commands me to do X' without understanding 'I ought to do X'. In understanding 'God commands me to do X' I must

---

[4] I should not at all like to suggest that these are the only grounds on which they rejected Christianity. They were, however, for Mill and McTaggart very central considerations.

[5] D. A. Rees, 'The Ethics of Divine Commands', *Aristotelian Society Proceedings* (1956-57), p. 86.

understand that there is an intended reference in this use of language to right action. 'God commands me to help the poor' is normally both a religious and a moral utterance. To fail to understand this is to fail to understand the use of this utterance.

To take this more plausible road is to surrender far, far too much however, if it is anyone's continued intention to argue that religion and morality are not independent and that morality must be based on religion. 1. To admit that 'God commands me to do X' and 'I ought to do X' are not equivalent and that the latter expression can be understood independently of the commands or will of God is to admit that a morality can be independent of religion. But this is just what Barth, Brunner, Copleston *et al.* are denying when they claim morality *must* be based on religion. 2. The above argument does not show that Christian moral beliefs can be derived from non-moral beliefs, but only that some Christian moral beliefs can be derived from some other Christian or theistic *moral* and religious beliefs. But was this ever in doubt? It has not been shown that we can discover what we *ought* to do from discovering that a purely non-moral command has been issued or from discovering that there is a God or a 'Necessary Being' (whatever they may mean). If a religious utterance is not a moral utterance no moral inferences can be derived from it; and if it is a moral utterance as well, it obviously does not license us to say that any moral beliefs at all are based on religion. In either event morality remains autonomous, though if all religious utterances were in part moral it would seem that religion is not itself independent of morality. The converse, however, would not be the case.

To this last argument it may be replied: the crucial feature here has been missed. Basic religious statements are never just discoveries about what there is. They are never morally neutral. 'God exists' or 'There is a God' can only be understood 'in terms of, such propositions as "God is loving", "God is forgiving", "God knows the secrets of all men's hearts", "God commands men to love one another" ' and the like.[6]

Now even if we grant this (and I do not think we have to) it is still the case, if we are to continue to use religious discourse as Christians and Jews have used it in the past, that a claim about what kind of beings there are in the universe is analytically distinguishable (though perhaps not in fact separable) from the moral evaluation involved in religious language. We say 'God exists'. In

6 *Ibid.*, pp. 105-106.

the Athanasian Creed we speak of 'The Father eternal, the Son eternal: and the Holy Ghost eternal'. The creed also speaks of 'God, of the substance of the Father, begotten before the worlds'. We also say 'God is love', 'God is good' and the like. Now the 'is' in these last two utterances cannot be the 'is' of identity. 'God' and 'good' and 'love' would then be equivalent and we could not in any literal sense say that God is of the substance begotten before the creation of the worlds. If 'God' and 'love' are equivalent there can be no literal sense to the Apostles' Creed where we say, 'I believe in God the Father almighty, maker of heaven and earth. . . . ' 'God' can no longer refer to a transcendent being, 'the ground of being' or to any reality at all. 'God' like 'good' and 'love' becomes an evaluative term and not a name of a person or of some reality or ground of reality. One can agree with someone like Hare when he claims that 'God' usually functions evaluatively as well as descriptively; but it still essentially functions descriptively; and it functions descriptively in a very peculiar way.

If to this it is objected: 'You are too literal. No one can have much religious awareness if he treats religion as an effort to make certain factual claims and nothing else. As Penelhum has said, 'Into the believer's utterances is packed a whole attitude to living and a whole range of feeling quite foreign to the literal-minded man: hence the great beauty of the classics of religious writing.'[7] Religious utterances have rich emotive, performatory and ceremonial uses. You should not look upon them as literal statements of some odd kind of fact but as mythical or legendary utterances.

Now to argue thus is to in effect give up the great Catholic and Reformation claims. It amounts to a radical proposal to *change* theistic discourse and theistic beliefs and not to *interpret* them in the way that they have been historically understood. This may be all to the good, but then Christianity becomes hardly distinguishable from ethical ways of life like humanism. Presbyterianism and the Society for Ethical Culture would only differ in terms of some of their moral appraisals and in terms of the stories they entertained. Father Copleston and Mascall were quick to see this and fully rejected Braithwaite's attempt so to reduce religious language in his 'An Empiricist's View of the Nature of Religious Belief'. And Penelhum also justly remarks: 'although religious statements have all these non-fact-stating functions, I also think they would not have them, that no one would entertain quite the

[7] Terence Penelhum, 'Faith, Fact, and Philosophy', *Toronto Quarterly* (1956-57), p. 99.

attitudes they express, if it were not thought by those who uttered them that they stated facts as well.'[8] But then 'God is love' or 'God is good' cannot bear an interpretation in which the 'is' is an 'is' of identity. And if the Christian under pressure wishes to re-define all his religious utterances into moral ones he might well reflect on Hägerström's claim that 'Christianity as a positive re-ligion . . . consists in faith in an *objective power*, to which one can turn and from which one can draw strength to attain that which one strives after in one's innermost being; strength to resist temptations and a final hope of blessedness in a future life.'[9]

If, on the other hand, the Christian says that 'love' and 'good' are words standing for the attributes of God and are not really identical with the word 'God', then there is a difference in logical function between utterances like 'God is good' and 'God is love', and 'There is a god', and 'God is real'. The *believer* can say 'God commands me to do X' implies 'I ought to do X' only because he has made the logically prior moral judgments that 'Whatever God commands is good' and 'God is good' or 'God is love'. But how, except by his own moral understanding, can he know that this Objective Power is good or is a Being whose commands we ought to obey? If he is powerful enough we might decide that it would be 'the better part of valour' to obey him but this would not at all entail that we ought to obey him. How do we know that this being is *good*, except by our own moral discernment? We could not discover that this Being is good or just, by discovering that he 'laid the foundation of the world' or 'created man in his image and likeness'. No information about the behaviour patterns of this Being or Person would of itself tell us that he was good, righteous or just. We ourselves would have to decide that, or—if we must use the misleading language of the ethical intuitionist—we would have to intuit or somehow come to perceive or understand that the unique ethical properties 'good', 'righteous' or 'just' applied to this strange Being or 'ground of all being' that we somehow discover to exist. Only if we independently knew what we would count as 'good', 'righteous', 'just', etc., would we be in a position to know whether this Being is good or whether his commands ought to be obeyed. That most Christians most of the time un-questionably assume that he is good only proves that this judgment

    [8] *Ibid.*, p. 100. In addition see J. A. Passmore, 'Christianity and Positivism', *Australasian Journal of Philosophy* 35 (1957), pp. 125ff.
    [9] Axel Hägerström, 'Lectures on So-called Spiritual Religion', *Theoria* 14 (Part 1, 1948), 34-35.

is for them a most fundamental *moral* judgment. But this should hardly be news.

At this point it is natural to reply, 'Still, we would not even call this being "God" unless he was thought to be good. God, whatever else he may or may not be, is a fitting or proper object of worship.' A person so arguing might continue: 'This is really a material mode statement about the use of the word "God"; that is to say, we would not call a Z "God" unless that Z were a fitting or proper object of worship or a Being that *ought* to be worshipped. And if we say "Z is a fitting object of worship" or "Z ought to be worshipped" we must also be prepared to say "Z is good". Z could not be one without being the other; and if Z is a fitting object of worship Z necessarily is a Being we would call "God". Thus if Z is called "God" then Z must also of necessity be called "good" since what ought to be worshipped must also be good. (This is a logical remark about the use of the phrase, "ought to be worshipped".) "God" by definition is "good". Though the word "God" is not equivalent to the word "good", we would not call a being of power "God" unless that Being was thought to be good.'

The above point is well taken, but it still remains the case that the believer has not derived a moral claim from a non-moral religious one. Rather he has only indicated that the word 'God', like the words 'Saint', 'Santa Claus', 'Hunky', 'Nigger', 'Mick' or 'Kike', is not a purely descriptive term; as we remarked before, 'God' like 'Saint', 'Santa Claus' or 'Marilyn Monroe', has an evaluative force; that is to say, it expresses a pro-attitude on the part of the believer and does not *just* designate or even describe a 'Necessary Being' or 'Transcendent Power' or 'Immanent Force'. Such a believer—unlike Schopenhauer—means by 'God' something toward which he has an appropriate pro-attitude; employing this word with its usual evaluative force he could not say, 'God commands it but it is really evil to do it'. If, on the other hand, we simply think of what is purportedly designated or described by the word 'God'—the descriptive force of the word—we can say, for example, without paradox, 'An Objective Power commands it but is evil to do it'. By simply considering the reality allegedly denoted by the word 'God' we cannot discover whether this 'Reality' is good. If we simply let 'Z' stand for this 'Reality' we can always ask 'Is it good?'. This is never a self-answering question in the way it is if we ask, 'Is murder evil?'. Take away the evaluative force of the word 'God' and you have no ground for claiming that it *must* be the case that God is good; to make this claim we, with our admittedly fallible moral understanding, must decide if this Z is good.

'But'—it will be countered—'you have missed the significance of the very point you have just made. As you say yourself, "God" is not just a descriptive word and God-sentences are not by any means used with a purely descriptive aim. "God" normally has an evaluative use and God-sentences have a directive force. You cannot begin to understand them if you do not take this into consideration. You cannot just consider what Z designates or purports to designate.'

My reply to this is that we can and must if we are going to attain clarity in these matters. Certain crucial and basic sentences like, 'God created the Heavens and the earth', and 'God is in Christ', are by no means just moral or practical utterances and they would not have the evaluative force they do if it were *not* thought that in some strange way they described a mysterious objective power. The religious quest is a quest to find a Z such that Z is worthy of worship. This being the case, the evaluative force of the words and of the utterance is dependent on the descriptive force. How else but by our own moral judgment that Z is a being *worthy* to be worshipped are we enabled to call this Z 'My Lord and my God'? Christians say there is a Z such that Z should be worshipped. Nonbelievers deny this or remain sceptical. Findlay, for example, points out that his atheism is in part moral because he does not believe that there can possibly be a Z such that Z is a worthy object of worship. Father Copleston, on the other hand, says there is a Z such that Z *ought* to be worshipped. This Z, Father Copleston claims, is a 'Necessary Being' whose non-existence is in some important sense inconceivable. But both Findlay and Copleston are using their own moral understanding in making their respective moral judgments. Neither is deriving or deducing his moral judgment from the statement 'There is a Z' or from noticing or adverting to the fact—if it is a fact—that Z is 'Being-itself', 'a reality whose non-existence is unthinkable', 'the ground of being' or the like.

Mr Rees and the Crisis Theologians notwithstanding, Plato's point here is still correct. Morality cannot be based on religion. If anything, the opposite is partly true, for nothing can be God unless he or it is an object worthy of worship and it is our own moral insight that must tell us if anything at all could possibly be worthy of worship.

It is true that if some Z is God, then by definition Z is an object worthy of worship. But this does not entail there is such a Z; that there is such a Z would depend both on what is the case and on what we, as individuals, judge to be worthy of worship. 'God is worthy of worship' is—for most uses of 'God'—analytic. To understand this sentence requires no insight at all but only a knowledge of English; but that there is or can be a Z such that Z is worthy of worship depends, in part at least, on the moral insight —or lack thereof—of that fallible creature that begins and ends in dust.

In her puzzling article, 'Modern Moral Philosophy', Miss Anscombe has made a different sort of objection to the type of approach taken here. Moral uses of 'ought' or obligation statements, she argues, have no reasonable sense outside a divine-law conception of ethics.[10] Without God such conceptions are without sense. There was once a context, a religious way of life, in which these conceptions had a genuine application. 'Ought' was once equated, in the relevant context, with 'being obliged', 'bound', or 'required'. This came about because of the influence of the Torah. Because of the 'dominance of Christianity for many centuries the concepts of being bound, permitted, or excused became deeply embedded in our language and thought'.[11] But since this is no longer so unequivocally the case these conceptions have become rootless. Shorn of this theistic Divine Law, shorn of the Hebrew-Christian tradition, these conceptions can only retain a 'mere mesmeric force' and cannot be 'inferred from anything whatever'.[12] I think Miss Anscombe would say that I have shown nothing more than this in my above arguments. What I have said about the independence of morality from religion is quite correct for this 'corrupt' age where the basic principles of a divine-law conception of ethics appear merely as practical major premises on a par with the principle of utility and the like. In such contexts a moral 'ought' can only have a psychological force. Without God it can have no 'discernible content' for the conception of moral obligation 'only operates in the context of law'.[13] By such moves as I have made above I have, in effect, indicated how moral obligation has *now* only a delusive appearance of content. And in claiming that without God there still can be genuine moral obligations I have manifested 'a detestable desire to retain the atmosphere of the term' 'morally obligatory' where the

[10] G. E. M. Anscombe, 'Modern Moral Philosophy', *Philosophy* 33 (January 1958), 8.
[11] *Ibid.*, p. 5.   [12] *Ibid.*, p. 8.   [13] *Ibid.*, p. 18.

term itself no longer has a genuine use.[14] Only if we believe in God as a law-giver can we come to believe that there is anything a man is categorically bound to do on pain of being a bad man.[15] The concept of obligation has, without God, become a Holmesless Watson. In our present context, Miss Anscombe argues, we should, if 'psychologically possible', jettison the concepts of moral obligation, moral duty and the like and approach ethics only after we have developed a philosophical psychology which will enable us to get clear about what pleasure is, what a human action is and what constitutes human virtue and a distinctively 'human flourishing'.[16]

I shall not be concerned here with the larger issues raised by Miss Anscombe's paradoxical, excessively obscure, yet strangely challenging, remarks. I agree, of course, that philosophical psychology is important but I am not convinced that we have not done ethics and cannot profitably do ethics without such a philosophical psychology. I shall, however, be concerned here only to point out that Miss Anscombe has not shown us that the notion of 'moral obligation' is unintelligible or vacuous without God and his laws.

We have already seen that if so-and-so is called a 'divine command' or 'an ordinance of God', then it is obviously something that the person who believes it to be a 'divine command' or 'ordinance of God' ought to obey, for he would not call anything 'a *divine* command' or 'an ordinance of *God*' unless he thought he ought to obey it. But we ourselves by our own moral insight must judge that such commands or promulgations are worthy of such an appellation. Yet no moral conceptions follow from a command or law as such. And this would be true at any time whatsoever. It is a logical and not a historical consideration.

Now it is true that if you believe in God in such a way as to accept God as your Lord and Master and if you believe that so-and-so is an ordinance of God then you ought to try to follow this ordinance. But this is not so because we can base morals on religion or on a law conception of morality; rather it is true for just the opposite reason. The man who can bring himself to say 'My God' uses 'God' and cognate words evaluatively. To use such an expression is already to make a moral evaluation, the man expresses his decision that he is morally bound to do whatever God commands. 'I ought to do whatever this Z commands' is an expression of moral obligation. To believe in God, as we already have seen, involves the making of a certain value judgment; that is to say, the believer

14 *Ibid.*, p. 18.   15 *Ibid.*, p. 6.   16 *Ibid.*, pp. 1, 15, 18.

believes that there is a Z such that Z is worthy of worship. But this value judgment cannot be derived from just examining Z, or from hearing Z's commands or laws. Without a pro-attitude on the part of the believer toward Z, without a decision by the individual concerned that Z is *worthy* of worship, nothing of a moral sort follows. But no decision of this sort is entailed by discoveries about Z or by finding out what Z commands or wishes. It is finally up to the individual to decide that this Z is worthy of worship, that this Z ought to be worshipped, that this Z ought to be called his Lord and Master. We have here a moral use of 'ought' that is logically prior to any law conception of ethics. The command gains obligatory force because it is judged worthy of obedience. If someone says, 'I don't pretend to appraise God's laws, I just simply accept them because God tells me to', like considerations obtain. This person judges that there is a Z that is a proper object of obedience. This expresses his own moral judgment, his own sense of what he is obliged to do.

A religious belief depends for its viability on our sense of good and bad—our own sense of *worth*—and not vice versa. It is crucial to an understanding of morality that this truth about the uses of our language be understood. Morality cannot be based on religion and I (like Findlay) would even go so far as to deny in the name of morality that any Z whatsoever could be an object or Being worthy of worship. But whether or not I am correct in this last judgment, it remains the case that each person with his own finite and fallible moral awareness must make decisions of this sort for himself. This would be so whether he was in a Hebrew-Christian tradition or in a 'corrupt' and 'shallow' consequentialist tradition or in any tradition whatsoever. A moral understanding must be logically prior to any religious assent.

9

MORAL JUDGMENTS AND
GOD'S COMMANDS

Ian T. Ramsey

I PROPOSE to begin my comments on the logical problems involved in talking of duty or goodness as God's will by reference to a recent book, *The Theological Frontier of Ethics*,[1] by W. G. Maclagan. In that book he summarizes very clearly what seems to him to be the basic difficulty in this way of talking. To say that 'x is good' or 'x is my duty' because God wills x, or God commands x; that 'x is good' or 'x is my duty' is equivalent to, or is entailed by 'God wills x' or 'God commands x' is, for Maclagan, to be on the horns of a dilemma. He comments: 'If we are not to use anthropomorphic concepts the theory cannot be stated, and if we are to use them it cannot be defended; and one or other we must do.'[2] To recognize that something of the same dilemma arises for all discourse about God—if we are not to use anthropomorphic concepts like love, power, wisdom, we cannot talk about God; but if we *do* use them, how do we manage to talk of God and not man?—only underlies the fundamental character of the logical problems which talk of Duty as God's will generates.

Undoubtedly by speaking of the 'will' of God, or of God's 'commands', the theory trades in anthropomorphisms. In its very formulation the theory appears to speak of God as though he were some Oriental potentate, Headmaster or Sergeant-Major.[3] Yet once it does this, it runs into a difficulty that can be variously expressed.

It may be said, for instance, that the fact that there is a person

---

[1] Allen and Unwin 1961.   [2] *Ibid.*, pp. 68-69.
[3] As Mr G. de Graaff reminds us, p. 32 above.

who issues commands, or who wishes something to be done, does not by itself ever tell us what we ought to do, or what is good. The one question about a fact must be distinguished from the other question—about morality. The mere fact that someone—God—commands something x, or that it is his will that y should be done, no more obliges us to do x or y, no more entails that 'x is my duty' or 'y is good' than if (say) Hitler or Lord Shaftesbury had commanded or wished it. The question of duty or goodness must be distinguished from any question about a mere matter of fact such as whether someone commanded x or wished y to be done.

Maclagan would put the matter in another way. Duty, he would say, no doubt echoing Kant, is intrinsically binding. But if whatever was morally binding was only made so by God's commanding it, there would be a collision between the contingency of this existential fact about a will, and the intrinsic necessity (as Maclagan would see it) of some specific obligation. If Duty is intrinsically binding, if ethics is autonomous, there must be no sort of 'subordination' of duty. The autonomy of Duty must not be compromised by being derived from somebody's will as its source. Not even God's will is an exception. If a traditional theist now said that in all this, Maclagan was treating God as if he were an ordinary person, or (more intricately) that God's existence and so his will, is not contingent but necessary, so that there is after all no conflict here between necessity and contingency, Maclagan would say, with some plausibility, that the command theory is then emptied of all significance. The theory only allows for the autonomy of ethics when it takes such a view of God as excludes the possibility of talking of God by means of ordinary human concepts like will and command.

So far it might seem as if Maclagan only underlines the difficulties on which Nowell-Smith has gone to town.[4] But Maclagan is unwilling to be entirely negative; he is unwilling to be wholly ruthless towards talk of moral obligations in terms of God's will or commands; and once he has made the autonomy of ethics clear beyond doubt he makes some remarkable suggestions to which we may attribute the status of second thoughts. There are four passages in the book where these surprising suggestions are made.[5]

On page 64 Maclagan says that 'moral experience', once it has

[4] See above, ch. 5.
[5] The next two paragraphs, as well as some of the phrases in the preceding paragraph are, with certain additions, taken from my review of Maclagan's book in *Mind* NS 72, No. 286, April 1963.

been 'left to stand on its own and to make sense of itself', 'may then reveal itself as more than it is ordinarily acknowledged to be'. Even though he has been broadly inclined to make the word 'God' no more than a synonym for 'Moral Law' or 'Moral Demand' (a move with no other merit—if that—save typographical economy), never-theless on pages 81-2 he acknowledges that 'the term "God" may well mean a great deal more than is meant by "moral law" and the more may be of the utmost significance to our lives. . . .' It is only 'in so far as the consciousness of moral demand is considered in and by itself (that) "God" can mean nothing different from "moral law",' only then that 'the theological term renames without eluci-dating'. So he can say (somewhat surprisingly in view of other state-ments) that there may be 'a legitimate overplus of meaning attach-ing to the term "God", additional to what is signified by "moral demand"'; an overplus which 'will derive from elements or "moments" in experience other than that of confrontation by the moral demand itself . . .'. Whereupon 'a theologian might . . . say that illumination in this sense, by lateral enrichment, so to call it, and not by vertical grounding, is all that he ever looked for.' The same distinction recurs a little later when, on page 89, Maclagan, rejecting another quasi-theological crudity which would suppose that values can be provided by theology with a sort of 'solidity' which keeps them from being 'flimsy' (whatever all that means), nevertheless allows that 'theistic beliefs otherwise acquired might throw . . . light on the concept of an order of values' by 'a sort of lateral, not a vertical illumination'. Last of all we may quote page 171. Though Maclagan has been willing to allow that a man's moral *response*, formulated in concepts of prayer and of grace as 'environ-mental succour', affords some justification for talking of God as personal, yet in so far as he assimilates 'moral *demand*' and God, the personality of God (as he readily acknowledges) seems to be com-promised. So we may be all the more surprised to find Maclagan on pages 171 and 172 allowing not only that there may be some occa-sions when God can be spoken of as personal, but that God may be so spoken of in relation to the demands of the moral law. Speaking of the possibility after all of using the concept of personality of God, he says that 'we may certainly apply the concept of "person" to God, meaning by it just what we ordinarily mean, as a sort of final, and so to say despairing "gesture of affirmation" regarding a being that we do not think it really fits, but in the conviction that to deny what is thus affirmed could be even less appropriate . . .' and he continues (p. 172 and despite the whole of ch. 3) '. . . so far as there is propriety at all in using of God the language of personality it will be natural and even proper to describe the "moral law" or "order of values" as being or expressing the will of God'. 'But' (he continues) 'it will be vitally important to remember . . . that this is no more than a manner of speaking; a permissible description indeed (and even as description no more than permissible, rather as one might be permitted to speak of Scott as "the author of *Waverley*" even in talking of his work not as novelist but as sheriff), but still in no sense an explanation of the moral facts. Explanation, however, is just what has been pretended', i.e., Maclagan would say, in traditional theology.

In such ways as these, then, and despite what the casual reader might suppose, Maclagan allows the possibility of theological concepts affording a wider interpretation of moral experience, though he would make two important qualifications: (*a*) The links in this wider interpretation are not causal. God must not be supposed to be a source of morality *if this means* providing a causal explanation of it. Duty is not binding because (in a causal sense of 'because') it is God's will; (*b*) no one, neither religious believers nor (say) Professor Nowell-Smith, must suppose that God, pictured as a person, is anything more than 'a manner of speaking', what some would call a model. But providing we remember this, we may (despite what Maclagan has said in chapter 3 of his book) approximate to the logic of God by using the model of a personal will, so that even duty can be talked of as '*a kind* of "hearing God addressing and commanding us"' (p. 56, italics mine).

In these ways I think Maclagan helps us to see two crucial problems which cluster around talk of Duty and Goodness in terms of God's will and commands, and it is with these two problems that this paper will now be largely concerned.

I. The first problem concerns the autonomy of ethics. What is meant by claiming autonomy for ethics? Is it possible to have autonomy while allowing for what Maclagan calls 'lateral enrichment', or 'lateral illumination' of the language of morals by the language of theology?

II. The second problem is a more particular one and concerns the logical status of phrases like 'God's will' and 'God's commands'.

Let us look at each of these problems in turn.

I

One of the clearest accounts of the 'autonomy of ethics' is that given by Dr A. C. Ewing in his paper with that title in a symposium titled *Prospect for Metaphysics*.[6] By 'autonomy of ethics' Dr Ewing expresses 'the contention that ethical and indeed valuational concepts generally are quite distinctive and cannot simply be reduced to those of any other branch of thought (or any combination of them).' He continues: 'The autonomy of ethics has been defended especially against "naturalism", which sought to reduce ethical concepts to empirical concepts falling within the sphere of a natural science, usually psychology: but I should, like Kant and Moore, the two most famous protagonists of autonomy, regard it as excluding also their reduction to concepts of metaphysics or theology.'

The impossibility of reducing value-terms to terms in the natural sciences, metaphysics or theology is, Dr Ewing would say, a logical impossibility which arises because, as he agrees with R. M. Hare, value-terms have the special function of commending, which if not done by value-terms cannot be done by any other. The consequence is that not only is there an autonomy about ethics in so far as 'ethical judgments cannot be *reduced* without residium to judgments that fall within a natural science'[7] or, we may add, philosophical theology; this autonomy also implies that ethical judgments cannot be *deduced formally* from such judgments either.

But, as Dr Ewing sees, the point must not be over-argued. There is plainly not such an autonomy about ethics that it is altogether independent of factual judgments—that would be absurd. 'We judge what we ought to do because of what the situation is or at least appears to us to be; we judge something to be good or bad because of its factual nature.'[8] In this kind of way, ethical judgments are based on matters of fact. But granting this dependence, autonomy is still preserved because 'from no factual proposition whatever can we infer that things which have (certain) properties will be intrinsically good or bad, and similarly from factual propositions alone we cannot infer that any act of a given kind in a given situation will be morally wrong or right'. We are thus back at the old point that there can neither be reductions of moral assertions to, nor formal derivations of moral assertions from, assertions in, e.g., natural sciences or philosophical theology. At the same time

---

[6] Ed. Ian Ramsey, Allen and Unwin 1961.
[7] *Prospect for Metaphysics*, p. 37.   [8] *Ibid.*

Dr Ewing, and I think rightly, makes it plain that this kind of logical independence does not exclude any and all links between 'facts' and 'values'. 'The link between facts and values' he says, 'must be grasped by a specific ethical insight', but again he adds, so as to avoid any possible misunderstanding, 'for which no metaphysical substitute can be provided.'[9]

It is clear then that the autonomy of ethics, though it excludes certain views as to the relation of ethics to the natural sciences and theology, need not deny any and every kind of relation between ethics and theology, any more than between ethics and the natural sciences. Indeed, Dr Ewing, at the end of his paper, makes various concessions, the most important of which for our purpose is that while theism 'cannot create ethics' it can nevertheless 'add a new tone to ethics'. We are reminded of Maclagan's phrases such as 'lateral enrichment' and 'lateral illumination'. It looks as if even a claim for the autonomy of ethics allows for, and leaves room for the possibility of *some kind* of theological interpretation.

Before trying to elucidate further the possibility of and conditions for such reliable interpretations, in a field where most interpretations are tangled, it will be useful to look first at two other examples of theologically interpreted ethics, both of which seem to escape the logical blunders of cruder theories, and neither of which it would appear need compromise the autonomy of ethics.

The first example is given to us by the Rev. Patterson Brown[10] in the same issue of *Mind* to which I have already referred. In the context of a discussion of the problem of evil, Patterson Brown gives his view of the relation between moral and religious concepts which, as he argues, 'so many philosophers have utterly misconstrued'.[11]

'The first point which must be made' he says 'is that "God" is ordinarily a partially moral term. In our civilization, and thus in our language, it would not be strictly proper to call a being "God" whose actions were not perfectly good or whose commands were not the best of moral directives. That God is good is a truth of language, and not an ethical contingency, since one of the usual *criteria* of Godhood is that the actions and commands of such a being are perfectly good. In referring to some being as "God", we would in part be saying that he was morally faultless.'[12] In this way, 'God is good' becomes trivially true in the same way as 'Saints are good'.[12]

[9] *Ibid.*   [10] 'Religious Morality', *Mind* NS 72, No. 286, April 1963, pp. 235-244.
[11] *Ibid.*, p. 235.   [12] *Ibid.*, p. 238.

But, he hastens to add, 'There remains . . . a crucial difference between the necessary goodness of God and the necessary goodness of Saints. To say that Saints are by definition morally faultless is to say that we will withhold the title of "Saint" from anyone who is not perfectly good by Christian standards. To say that God is by definition perfect, however, is to say more than this. Not only would we withhold the name "God" from any being who was imperfect by Christian standards; in addition, the appellation "God" is reserved for that particular being who is the ultimate Christian *criterion* of the good. The saint is good because he follows God's will; but God is good because he is the standard of goodness. Thus, it is rhetorical to ascribe goodness both to Saints and to God, since only that being is called "God" who is the supreme paradigm of goodness, and no one is called "Saint" unless he is Godly. "God is the ultimate standard of the good" is true by definition, and this entails that "God is good" is trivially true. Therefore in addition to stating that there is an omnipotent, omniscient and transcendent Creator and that he is perfectly good, "There is a God" also serves as a moral commitment to that being as the basis of Christian morality. So, quite clearly, the statement "If God commands something, then it ought to be done" is pleonastic. If we are not unconditionally obliged to do whatever x commands, then x is by definition not God. Belief in the Judeo-Christian God, then, can entail normative conclusions just because it presupposes a moral commitment. In becoming a Christian theist, one commits oneself to the will of the Creator—who must first, of course, be assumed to exist— as one's own highest ethical standard.'[13]

In this way, he differs from Professor Nielsen, from whom he quotes,[14] and who would say that 'The statement "God wills x" is not a moral pronouncement.' Likewise Patterson Brown would presumably take issue when Professor Nielsen says, ' "God wills x" or "God commands x" is not equivalent to "x is good", as "x is a male parent" is equivalent to "x is a father". "God wills it, but is it good?" is not a senseless or self-answering question like "Fred is a male parent, but is he a father?".'[15]

---

[13] *Ibid.*, pp. 238-9.

[14] 'Religion, Morality and Bertrand Russell', *The Amherst Review* (Spring 1959), p. 15, though Patterson Brown recognizes that Professor Nielsen 'has considerably modified and extended his argument' in the paper included in this present book, even if he still adheres 'to his earlier conclusion that morality must be logically prior to religion', which is the point Patterson Brown wishes to contest. See further above, p. 140 n. 1.

[15] *Mind* 70, No. 278, April 1961, p. 175. See above, p. 141.

As for Professor Nowell-Smith, from whom he also quotes,[16] while it can be said of him as of Professor Nielsen and many others, 'they take "God is good" to be an ordinary moral judgment rather than a truth of language', a further word may be called for in relation to Nowell-Smith's remark that 'For religious people the fact that God has commanded them to do something is a sufficient reason, perhaps the only reason, for thinking themselves obliged to do it. But this is because they have a general pro-attitude to doing whatever God commands.'[17] Presumably, Patterson Brown would take no exception to the first sentence; what he would say however is that *in so far as* the second sentence assumes that there are commands of God which the religious person contemplates and then evaluates and judges, it misconstrues the logic of at any rate Christian assertions. He remarks that 'the actual religious "evaluation", if it can be called such, is that of committing oneself to a God-centred morality in the first place. Subsequently to pass independent judgment on God's actions or commands would be a straightforward abandonment of Christian morality, since some other moral principle would then have been accepted as more fundamental than the Creator's will. So that to judge God is in effect to deny that he is *God*.'[18]

Here then is the first example of a less crude theological interpretation of ethics and it is one which derives from the view that ' "God" is ordinarily a partially moral term'.

My second example is to be found in the writings of Dom Illtyd Trethowan.[19] Of this view he himself says that 'it is the view that the existence of God is apprehended *in* the recognition of moral obligation or that the recognition of moral obligation occurs *in* the apprehension of God. The apprehension of God *is* the recognition of moral obligation and vice versa.'[20] Here is a view which neither tries to prove the existence of God from a sense of duty nor tries to validate a sense of duty by calling in God. Rather 'it is asking for recognition of the fact that the experience to which people refer when they speak of being *obliged* to live up to a moral standard, and the experience to which people refer when they speak of discovering

[16] *Ethics* (Pelican Philosophy Series).
[17] *Op. cit.*, pp. 192-193.
[18] *Art. cit.*, p. 239.
[19] I shall quote from his paper, 'The Philosophical Concept of Morality' in the Downside symposium *The Springs of Morality*, ed. John M. Todd (Burns and Oates 1955). But it is only fair to Dom Illtyd to mention that in the article he refers the reader to other of his works where he develops his case at greater length, e.g., *Certainty* (Dacre Press 1948) and *An Essay in Christian Philosophy*, Longmans 1954.
[20] *Loc. cit.*, p. 17.

God in his action upon them are the same experience.'[21] Dom Illtyd continues later: 'Some awareness of God arises, we may suppose, in everyone's history, as the recognition that some *standard* imposes itself upon him, although he may not realize that this is what the theists are talking about. But if the awareness is to "take", he must be willing to be interested in it, and he may use his freedom to reject the standard; he can avoid the imposition. He may move so far away from this experience of absolute value that he may need a complete re-education if he is to recover it. That is the position in which so many of our contemporaries seem to be; for them God's existence is certainly not self-evident.'

To speak of an apprehension of God which is the recognition of moral obligation is to appeal, Dom Illtyd would say, to an 'experience' of God which is a 'mediate experience', and he recognizes that there are difficulties to be cleared up about this concept. He speaks of making the appeal to what 'is rather the undercurrent of experience', and, he adds, 'the word "experience" is used in the widest sense'.[22] He continues: 'I have been in the habit of using a spatial metaphor' for this awareness of God 'and calling it a "background" knowledge: since it is obviously of a unique kind, it can be indicated only by a metaphor, and I must be content to leave it there.'

Here then is Professor W. G. Maclagan, the Rev. Patterson Brown and Dom Illtyd Trethowan, and even Dr A. C. Ewing, allowing in different ways for the possibility of some kind of theological interpretation of obligation and value-judgments generally, which nevertheless does not compromise the autonomy of ethics. Can we do anything to elucidate further this possibility? Can we say anything more to illuminate those phrases which they severally use and which speak of theology affording a 'lateral enrichment' or a 'lateral illumination' of ethics, or 'adding a new tone to ethics'; of 'God' as being 'ordinarily a partially moral term'; or of the apprehension of God being the recognition of moral obligation and vice-versa?

My answer begins by recalling R. M. Hare's account of the language of morals, and it eventually takes up some of the points made in my recent discussion of A. C. Ewing's views. I approach my answer this way to show just how it arises in relation to what is currently the most influential view of the logic of moral judgments.

Hare's account may be expressed succinctly as follows. Moral judgments, e.g. 'It was good of the Samaritan to come to the traveller's aid when he was lying helpless on the road', are not only, as

21 *Ibid.*, p. 17.   22 *Ibid.*, p. 18.

they plainly are, descriptive, they are also prescriptive, or as it is sometimes expressed, evaluative. To evaluate an action is not to assert the existence of some new quality; it is not to be descriptive of that action in some special kind of way, it is not to describe it at all. Instead it is to adopt an attitude towards the action. So if for example we have called an action 'good' we shall have prescribed that action for ourselves, we shall have committed ourselves to that action when appropriate circumstances arise. Further, not only shall we have commended the action in this sense of declaring our own allegiance to it, we shall also have commended it by prescribing similar conduct for others in like circumstances. Moral judgments are thus not only prescriptive—a characteristic they share with imperatives, for example—they are also in this way universalizable and so lead to moral principles, which provide us with guides to conduct. Here is Hare's view in its full perspective, and it will I hope be clear why he chooses 'universal prescriptivism' as the title for it.[23]

In *Freedom and Reason* Hare remarks that 'when we are trying, in a concrete case, to decide what we ought to do, what we are looking for . . . is an action to which we can commit ourselves (prescriptivity) but which we are at the same time prepared to accept as exemplifying a principle of action to be prescribed for others in like circumstances (universalizability).'[24] Further, Hare suggests that it is because of this complete universalism which belongs to moral judgments that moral judgments are sometimes invested with a quasi-factual character.[25] But of course they must not be confused with statements of fact; indeed the combination of prescriptivity and universalizability avoids both naturalistic reductions on the one hand (as we saw in our discussion of A. C. Ewing above) and also what Hare calls 'old-fashioned subjectivism' on the other. He continues:[26] 'My own view is rather that, if a man is thinking morally (or even in general, evaluatively) he is compelled to universalize his volitions: (but) his judgments remain prescriptive, and therefore cannot be deduced from any statements of fact.' Or again, he remarks that 'an illuminating way of approaching the thesis which I am maintaining (namely universal prescriptivism) is to look upon it as retaining what is sound in descriptivism (natural and non-natural), and adding to it an account of the other essential element in the meaning of moral judgments, the prescriptive'.[27]

---

[23] *Freedom and Reason*, p. 21.   [24] *Op. cit.*, p. 89-90.   [25] Cf. *Language of Morals*, p. 179.
[26] *Freedom and Reason*, p. 199.   [27] *Ibid.*, p. 21.

So far I can register nothing but indebtedness to Hare for the light he has thrown on the logic of moral judgments. But it seems to me that a legitimate place can be found for theological interpretations if Hare would allow us to develop his view at a point where it seems to me both to need, and to allow for, development. When in speaking of an action as 'good' we commit ourselves to it, are we not recognizing a prior claim which that action makes on us; isn't a commitment always a response to something which is discerned? Further, does not the feature of universalizability imply that others in like circumstances will have a like discernment?

Does not Hare, then, like R. B. Braithwaite whom I mention below, overlook a third feature which belongs to moral judgments, and it is a feature which is presupposed *by* prescriptivity and universalizability, as much as these presuppose descriptivity. Let it be granted that no one can say, 'You ought to do x' or 'It was good of you to do y' without indulging in some description. Further, Hare has shown how both assertions, being moral judgments, must be prescriptive and universalizable. But without in any way denying those important analytical insights, my point is that something more yet remains to be said, viz. that both judgments *presuppose* that x and y are *claim-possessing* circumstances, whose claims I acknowledge in making the moral judgments I do.

I think that there may be ambiguities in the concept of prescriptivity which conceal this presupposition. When I say, 'You ought to do x' it looks as if *I* am prescribing x, which in one obvious sense of course I am; but before *I* could prescribe x to another person B, *x* must already have *claimed* this attitude, this commitment, from me. What is more, before there can be universalizability, and before B can with freedom and reason himself do x in responding to my prescription, he must share with me the claim which I acknowledged when I prescribed x in the first place. So 'prescriptivity' seems to cover both self-prescription, and prescription for others, though these are not on logical all-fours.

Prescriptivity, when it refers to self-prescriptivity, commitment on my own part, is the adopting of a certain attitude, the expression of a decision, all of which have the character of a response to a value-claim which they acknowledge and in this sense presuppose. But prescription for others is an endeavour to recreate that value-claim for them, so that prescriptions are not transferable from myself to others in the straightforward self-guaranteed way in which descriptions are. For prescriptivity only arises when there is a situation

which can be characterized as a discernment as well as a commitment, which exhibits a *claim* as well as a response, and such a claim
has to be 'seen' and acknowledged before it is action-compelling. In
brief, such 'seeing' is the correlate of a disclosure. This is the point
I would now like to argue in further detail, and in particular that
prescriptivity in so far as it is associated with universalizability,
acknowledges a claim which, I would say, it presupposes and which
has to be 'seen' before it is sufficiently compelling.

Nor do I think that this is a point with which Hare need disagree,
and I will develop my view keeping close to his exposition. He
remarks that 'both naturalism and my own view lay great stress on
the fact that, when we make a moral judgment about something, we
make it *because* of the possession by it of certain non-moral properties'.[28] As he has said earlier, 'The truth in naturalism is that moral
terms do indeed have descriptive meaning' and it is 'in virtue of
possessing this descriptive meaning' that 'moral judgments are
universalizable, and naturalism has the merit of implying this'.[29]
Now it seems as if Hare believes that the universalizability which
belongs to moral judgments is a characteristic which they share with
'all judgments which carry descriptive meaning',[30] and that descriptive judgments and 'moral judgments are, *in the same sense*,
universalizable'.[31]

This may be true, but I do not think it follows that the 'facts' with
which moral judgments are concerned are in every respect like the
facts with which descriptive perceptual or scientific judgments are
concerned. Indeed if descriptivity and universalizability were in
every respect the same for moral and non-moral judgments it is
difficult to see how prescriptivity could arise distinctively in the
moral case. My point is that there is a feature of a moral situation
which involves no new facts of a perceptual or scientific sort, but
which is nevertheless precisely that which leads to moral judgments
having the prescriptivity they have: this feature is a *claim* arising
around and out of the facts to which the prescriptivity is a response.

It is in terms of this feature that I would see both the need and
the possibility of developing Hare's account of the logic of moral
judgments so as to allow for legitimate theological interpretations.
I would even think that in the last chapter of *Freedom and Reason*
Hare himself moves in the direction I am concerned to go along. He
rightly remarks that in the practical consideration of moral prob-

[28] *Op. cit.*, p. 21.
[30] *Ibid.*, p. 10.
[29] *Ibid.*, p. 21; cf. p. 10.
[31] *Ibid.*, p. 12.

lems, 'we are logically prohibited from making different moral judgments about two cases, when we cannot adduce any difference between the cases. . . .'[32] This as he says is 'one way of stating the principle of universalizability' and 'Since the Nazi cannot justify his different treatment of Germans and Jews without adducing some difference between their cases, he invents a difference': [33] the lack of a significant factor in their heredity which the Germans have.

But the important word which I have deliberately included is 'significant'. The factor must be such, or more accurately be so talked about, that its occurrence creates a claim which calls from the Nazi a commitment which leads him to make his prescriptive universalizable judgments about the Jews. The factor will never be given by a mere listing of some fact or facts. As Mr Hare is anxious to recognize, the major difficulty in moral reasoning about some difficult moral problem is not to produce a universal principle, a ground for moral reasoning, but to ensure that it is held, where the stress is on '*held*'. Quoting aptly from Kant, Mr Hare remarks, 'It is necessary not merely to *quote* a maxim, but . . . to *will* it to be a universal law'; and here as we would expect prescriptivity arises.[34] In particular, willing anything to be a universal law involves willing it to apply even when the roles played by the parties are reversed, a specially relevant reflection for the discussion of racial problems.

We may take this with what Mr Hare says somewhat later: 'To get people to think morally it is not sufficient to tell them how to do it; it is necessary also to induce them in the wish to do it.'[35] But it is surely more than the wish: there must be the will. What in fact is involved in 'enlightened politicians, journalists, commentators, preachers, novelists affecting a change for the better'?[36] What is involved in bringing people to think morally? Is it something which can be done without a growth in sensitivity or what Hare would call cultivating the imagination? No. The fanatic and the bear-baiter certainly need to be cured of their 'insensibility or lack of imagination'.[37] We shall never help people both to think and to act morally unless we ourselves have a clear idea of the logic of the moral judgments which we are hoping they will make.

But there is more to it than that. My point is that there is an element in this logic which even Mr Hare's lucid and brilliant exposition neglects: a claim-acknowledging element. To be clearer

[32] *Ibid.*, p. 216.   [33] *Ibid.*   [34] *Ibid.*, p. 219.
[35] *Ibid.*, p. 224.   [36] *Ibid.*   [37] *Ibid.*, p. 232.

about moral judgment we must make evident the prior claim to which the moral judgment is a response, the claim which arises out of and around the facts of the situation which are considered relevant. People will never think or act morally until they recognize that to think (or act) morally is to think about a response (or to respond) to a certain kind of claim; and it is because there is a situation possessing this kind of claim that moral judgments have both their descriptive-universalizability and their prescriptivity. They have both because they are claim-acknowledging: descriptivity leads to prescriptivity and affords universalizability because all features go back to a claim-possessing situation.

It is because of this claim element in a moral situation, to which moral judgments arise as a response, that there arises the possibility of legitimate and significant theological interpretation of morality; but before developing that point, I would first like to explain my contention somewhat further, and I begin by illustrating my view by reference to two other moral philosophers, Professor R. B. Braithwaite and Dr A. C. Ewing.

On the view I am putting forward, then, moral judgments are descriptive and prescriptive and both in a way which permits of universalizability *only because* they are also responsive, having the character of being responses pointing to a prior claim they presuppose. In this way they point beyond themselves, but in a way which as we shall see in no sense compromises their autonomy. We can now see, I suggest, why Professor R. B. Braithwaite's account of the logic of religious assertions[38] is inadequate. It is inadequate because it does no justice to this character or moral assertions as responsive, and so does not recognize that it is the point of the stories, characteristic of the religious man, to describe the claim which that response acknowledges, and to which a response is made when a moral judgment occurs. The stories do not only encourage his behaviour: they make that behaviour possible in so far as they contrive to express a claim to which the behaviour is a response.

What I say about claim and response may also, I hope, illuminate what Dr Ewing may have had in mind when, in speaking of moral judgments as being evaluative, he said that to evaluate 'is not to assert the existence of new special qualities in what is being evaluated', but is 'rather to adopt an attitude for or against it', and then made the—for me—important acknowledgment that 'that attitude is justified by the nature of the object'.[39] Or as he said in a quotation

---

[38] See ch. 3 above.   [39] *Op. cit.*, p. 36.

I gave earlier: 'We judge what we ought to do because of what the situation is or at least appears to be: we judge something to be good or bad because of its factual nature.'[40] What I have said about a claim leading to an acknowledgment in a moral response is an endeavour to explicate further this 'factual nature', 'what the situation is', and just how 'the nature of the object' justifies the attitude.

I will now say a little more to develop my contention about moral judgments being a response to a claim, and I begin from a remark which Dr Ewing makes a little later. Granting that value-judgments are 'not just factual judgments telling us of the existence of certain natural properties'—that is the error of naturalism—nevertheless (he says) 'they are based on' though they 'are not themselves judgments about, natural properties'.[41] How then may we think of the claim arising from the 'natural facts'? My answer is that a value-judgment occurs as and when a group of natural properties 'come alive', 'take on depth', in this sense disclose a claim emerging from them, a claim to which we respond in a 'free' decision. We make a value-judgment rather than a plain, descriptive judgment, when there arises around a group of plain 'facts' what I have called elsewhere a 'disclosure', what might be called 'ethical insight'. We are all aware of what happens when (as we'd say) a puzzle picture suddenly comes to life, when a flat set of straight lines takes on depth, when yet another hand in a formal reception is that of a friend. The plain, flat situation, in Dom Illtyd's phrases 'takes', mediates something else, reveals an 'undercurrent'. Around and out of the 'plain facts' a disclosure occurs. I have given examples elsewhere of how in this way moral obligations or, more generally, value-claims, are disclosed through and around plain facts, and I would respectfully refer the reader to them.[42]

Now such a claim disclosed through and around plain facts has been traditionally spoken of by terms like 'Duty' or the 'Moral Law' and a theological interpretation arises as and when such terms are theologically contextualized. The possibility of theology affording a 'lateral enrichment' of ethics, of theology 'adding a new tone to ethics', of 'God' being partially a moral term, or of speaking of apprehending God in a moral obligation—all these possibilities arise because moral judgments have the characteristic of being responsive, and in having this characteristic acknowledge a value-

[40] *Ibid.*, p. 37.   [41] *Ibid.*
[42] *Freedom and Immortality*, SCM Press 1960, pp. 28-38.

claim to which they express a response. What a theological interpretation does is to set this value-claim in a wider context.

Does this view compromise the autonomy of ethics? Now in so far as all moral judgments presuppose a prior value-claim—in being prescriptive responses to such a value-claim; in presupposing such a value-claim as that to which the universalizable description points in the case of moral judgments—this value-claim might be called the 'basis' of ethics. But it would still be of the highest importance to recognize that the value-claim affords *no basis* whatever for ethics, *if* a 'basis' is thought to be something which entails moral principles, which are thus to be derived from it. It is only a 'basis' in the sense of being presupposed by moral judgments having the character they have. There is therefore no threat whatever to the 'autonomy of ethics' in the sense in which Dr Ewing uses the phrase and which is the sense we accept above. That the value-claim, presupposed by moral judgments, can bear a theological interpretation no more compromises the autonomy of moral judgments than the fact that moral judgments presuppose facts which bear a scientific or 'naturalistic' interpretation. There is no fallacious heteronomy, and no illegitimate move of a naturalistic kind from an 'is' to an 'ought'.

Further, the theological interpretation in no way modifies the value-claim or otherwise compromises it. In so far as it is intrinsically justified it simply provides us with a wider context which sites the value-claim in relation to other, chiefly non-moral, features of the Universe. At the same time, we need not deny that in doing this a theological interpretation may provide us with some distinctive 'reasons' for a moral judgment. But these will *never* be entailing reasons for a moral judgment. This is a position not unlike that of Kant for whom there could be no entailing reasons for Duty, least of all reasons which appealed to happiness, but who could nevertheless recognize an appropriateness in virtue being accompanied by a due measure of happiness, and presumably there thus arise, even for Kant, some non-entailing reasons for doing our duty. Theological considerations might add to the reasons for doing an action—but could never add to or in any way prejudice the character of the value-claim to which that action was a response.

One further point, and though for obvious reasons it can be given no more than outline treatment, it will act, I hope, as a transition between parts I and II of the paper.

For the sake of argument let it be granted that belief in God arises when there occurs a disclosure of such a range and extent that it might be called 'cosmic'; and suppose that the traditional arguments for the existence of God are to be regarded as discourse designed to evoke such a disclosure by talking of 'the most perfect being', or of purposive patterns in the universe, or even by asking questions such as 'Why is there anything at all?' Suppose further that when a cosmic disclosure occurs, when insight is generated in this way, the word 'God' is justifiably used of what is disclosed.

It is important to recognize that the word 'God', introduced in this way, can never have the logic of words which stand for human beings. For it is used in relation to disclosures which are cosmic, infinite in character as compared with those circumscribed finite disclosures by which persons are revealed. So it is that while theological discourse contains 'anthropomorphisms'—using of God words which relate to human beings, e.g. will, mind, personality, words indeed which can witness to the routes by which the cosmic disclosure has been reached, words which supply us with models— the discourse must also contain qualifying words like 'perfect', 'infinite'. Models and qualifiers together point us to a cosmic disclosure as the situation where their reference will be found; qualifiers are logical reminders never to be content with talk about God as if he were a human being.

It is this theological dependence on disclosures—not all of which are moral—which affords the reason why there can be a legitimate theological account of morality, why theology can provide some 'lateral enrichment', add 'tone to ethics' and so on, without compromising the claim which a moral disclosure makes on our will and behaviour. But it will be noticed that part of the price paid by theology for having its foundation in a cosmic disclosure is that theology, without essential logical qualification, cannot talk of God in terms of 'will' or 'command', and certainly must not assimilate 'God' to words which stand for human beings.

We have now been brought to points which are highly relevant to the second part of our discussion.

II

Having now established the possibility of a theological interpretation of ethics which does not compromise the autonomy of ethics, the next question is how legitimate it is to develop this interpretation in terms of God's commands.

Let us acknowledge at once the strength of this particular interpretation. As Hare recognizes, his universal prescriptivism, at least in so far as it deals in prescriptives, high-lights the significance of imperatives; and we might further say that in so far as a moral judgment is responsive, the value-claim may be usefully compared with the claims another person makes on us in social behaviour. In short, we can see that, once we talk of prescriptivity or responses, and in these ways acknowledge the significance of imperatives or value-claims, then these imperatives and value-claims come to be talked of in terms of metaphors or models of human commands, a person's will and so on.

It is important of course to realize that as far as the language of morality goes this may be no more than a picturesque way of talking about and high-lighting the value-claim which is at the basis of moral judgments, and hardly, if at all, explicates that claim. But if on independent grounds we have reason to believe in God on the basis we outlined above, we begin to see how this could be more than a merely picturesque way of talking. At the same time, it was very evident from the discussion that, even now, we could only with the greatest circumspection talk of God's commands or God's will. It would always be, as Maclagan said,[43] no more than a 'manner of speaking', what I have called a model. We can only talk of Duty as '*a kind of* "hearing God addressing and commanding us" '.[44] For however we explicate belief in God it will somewhere and in some way become abundantly clear that the logic of 'God' is not that of a human being, so that 'God' cannot be substituted for the subject in sentences such as 'It is the Headmaster's will that we should do y', or 'The Sergeant-Major commands us to do x'.

Yet as we have seen earlier this is precisely how such a sentence as 'It is God's will that we should do y' or 'God commands us to do x' is often construed, and by believers and unbelievers alike.

Even a critic as sympathetic as Dr Ewing can speak of 'the simplest and most radical way of making all ethical principles dependent on God' being 'to say that their validity just depended on their being decrees fixed by the will of God'.[45] Now whatever difficulties such a view might have as a moral theory, talk of God fixing decrees in any case positively bristles with philosophical and theological difficulties. Again, Dr Ewing might well ask of all of us, 'What is goodness except doing the best because it is the best?'[46] but unless the logic of God was identical with that of human beings we cer-

---

[43] *Op. cit.*, p. 172; quoted above p. 155.
[44] *Op. cit.*, p. 56. Italics mine; quoted above p. 155.
[45] *Op. cit.*, p. 39.   [46] *Ibid.*, p. 49.

tainly could not conclude, as Dr Ewing does that 'therefore even God's actions presuppose, as logically prior, the recognition of ethical principles'. Patterson Brown has exposed some of the difficulties involved in making any such assimilation.

There is no doubt that much of the discussion in this field is rendered pointless and futile by a failure to do justice to the logic of God. My colleague Richard Robinson for example moves without the slightest raising of a logical eyebrow between talk of a father, of God and of a mistress, so that there is no *logical* difference for Mr Robinson between a man adopting a way of living from a desire to please one or other of these individuals, or from a decision to obey his or her commands.[47] But my loudest warning would be to believers. Even if (as I hope I have shown) it is the case that a theological interpretation need not compromise the autonomy of ethics, and even if (as I also hope I have shown) there are some good reasons for using phrases like 'God's will' or 'God's command' to develop this theological interpretation, the need to be logically circumspect in developing these ways of speaking about God remains paramount.

When, for instance, in the second part of his paper, Patterson Brown outlines, as I have shown, a legitimate theological interpretation of ethics, it is a pity that later in the same part he speaks of God, and God's will, and God's commands, in a way which lends itself at once to the kind of misconstruing of which he accuses Professor Nowell-Smith and Professor Nielsen.

For example, with as little logical caution as Mr Robinson he can invite us to consider the assertion, 'There is a God, and he commands y'—the very kind of talk to which Mr Robinson might well appeal in defence of saying what he does. Nay more, it is not one single sentence, but a whole context which is developed incautiously. 'The Christian', he says, 'has two sorts of ways to find out what is good or what ought to be done according to his morality. Firstly, one can be *told* by God what is best, either directly through personal revelation, or indirectly through the Church or the Bible.'[48] It is true that he immediately allows—'The numerous philosophical difficulties attending these notions would occupy an essay in themselves.' But isn't the major difficulty that raised by the definitive phrase '*told* by God'? He continues: 'Secondly, one can *infer* by means of reason alone, *i.e. via* the Natural Law, what God would command. For we can presumably ratiocinate, at least to

[47] *Op. cit.*   [48] *Art. cit., Mind* NS 72, No. 286, April 1963, p. 241.

some degree, what a supremely intelligent, loving and just being would will.' We may pass over the difficulties of doing anything *via* the Natural Law.[49] But even with the qualification which Patterson Brown makes, does not this way of talking only serve to mislead unbelievers, to confirm them in their criticisms, while it encourages believers to continue to make assertions in sermons and devotional literature which are at best incautious and may be logically disastrous? If we have had any understanding of the complex logic of the word 'God' let us be faithful to it at all points, and not develop discourse in a way which pays no heed to lessons we ought to have learnt before. It is disingenuous, if nothing else, to meet objections to theological assertions by rightly appealing to their logical peculiarity, and then to indulge in theological discourse which uses those assertions as if they were logically fool-proof. It is specially disastrous to do this when, as in the case of moral judgments and God's commands, both moves take place in the same discussion.

I have tried to argue, then, that there can be a theological interpretation of ethics which in no way compromises its autonomy, while it makes possible that 'lateral enrichment' of which Maclagan speaks. Further, this wider theological interpretation can incorporate with some reason phrases like 'God's commands' and 'God's will'. But if it does so, it must use these phrases in a way which does not at the second move forget the logical points implied in the first move. This means that the believer must remember that in talking of God's will or God's command he is talking about God and not about man, and that the unbeliever must be prepared to allow that if sentences containing the word 'God' have any logical viability at all it will not be one which enables the word 'God' to be worked interchangeably with the name of a human being.

Meanwhile, we may regretfully admit that, as is so often the case, the unbeliever, anxious to destroy any theological interpretation of morality, gets all the fuel he needs for his fire from believers who are careless enough in their expressions not only to neglect the logic of their assertions, but on that account to talk sometimes in a way that is near-blasphemous.

[49] Some of them are considered later in this volume, ch. 20.

10

THE VOICE OF CONSCIENCE AND
THE VOICE OF GOD

H. D. Lewis

I T I S not surprising that, in the present state of religion, some Christian apologists should have to recourse to rather desperate expedients. Many, for example, have tried to come to terms with the prevailing empiricism in philosophy by seeking to give an account of religion in exclusively empiricist terms. The varieties of this procedure have been much discussed of late and I will make no attempt to repeat here a tale that has by now been told perhaps too often. Readers of this book will be familiar with Professor Braithwaite's view that the essentials of a religion can be found in the moral teaching it commends;[1] and they will know of the sharp criticisms—to my mind unanswerable ones— which it has elicited.[2] They will also know of many theological attenuations of faith, like those of Tillich and his popularizers, which reduce religion to some attitude we adopt towards our problems in the present world—an attitude, moreover, which involves much ethical relativism. But it is not very well understood how insidiously this short way with the dissenter has infected the work of seemingly much more orthodox thinkers. The example which comes to my mind especially is that of John Baillie. Baillie was passionately anxious that people should believe in God, and in his zeal to convince them of the truth of the Christian faith he would often maintain—this is indeed the main theme of his major works—that they in fact believe already. All that is needed is for them to realize 'at the top of their minds' what they know well 'at the bottom of their hearts'. This, in my view, is a very

---

[1] [See ch. 3 above. *Editor.*]   [2] [See ch. 4 above. *Editor.*]

misguided policy, and it fails altogether to take the measure of contemporary scepticism. It does not show the sceptic the respect he deserves. But it will not be out of place in this book to look at one form
of the procedures Baillie adopts in the attempt to prove his case.
The arguments he advances are many, and some of them make what
seems to me a very questionable reference to what we are supposed
to learn from the case books of recent psychologists. But what I wish
to note here is the case with which Baillie, despite his originally
orthodox theological position, tends, at the crucial points of his
books, to equate religious conviction with the awareness of a moral
obligation and kindred ethical matters. No one, it is thought, can
deny that he has a conscience—although I think many would do so
in the sense that Baillie intends. But to admit to a conscience is
tantamount, so the frustrating argument goes, to finding oneself in
the Christian fold.

It is in this vein that we are assured that everyone has an 'uneasy
conscience' and that 'ultimate reality meets us, not in the form of
an object that invites our speculation, but in the form of a demand
that is made upon our obedience'. Now there may be such a demand
and it may be possible to show that everyone has an 'uneasy conscience', although this is far from obvious. But even if all this were
plain, how much does it give us? We may wrap it in religious terminology, conferring on the 'Absolute Obligation' the dignity of
capital letters. But have we in effect anything of substance which
goes beyond the religion as morality of Professor Braithwaite? Admittedly Baillie speaks in more orthodox terms and converts the
voice of conscience sometimes into a haunting numinous presence.[3]
But when we look at the substance of what he says, especially when
it becomes hard for him to prove the universality of religious belief,
it is the allegedly inescapable character of a moral sense that is really
stressed. Even here the ground may not always be firm; there are
moral as well as religious sceptics and there are certainly many who
do not believe in an absolute duty. But even if we could get over
these ethical difficulties, how far would we have got towards establishing the claims of religion? Professor Baillie's procedure is indeed
high-lighted in his reference to 'L. P. Jack's shoemaker who "spent
his breath proving that God did not exist, but spent his life in
proving that He did" '.[4] The point seems to be that no matter what
the shoemaker sincerely professed, his fine conduct amounted to
religious belief. That is, I think, how this cryptic remark is to be

[3] E.g., *Our Knowledge of God*, O.U.P., 1939, p. 4.   [4] *Ibid.*, p. 66.

taken in its context, and if I am right we have at any rate come dangerously near that attenuation of faith which equates it with merely moral beliefs and attitudes.

Consider again the following passage:

We should ask ourselves whether some who profess belief in God are not much more genuinely atheistical than are many of our rationalist and communist friends who take to themselves that name. The real unbeliever is not he whose life witnesses to a belief that he thinks he does not possess; but rather he whose life proves that he does not really believe what he thinks he believes . . . if the fruits are truly manifest, some germ of faith must then be there, however unrecognized.[5]

There is of course much truth in this passage. A profession of faith is suspect, to say the least, if it finds no reflection at all in the way we live. If we learn of some member of a Christian Church that he always behaves meanly and selfishly, that he consistently takes advantage of people in his power, that he leads secretly a dissolute life, then we are apt to exclaim, 'A sorry sort of Christian he makes.' There is no substance in the Christian witness of such a person; he is a liability and not an asset. The Church, we say, would be better without him. Even so it does not follow that all his profession of faith is base dissimulation. There may be much that he believes, and in some moods believes profoundly, in spite of falling so far short of the ideals to which he is committed. This may come about in two ways. Firstly, we are not bound to behave in the way we think we ought to behave; to recognize an obligation is one thing, to discharge it another. Secondly, there are aspects of religion other than the moral ones, and lack of respect for moral ideals is no unfailing indication of the strength or feebleness of faith in its other regards. How far it is possible to have a genuine Christian belief and be unmindful in practice of Christian ideals is a moot point. I should be inclined to say that someone who does not mind at all how he lives can hardly be credited with genuine belief in a Christian God. On the other hand, the measure of our lapses is no sure indication of the firmness and depth of a belief in the God whom Christians worship.

There are, I believe, many subtle and complicated aspects of the question of faith and practice which Baillie does not pause to examine; and it is certain that no one is perfectly co-ordinated and consistent within himself. But even if these points had little sub-

[5] *Our Knowledge of God*, p. 66.

stance, or if we disregarded them for the moment, there would remain to be made one observation which has much greater relevance in the present context.

It is that, even if it is true that no one who is unmindful of Christian behaviour can seriously be credited with Christian belief, the contrary is not true. A person may behave in a Christian spirit without having a Christian belief. This would not of course be true if- we understand by Christian behaviour and Christian spirit the conduct or attitudes which are expressly inspired by Christian faith in its fullness. But it is certainly possible to show in extensive measure the sort of charity, selflessness, forgiveness and so on which the Christian requires of himself and others without believing in a Christian God—or in any God at all. Do we not know many who have done so?

It may also be admitted that, in the sight of God, it is much better to live in a Christlike way, even without Christian belief, than to profess a belief in Christ, and even have genuine belief in him, and betray him in practice. Conduct may in this way be much more important than belief, but this does not equate belief and conduct; nor does it make belief insignificant or of little account in all that we fully mean by Christian salvation. It is the conflation of belief and conduct that has led to some of the worst confusions in Christian understanding of late; and this shows itself not only in the elevation of practice over belief but also the other way round, to the very serious detriment of the due appreciation of Christian standards— as may be seen in much of the so-called Continental Theology which I have ventured to criticize elsewhere.

The cause of true understanding is in fact never served by blurring important distinctions, and there are few more important distinctions in religion than that between belief and practice. It is by properly noting the distinction between these that we can also arrive at a sound understanding of the relation between them and of their place in a rounded Christian conception of salvation.

This is well shown in another feature of Baillie's thought. The sort of ethical theory to which he subscribes is a very Socratic one, that is he believes that human beings are invariably attracted to the good. We only do evil because we mistake it for goodness. Baillie thinks this is the liberal alternative to pessimistic doctrines of total corruption. Man is not at all corrupt at heart, he is invariably drawn to the good, but he is often sadly deceived. This is where the devil gets his opportunities; if we recognized him we would always flee

him. Evil would not appeal to us did it not always have 'the form of
goodness'.[6] The devil tempts us in the form of 'an angel of light'.[7]
This seems to me very questionable. The dignity and responsibility
of men consists in their power of deliberately choosing to do wrong
as well as right, and this seems to me the basic element in the liberal
alternative we must offer to pessimistic theological doctrines. But
these are matters that many writers have sufficiently ventilated elsewhere. The main point at the moment is this.

Holding this very questionable notion that we always aim at the
good but often fail to recognize it, Baillie is led to describe this
situation in the language of traditional Christian theology, speaking much of sin and 'the shadow of the Cross'. In my view this fails
to do any justice to the distinctive Christian notions which such
terminology expresses. To do them justice we must certainly heed
ethical matters carefully, and also, I may add, take more pains to
understand ethics properly on its own account than many theologians, among whom I fear we must number Baillie himself, are
prepared to do. But we have also to consider these ethical matters in
a wider context of man's total aspirations and his relation to God.
The situation to which the Christian doctrine of salvation is addressed cannot be understood exhaustively in ethical terms without
very misleading simplification. But that, it seems to me, is just what
John Baillie is apt to overlook; and in this alas he is far from being
a solitary figure today.

It is indeed surprising how much of the most emphatically transcendentalist theology of today, including the Barthianism to which
Baillie considers himself to be supplying an alternative, reduces in
substance to the presentation of tortuous and confused ethical thinking baptized into the terminology of traditionalist theology but
with little room at the centre for the reference beyond to the
allegedly transcendentalist elements of Christian theology. But this
is much too long a story to be told here.

It does not follow from the line of criticism outlined in this paper
that there is no sense in which the voice of God may be thought to
be pre-eminently the voice of conscience. We have acquired today—
largely in the encounter with empiricist critics—a very sharp understanding of the sense in which God is transcendent and thereby
elusive and mysterious. We cannot, as has been much stressed, know
what divine reality is like in itself or know the essence of God. We
can know that God must *be* as the supreme or absolute or uncon-

⁶ *Our Knowledge of God*, p. 32.   ⁷ *Ibid.*, p. 33.

ditioned ground of all other being, but from the nature of the case we can know nothing else directly about him. But the indirect knowledge we have of God as he manifests himself in our own experience comes to us especially in the association of the sense of God with moral experiences of various sorts; there is a certain toning of our ethical insights[8] that comes about especially in religion, and further developments of our religious life take the form of a religious significance which is acquired by certain situations of a predominantly ethical character—as when the sense of the transcendent is, on the one hand, disrupted and deadened by consciousness of guilt and, on the other, unexpectedly renewed in the experience we come to recognize as the insistent seeking of us by a God of reconciliation and grace. In the substance of the dealing of God with us in these and kindred ways there is little we can describe beyond the significant changes in the character of the situation by which this comes about, although the decisive feature of such situations in their full religious character is the reference in them to a reality beyond themselves by which they are shaped.

There is thus a very important sense in which the voice of God is to be heard especially in our own moral awareness, and many of John Baillie's observations suggest just this, especially when he speaks of the sense of moral obligation acquiring a numinous character, of the moral reality becoming alive as a 'haunting presence'. The unfortunate thing is that, in seeking to explain how this comes about, Professor Baillie is both too bold and too timid—too bold because he tries to provide an elaborate explanation of a situation which it is more proper to recognize in its simplicity as at once a religious and an ethical one, too timid because he wants to discover in the complexities of the moral life as such the sort of distinctively religious and transcendent reality which must be expressly recognized on its own account.

God is, then, found pre-eminently in moral situations which are more than moral, but 'more' in the sort of way which cannot be explicitly described except in terms of something distinctive which is happening to the moral experience in its various forms.

This is one of the matters most overlooked by recent humanist critics of religion. They have often directed their main criticism to specifically ethical aspects of religion, and the substance of their complaint has been that the morality we associate with religion is bound to be authoritarian and absolute—absolute, that is, in the

[8] [Cf. ch. 9 above, pp. 153–5 and 157–67. *Editor.*]

objectionable sense of holding without the possibility of exceptions to moral rules.[9] This is believed to be true of religion because it is assumed that the religious person derives from his religion directly a set of infallible moral insights, as if he were lifted out of the complexities of the situations we actually meet in the world and were given by God—from behind the scenes as it were—a body of principles which, in having this explicit divine sanction, apply without exception or deviation in all circumstances. In deriving from God as absolute or ultimate, the principles are thought to be absolute too.

Nothing could be further from the truth of moral situations as they develop within a genuine religious experience. Nor could anything be further removed from the history of the development of religion and the refining of the ethical understanding to be found within it. The prophets have no doubt spoken with firmness and vigour, conscious of being the mouthpieces of God, but their message has come to them also in the strains and tensions of their own experience or that of the people with whom they were especially identified. This has involved also much correction of what was said 'of old'. It follows that, although religion goes deeper and extends our moral insights, we have not to suppose that religious persons are lifted above the level of agonizing moral perplexities. On questions of fact, as they bear on ethical decisions, there is no reason to expect a religious person to have invariably a sounder understanding than his secular neighbour; sometimes he may be badly out on his facts. But his moral insights as such are also fallible, and may sometimes be very uncertain. This is because God does not put his saints in a privileged position; he does not speak to them as if they were also God—the gravely mistaken supposition we find in so much Barthian theology. God speaks to men in the way they can understand as men and through the limited faculties he has bestowed upon them as limited created beings. They have to agonize like others over moral decisions, although they do not do so without distinctive help.

There may be some substance historically in the accusation that the morality we find in religion tends to be authoritarian and absolute. Many vested interests have been identified with religion and, in the institutionalizing which is an unavoidable feature of the perpetuation of religion, the voice of harsh and undiscerning authority may often have been loud and distressing. But this is certainly no more than one side of the picture, and when we find religion most

---

[9] [See chs. 5 and 6 above; and cf. ch. 9, pp. 168–71. *Editor.*]

certainly true to itself, the emphasis is not on the magisterial voice of a moral censor outside us but on the Kingdom of Heaven within and the illumination of mind and heart through the influence of a long-suffering and seeking God who deals with us as persons and deepens our understanding of his will for us in the refinement and deepening of our own moral understanding. Nothing could be further removed from the spirit of authoritarianism than the teaching and example of Jesus.

At the opposite extreme to the travesty which recent humanists set up as a target for criticism is the flabby relativism we find in so much recent Christian apologetics. It is assumed that because the Christian cannot meet the complexities of personal and public ethical situations of today armed with infallible insights and invariable rules, there is nothing very specific which he can affirm in morality. This is another aspect of the evasiveness and easy accommodation with the way of this world into which some avowed defenders of the faith have lapsed. Involved in this attitude are many confusions, some of them quite elementary, about ethics as such and the various ways in which ethical principles may be said to be, and not to be, absolute. Much of that could have been avoided if religious thinkers, in pronouncing on ethical matters, had paid closer heed to what moral philosophers have said about them.[10] But this is also a story too long to be properly unfolded here. What matters more at the moment is that, in claiming that God speaks to us within ourselves and in the refinement of our fallible ethical insights, we must not overlook the genuineness of such insights and the objectivity they have on their own account. There is nothing in the inwardness and flexibility of genuinely religious ethics to warrant a lax and fumbling ethical attitude, least of all on matters where even elementary ethical principles at their own level are precise and certain. When the voice of God is heard within the voice of conscience it is not the voice of easy accommodation but that of a deepening of all that we already associate with conscience and with the accumulation of ethical wisdom in the past.

On no side of what I have said are the issues substantially affected by special views we may hold as Christians about the work and person of Christ. For in recognizing Jesus as an incarnation of God in the world we have not to suppose that he speaks to us differently from the way God always speaks. Both in the ethical elements in our recognition of his divinity and in the assimilation to our own lives

[10] [In this volume see e.g. many of the contributions to Section IV and ch. 20. *Editor.*]

and problems of the teaching which carries his authority, we have to appreciate that he speaks to us as the sort of creatures God made us and in the situations in which we are set. This means that Christian insight, in moral as in other matters, has to be won, to be made alive and insistent in the fires of our own experience. And here as elsewhere we must avoid the easy alluring simplifications of the 'short way', whether in the form of an obtuse authoritarianism or of the sort of false toleration or latitudinarianism which makes it very uncertain whether we are truly bringing our consciences to God to be sanctified, like his other gifts, in his own service.

This will in turn have much bearing on other questions. It will have much relevance to the prominence appropriately given in a Christian context to the distinctiveness and worth of persons—as it is sometimes put. We shall likewise see better what is amiss in attempts to base the objectivity of ethics on some further metaphysical or religious ground. Ethics has firm objectivity in itself, and it is not an argument from morality to religion that we must seek but a cultivation of the sense in which the voice of God may be heard within the voice of conscience itself.

As a witness to the sense in which God comes to us as a haunting presence in the moral life which we have as men, the work of John Baillie and his insistence, in the words of the title of his latest and posthumous book, on 'the Sense of the Presence of God', may be warmly welcomed. But in the proclivity, which dominates so much of the details of his work, to equate the sense of God with our sensitivity to exclusively ethical matters, we must learn to recognize one of the most persistent and grave temptations that beset the eager apologist. However closely intertwined with ethics, religion is vastly more than ethics and any other human feature of human situations. We may win converts, win them almost by definition, by equating religion with morality; and indeed since it is not likely that any human person is without some discernment of ethical matters we may seem to have proved the universality of faith. But if ever there was a Pyrrhic victory this is certainly one—most of all for Christian faith.

IV · MORAL DECISIONS:
THE PLACE OF IDEALS AND PRINCIPLES, AUTHORITY AND REASON

II

VISION AND CHOICE IN MORALITY

1. *R. W. Hepburn*

1. STORIES AND FABLES

M O S T recent British moral philosophy has been dominated by the 'rule-obedience' model: moral judgment as the endorsing of principles, commitment to universalizable policies. There have been lately, however, some reminders that, whether or not rule-obedience may be the most satisfactory analysis of moral language, very different models are quite often in fact held by morally sensitive people— by those, for instance, who see moral endeavour as the realizing of a pattern of life or the following out of a pilgrimage. Contemporary ethical writing certainly says little or nothing about whether such models are logically confused and benighted, or are witnessing to a philosophically neglected, but logically legitimate, way of viewing morality.

One can, of course, see reasons for the neglect. The language of 'resolutions', 'decisions of principle' is compatible with no-ghost-in-the-machine; but it is not so plain that we could work out the other models without reference to the spectral landscape of an 'inner life'. Secondly, the analysis of myth, parable, pilgrimage would involve considering language with far higher descriptive content than those terms (notably 'good' and 'ought') which have been the focus of recent study. More seriously, many people who speak the language of 'bringing into being a pattern in one's life', speak of the pattern or pilgrimage not only as relevant to the question 'what shall I do?'

but also to those very embarrassing questions—'what does my life add up to?' 'what is its meaning?' 'is it coherent, integrated, or formless, chaotic?' 'have I maintained initiative, been successfully creative; or has life gone past in uncreative passivity?' What can be said about these alarming violations of that jealously guarded ethics-aesthetics frontier? Can the philosopher of language address himself to such utterances without forfeiting all precision? Or, more to the point—is the language itself logically confused, merely picturesque or rhetorical?

I should perhaps have thought it was, were there not certain unassuming, unrhetorical people who feel compelled to use it in writing of their lives. A prime example is an autobiography like that of the poet and critic Edwin Muir, the first version of which he entitled *The Story and the Fable*. Significantly titled; for Muir contrasts the 'story' of his life (the bare narration of events) with its 'fable'—a slowly developing, often elusive, cluster of personal symbols, compounded of childhood memories, foci of aspiration, discoveries in literature, with reference to which his whole life is orientated, and his autobiography knitted into a natural unity, a unity different from any conventional articulation into a life's phases. One is forced to recognize that the 'form' of the life lived and the literary form of the autobiography in a strange way coincide. Thus, a personal myth of primal innocence and 'cosmic fall' is fashioned from Muir's years on Orkney farms, out of the mad rush of cattle to the fields at the start of Spring, the recurrent guilt of the killing of animals, the archaic simplicity of life and landscape, the 'stationary', dependable, family circle, and the earliest memory—a shaft of sunlight shining through motes of dust. These become the touch-stones (interlinked symbols, not rules, a fable, not a sheaf of principles) by which Muir the adult evaluated what he saw and in the light of which he set himself his tasks. In a single phrase he gathers his vision into one burning focus—an 'image of timeless human life as intersection and interpenetration of a stationary beam falling from heaven and the craving, aspiring dust rising for ever to meet it . . .'.

There is nothing easily won in this pattern-realizing: indeed there are desolate tracts in the autobiography where the 'story' stubbornly refuses to be transmuted into 'fable'. 'Nothing, it seems, can redeem this terrifying vision of overwhelming chaos and disjointed pathos: least of all some pat superficiality of material success. A life is a life, how can it be more?' Nevertheless, 'by the end this some-

thing more has indeed transpired, though the author modestly gives
no overt hint of it'.[1]

Berdyaev (who gave his autobiography a suggestively similar title
to Muir's, *Dream and Reality*) is more explicit: 'my work . . .
revolved round a single axis and has a number of constant dominant
themes, which give it an inward unity'.[2] Here again is the striving
after pattern, the interpretation of life through 'fable', the insistent
language of 'creativity' not *vis-à-vis* the arts but *vis-à-vis* life itself.
Similarly, Yeats, 'deprived . . . of the simple-minded religion of
. . . childhood', could not live without *some* fable, and constructed
'almost an infallible Church of poetic tradition, of a fardel of
stories, . . .'.[3]

Even the outwardly very different autobiography of Arthur
Koestler reveals a comparable aim—as witness the titles of two of
its instalments, *Arrow in the Blue* (symbolizing boundless aspiration, quest for the transcendent) and *The Invisible Writing* (very
roughly analogous to Muir's shaft of sunlight).

What, then, is the philosopher to say to all this? In the first place,
these symbols and fables have plainly many functions besides
answering, 'What shall I do?' Only some exploratory probing can
show how far these can be plotted logically. The notorious quasi-
aesthetic language needs scrutiny: how can it fail to be wildly
misleading? Can there be anything like a consistent system of
appraisal for patterns, fables and pilgrimages; and do we have in
them, as some claim, a serious alternative to the rule-model? What
is the logical status of the descriptive elements in the fables and
parables themselves?

II. 'CREATIVITY' AND 'INTEGRATION'

I wish first of all to examine the claim, made by some (but by no
means all) of those who see their lives in the way outlined above,
that 'man makes himself', that men may be considered as artists,
their own lives the artefact. For here the aesthetic intrusion seems
most extravagant, most liable to lead to cloudy nonsense. Granted,
the metaphor of the artist is not wholly absurd—artist and artefact
may be said to be one, when, for instance, a dancer performs a dance

---

[1] Dr John Holloway, reviewing Muir's *Autobiography* in *The Hudson Review* (Summer
1955), p. 308. Stephen Spender says of Muir that 'he had the purpose which converted a
life of shifting jobs into a spiritual pilgrimage.'
[2] Nicolas Berdyaev, *Dream and Reality*, Bles 1950, p. 285.
[3] W. B. Yeats, *Autobiographies*, Macmillan 1926, p. 142.

of his own devising; but something more precise is required than metaphor. I shall say, then, that 'man makes himself' is partly often a rhetorical way of expressing the irreducibility of value-decisions to statements of facts, and a revolt against any sort of 'heteronomy'. In this sense (sense 1) 'man makes himself' is true, a truth of logic. But it also can bear the meaning (sense 2), 'men make themselves by the strengthening or weakening of habits and dispositions, both good and bad, through the decisions they make'. (Remember William James's famous harangue on habit: 'The molecules are counting. . . .') In both senses 1 and 2 self-making is (in different ways) inescapable. In so far, therefore, as the language suggests conscious craftsmanship, the calling of some but not all men, it is rhetorically misleading. But a third sense remains, not often clearly distinguished from 1 and 2, namely, that one may look upon the 'material' of one's life, one's dispositions, station in life, intellectual and emotional resources as they are at any moment 'given', rather as an artist regards his canvas and paint or a sculptor his stone. Sense 3 concerns us most here, and there is no doubt that within limits this conception is perfectly intelligible and quite familiar. It *is* very much up to a moral agent how he fashions his character by the culture of his imagination, by contemplation of the noble or debased; and the parables, symbols of ideals and the concatenations of these which I am calling 'fables' may clearly play a large part in this. But this is plainly not a *creatio ex nihilo*. Justice must be done to both the existentialists' emphasis on freedom, self-creation through decision, and to the unavoidably *given* elements, psychological and environmental, including what our decisions of the past have made of us. In British philosophy the tension between these poles is perhaps visible in the contrast between R. M. Hare's emphasis on 'decision' and P. Nowell-Smith's on 'human nature'.

Another important limitation upon creativity is the logical impossibility of wilfully altering one's fundamental value-judgments, since it is only in response to these that any self-criticism or -transformation can be undertaken. Hence the misleadingness of saying 'we create our values'. If this means no more than 'valuing is something we do', then there can be no quarrel: but it misleads if it suggests that we are aware of a *choice* between a range of 'optional' values.

Some users of the 'creativity' language, however, intend more by it than this.

1. Quite apart from concern with self-creativity, they have wished (very properly) to emphasize the fact that by no means all moral situations demand a single, unambiguous course of action. 'Duties of special obligation' come nearest this—there is often little *Spielraum* in keeping a particular promise or fulfilling a contract. But there is a great deal of *Spielraum* (giving scope for 'creativity' in a sense beloved of Gabriel Marcel) in, say, educating a child or conducting one's relations with one's husband or wife or (often) in choosing one's own career and manner of life. Even moral 'tight spots' leave room for some. An example from Marcel describes a man, compelled to work in a 'security police' organization directed against his own countrymen, who nevertheless uses this position to help, not to harm, his friends.[4] Rather as 'self-creation' may mean to cope imaginatively with given personal resources and environment, often recalcitrant 'material', so does this new sense involve coping with complex moral situations for which no rule of thumb legislates, where there is room for spontaneity and originality,[5] although (as in Marcel's case) again the material can be stubborn and exacting. The nearest aesthetic analogy is perhaps the scope for originality offered by fugue or canon within its rigorous formal structure.

On the other hand, Stuart Hampshire in his article, 'Logic and Appreciation',[6] wishes to point the most abrupt contrast between the situations of artist and moral agent. The artist sets *himself* his problem, he could by-pass it altogether if he wished: the moral agent has his problem set for him—'Action in response to any moral problem is . . . imposed.' Two comments on this: while Hampshire's distinction certainly is crucial, his language misleadingly *suggests* that all or most moral situations are cases of being under some duty of special obligation (with, therefore, little or no *Spielraum*, scope for 'creativity'); and second, it *under*-estimates the strong sense of constraint which a human problem may lay upon an artist. In both these ways the undeniable gap between ethics and aesthetics is unwarrantably widened, to the distorting of both. This is true also of his argument that uniqueness, inimitability characterize the work of art, whereas morality concerns the repeatable and imitable. 'To copy a right action is to act rightly; but a copy of a work of art is not necessarily or generally a work of art.' I suspect

---

[4] Gabriel Marcel, *Men Against Humanity*, Harvill Press 1952, p. 17.
[5] A. D. Lindsay, *The Two Moralities* (1940), Eyre & Spottiswoode 1948, p. 47: ' "Gracious" conduct is somehow like the work of an artist.'
[6] *Aesthetics and Language*, ed. W. Elton, Blackwell 1954, pp. 161 ff.

that the contrast here depends on an unnoticed ambiguity in 'copy'. In its first appearance a 'copy' is something similar in all (morally) relevant respects; in the second (of a work of art) it carries the nuance 'imitation by an inferior hand', 'similar in many, but *not* all (aesthetically) relevant respects': an expert could detect the difference. But if he could not; if nobody could; if the 'copy' were in fact indistinguishable in every respect from the original, then I should say it must possess the *worth* of the 'original', since the features considered relevant to appraising the first are without exception present also in the second. *Both* the artist's and the moral agent's performances may be original, unique, exhibitions of 'creativity', although in identical senses their performances are (theoretically) repeatable, imitable. But I am very far from claiming that 'creativity' is used in identical senses with regard to both. I am attempting only to show that in exploring the aesthetics-ethics analogy nonsense is not reached quite so rapidly as some of us have tended to fear.

2. The next aspect of 'creativity' language I wish to comment upon ('*self*-creativity' again) may smack too much of metaphysics for analytical palates: but something important would be omitted if it received no mention; and once more it seems that perfectly good sense can be made of it. It concerns the 'unity of being' which the subjects of our study strive to attain through self-knowledge and 'self-creation'. What kind of unity is sought may best be discovered by considering a confessed failure to achieve it. Muir supplies one: his years in Glasgow saw the shattering of his Orkney pastoral dream, the deaths of several intimate relatives and a general disorientation of his intellectual and imaginative life. With these barren years he can 'do nothing'; they lie in his memory 'like a heap of dull immovable rubbish'. They are eccentric to the fable; that is to say, he has no symbol which can cope with, give him 'command' over, these events; no image, 'motif', 'theme' is available through which his resources may be organized and initiative recaptured. (One would say fancifully, it is as if the category were lacking through which alone chaos could be reduced to perceptual order.) 'Despair' might be described as the recognition of *complete* failure to regain initiative in such a situation.

Generalizing: various causes may produce this sort of breakdown. The symbols may have been adequate to cope with adolescence but not with adult life; or, they may have been inadequate to cope effectively with *any* stage—like the popular myth of romantic love, the quest for the one 'destined' lover. Again, there may have been a conflict within the fable itself: marital happiness, for instance, being the earnestly wished for goal, while the imagination stubbornly holds to a memory or vivid image of homosexual friendship as the apotheosis of love. In each case, though in different ways, the task for creativity will be the re-fashioning, or re-interpreting of the old motifs so as to give coverage to the new situation. To tackle the task may be an 'ought', but the consistent achievement of it, being psychologically and imaginatively beyond the power of almost everyone, cannot be.

The 'unity' sought for, then, is some sort of imaginative unity, again most illuminatingly captured in quasi-aesthetic language; for instance the words of Cleanth Brooks about poets: the poet gives 'an insight which . . . triumphs over the apparently contradictory and conflicting elements of experience by unifying them into a new pattern'.[7] A musical analogy—from the exposition, development and recapitulation of themes—could make the same point, and in addition suggest quite close parallels, between the awareness of *time* in music and in the 'fabled' life. But to develop these would take more than our allotted space.

3. Drawing together those different ways in which one may meaningfully speak of 'design' being given to life, it may be claimed that the genuinely religious life most clearly exemplifies these and exhibits in addition other ways in which 'unity of being' can be achieved. The religious person has his vision of the good life, to the attainment of which all activity is subordinated. All the teachings and actions of the central figure of the religion are charged with the high solemnity and authority of his person. The solemnity is carried back into the believer's conception of what he is doing in performing the humblest moral action; whatever it is, it finds its 'position' in the pilgrimage, its solemnizing context in the 'fable' of that religion. 'Inasmuch as ye have done it unto one of the least of these my brethren, ye have done it unto me.' 'Who sweeps a room, as for thy laws, Makes that and the action fine.' Similarly in parable, a characteristically religious mode of moral teaching, a whole slice of life is presented, not an isolated maxim; and the *effects* of the prescribed conduct (often too the effects of its omission) may be built into the one economical story. In meditation, the believer disciplines his imagination, so as to bring into alignment his own unique conception of his life and the *public* fable of his faith.

[7] Cleanth Brooks, *The Well Wrought Urn*, Dobson 1949, p. 195.

. . . Not the intense moment
Isolated, with no before and after,
But a lifetime burning in every moment
And not the lifetime of one man only . . .[8]

III. Appraising Patterns and Fables

How far does this entire subject-matter depend on a naïve conception of the 'inner life' in all its ghostliness, a private realm
accessible only to the agent, whose revelations concerning it are
infallible? Worse: what is the logical status of this 'self' which is
being 'created'? Thirdly: is there a dubious assumption here that
the culture of the inner life is the one supremely valuable thing?
For all those questions might well beget uneasiness in the reader.

1. Although some of my specimen autobiographers would deny
my analysis, I have not myself presupposed any shadowy substantial 'soul' which is the artefact. Indeed, the articulation of memories, the patterning of symbols, described above, may be for the
sceptic a sort of *substitute* for the loss of belief in any indestructible
soul. All I have presupposed is that we can meaningfully speak of
selecting, ordering and dwelling upon memories and images, plus a
capacity to let certain of those function as symbols.

2. Talk of the inner life does not imply infallible description of a
private landscape. The sincere autobiographer admits that memories may become falsified, distorted. A friend's information about
one's own past *may* lead to the refashioning of one's 'fable'.[9]

3. I have avoided speaking of an hypostatized 'self', objectionable
both grammatically and logically. When our autobiographical subjects say, 'I was estranged from myself . . . at one with myself . . .
out of touch with myself', it is *our* nonsense, not theirs, if we translate 'myself' into 'my self', implying two beings, one a true, or real,
'self'. These uses, rather, are analogous to the familiar—'It's Joe all
right—but he's not himself today'; he is acting uncharacteristically.
In 'I was estranged', etc., 'myself' means something like 'that orientation, that patterning of my life's motifs, etc., which I endorse in
moments of reflection, in a "cool hour" '. To be at one with myself
is to be engaged fruitfully in bringing experience into alignment
with the pattern; to be estranged is to fail or to stop trying.

---

[8] T. S. Eliot, *Four Quartets*, Faber 1944, p. 22.
[9] This is one cardinal difference between the 'fables' of the sane and the psychotic.

4. There is no good reason why these activities should be prized above all others. Thinking-of-oneself is not being claimed as more important than thinking-of-others. Indeed, as a result of the study of fables and patterns one's openness to others, *disponibilité*, may rather become more sensitive to the vision of their own lives which we glimpse in those we intimately know.

The last few sentences have strayed from meta-morals (or phenomenology of morals) into morals proper. We may be well to continue there for a little, not in order to play the pontiff, but to see if there is any necessary clash between moral assessments which we may wish to defend and those which may appear to be implied by the model under discussion. Theories can be confirmed or upset by such tests. Most pertinently, the 'aesthete's' conception of life and that of 'self-realization' theorists are both relevant to our theme and (when not vacuous) are notoriously open to just this sort of challenge.

From the autobiographical writings which are our data, I think the following criteria could be drawn up of an adequate pattern or fable as these writers tend to conceive it. (i) *Coherence:* the 'hanging-together' of symbol, motif and the rest into one fable. Differences of opinion will be found over what *counts* as coherence achieved;[10] and over what grounds there are for excluding a fatuous claim like 'things always happen to me in threes'. Some account of this sort of evaluation will be attempted below in elucidating 'superficiality' in patterns and fables. (ii) *Comprehensiveness:* ability to assimilate every sort of experience, however recalcitrant; resilience and toughness under intrusion. The 'tragic pattern' and religious patterns notably attempt to 'cope with' the most recalcitrant element of all—death. (iii) The symbols should be personally vivid, not second-hand, furthering the development, not the ironing out of individuality. (iv) They should 'back up', not fight against, the value-decisions of the person concerned; so that duty does not appear to demand a violating of the pattern, a stepping outside the fable. Section IV below develops this point.

If I had to defend these criteria, I should do so (*a*) by a straightforward *moral* judgment (discipline of the imagination leading to moral sensitivity); (*b*) by appraising their *psychological* value,[11] and (*c*) by a quasi-*aesthetic* judgment not unlike J. S. Mill's: it is only

[10] See Paul Welsh in *The Philosophical Quarterly* (1955).
[11] See, for instance, Erich Fromm's *Man for Himself.*

'by cultivating and calling forth' all that is individual in man that he 'becomes a noble and beautiful object of contemplation'.[12]

Any number of things can, of course, go wrong with the enterprise. For example, one criterion may be over-emphasized and others neglected. Individuality collapses into eccentricity: 'toughness' and 'resilience' become escape to the ivory tower, or even into the psychoses which epitomize indestructible fables. If criterion (iv) is neglected, we have the aesthete's manipulation of others, to facilitate his own self-dramatization. ('I grew careless', said Oscar Wilde, 'of the lives of others.'[13]) If self-realization means more than 'realize what *ought* to be realized in your actions, etc.' (i.e. 'do what you ought to do'), then it too comes under the same condemnation, being either *confusedly* egoistic ('the important thing about "moral" action is what it does to me'), or else blatantly so—'realize oneself, and others be damned'. In less catastrophic ways, a fable may become a screen against self-knowledge instead of a powerful aid to it, as when the springs of one's conduct (say in acting the philanthropist for ultimately selfish ends) are obscured by 'some melodramatic scenery' which we have erected to hide them from ourselves.[14] Summing up: the pattern must be open to moral claims from without, must be ready to admit its own inadequacy.

Again, fable-elements (like those of the historical religions, and elements drawn from childhood and youth) readily become 'fossilized' at the level of the (historical or immature) situations to which they *explicitly* refer; benevolence, for example, being wholly confined to intimate personal encounters (*à la* Good Samaritan, the prototype), and not extended to, for example, state-planned welfare, organized famine-relief, since these are (in their details) too unlike the parable-situation. The outcome is a quite senseless prejudice against the 'coldly scientific' and 'impersonal' in the name of charity.

In whatever way Muir's life could be redeemed from the chaos of 'one thing after another', it could *not* be redeemed by 'some pat

[12] *Liberty* (Everyman), p. 120.

It may seem needless to point out that these cannot be other than value-judgments. Some writers, however, blur their logic by semi-descriptive, covertly evaluative language. According to Kierkegaard, one becomes an 'individual' only by giving one's life a freely chosen 'shape'. Keats denied that people without distinctive individuality have any 'identity'. Marcel provides an example of a moral judgment presented as if it were a logical implication of 'creativity' language: 'the idea of being creative . . . always implies the idea of being open towards others' (*Men against Humanity*, p. 17).

[13] *De Profundis*, Methuen 1949, p. 78.

[14] Keats, *Letters* (ed. Forman), p. 315. [Cf. pp. 333–6. *Editor.*]

superficiality of material success'.[15] But what is it to be 'superficial' here? It is to shirk the task of finding one's own fable, which stems from one's own moral judgments, aspirations, memories; and to accept one prefabricated—like those of Sartre's complacent civic dignitaries in the Bouville museum.[16] Further differences between 'superficial' and 'serious' pattern may appear when one asks what happens when a pattern is maintained 'in spite of . . .': in spite of changes in personal circumstances, break-up of a career, outbreak of a war, and so on. Suppose I am playing the role of 'a person-of-wealth-and-influence'; then how ludicrous to maintain it in spite of, e.g., retirement to a new community after loss of my capital through speculation. Compare the 'fond parent', who exists simply *as* such, but whose child insists on growing up. Certain kinds of 'leadership' exemplify a slightly more flexible pattern; change the circumstances from battle to prison-camp or rubber dinghy and still the pattern may be appropriate; though again one can readily imagine circumstances in which to play the leader would be quite absurd. The comprehensiveness and toughness criteria might be rephrased, then, as the striving after a pattern or fable or vision of pilgrimage, sufficiently flexible to accommodate vicissitudes without resulting in moral catastrophe or absurdity when maintained under widely different conditions.

IV. RULES AND PATTERNS

If a fable is to come under moral criticism and control, that criticism may find expression in maxims, principles, or it may itself appear as fable. For example: Jesus sought to 'fulfil' the Old Testament fable, partly by precept but far more by acting out 'prophetic symbolism', by parable and by the re-interpreting of religious images like the Throne of David and the Son of Man. That is, to undertake moral control does not *necessarily* mean stepping quite outside the language of 'pattern' into what would then appear as the more fundamental language of 'rule'. We have still to ask, then, Is the fable a picturesque embroidery upon the rule, or is the rule a legalized, abstracted version of the fable, or are the two *equally legitimate* models?

The second of these possibilities recalls the distinction made in A. D. Lindsay's *The Two Moralities* between the morality of rule (my station and its duties) and the morality of grace and love, in

---

[15] John Holloway, in the review quoted earlier.
[16] *La Nausée*, Paris 1938, 1944, pp. 107ff.

sharp contrast to any 'laboured obedience to a theory or rule'.[17] 'Rule' in this context means, of course, an explicitly formulated elementary rule of thumb of the kind that keeps disaster from social relations, but no more. This is *not* the sense in which most philosophers use the word today. For them a 'rule' is implied by any universalizable judgment (even though to state it might require many words), whether or not it exists as a formulated copy-book maxim. In this sense any judgment that could be called 'feature-dependent' may be called the expression of a rule or principle—the same features, the same judgment.

The 'two moralities' distinction, although not the one we are directly concerned with, is indirectly most instructive. For I suspect that some of the people who have been wondering lately whether parable, fable, etc., may provide an alternative to the 'rule' model have in fact been thinking of rules in Lindsay's sense—maxims commonly formulated and taught. Understandably so, for since parables and fables not only prescribe policies of conduct, but are also interested in the agent's motivation, they can be at least strong allies of his 'above rule' morality.

But in the *other* sense of 'rule', which claims to refer to the necessary logical form of any judgment which can meaningfully be called 'moral' (*including* Lindsay's 'above rule' judgments) a judgment expressed in fable, parable is just as inescapably a 'decision of principle', the endorsing of a rule, the expression of a resolution, as any other moral judgment. If a story is entertained as a parable, it is seen not as a set of events which happened in the past, not as facts about the world, but as the commendation of a universalizable programme for action in any similar case to the case cited. Therefore it is irrelevant whether or not the events of the parable happened in history: to entertain it morally is to be indifferent to the question. Imaginary may be substituted for historical, with no loss. If, however, the prospect of this substitution *is* found embarrassing, something other than moral is at stake; perhaps a desire for psychological reassurance—'X (of whom the parable speaks) carried out this commended policy; so it may be within my power after all'.

I conclude that if the 'rule model' does no more than affirm the feature-dependent nature of any moral judgment, then the 'parable model' cannot displace it, cannot even conflict with it; for it

---

[17] *The Two Moralities*, pp. 40ff. The words quoted are George Eliot's (*Westminster Review*, Jan. 1857). The absence of such laboured obedience, she claims, should characterize both the moral agent and the artist.

assumes it. The parable-obeyer need not formulate his rule as a rule: it suffices that he entertains his parable in a particular way. Certainly, in thinking of morality in his own way he is not logically blundering. There need be no recalling him in maxims. With three provisos. 1. One parable is never logically equivalent to the expression of one maxim; built into it, often with remarkable economy in words are 'flash backs' of the total way of life to which it belongs, and even sometimes aids to its own implementation (such as ways of penetrating the agent's complacency and self-deceit). 2. (A *moral* proviso)—In all ethics which stress the state of mind of the agent at least as much as what he does, there is danger in supposing that if one looks after the character the actions will look after themselves. On the contrary, there is an important place in moral thinking for the most sober calculation of consequences.[18] 3. (Again a moral, not meta-moral problem)—A person who habitually thinks in terms of parable and fable, most of all a fable of the highly organized sort which we call a religion, has a difficulty about *altering* an individual moral judgment, which is not experienced by the follower of principles. A single *principle* can readily be exchanged for another if a person changes his mind over its soundness. But there is a great pressure on the fable-follower not to violate the unity of his pattern—a pressure which may readily tempt him away from moral integrity; he meets also the problem (intractable to all but the imaginatively inventive) of how to sew in the new evaluation to the old fabric.

v. How far is Religious Language 'Resolution' plus 'Fable'?

I have suggested that *in part* at least the propositions of the Christian religion can be construed as the specification, through fable, of a way of life. If it is no more than this, then the Christian should be very nearly indifferent whether the events narrated in Old and New Testament did or did not happen. Some Christians and some atheists too have held positions of this kind. 'Historicity' is no problem to them, and they deny that the philosophically baffling religious propositions are essentially statements of fact. They hold to the biblical narrative as to a *moral* blueprint.[19]

[18] Compare John Laird, 'Act-Ethics and Agent-Ethics', *Mind*, 1946.
[19] Notably R. B. Braithwaite's *An Empiricist's View of the Nature of Religious Belief*. Professor Braithwaite uses the word 'story' for what I have been calling 'fable' within a religion. 'Story', being neutral regarding factual occurrence, is a better general purpose

There are difficulties in this, if one took it as an *analysis* of traditional Christianity. 1. If it is true, then *The Pilgrim's Progress*, the
New Testament contents and the theologians' accounts of the faith
are unsuspectedly homogeneous. In none is descriptive language
logically crucial; in all, moral prescription *is*. Most Christians would
agree that it did not matter whether or not historically the Pilgrim's
burden fell off his back before the Cross. A few would say the same
regarding the historicity of Jesus' resurrection, though most would
deny it. But even these few would insist that the theologian's account of 'God's reconciling love' was in some sense description
of the activity of a being other than man. 2. Most Christians (not
only Professor Braithwaite's 'unsophisticated Christians') would
insist that in prayer also the believer posits a being not oneself;
that belief in a hereafter (*partly* moralizable as how we ought to
see the here-and-now) involves more crucially an expectation concerning a limitless future, different from the expectation of nonbelievers; and that Christ's resurrection does crucially involve
'expectations' regarding the past, different from those of nonbelievers.

I should not wish to withhold the word 'religion' from the
position which denies all those claims but retains the 'fable' (indeed
I find the view a most attractive one); but we do require some
linguistic means of distinguishing it from historical Christianity, of
which it most certainly is not an analysis. The characteristic zeal of
the Christian for the authentication of his canonical documents by
historical research, his insistence that *those* stories and no others
(even others with identical 'agapeistic' implications) are authoritative, bear witness to his refusal to count descriptive meaning as
secondary: his propositions cannot be analysed without remainder
into the specification and commendation of a pattern of life.[20] St
Paul for one thought not. 'If Christ has not been raised . . . then
those who have died in Christ have perished.'[21] A Braithwaite
analysis must come to grief here: for 'those who have died',
although they died 'in Christ' (that is, living out the agapeistic life),
have nevertheless perished in some other important sense. Paul is

word than mine. I retain 'fable' here simply because I started the paper in the language
of Muir's *The Story and the Fable*. [For Professor Braithwaite's views, see II. 3 above.
Editor.]

[20] This is not to say that *no* metaphysical or religious proposition may be so analysed.
'The world is a vale of Soul-making' seems a promising instance. No 'is/ought' confusion
is involved if one 'reads off' value-judgments from such a (grammatically) descriptive
proposition.

[21] I Cor. 15.17f. (Revised Standard Version).

still horrified at what they would still have forfeited, if death ended all. If, then, the descriptive meaning of 'God', 'hereafter', etc., fails to bear up under logical analysis, we can retain their *pre*scriptive meaning only within a radically transformed religion, and only by walking a razor-edge of redefinition.

This paper has attempted no more than to open up a set of problems, some which have been unjustly neglected in recent ethics and aesthetics, with their concentration upon the most 'purely' normative words and their impatience with the phenomenology of less usual ways of looking at life, such as Muir's, Berdyaev's, Yeats'. A study of these raises a variety of problems: the place that aesthetic and quasi-aesthetic concepts may have in the moral life; the many different ways in which a life may be seen as 'patterned', whether by a personal or a public mythology or by a combination of the two; the logical relation between morality seen as the following of rules and as the realizing of fables and parables, and finally the extent to which such an analysis might embrace an historical religion. Each of these problems brings its own tasks for analysis, tasks which this paper scarcely begins to tackle—the analysis of 'initiative', 'cope', 'integrate', 'cohere', and related concepts. Throughout, I have intentionally minimized the historical links between many of these ideas (or variants of them) and philosophical systems—idealist or existentialist, in order not to identify the question of their *individual* tenability with that of the systems in which they have appeared.

2. *Iris Murdoch*

I agree very much with the general direction of Mr Hepburn's argument. My main criticism will be that he has not made enough of his case. He wishes to draw our attention to certain aspects of our life as moral beings which have been neglected in the models offered by philosophers; he argues that 'fables' and 'patterns', rather than rules, are for many people the form which their morality most naturally takes, and that there are familiar ways of appraising the claims of these fables to act as moral guides. Mr Hepburn asks himself whether the inclusion of such phenomena under the heading of 'the moral' would conflict with current views either of 'the

mind' or of moral judgment itself, and decides that there is no conflict. The inclusion of the new material is therefore neither morally
nor philosophically objectionable. He concludes by indicating a
contrast between the 'subjective' moral fable and the 'objective'
religious story.

I want to begin by discussing the type of argument which is
appropriate to the kind of investigation on which Mr Hepburn has
embarked. It is a peculiarity of ethics that the initial segregation of
the items to be studied is less easy than in other branches of philosophy. Mr Hepburn himself moves, quite frankly, between moralizing and philosophizing in his paper, and at one point, when considering different modes of appraising fables, says that 'theories can
be confirmed or upset by such tests'. By this I take him to mean that
if it should turn out on investigation that fable-making was something which we always judged to be detrimental to morality, then
we should have to exclude it from the field of study of the moral
philosopher. Now it has been assumed, roughly since Moore, that
we can distinguish two questions: 'What is my morality?' and
'What is morality as such?' After an initial period of excitement
over this distinction, ethics is moving in the direction of finding it
less simple. When we survey the feuds of our recent ancestors who
are not in the linguistic tradition, for instance, the differences of
opinion of Joseph, Taylor, Ross, Prichard, it is easy to see that these
philosophers had very different interests and attitudes to the world,
and were concerned accordingly to display different aspects of the
moral life. Can it be safely assumed that linguistic philosophers are
immune from such partiality, being able to derive from the study of
language some sort of initial definition and subsequent analysis of
morality which shall have the prestige and neutrality of logic?
Here it is especially important to attend to the initial delineation
of the field of study, observing where and in what way moral judgments may be involved, and then to consider the relations between
the selected phenomena and the philosophical technique used to
describe them. A narrow or partial selection of phenomena may
suggest certain particular techniques which will in turn seem to
lend support to that particular selection; and then a circle is formed
out of which it may be hard to break. It is therefore advisable to
return frequently to an initial survey of 'the moral' so as to recon-
sider, in the light of a primary apprehension of what morality is,
what our technical devices actually *do* for us. Why do we do moral
philosophy anyway? For the sake of 'completeness'? It is the great

merit of Mr Hepburn's paper to redirect our attention to a particular, perhaps neglected, group of these original phenomena.

What impact such a study should have upon current views is not immediately clear. Hepburn speaks of his fables as an alternative 'model'. Strictly speaking, they do not constitute a philosophical model at all in the sense of a 'logical picture', valid irrespective of the content of the morality or the consciousness in question. They are ideas which are consciously entertained as an aid to, or as a part of, morality; nor is it immediately clear that they can be regarded as forms or vehicles fit to receive all and any moral content. Whether a comprehensive and clear distinction between form and content can at all be made in morality is precisely one of the questions which, it seems to me, is raised by consideration of Mr Hepburn's new material. This material, furthermore, is extremely rich and various, and an important distinction is made at the very end of the paper. I shall attempt to proceed by dividing and classifying further the phenomena in question and trying as I do to make clear the implications for current philosophical techniques of the inclusion of these phenomena within the field of 'the moral'.

I shall begin by outlining the view with which I want to bring our fresh evidence into relation, and perhaps into conflict, emphasizing its main points of interest and attraction. It may be that no one individual completely adheres to this position, but I think that it will sound familiar and may pass as a summary of what has quite lately been maintained and not authoritatively or as a whole displaced. I shall call it, with apologies to those who do not hold it, the 'current view'. The remote ancestors of this view are Hume, Kant, and Mill; its more immediate determinants are Rylean behaviourism and the view of meaning, together with its anti-metaphysical corollaries, which we connect with the 'verification principle', but which also has its background in the works of Russell and the British empiricists. On this view, the moral life of the individual is a series of overt choices which take place in a series of specifiable situations. The individual's 'stream of consciousness' is of comparatively little importance, partly because it is often not there at all (having been thought to be continuous for wrong reasons), and more pertinently because it is and can only be through overt acts that we can characterize another person, or ourselves, mentally or morally. Further, a moral judgment, as opposed to a whim or taste preference, is one which is supported by reasons held by the agent to be valid for all others placed as he, and which would involve the objective specification of the situation in terms of facts available to disinterested scrutiny. Moral *words* come into the picture because we not only make choices, but also guide choices by verbal recommendation. This group of words have their meaning, in accordance with the situation outlined above, through the two elements of recommendation and specification (evaluative and descriptive meaning). The specification (of good-making criteria) will differ according to the moral code of the agent, while the element of recommendation will remain constant. A moral concept then will be roughly an objective definition of a certain area of activity plus a recommendation or prohibition.

The charms of this view are obvious. It displays the moral agent as rational and responsible and also as free; he moves unhindered against a background of facts and can alter the descriptive meaning of his moral words at will. The view thus combines the philosophical insight of Hume (we live in a world of disconnected facts) with that of Kant (morality is rational and seeks universally valid reasons), while more surreptitiously it embodies the morality of Mill ('a creed learnt by heart is paganism'). All this is achieved, moreover, by a 'linguistic' method which provides a meaning for moral words which eschews earlier errors and construes these words as nearly as possible on the model of empirical terms, giving them definite factual criteria of application, and without reference to transcendent entities or states of consciousness. Morality can then be shown to be rational after its own fashion,[22] while at the same time a method is provided whereby we can analyse any morality, reflective or unreflective, our own or someone else's. This neatly reconciles the opposite ways in which Hume and Kant reached the same conclusion about heteronomy of the will. The points in this, I am afraid very condensed, account which I should like to emphasize for future reference are these: the behaviouristic treatment of the 'inner life', the view of moral concepts as factual specifications plus recommendations, the universalizability of the moral judgment, and the accompanying picture of moral freedom. Of these points, the first and third are explicitly raised by Mr Hepburn, and the last is, I think, implicitly raised by the conclusion of his paper.

I have suggested that Mr Hepburn's initial argument whereby he draws our attention to a certain range of moral phenomena, needs

---

[22] Those who prefer Burke to Mill may find the 'unconscious' version of the model more attractive, wherein morality appears as habit, and moral remarks are rules for beginners.

further consideration in that the phenomena indicated are rather various. I want now to begin to sort out these phenomena and bring them into relation with the current view. In a philosophical analysis of morality what place should be given to the 'inner life'? Mr Hepburn apparently does not wish to dissent from the current treatment of the inner, but wishes merely to show the importance of the 'fable' in the moral life of certain kinds of imaginative people. He suggests that these people have a 'less usual way of looking at life'; he also implies that a fable *ought* to be comprehensive and coherent, as in the examples which he cites. This seems, however, to be an arbitrary and unnecessary limitation of the field. To begin with, why insist that a fable be comprehensive? There may be brief fables (stories which order small segments of our lives); there may, on the other hand, be highly integrated and comprehensive systems of rules, either held consciously (as in a legalistic morality) or unconsciously (in an habitual morality). What doubtless lies behind Mr Hepburn's view here is a moral judgment to the effect that if one is going to understand one's life imaginatively one must aim at completeness. But the point is rather (and this Mr Hepburn also says) that we know how to assess these fables from a moral point of view; and we do not in practice think that completeness must be had at any price. In fact, and this is to turn to the other point, are these ways of looking at life really so unusual? If we drop the insistence that fables must be highly coherent and comprehensive, is not fable-making a fairly natural and ordinary activity of human beings and is it not continuous with our most everyday methods of reflecting on and understanding our lives? Here one may distinguish a number of different but similar things which merge into each other. There is the highly reflective and imaginative personal fable (which is what Mr Hepburn mainly has in mind), the 'story of one's life', of which, whether kept privately or displayed to others, most people have formed some conception, more ephemeral and disconnected stories and shapings of particular incidents or periods, metaphors explanatory of situations or changes, miscellaneous personal attitudes and visions which may show dramatically in special modes of description or in a more diffused manner in the selection of explanatory concepts. This indicates, of course, a region much wider than that with which Mr Hepburn was concerned: a region in which the 'personal visions' in question may be overt or secret, more or less pictorial, and, in the ordinary sense of the word, imaginative or unimaginative. This, however, is the variegated region to which we must attend if we are to meet the problems raised by Mr Hepburn's fables, which are themselves a section quite arbitrarily, as it seems to me, isolated.

Now if we ask how this region is treated on the current view, the answer is complex and it is at once necessary to make a distinction. What must here be clearly separated is the notion of inner or private psychological phenomena, open to introspection, and the notion of private or personal vision which may find expression overtly or inwardly. There has, I think, been some tendency for the discrediting of the 'inner' in the former sense to involve the neglect of the 'inner' in the latter sense. Recent philosophy has concentrated upon the task of resolving 'the mind' into sets of identifiable activities, where the problem is first, how to isolate and identify such of these activities as are purely introspectible ones, and second, how to assess the importance of these inner proceedings as criteria for the application of words descriptive of the mind. The arguments on both these points are familiar. Introspectible entities present difficulties of identification; however, it may be conceded that 'mental events' exist, in the sense that there are mental images, speeches uttered to oneself, and perhaps more obscure occurrences which ask for metaphorical descriptions.[23] These events, however, are in no way privileged, either as being causes of more outward activity or as being the hidden core or essence of individual minds. The concepts which we use to comprehend and describe the mind depend almost entirely on overt criteria.

How does this affect ethics? On the one hand, in a legitimate way through the elimination of hypostatized and non-observable 'qualities', 'sentiments' or 'acts of will' which might have been thought to be bearers of moral value. On the other hand, our by now fairly modified mental behaviourism has tended, in the field of ethics, to lend support to a more rigid moral behaviourism, which has much more extensive implications; this is partly because, as we have constantly seen, modern ethics lags behind other branches of philosophy and assimilates their findings at first in a crude form, and partly because of more or less conscious *moral* attitudes which favour a behaviouristic picture. That is, it has been readily assumed that in assembling the data (initial definition) for the moral philosopher to work on, we can safely leave aside not only the inner monologue and its like, but also overt manifestations of personal attitudes, speculations, or visions of life such as might find

[23] See Professor Ryle in *Aristotelian Society, Supplementary Volume*, 1951.

expression in talk not immediately directed to the solution of specific moral problems. In short, the material which the philosopher is to work on is simply (under the heading of behaviour) acts and choices, and (under the heading of language) choice-guiding words together with the arguments which display the descriptive meaning of these words. Here two philosophical conceptions reach out towards each other and, in a hazy region, seem to meet. On the one hand, there is no inner life, and moral concepts too must have meaning through definite external criteria. On the other hand, morality is choice, and moral language guides choice through factual specification. The result is a picture, which seems to have the authority of the modern view of the mind, of the essence of the moral life as sets of external choices backed up by arguments which appeal to facts. The picture is simple, behaviouristic, anti-metaphysical, and leaves no place for commerce with 'the transcendent'. It gathers force too from the exaluation which it implicitly contains and which may be put in the form of an appeal to 'the moral life as we know it': surely we see that morality is essentially behaviour. 'If we were to ask of a person "what are his moral principles?" the way in which we could be most sure of a true answer would be by studying what he *did*.'[24]

Now clearly, as a piece of moral advice it might be wise to tell somebody: don't speculate, just concentrate on *this* state of affairs and see what is to be done. It is an important fact that our lives occur temporally in the way that they do, and that we tend, for purposes of getting on to the next thing, to construct them into a series of situations. However, if one is, as a moral philosopher, exclusively interested in this fact one will miss certain important aspects of morals. I suggested earlier that care must be taken in the initial assembly of data, as this may affect the subsequent techniques which will in turn seem to endorse the data. I shall now briefly discuss the area in question (the 'inner life' in the sense of personal attitudes and visions which do not obviously take the form of choice-guiding arguments) from the point of view of its claim to form part of the data of ethics; and I shall then go on to discuss the compatibility of these data with current techniques.

Ethics need not have any quarrel with the argument against the inner in its most modified form. At any rate, I do not at this point wish to propose any quarrel. The data in question are all 'events' and 'activities' which are either overt (conversation, story-telling) or

[24] R. M. Hare, *The Language of Morals*, p. 1.

if introspectible are identifiable and in principle exposable (private stories, images, inner monologue). Now activities of this kind certainly constitute an important part of what, in the ordinary sense, a person 'is like'. When we apprehend and assess other people we do not consider only their solutions to specifiable practical problems, we consider something more elusive which may be called their total vision of life, as shown in their mode of speech or silence, their choice of words, their assessments of others, their conception of their own lives, what they think attractive or praise-worthy, what they think funny: in short, the configurations of their thought which show continually in their reactions and conversation. These things, which may be overtly and comprehensibly displayed or inwardly elaborated and guessed at, constitute what, making different points in the two metaphors, one may call the texture of a man's being or the nature of his personal vision. Now with regard to this area various attitudes may be adopted by the moral philosopher. It may be held that these elusive activities are irrelevant to morality which concerns definite moral choices and the reasons therefor. It may be held that these activities are of interest in so far as they make choices and their reasons more comprehensible. It may be held that these activities can be regarded as being themselves moral acts resulting from responsible choices and requiring reasons. All these three positions would be in different ways compatible with the current view. Or finally, it may be held that these activities are themselves direct expressions of a person's 'moral nature' or 'moral being' and demand a type of description which is not limited to the choice and argument model.

It may be said at once (in answer to the first of the four views mentioned above) that we do to a considerable extent include the area in question in our moral assessments of others and indeed of ourselves, and we usually know very well in practice how to balance definite performance against apprehended 'being' in our judgments. The question is, what technique is suitable to the analysis of such material. It is proposed on the current view that we regard moral differences as differences of choice, given a discussable background of facts. Moral arguments will be possible where people have similar criteria of application (share descriptive meanings of moral terms) and differ about what exactly the facts are. Moral arguments will be difficult or impossible where the differences are differences of criteria. This picture seems plausible if we take as the centre of 'the moral' the situation of a man making a definite choice (such as whether to join a political party) and defending it by reasons containing reference to facts. It seems less plausible when we attend to the notion of 'moral being' as self-reflection or complex attitudes to life which are continuously displayed and elaborated in overt and inward speech but are not separable temporally into situations. Here moral differences look less like differences of choice, given the same facts, and more like differences of vision. In other words, a moral concept seems less like a movable and extensible ring laid down to cover a certain area of fact, and more like a total difference of *Gestalt*. We differ not only because we select different objects out of the same world but because we see different worlds.

I take it that it is part of Mr Hepburn's purpose to suggest that morality is understanding, interpretation and reflection as well as 'choice'. Mr Hepburn is cautious, however, in that he seems content to regard these as merely preliminaries to choice. Whereas I would argue that we cannot accommodate this aspect of morals without modifying our view of 'concepts' and 'meaning'; and when we do this the idea of choice becomes more problematic. In construing meaning for purposes of ethics, philosophers have been anxious to keep as near as possible to a model suitable for simple empirical terms. 'Good' is to have meaning in the same way as 'red', except that the factual criteria may vary and a recommendation is added. This is one result of assuming that moral philosophy can be made linguistic simply by putting 'good' into inverted commas. That this is insufficient may be overlooked so long as we construe the moral life behaviouristically as strings of choices and recommendations backed up by reference to facts. In such a world 'good' and 'right' *could* be the only 'moral words'. But if we attend to the more complex regions which lie outside 'actions' and 'choices' we see moral differences as differences of understanding (and after all, to view them so is as old as moral philosophy itself), more or less extensive and important, which may show openly or privately as differences of story or metaphor or as differences of moral vocabulary betokening different ranges and ramifications of moral concept. Here communication of a new moral concept cannot necessarily be achieved by specification of factual criteria open to any observer ('Approve of *this* area!') but may involve the communication of a completely new, possibly far-reaching and coherent, vision; and it is surely true that we cannot always *understand* other people's moral concepts.[25]

[25] On this and related topics see Mrs Foot's excellent paper, 'When is a principle a moral principle?', *P.A.S.* Supp. Vol. 28, 1954.

If we take the view that moral differences are in this sense 'conceptual' and not exclusively behaviouristic we shall also be able to see moral philosophy itself as a more systematic and reflective extension of what ordinary moral agents are continually doing, and as able in its turn to influence morality. Great philosophers coin new moral concepts and communicate new moral visions and modes of understanding.[26]

It is not difficult to see why such a view of morals and of moral philosophy is regarded in some quarters with suspicion. Briefly, there are at least three reasons, two of them predominantly moral, and one more philosophical. First, it is felt to be dangerous to regard morality as insight (or understanding or sensibility) rather than as action plus argument closely related to action. This view is partly perhaps a reaction against emotivism, which tended to confuse insight with emotion; mainly, however, it represents a determination to value action as against understanding or meditation. Notice with what passion philosophers hastened to correct the error of Moore, who separated insight from action. Here, all I can say is that in this complicated matter most moral agents know how to proceed. Moral insight, as communicable vision or as quality of being, *is* something separable from definitive performance, and we do not always, though doubtless we do usually, require performance as, or allow performance to be, the test of the vision or of the person who holds it. The second point concerns freedom. On the current view the moral agent is free to withdraw, survey the facts, and choose again. There is, moreover, an open field for argument of an empirical fact-investigating kind among those who have similar principles. This view is Kantian in atmosphere: moral beings, or those of them who can communicate, live in the same world. It is also Humian: only carelessness and inattention, that is habitual and traditional attitudes, separate us from 'the facts'. Argument or tradition may then be stressed, according to taste. If, however, we hold that a man's morality is not only his choices but his vision, then this may be deep, ramified, hard to change and not easily open to

---

[26] We may reflect here upon the attitude which certain modern philosophers take up toward their predecessors. Mr Weldon (*Vocabulary of Politics*) argues that most political philosophies are tautologous conceptual structures surrounding empirical recommendations. Mr Hare (*Proceedings of the Aristotelian Society*, 1954-55) speaks of 'the oldest and most ineradicable vice of moralists—the unwillingness to make moral decisions'. (Hence the search for Golden Rules and other such simplifications.) It is easy to see how both these attitudes arise from the current view of morality as surveying the facts and making a choice. But great moral and political philosophers offer us new concepts with which to interpret the world, and they simplify because they are philosophers. What these linguistic analysts mistrust is precisely language.

argument. It is also less realistic to say that it is itself something which we choose; and then it may seem that our conception of moral freedom is in danger. Here it may be said that those who think that freedom is absolute in the 'withdraw and reflect' sense confuse the wish with the fact—and that in any case there is no need to equate the freedom needed to ensure morality with a complete independence of deep conceptual attitudes. It may be argued that we *ought* always to assume that perfect communication and *disinterested* reflection about facts can precede moral judgment, and it is true that such an attitude may often be desirable. But this is itself a Liberal ideal. Finally, the notion that moral differences are conceptual (in the sense of being differences of vision) and must be studied as such is unpopular in so far as it makes impossible the reduction of ethics to logic, since it suggests that morality must, to some extent at any rate, be studied historically. This does not of course imply abandoning the linguistic method, it rather implies taking it seriously.

So far I have been attempting to bring certain moral data, covering a rather wider field than that originally indicated by Mr Hepburn, into conflict with two related dogmas: moral behaviourism and the descriptive-evaluative view of moral concepts. I shall now go on to the cases, which Mr Hepburn took as the centre of his argument, of more coherent personal fables, and attempt to bring this data into conflict with certain current views about universal rules. I shall want here to distinguish the personal fable as such from 'personal vision' or 'moral being', on the one hand, which I have just been discussing, where differences may be conceptual without being uniquely personal or pictorial, and from theological structures on the other hand, which may be thought of as 'transcendent realities', and which I shall be discussing later. Here my first argument will be brief and negative: why insist on forcing moral attitudes into the 'universality' model when this is contrary to appearances? My second argument will be to the effect that certain moralities make use, positively, of a quite different model.

Mr Hepburn says readily that a fable will imply rules of conduct. Now clearly any fable, if it is connected with practice, and is not merely a private film show *à la* Walter Mitty, will imply rules since a discipline is required to put any plan into action. The question which we need to answer in order to relate this phenomenon to the current view is whether a morally important fable will always imply universal rules. It has been powerfully argued, especially by

Mr Hare,[27] that a *moral* decision is one which is supportable by reasons which are universalizable. Here we may get the full force of what is meant by a philosophical model. We are being asked to conceive of a structure of would-be universal reasoning as lying at the core of any activity which could properly be called moral.

How do we decide whether a fable is morally important? If my' argument (which forms an internally connected edifice, just as the current view does) is accepted so far, then it will be conceded that a considerable area of personal reflection is morally important in the sense of constituting a person's general conceptual attitude and day-to-day 'being', which will in turn connect in complex ways with his more obviously moral 'acts'. And here must be included a man's meditation upon and conception of his own life, with its selective and dramatic emphases and implications of direction. Again, we have in practice ways of distinguishing fables which are morally relevant from those which are more purely decorative,[28] and it suffices for the argument if fables are sometimes of the former kind. Such fables may be more or less closely and more or less obviously connected with 'action' and 'choice'.

For purposes of the present question let us consider the cases where fables are fairly closely related to action. Now clearly a fable may very well have practical implications which *can* be regarded as universal rules. This will be so especially when the fable expresses some sort of generally accepted and comprehensible social pattern. Parables of widely held religions, which have the concreteness of personal fables, may have universalizable implications for similar reasons. Such will, however, not so obviously be the case, either where the fable is elaborately personal, or where the fable includes the conception that the individual is unique. If one is Napoleon one does not think that everyone should do as one does oneself. Let us consider these cases.

A man may penetrate his life with reflection, seeing it as having a certain meaning and a certain kind of movement. Alternatively, and in fact the alternatives can shade into each other, a man may regard himself as set apart from others, by a superiority which brings

---

[27] *P.A.S.* 55, 1954–55, pp. 295–312.

[28] There are forms of unity in life stories which can safely be said to be of purely aesthetic interest. Vladimir Nobakov, for instance, in his autobiography, *Speak, Memory*, tells how General Kuropatkin, who once played with matches with him as a child, was recognized by his father years later, when disguised and fleeing from the Bolsheviks, by a flaring match light. Nobakov adds, 'The following of such thematic designs through one's life should be, I think, the true purpose of autobiography.' The king of this region is Proust.

special responsibilities, or by a curse, or some other unique destiny. Both these fables may issue in practical judgments, possibly of great importance. Now, does the question whether these are moral decisions really depend on the answer to the question: would you wish anyone else so placed to act similarly? If faced with this somewhat surprising query the fable-makers might reply, 'yes, I suppose so'; or possibly they might reply (in the first case), 'But nobody could be in *this* position without being *me*', or (in the second case), 'No, for nobody else has *my* destiny'. It will then also be so that, when asked for reasons for their actions, the first man will answer, 'You wouldn't understand', and the second man will give reasons which will only be cogent if one agrees that he is unique. My point is that here the 'universal rules' model simply no longer describes the situation. One can force the situation into the model if one pleases, but whatever is the point of doing so? To do so is to blur a real difference, the difference between moral attitudes which have this sort of personal background and these which do not. Whether such attitudes seem to us desirable or praiseworthy is quite another question.

I leave my negative argument here and go on to the second argument. It is at this point that one may raise the question, touched on by Mr Hepburn, of the contrast between art and morals. I agree here with Mr Hepburn's criticisms of Mr Hampshire, but again would wish to carry the matter further. Some people stress the dissimilarity between art and morals because they want to insist that morality is rational, in the sense of legislating for repeatable situations by specification of morally relevant facts. Other people stress the similarity between art and morals because they want to insist that morality is imaginative and creative and not limited to duties of special obligation. Is there a conflict here? Let us consider the latter case. In the paper already mentioned[29] Mr Hare excellently emphasizes the importance of distinguishing the pair general and specific from the pair universal and particular. Accepting this distinction, one may say that a moral agent may explore a situation imaginatively and in detail and frame a highly specific maxim to cover it, which may nevertheless be offered as a universal rule. This would seem to reconcile the two parties mentioned above; and I think that this would also be the position that Mr Hepburn would take up.

I have already argued that there are kinds of moral outlook which it seems pointless to crush at all costs into the universal rules

[29] *P.A.S.* 55, pp. 295-312.

formula. I want now to consider whether there are not positive and radical moral conceptions which are unconnected with the view that morality is essentially universal rules. I have in mind moral attitudes which emphasize the inexhaustible detail of the world, the endlessness of the task of understanding, the importance of not assuming that one has got individuals and situations 'taped', the connection of knowledge with love and of spiritual insight with apprehension of the unique. Such a description would in fact roughly fit types of moral attitude in other ways very dissimilar: certain idealist views, certain existentialist views, certain Catholic views.[30]

Now it may be argued that one may well meditate upon the mysteriousness and inexhaustibility of the world, but meanwhile one has continually to make judgments on the basis of what one thinks one knows, and these, if moral, will claim to be universal. Here again, let us pause and consider what after all a philosophical model is for. If we give in here and agree that somebody whose belief and moral inspiration was of the kind mentioned above would of course, when he acts, wish others so placed to act as he does, what does it profit us? We have won a similarity, but we have lost a much more important and interesting difference. There are people whose fundamental moral belief is that we all live in the same empirical and rationally comprehensible world and that morality is the adoption of universal and openly defensible rules of conduct. There are other people whose fundamental belief is that we live in a world whose mystery transcends us and that morality is the exploration of that mystery in so far as it concerns each individual. It is only by sharpening the universality model to a point of extreme abstraction that it can be made to cover both views.

One may suspect, in fact, that much of the charm of 'universality' is borrowed surreptitiously from 'generality'. Mr Hampshire,[31] for instance, who does not explicitly make Mr Hare's distinction, emphasizes the repeatability of moral situations; and Mr Hare himself says 'we steer a middle course' between the 'hidebound inflexibility'

[30] I regret mentioning without expounding, but to elaborate these themes here would take too long. Miscellaneous examples of the kind of view I have in mind, may be found in Nédoncelle, *Vers une Philosophie de l'Amour*; Marcel, *Être et Avoir*; Rousselot, 'Synthèse aperceptive et philosophie de l'amour', *Revue de Philosophie*, 1910. Behind the current view lies British empiricism. Behind these views lie idealism and perhaps certain aspects of Thomism. See Marcel on his debt to Bradley in the *Journal Métaphysique*. It is Kierkegaard who most specifically, though in some ways tiresomely, displays the transformation of an idealist philosophy into a phenomenology of individual moral struggle.

[31] His article 'Logic and Appreciation' in *Aesthetics and Language*, edited by William Elton.

of the man who never adjusts rules to situations, and the 'neurotic indetermination' of the man who always hesitates because he fears he has not understood.[32] But who steers this middle course? To select the middle course is itself a moral choice: the choice which, transformed into a description of morality, Mr Hare wishes us to make true by definition. We do continually have to make choices—but why should we blot out as irrelevant the different background of these choices, whether they are made confidently on the basis of a clear specification of the situation, or tentatively, with no confidence of having sufficiently explored the details? Why should attention to detail, or belief in its inexhaustibility, necessarily bring paralysis, rather than, say, inducing humility and being an expression of love?

Mr Hare and Mr Gellner[33] caricature a person whom they call an 'existentialist' who seems to have nothing to say for himself except that he thinks he has a duty to do a certain action, but has no views on whether anyone else so placed should act similarly. With no further explanation this views seems absurd, especially when we contrast it with everyday ideas of morality as rules which are not only universal but also general. However, no real existentialist is so tongue-tied. Any attitude may be made to look absurd if its conceptual background is removed. A morality, if I am right, is a ramification of concepts, and this only appears, in current writings, not to be so because on the one hand the key concepts of our general social morality (freedom, tolerance, factual arguments, etc.) have become practically unconscious and are taken for granted, and on the other hand because the concepts are what they are (insistence on specification of generally observable facts, etc.), whereas a man who hesitated, always acted with an air of doubt, thought it meaningless to legislate for others, and so on, might well be able to explain his conduct rationally in terms of different concepts.

Here again, it is not difficult to see why such views are met with hostility and why the current model is defended with passion. Doubtless 'everyday morality', in our society at any rate, is of the kind currently described, where rules are universal, fairly general without being too general, and where clear and above-board factual reasoning is required to justify choices. It is felt (Mr Gellner obviously feels[34]) that other attitudes will tend to be non-rational and

---

[32] *Op. cit.*, p. 310.
[33] *P.A.S.* 55, 1954-55, pp. 157-178.
[34] Mr Gellner contrasts U-type evaluations (which claim universality) with E-type

possibly non-democratic; whereas Hare would perhaps suspect
that a refusal to accept his picture constituted a sort of moral
evasion, an attempt to avoid responsibility by pretending that
everything is too difficult: and clearly there are views and attitudes
which would justify both fears. However, on the one hand, even a
disreputable view may still be a moral view,[35] and on the other
hand, if we look with understanding, these alternative views are
not by any means so sinister or so unusual. Let us consider in more
detail some of the reasons for mistrust.

It may be held that views which emphasize 'particularity' and
'inexhaustibility' will involve inability to describe and specify and
hence breakdown of communication, and it may be felt that this
will at best condone slackness and at worst encourage violence. Mr
Hare says briskly that individuals (and doubtless situations) 'can be
described as fully and precisely as we wish'. Now, with the best will
in the world, this is not always so. There are situations which are
obscure and people who are incomprehensible, and the moral agent,
as well as the artist, may find himself unable to describe something
which in some sense he apprehends. Language has limitations and
there are moments when, if it is to serve us, it has to be used creatively, and the effort may fail. When we consider here the role of
language in illuminating situations, how insufficient seems the
notion of linguistic moral philosophy as the elaboration of the
evaluative-descriptive formula. From here we may see that the task
of moral philosophers has been to extend, as poets may extend, the
limits of the language, and enable it to illuminate regions of reality
which were formerly dark. Where the attempt fails, and one has to
choose without having understood, the virtues of faith and hope
have their place. It is very well to say that one should always attempt
a full understanding and a precise description, but to say that one
can always be confident that one has understood seems plainly unrealistic. There are even moments when understanding *ought* to be
withheld.

The insistence that morality is essentially rules may be seen as an
attempt to secure us against the ambiguity of the world. Rules may
be ambiguous in that we have to decide how to apply them, but at

---

ones (which do not), and connects the former with rational argument, and the latter
with disreputable things such as the *Fuehrerprinzip, credo quia absurdum,* and romantic love.
   [35] It may be noted that Mr Gellner regards both the systems which he describes as
'moralities', and admits that he does not see 'by what standard external to both one could
choose between them'.

least in attempting an ever more detailed specification one is moving in the direction of complete clarity. If I am right, however, this cannot properly be taken as the only structural model of morality. There are times when it is proper to stress, not the comprehensibility of the world, but its incomprehensibility, and there are types of morality which emphasize this more than is customary in utilitarian Liberal moralities. We may consider here the importance of parables and stories as moral guides. Mr Hepburn says that parables will imply maxims, but rightly adds that 'one parable is never logically equivalent to the expression of one maxim'. How ambiguous a parable appears to be will depend on the coherence of the moral world in which it is being used. Certain parables or stories undoubtedly owe their power to the fact that they incarnate a moral truth which is paradoxical, infinitely suggestive and open to continual reinterpretation. (For instance, the story in the New Testament about the woman who broke the alabaster box of very precious ointment, or the parable of the prodigal son.) Such stories provide, precisely through their concreteness and consequent ambiguity, sources of moral inspiration which highly specific rules could not give.[36] Consider too the adaptability which a religion may gain from having as its centre a person and not a set of rules. (For a determined rejection of such 'concrete' guidance, see Kant's remarks about Christ in the *Grundlegung*.) It may be said, that a moral attitude which lays emphasis on ambiguity and paradox is not for everyday consumption. There are, however, moments when situations are unclear and what is needed is not a renewed attempt to specify the facts, but a fresh vision which may be derived from a 'story' or from some sustaining concept which is able to deal with what is obstinately obscure, and represents a 'mode of understanding' of an alternative type. Such concepts are, of course, not necessarily recondite or sophisticated; 'hope' and 'love' are the names of two of them. And there are doubtless some people who direct their

---

[36] Mr Hare says that it is odd that existentialists like to discuss moral questions by writing novels since 'no work of fiction can be about a concrete individual' (*P.A.S.* 1954-55, p. 310). This seems a strange view. We *imagine* fictitious characters as concrete individuals and although it is true that the information which we have about them is limited, this may be so also in the case of real people, and anyway the information is endlessly open to reinterpretation. In fact, we may, in the course of time, alter our assessment of a fictitious character. We do not see the same Stavrogin or the same Charlus at forty that we saw at twenty. Why existentialists like writing novels is plain. A novelist can readily *represent* a situation in which the agent is immersed, which he only partly understands, and whose solution may involve a clash of irreconcilable moral viewpoints. Whether and in what circumstances such a 'representation' constitutes an 'explanation' is, of course, another question.

whole lives in the latter way. The 'moral' dangers of such attitudes are plain. All that can be said is that we know roughly how to deal with these dangers and part of the moral life is dealing with them.[37]

I come now at the end of my paper to a matter of great importance which must, however, be dealt with briefly. What I have attempted to do so far is, by appeal to a certain range of 'moral data', to suggest that the current model illuminates and describes only a certain type or area of moral life, and that if we attempt to construe all moral activities in terms of it we are led to ignore important differences. In order properly to analyse these differences, I argued, it was necessary to think of morality not solely as choice and fact-specifying argument, but as differences between sets of concepts—where an exclusive emphasis on choice and argument would be itself one conceptual attitude among others. What I have said so far has been said without raising the question of naturalism.

I think that a good deal of the power of the current view derives from a feeling that it constitutes a defence against the fallacy of naturalism; and it does appear to do this, since patently no argument can proceed directly from fact to value if it has to go *via* the agent's choice of good-making criteria. Let us, however, see how the position is affected by the alternative view I have outlined above. Is there in fact a knockdown argument against naturalism? The argument against it may be divided, I suggest, into the following components. 1. An argument against metaphysical entities. This may come in a strong form which claims that all concepts of metaphysical enties are empty, or in a weak form which merely holds that the existence of such entities cannot be philosophically established. 2. A closely related dogma concerning meaning, which I have discussed above, to the effect that empirical terms have meaning *via* fixed specification of empirical criteria, and moral terms have meaning *via* movable specification of empirical criteria, plus recommendation. This will imply that a moral term cannot be defined by a non-moral term. 3. The use of these insights to point

---

[37] If time and space permitted it would be tempting to digress here on the subject of 'symbols'. Symbols ('the language of the unconscious') may play, in ways which are still largely obscure, a spiritually liberating role. Jung (*Answer to Job*, Routledge 1954, p. 172) contrasts the maternal attitude of the Catholic Church, which 'gives the archetypal symbolisms the necessary freedom and space in which to develop' with the paternal attitude of Protestantism with its more rationalistic rule-conscious viewpoint. Whether or not one cares for Jung's general attitude (which seems to make absolute some rather dubious concept of 'psychic vitality') there is a contrast here and an interesting one. A deeper realization of the role of symbols in morality need not involve (as certain critics seem to fear) any overthrow of reason. Reason must, however, especially in this region, appear in her other *persona* as imagination.

out that any argument which professes to move directly from fact to value contains a concealed evaluative major premise. 4. A *moral* argument or recommendation of a Liberal type: don't be dogmatic, always reflect and argue, respect the attitudes of others. Behind the first two points lie the assumptions of British empiricism, and behind the fourth lie the moral attitudes of Protestantism and Liberalism.

The total argument has sometimes been presented as if it were the exposure of a quasi-logical mistake; if we dismember it, however, we can see that only (3) has a strictly logical air. We can also more coolly decide which parts are acceptable and what it is able to prove. For myself, I accept the weak form of (1). (For instance: there are no philosophical proofs of the existence of God, but it is not senseless to believe in God.) Where (2) is concerned I have attempted to offer an alternative view of moral concepts which shows moral differences as differences of vision not of choice. What effect does a modified acceptance of (1) and a rejection of (2) have upon one's view of alleged arguments from fact to value? Such arguments, it would be currently held, can be faulty either because they involve a definition of moral terms in non-moral terms (the case dealt with by (2)) or because they are elliptical (the case dealt with by (3)). These alleged mistakes are closely related but not identical. Someone who says 'Statistics show that people constantly do this, so it must be all right' (pattern of certain familiar arguments) should have it pointed out that he is concealing the premise 'What is customary is right.' He must also realize (it would be argued) that 'What is customary is right' is a moral judgment freely endorsed by himself and not a definition of 'right'. The notion that 'customary' defines 'right' may be the psychological cause of, or the would-be reason for, the curtailing of the argument, but it is not the same thing as the curtailing of the argument. The man may publicize his premise, still insisting on the definition. In many cases, of course, the exposure of the premise destroys the appeal of the argument, which may depend (as in the example above) upon the hearer's imagining that he has got to accept the conclusion or deny the plain facts; and I would certainly want to endorse many arguments of type (3) whose purpose is solely to achieve such an exposure. I turn now to the other contention, which is the more interesting one.

Why can moral terms not be defined in non-moral terms? The answer to this question is given by the world picture which goes with the current view, and whose purpose at this point is to safeguard a certain conception of freedom. The descriptive-evaluative distinction is simply another way of saying that moral terms cannot be *defined* in non-moral terms because the agent *freely* selects the criteria. The moral word cannot *mean* the empirical state of affairs it commends since it can be used to commend others without change of essential meaning. This can be plausibly illustrated in the case of 'good'. If, however, we do not accept the current view of moral concepts as commendations of neutral areas, and consider rather the way in which a moral outlook is shown in ramifications of more specialized concepts which themselves determine a vision of the world, then the prohibition on defining value in terms of fact loses much of its point. It is, of course, the case that moral arguments may proceed by appeal to facts; but what may be lost to view, especially if we consider only simple utilitarian arguments, is that such arguments take place within a moral attitude where some sovereign concept decides the relevance of the facts and may, indeed, render them observable. The too rigid affirmation of a link between certain facts and an evaluation could appear here either as a *moral* error or as a *linguistic* error. The moral error could be, for instance, 'lack of realism' (lack of a suitably wide and reflective attitude to facts) and would be judged as such in the light of a rival moral attitude concerning what was morally relevant. The linguistic error could be, for instance, a failure to understand the customary degree of generality of a moral word; although here one might need further information before deciding whether an unusual use of a word represented a linguistic misunderstanding rather than a moral difference. My point is that if we regard the current view, not as a final truth about the separability of fact and value, but as itself representing a type of moral attitude, then we shall not think that there is a *philosophical* error which consists in merging fact and value. On the alternative view which I have suggested fact and value merge in a quite innocuous way. There would, indeed, scarcely be an objection to saying that there were 'moral facts' in the sense of moral interpretations of situations where the moral concept in question determines what the situation is, and if the concept is withdrawn we are not left with the same situation or the same facts. In short, if moral concepts are regarded as deep moral configurations of the world, rather than as lines drawn round separable factual areas, then there will be no facts 'behind them' for them to be erroneously defined in terms of. There is nothing sinister about this view; freedom here will consist, not in being able to lift the concept off the otherwise unaltered facts and lay it down elsewhere, but in being able to 'deepen' or 'reorganize' the concept or change it for another one.[38] On such a view, it may be noted, moral freedom looks more like a mode of reflection which we may have to achieve, and less like a capacity to vary our choices which we have by definition. I hardly think this a disadvantage.

It is from here that we can see what the problem of naturalism really is. We have noted the anti-metaphysical argument (1), the argument against concealment of premises (3), and the dogma about the essential separability of fact and value (2). There remains a question which is fundamentally an evaluative one concerning how we picture morality and its source. I think that much of the impetus of the argument against naturalism comes from its connection with, and its tendency to safeguard, a Liberal evaluation (4). It is felt to be important that morality should be flexible and argumentative, centred upon the individual, and that no alleged transcendent metaphysical realities, such as God, or History, or the Church, should be allowed to overshadow the moral life. But, and this is the point to which I have been wanting to get, if I am right in accepting the weaker version of (1) and in rejecting (2), then there is nothing in the so-called argument against naturalism to prove that *belief* in the transcendent can form no point of a system of morality.

We may now turn back to the real world and consider with an open mind what part such belief does play in morals. There is surely an important and philosophically interesting difference between the man who believes that moral values are modes of empirically describable activity which he endorses and commends and the man who believes that moral values are visions, inspirations or powers which emanate from a transcendent source concerning which he is called on to make discoveries and may at present know little. Whether such deep differences of outlook correlate with obvious differences of moral procedure will depend on further details of the beliefs and society in question. It has been possible to ignore such differences in England partly because the Protestant Christian and the Liberal atheist have, for historical reasons, so much in common. If, however, we interest ourselves in the concep-

---

[38] In certain cases, whether we speak of deepening or of changing a concept will be a, not necessarily unimportant, question of words. When we deepen our concept of 'love' or 'courage' we may or may not want to retain the same word.

tual background of choice, and the 'vision' and 'moral being' of the chooser, we shall see naturalism not as a fallacy but as a different system of concepts. The current model, so far from refuting naturalism, merely summarizes a non-naturalistic moral attitude. The true naturalist (the Marxist, for instance, or certain kinds of Christian) is one who *believes* that as moral beings we are immersed in a reality which transcends us and that moral progress consists in awareness of this reality and submission to its purposes.

The defender of the current view may maintain that in so far as the naturalist's arguments are not erroneous philosophical ones (which we have already excluded) they are mere blind appeals to non-rational conceptions and cannot be called proper moral reasons. Here I can only reply that I do not accept the implied definition of 'rational' and 'moral' and have already argued this at length. Whether a particular argument is rational or (in some sense of 'seriously offered') moral is something which we decide, in ways which are hard to summarize, by considering the weight and coherence of the total attitude—and we may assess in this way arguments which conform to the current pattern just as much as those which do not.

The final argument of the defender of the current view will be the deep one that whatever set of concepts incarnate a man's morality, that man has *chosen* those concepts, and so at one remove the familiar pattern can re-emerge. It may be felt that this argument at least is inescapable; Mr Hepburn apparently thinks so, since he says that it is a truth of logic that the will is autonomous. Here one can only come back again to the question: what is a philosophical model for? The Liberal wants all the time to draw attention to the *point of discontinuity* between the choosing agent and the world. He sees the agent as central, solitary, responsible, displaying his values in his selection of acts and attitudes. The naturalist on the other hand, differs from the Liberal precisely in *not* seeing the moral agent in this way; and whereas the Liberal thinks that the naturalist has certain erroneous beliefs and fails to realize the responsibility which he nevertheless has, the naturalist thinks that the Liberal fails to understand the truth about the universe and wrongly imagines himself to be the source of all value. (Remember Belloc's remark about the lady who decided to give the universe a piece of her mind.) Different conceptions of moral freedom, which would need to be explained at length, go with these two views. Why should they be planed down and assimilated to each other?

It was Mr Hepburn's intention to lead us back from abstract philosophical formulae to the patterns and models which are really used by moral agents. I have argued, I hope, in the spirit of that intention. I have wished to deny the claim of the current view to picture morality as such. The current view pictures a type of morality. Philosophers have been misled, not only by a rationalistic desire for unity, but also by certain simplified and generalized moral attitudes current in our society, into seeking a single philosophical definition of morality. If, however, we go back again to the data we see that there are fundamentally different moral pictures which different individuals use or which the same individual may use at different times. Why should philosophy be less various, where the differences in what it attempts to analyse are so important? Wittgenstein says (*Untersuchungen* 226e) that 'What has to be accepted, the given, is—so one could say—*forms of life*.' For purposes of analysis moral philosophy should remain at the level of the differences, taking the moral forms of life as given, and not try to *get behind them* to a single form.

I suggested above that ethics had in the past, in one of its aspects, been continuous with the efforts of ordinary moral agents to conceptualize their situations. This kind of imaginative exploration of the moral life is being practised by contemporary continental philosophers, often without special metaphysical pretensions; and there is no reason why such exploration should be combined with erroneous philosophical arguments. It has been largely abandoned in this country since philosophers have been under the impression that ethics must be neutral analysis or nothing. I have argued that in so far as ethics sets out to be analysis rather than exploration it can attain only a precarious neutrality, like that of history, and not the pure neutrality of logic. This will also imply that ethics is in certain important respects discontinuous with the rest of philosophy, as political philosophy, with its more detailed historical implications, is usually conceded to be. Ethics surely is in fact, as it has always *mutatis mutandis* been, both exploration and analysis; nor can we assume that even if we try explicitly to separate these two activities we shall necessarily be successful.

Here, if we abandon the notion of a pure formula, we shall be able once again to see how deeply moral attitudes influence philosophical pictures of morality. (This present writing is doubtless no exception.) There is perhaps in the end no peace between those who think that morality is complex and various, and those who think it is simple and unitary, or between those who think that other people are usually hard to understand and those who think they are usually easy to understand. All one can do is try to lay one's cards on the table.

12

MORAL CHOICE AND DIVINE AUTHORITY

Helen Oppenheimer

I

T H E most intractable problem for Christian ethics is the question of the permissible, of how to apply the dichotomy 'optional/compulsory' to the things a Christian believes he ought or ought not to do. This problem is not just a set piece for casuists, luring one into the intricate mazes of tutiorism, probabilism or probabiliorism. To fix its importance, one might characterize it as a way of transposing from history or metaphysics to morals the question: 'What think ye of Christ?' It asks not simply what moral teaching Christianity propounds, but what kind of moral teaching.

It arises because as a system of ethics Christianity is both perfectionist and universal in its claims. This is both its fascination and its dilemma, that it expects of all what in fact we know perfectly well is only feasible for some, if any. Admire it simply as a beautiful ideal and no trouble arises; but once ask, 'And *must* I really?', and the problem of the permissible has to be faced. Nor is it just a practical problem. If human weakness were all we were worried about, a stiff doctrine of grace or of original sin, or both, would solve the problem. 'You can with God's help' or 'You cannot and that shows how evil you are' are in their way practical answers. They do nothing to solve the theoretical problem: '*Ought* I to be perfect? Can it be expected of me?' Of course it cannot fairly be expected, but to ask less when perfection has been set before one is equally obviously a moral decline. 'A doubtful law does not oblige'—but can any law really be doubtful once it has commended itself to my conscience as a fine ideal? Am I not bound to follow the highest principles I can devise? But that way madness lies.

Yet on the other hand to stop short of taking the loftiest flights as compulsory, to ask to be let off, is to have deserted the high moral point of view of right for right's sake. 'What need I do to be morally safe?' is hardly more than a decently obscure wording for the blatant 'How much can I get away with?' The concept of the permissible gives no secure foothold, but turns out to be an unstable and uncomfortable halfway house between the required and the forbidden. To deny it is unjust; to take one's stand at all firmly upon it is generally to make dangerous inroads upon moral values themselves.

11

The next move, and a promising one, is to suggest that all this difficulty comes from treating morality as essentially a matter of rules. If one has been brought up to identify moral behaviour with self-discipline and the overcoming of temptation, this assumption of a rule-morality is likely to be very deeply embedded. One is convinced that in any given situation there is some specific act which *ought* to be done. Moral choice is seen as a matter of finding *the* right answer to a problem, on the analogy of a computer suitably programmed to give reliable answers. To become aware of more and more intricate moral problems and more and more conflicting considerations on either side does not necessarily upset this model: rather the contrary. The more complicated the question, the more we feel challenged not to give up the struggle, but to master its intricacies. Of course, if our computer is inadequately programmed, the results it will yield will be unreliable, but that is up to us. If for example we have only fed into it the principle 'never tell lies', we cannot expect it in a given case to balance the requirement of truthfulness against the rival requirement of not betraying one's friends. If we have indeed equipped it with every imaginable principle but have left out some of the empirical data we similarly cannot expect reliable results. If the man on trial turns out to be the witness's husband the question of whether she ought to tell the truth, the whole truth and nothing but the truth needs to be re-opened. This kind of perplexity, far from making us change our assumptions, merely leads us to hope that better and more accurate methods of calculation will eventually yield the definitive correct solution. Our casuistry is admittedly not yet a sufficiently delicate instrument to tell us, for example, whether a Christian must be in favour of unilateral nuclear disarmament. Conflicting answers have emerged, queried by other powerful computers; but we still tend to hope that one day with improved techniques we shall arrive at assured results.

The point is that once a definite answer to a question has emerged it is compulsory in the sense that all the other answers one might have guessed at are more or less wrong and to be avoided. If one is a Christian one's computer is programmed to give very strict answers, but having arrived at them one must obey them. One feeds in the datum 'someone has struck me on the right cheek' and out comes the result 'turn to him the other also'. The only alternative is to programme the machine differently, and some Christians think this ought to be done, while others maintain that it has been authoritatively programmed already in the only correct way.

But there is another alternative, and that is to abandon the rule-model and look for some entirely different analogy for moral decision. These difficulties about the permissible and the compulsory bring out into the open the lurking doubt whether in trying to resist muddle and make ethical issues cut-and-dried one is only becoming rigid rather than lucid. If it prepares the way for a more flexible idea of moral choice this doubt can prove not destructive but a positive liberation. It may arise when one is struck by the immense diversity of human aims and achievements and the many different ways in which people succeed in making sense of their lives. It suggests that it may be as well for a change to savour rather than to tabulate, to accept rather than to assess. To escape in this way from the tyranny of assured results and see morality from a different point of view, as an art rather than as a science, can come as a kind of revelation. One finds oneself thinking less in terms of right and wrong answers, of the optional and the compulsory, and more in terms of satisfying and unsatisfying patterns, patterns which are being formed by a process somewhat like craftsmanship rather than discovered by a process like calculation. The model of the computer is replaced by the model of the painter engaged upon his masterpiece.

This way of thinking, instead of being arrived at gently and gradually, may be forced upon one abruptly by the sheer intractability of actual moral predicaments, one's own or other people's, when they prove incapable of a tidy answer. This kind of 'intractability' is not merely a mathematical complexity. The considerations involved are not only intricate, they are imponderable. The problems are just as much moral problems, they require moral decision in what some people would call its highest form, but one feels that they cannot be systematized. They are concerned with specific individual situations, not with general principles. For example, a man has to obey his vocation in the light of his existing personal commitments; parents may have to balance the needs of a handicapped child against the needs of their normal children; a widow may be faced with the hard decision whether to remarry. It is highly characteristic of all these situations that to 'lay down the law' about where duty lies is to fail to appreciate the problem. Friends can perhaps supply additional data or considerations which may have been overlooked, but 'good advice', especially good advice of the form 'you must do such-and-such', is apt to be literally impertinent. What matters for the person who has to make the decision, is not the determination somehow to find *the* right answer and act upon it at whatever cost, but a deep conviction that the answer is not ready-made but has to be created. To see a moral predicament being resolved in this way, so that something completely new emerges which could not have been exactly foreseen or provided for by any kind of calculation, is to become permanently dissatisfied with restricted views of moral choice, and always to look on the 'optional/ compulsory' distinction with a certain suspicion.

This line of thought, which casts doubt on 'rule-morality' and proposes the analogy of a painter as a corrective to it, may seem to fit very well with the case put by R. W. Hepburn in his paper on 'Vision and Choice in Morality'.[1] He points out that, whatever philosophers may assume, morally sensitive people often see moral endeavour not as obedience to a rule, but as 'the realizing of a pattern of life, or the following out of a pilgrimage'.[2] He speaks of certain moral situations such as 'educating a child or conducting one's relations with one's husband or wife or (often) in choosing one's own career and manner of life'[3] as giving room for 'creativity'. But as he goes on he increasingly seems to see the pattern of 'fable' as something we must form for ourselves and then shape our lives by, more individual perhaps but in the end just as external as a set of rules. He concludes by discussing sympathetically the suggestion that a religious 'fable' such as the Christian might be used as a life-shaping pattern in this way by those who find it impossible to

[1] *P.A.S.S.* 30, 1956: reprinted above pp. 181ff.
[2] Page 181.   [3] Page 185.

believe in its literal truth. This may well be so, but it should not be
confused with the distinctive point the 'painter' analogy is trying to
make, that the moral agent creates his own pattern as he goes along,
not necessarily measuring his life against any ready-made rules *or*
story, but at each point performing a new creative act. Like painting, moral decision makes something original which can be judged
in its own context as successful or unsuccessful. To paint a picture
is, of course, as much a caricature of moral decision as to feed data
into a machine, but the question is whether the caricature is an
illuminating one.

Three criticisms immediately come to mind: that the 'painter'
analogy makes morality too strenuous, too unconventional, and too
much a matter of taste; but these are not unanswerable. First, one
recognizes that not all moral choices are of such an intense and
demanding kind as to suggest the bringing into existence of a
masterpiece; but equally, not every touch of the painter's brush has
to represent a striking creative act. There is plenty of straightforward craftsmanship about many works of art, the kind of skill
which can be taught and applied, needing care rather than genius.
It does not take a Raphael to paint a frieze of flowers and fruit
round a room, any more than it takes a St Francis to get up in time
for breakfast. There is no reason why the 'painter' model should not
be as well able as the 'computer' model to allow for ordinary good
behaviour as well as for the highest kinds of heroism.

Secondly, there is no need to over-emphasize complete newness.
Paintings can be of any degree of traditionalism, from the most rigid
Byzantine or ancient Egyptian conventions to the most revolutionary art of the twentieth century. Since profoundly successful work
can be done at both these extremes, there is no need to suppose that
to use the 'painter' analogy for moral choice commits one to wild
and unconventional moral views. In art and morality alike both
tradition and innovation can find honourable places. The one need
not be a dead hand any more than the other need lead to anarchy.
The originality which is important is not necessarily novelty but a
kind of unpredictable freshness for which no recipe can be given. It
is found in the work of artists who accept and of artists who reject the
conventions in which they have been educated, and it is perhaps its
moral equivalent which makes people comment upon the refresh-
ing diversity of the lives of the great saints. A Christian will look for
this quality and surely find it pre-eminently in the life and teaching
of Christ, accompanied by elements of both tradition and revolu-

tion which different temperaments will feel inclined to stress
differently.

Thirdly, none of this need lead one to suppose that according to
the 'painter' model morality is simply a matter of taste. Moral
decisions need be no more arbitrary than artistic decisions; they
can be criticized, rational grounds can be given for them, and some
are objectively better than others. The point is that the rightness of
a particular decision becomes apparent in its complete context and
cannot be schematized. 'Why does that tree in the foreground pull
the whole picture together although at first it might seem out of
scale?' 'Why did he give her the abrupt shock of telling her the
truth although it might have killed her?' 'Why does he do the sky
green?' 'Why won't he conform to conventional morality?' and so
forth.

Here it may be urgently protested that it is most misleading to
compare morality with 'what would make a good work of art'. We
cannot justify our actions by pointing out that they are aesthetically satisfying or would make a good story: far from it. This objection misses the point. The 'painter' analogy suggests that what
'aesthetically satisfying' means for a picture or a story is very like
what '*morally* satisfying' means for an action. A good picture or a
good act are not good in quite the same sense, but the procedures
for achieving them are, it is maintained, closely analogous. In each
case something is being made or done which has a claim to be
called unique, although it may be illuminated by all manner of
similarities and relations to other cases. Whether it is conventional
or novel, it cannot be determined by fixed rules whether it is to be
called successful or not; but nor is it a matter of individual taste.
To judge it successful is to appreciate it, and what one appreciates
one can learn from, although one would be unwise to copy slavishly.

The 'painter' analogy has led to a flat contradiction of an argument of Professor Hampshire's in his article 'Logic and Appreciation'.[4] 'Virtue and good conduct', he says, 'are essentially repeatable
and imitable, in a sense in which a work of art is not. To copy a
right action is to act rightly; but a copy of a work of art is not necessarily or generally a work of art.'[5] Mr Hepburn seeks to counter this
by urging that a perfect copy of a work of art 'must possess the
worth of the original'.[6] Whether this is convincing or not, I should
prefer to stand by the converse, that to try to make an exact copy is

---

[4] Printed in *Essays in Aesthetics and Language*, ed. W. Elton, Blackwell 1954.
[5] *Op. cit.*, p. 164.   [6] 'Vision and Choice in Morality': above, p. 186.

not the most promising way of producing something worthwhile in morals or art; whereas to learn from someone else's way of approach and work under his influence can be valuable in art as in morals.

III

So far then the 'painter' analogy for moral choice stands up well under attack, but this certainly does not mean that it can be taken as the whole truth about moral obligation. In pursuing its undoubted attractions and defending it against specific criticisms I have done scant justice to the profound conviction which underlies these criticisms, that there is something more basic wrong with the 'painter' analogy, that it has somehow missed the distinctive meaning of the word 'moral'.

This conviction reveals itself in stages. The first stage is to raise the surface objections I have already tried to deal with. The second stage goes deeper and brings to light the proposition that whatever ethics is about, it simply is not about unique situations. To many people the whole point of morality is precisely that it is not a matter of individual inspiration but the same for everyone. 'What is sauce for the goose is sauce for the gander' carries great conviction as a rough-and-ready formulation of Kant's criterion; and here the computer model comes into its own again. In one word, 'universalizability' is a promising slogan to which the 'computer' model remains soundly faithful. A computer after all is not unlike a just judge, showing no mercy admittedly but turning the same face to all, totally disinterested, no respecter of persons. It was rash to condemn too hastily 'the tyranny of assured results'. The worst mark of tyranny is arbitrariness; assured results, equal for all comers, the same data yielding the same answer, is a large part of what we mean by *deliverance* from tyranny. It is true that the whole vocabulary of data and calculation, of machines and results, seems arid and uninteresting compared with talk of harmonious patterns, craftsmanship, and creation; but why should one expect the subject-matter of morals to be aesthetically delightful?

Of course if one is determined to cling to the 'painter' analogy to the total exclusion of all others, one can simply continue the debate by trying to meet this new objection in its turn. It is plausible to argue that the ideal 'same data, same result' is a chimaera. The data never are exactly the same. A perfectly programmed computer is a computer apprised of a unique situation after all, so that 'universalizability' evaporates, by logical necessity, at the only moment when we can claim to have attained it. Either we have not fully specified our particular case, in which case generalization is unreliable; or we have fully specified it, in which case generalization is no longer possible.

But at this point a converse argument comes into play to show the equivalent inadequacy of the 'painter' model, by asking what it can mean to call a moral situation unique. 'In one sense', this argument runs, 'obviously every situation is unique as being *that* situation. If we mean that it contains exceptional features, if we are to take account of these they must be described by using terms which are general, in that they might also apply to other situations, however rare or unlikely.'[7] If this is the case the artist's ideal of uniqueness appears to be as much a chimaera as the calculator's ideal of universalizability. At the crucial point the two seem oddly to cancel each other out.

Continuing the debate in this way appears then to arrive at deadlock. Of course one could go on arguing: it would be foolish to suggest that the objections on either side are insurmountable. Computers do produce valid results and artists do create original masterpieces, and presumably some account could be given of how this is possible, but it is doubtful whether to give such an account would be particularly profitable, since after all neither computer nor artist is exactly what we mean by a moral agent. Analogies are points of view from which to see the facts in a new light, and will not stand being treated like scientific hypotheses, valid or invalid according to whether they ever break down or not.[8] The next stage is to accept the fact that no one analogy is going to prove absolutely helpful or unhelpful, and to try by a more general approach to bring to the surface what it is about the 'painter' model which, in spite of its merits, makes it deeply unacceptable to moralists.

Its strength, as I have tried to show, is its flexible and constructive account of moral decision, and here it certainly makes the ideal of 'universalizability' look inadequate. Miss Iris Murdoch, in her sensitive and convincing reply to Mr Hepburn's paper,[9] speaks of the 'unexhaustible detail of the world, the endlessness of the task of understanding, the importance of not assuming that one has got individuals and situations "taped", the connection of knowledge with love and of spiritual insight with apprehension of the unique',

---

[7] I owe both the argument and its wording to Professor Dorothy Emmet.

[8] See J. T. Wisdom, 'Other Minds', *P.A.S.S.* 20; reprinted in *Other Minds*, Blackwell 1952, *passim*, esp. pp. 195, 206.

[9] 'Vision and Choice in Morality': above, pp. 195ff..

and goes on, 'There are people whose fundamental moral belief is that we all live in the same empirical and rationally comprehensible world and that morality is the adoption of universal and openly defensible rules of conduct. There are other people whose fundamental belief is that we live in a world whose mystery transcends us and that morality is the exploration of that mystery in so far as it concerns each individual. It is only by sharpening the universality model to a point of extreme abstraction that it can be made to cover both views.'[10]

This line of argument would not only convince but also satisfy if morality consisted entirely in deciding what to do. But it also consists, and importantly consists, of feeling obliged to do one thing rather than another. Here at last the crucial weakness in the 'painter' model is uncovered, the reason for the moralist's constant inclination to insist on rules even with loss of flexibility. It is the stringency rather than the universality of rules which is really in question. 'Universalizability' turns out to be a sort of red herring. Undue emphasis upon it not only renders the moralist less able to cope with the creative and the unique, but also diverts his attention from the real nature of his disquiet about the 'painter' model. In the last resort the trouble is not that each painter's task is individual to himself, but that it is not properly analogous to the moral task of doing one's duty.[11]

This may seem a curious criticism in view of the almost notorious compulsion of the artist to create at all costs. A vocation is laid upon him: he cannot just please himself. There is a ruthlessness about him which seems to compare well with the inexorability of morality itself; but the more one emphasizes this inexorability the more one becomes aware that after all it *is* the inexorability of morality itself. Indubitably the artist is a man under a true moral obligation; his artistic integrity is a large part of what morality means to him; but this does not mean that his procedures are specially illuminating in understanding moral obligation, for here analogy is swallowed up in identity. In other words, if it is the stringency of morality that we want to emphasize, the 'painter' model, framed to emphasize the creativeness of choice, has no especial contribution

---

[10] Page 208.
[11] In *Freedom and Reason* (Clarendon Press 1963) Mr Hare is using the concept of 'universalizability' in a somewhat different sense which does emphasize the stringency rather than the universality of rules. They apply, not to 'everyone' but to 'anyone: even me'. But the criticism of Miss Murdoch remains that this usage is really 'sharpening the universality model to a point of extreme abstraction'.

to make. What is wrong is not so much a complete failure to apply but a sort of lack of fit. Loosely we may say that the struggle to bring a masterpiece to perfection is like the struggle to perform an act of heroism, while the filling in of minor details is like the carrying out of daily duties. This will pass muster but it will not clarify anything. The analogy is not doing anything for the concept it is trying to illuminate. It seems, as it were, to remain alongside it without shedding any actual light upon it or bringing any details into sharper focus.

v

This means of course that we have come back to the beginning. The proposed advantage of the 'painter' model, that it does not run into difficulties about the compulsory and the optional, has proved to be precisely its defect. In concentrating on the genuine and useful analogy between moral choice and artistic choice, the fact that both can be creative, the 'painter' model draws away the emphasis from the whole aspect of morality which is not choice at all but claim. It is no wonder then that it does not run into difficulties about which potential claims are truly binding upon us. It avoids the difficulty about the permissible by simply by-passing the question. Yet, in by-passing it, it has led into and opened up a territory which morality cannot be contented to exclude, the territory of what is the best thing to do whether or not we are strictly obliged to do it.[12] The question now is whether this territory can somehow be made accessible to a morality which takes full account of strict obligation.

What, in fact, are we to say about the ideals which go beyond duty? Are they supererogatory, or must the concept of duty be simply enlarged to include them? The moralist who is brought face to face in this way with the problem of the permissible will always be tempted to try to get rid of the concept altogether by translating 'may' willy-nilly into 'must' or 'must not'. Alternatively, in despair at the austerity of this programme, he will be inclined to water down 'must' and 'must not' into 'may'. Neither of these policies is satisfactory. It is much more promising to recognize that we have here come across a fundamental awkwardness in moral theory which is not to be resolved by forcing the data into a ready-made shape. We are indeed concerned with something very similar to a category

[12] Mr Urmson indicates the existence of this territory in his article 'Saints and Heroes' in *Essays in Moral Philosophy*, ed. A. I. Melden, Univ. of Washington Press 1958.

mistake. To say 'As well as being honest and respectable you must be loving' is superficially like 'When you have made progress in elementary mathematics you must go on to calculus'. It is worth asking whether it is not more significantly like 'This pupil has an aptitude for French and Latin but he must work hard at intelligence'.

To enquire whether it is my duty to turn the other cheek as well as paying my debts and telling the truth is a more sophisticated member of the same family as the mistake of enquiring whether I can see the University as well as the colleges. What these have in common is that to answer either 'Yes' or 'No' may mislead, because concepts are being put alongside each other which belong (for different reasons) on distinct levels. To say that we ought, that is that we have a duty, to do more than our duty, can function as a kind of 'useful nonsense' directing our attention to this discontinuity.

The lower level is the level of a rule-morality. Some will want to emphasize that it is basic, others that it is inferior. Its characteristic concept is the idea of fairness, of what may in justice be required of people; and of course the idea of 'universalizability' is very much at home here. It is essential to recognize that both the optional and the compulsory belong on this level, for if one can talk meaningfully about just demands one can also talk meaningfully about unjust demands. The line which demarcates the limits of what is required of one is the very same line as the boundary of the optional. The one concept defines the other, and neither makes sense if one is denied.

To leave either behind can only be achieved by leaving both behind; but it is an empirical fact that this can be done. The moral lives of human beings simply are not in total bondage to fairness and unfairness. There is a sphere in which the whole question of what is and what is not permissible can be unselfconsciously transcended: the sphere of live personal relationships. It is not that the boundary between the optional and the compulsory is re-drawn, but that people are not always obliged to live on the frontier. There are certain contexts, not exceptional but characteristically human, in which people do commonly behave in ways which go well beyond what a rule-morality could reasonably require of them, and take no credit for doing so.

A three-cornered comparison may explain the position best. First, ordinary duty requires, for example, that one should not tell lies. Secondly, one may find oneself under a stricter obligation which is still an obligation of the same sort. One may have given a promise, or one may have a debt to pay. Even a good resolution privately made can give rise to a duty which once accepted fits in alongside one's other duties as binding in the same sense as they are. But thirdly, once one is in a personal relationship one is exposed to a claim not just stricter than the claim of duty but different in kind. To recognize it at all is to recognize it in a different way from the lower-level claims which are compulsory or optional. It is to respond to it rather than to conform to it.

The lower-level claims of course remain valid. For example, a husband and wife owe each other duties in a perfectly straightforward sense. Legally, they can be sued for restitution of conjugal rights. Morally, they can be accused of telling each other lies or of being selfish. But in so far as their relationship is fully personal, to talk to them about duty is not so much incorrect as irrelevant. The claims which matter between them are not profitably understood in terms of duty. The mutual help, society and comfort that the one ought to have of the other is neither optional, for the word is 'ought' not 'may', nor compulsory, for here to compel is to destroy. This kind of claim makes no sense without the relationship, and within the relationship there is no need to make the claim.

This line of thought may be felt to substitute psychology for ethics. Why should the fact that people are sometimes more, sometimes less able to live morally be held to be relevant to the theory and not only the practice of morality? The interplay of theory and practice is here somewhat intricate. It is not just that people do sometimes for empirical reasons behave better or differently. It is rather that certain situations fundamentally alter what can morally be expected of one. If 'I ought implies I can', a radical enlargement of 'I can' may well engender a radical enlargement of 'I ought'.

To say that personal relationships transcend justice is therefore not a high-falutin' or sentimental piece of moral exhortation but a precise philosophical technicality. From the point of view of justice, personal relationships are 'the transcendent', that which cannot be talked about. That is why we get into acute *logical* difficulties when we try to say that the highest ethics are either fair or unfair. If we want to go on talking sense about justice, we must leave the ethics of personal relationships out altogether. This of course we are not willing to do. We are determined to talk about the transcendent, and for the usual reason: the empirical facts force us to it. We know what we mean by personal relationships because we actually have them: the level above justice has specific empirical content. We can see in practice that justice can be transcended, in the relationships of husbands and wives, parents and children, friends, colleagues, communities; but the essential point is that the relationship comes first and the claim depends upon it. When the relationship is still lacking, to exact the claim is literally unfair.

All this has a most immediate bearing upon Christian ethics. Indeed it can be taken as a lengthy paraphrase of a familiar Pauline text: 'The fruit of the spirit is love, joy, peace, patience, kindness, goodness, faithfulness, gentleness, self-control.'[13] The object of the paraphrase has been to sharpen its blunted meaning. It is not a pious platitude, 'If you are a Christian you should be virtuous', but a piece of accurate moral theory, 'The Christian virtues can be expected to grow as *fruit* of the Christian personal relationship.' To marry, to become a parent, to make friends, is to put oneself morally into a distinctive situation. *A fortiori*, to be made God's children by adoption and grace can be understood as a change of status capable of transforming one's elementary moral categories.

VI

But now a weighty objection presses upon me. I have said that the claims which matter between persons are not profitably understood in terms of duty; but surely if all this is to be applied to Christian ethics it must be applied first and foremost to the claim of God himself, and to say that *this* claim is not profitably understood in terms of duty is surely fantastic. It was after all for its lack of stringency that the 'painter' model eventually had to be left behind. Whatever is compulsory, surely to obey God must be, and if he commands one to be perfect, then to be perfect is surely in the strictest sense one's duty. If, as I have tried to show, the idea of a duty to go beyond duty is a kind of category mistake, then a Christian seems to be confronted with a profound incoherence in his whole moral system.

Part of the trouble here is a failure to take account of God's immanence, by thinking of him as *a* person, among other persons, who might or might not happen to be in relationship with one. To cherish one's wife now is a claim which does not lack stringency, but there was a time when to make her one's wife was simply optional. If God is likewise an individual person, however great, per-

[13] Gal. 5. 22-23 (RSV).

haps we can avoid his claim by never coming into relationship with him at all? To say either that we must or that we need not is not to transcend the optional-compulsory dichotomy but to smuggle it in at a different stage in the argument. What is required, and what, it is fair to point out, does exist in traditional Christianity, is some closer link between God and people, a link which will bring his personal claim to bear upon them as in some way fundamental, not just as one potential claim among many. Now one of the most difficult and often unacceptable parts of standard Christian doctrine is its insistence that God is not strictly speaking *a* person distinct from others but is in some more basic way involved with humanity.[14] Christ is the second Adam; Christians are his Body; they are the branches of the vine; he is potentially 'in' them and they 'in' him; to have dealings with one another is to have dealings with Christ. To approach these difficult doctrines as epistemological problems is apt to be a discouraging enterprise. To approach them from the direction of Christian ethics and consider what light they shed upon the nature of God's claim upon us is a more hopeful way of finding some meaning in them. The Pauline and Johannine theology may begin to seem less remotely metaphysical when it is brought into close relation with the apparent straightforwardness of the ethical teaching of Jesus, with 'Be ye therefore perfect', and 'Inasmuch as ye did it unto one of the least of these ye did it unto me'. To have seen the relevance of the doctrine of divine immanence to a particular problem, the moral problem of our obligation to God, should be at least some help in looking for its significance: a sound logical positivist dictum.

Be that as it may, the real difficulty remains untouched. Grant that God need not be thought of as one person among others, someone we happen to know who might have been a stranger. It is still highly paradoxical and almost offensive to insist that his claim upon us is a personal claim in such a way as to cast doubt on its being a claim of duty. If there is a God, duty to him is surely the duty of duties. Of course this is partly a matter of words. It is simple enough to use the same term 'duty' at both levels, the rule level and the personal relationships level, with a cautious awareness that one is doing this. One can speak without confusion, though also without any particular profundity, of our (high-level) duty to go beyond (low-level) duty. But the verbal question covers up a real problem

---

[14] The writings of C. C. J. Webb are very relevant here; especially *Problems in the Relations of God and Man, God and Personality, Divine Personality and Human Life.*

about the meaning of divine authority and it is as well to make this explicit.

One's 'high-level' duty to God is not so much incorrectly as inadequately characterized as a duty of obedience. To think of it in this way is to miss an opportunity rather than to make a mistake. The only purpose of moving on to the 'higher level' at all is to be able to speak in more personal terms. The higher-level claims are most usefully described not in terms of obedience but of relationship, a kind of commitment of the personality which makes the claiming of obedience irrelevant. If one timidly stops short of this conception of relationship when it is the divine claim one is trying to talk about, one loses a chance to enrich one's understanding of divine authority. Put one's preconceptions about 'obedience' as the basic concept of Christian morals aside for the moment, and one can see that this idea of 'commitment of the personality' when applied to God is not less than obedience but more: it is indeed worship. To reach the concept of worship in this way, not as something specifically theological but as the climax of the kind of commitment we owe to persons is not to belittle it but to give it content. Instead of saying, 'It is our *duty* to worship God because he is Transcendent Being', which sounds like a kind of metaphysical snobbery, we may say rather, 'Personal commitment goes beyond duty, and God is the proper object of the *degree* of personal commitment we call worship because he is Transcendent Person'.

To put it another way, personal relationships are relationships of love, swallowing up not invalidating moral obligation. Christians believe, for reasons which cannot here be gone into, that there is a God with whom one can, and in the last resort must, enter into personal relationship; and that on his side the love is unlimited. This means that his claim is unlimited, but to see what is meant by this is already to have transcended the distinction between the optional and the compulsory.

13

MORAL PRINCIPLES

I. M. Crombie

AN obvious difference between the discussions of moral matters that took place in the ancient world and those which take place among ourselves lies in the emphasis that we tend to put on moral rules, moral principles, moral codes. Whereas the ancients talked about 'the noble' and 'the base', about the *summum bonum*, about virtues and vices, and hardly at all about the principles in accordance with which one ought to act, we tend to talk hardly at all about the former, almost exclusively about the latter. A further feature of contemporary discussions of moral matters, at any rate at certain relatively unsophisticated levels, is that we tend to employ the notions of moral codes and moral principles with an extreme and dangerous vagueness. My purpose in this chapter is to try to examine the notion of moral principles both in order to see how this topic is related to other topics within the field of moral philosophy, and also in order to reiterate some fairly obvious but too often neglected distinctions between different kinds or levels of moral principles. My purpose therefore will be primarily academic, at least in the neutral sense of that word; but, in order to give it a little non-academic interest, I will begin by relating the discussion to a problem of practical relevance with which it is connected. The problem has also the merit of bringing out the two main themes of this essay: (i) What are moral disagreements about? and (ii) What is involved in applying a moral principle?

It is commonly held among Christians that we ought never to do evil that good may come of it. It is said that we cannot foresee the consequences of our actions, and that it is not our duty, nor even our right, to try to bring about situations which we judge to be valuable except when we can do so by performing actions which are praiseworthy or innocent. When circumstances put before us the painful choice between doing on the one hand something which is contrary to the moral law and permitting on the other the occurrence of something morally bad, then, many Christians are inclined to say, we ought not to do the action which is contrary to the moral law. Rather we should obey the moral law, leaving it to the divine wisdom to bring good out of evil; for we cannot search God's purposes, and are not called upon to play providence.

Experience does indeed seem to suggest that those who take it upon themselves to play providence in this way often do more harm than good. But there remains a difficulty in the position stated in the last paragraph. For it presupposes that there exists a set of moral principles—that which was referred to as the moral law—which combine the two characteristics (*a*) that we can know them to be correct, and (*b*) that they prescribe and forbid specific actions in specific circumstances. I cannot maintain that we should never do evil that good may come unless I am in a position to say what counts as doing evil. I cannot moreover in this context define doing evil in terms of the agent's motives. For he who does evil that good may come is of course acting with a laudable motive, namely the desire to produce something good. The 'evil' therefore that he does must be something which is evil whatever the motive from which it is done, and this means, surely, that it must owe its evil quality to the circumstance that it is a breach of some moral principle that one is not justified in breaking. But it does seem to be possible, both from the specifically Christian point of view and otherwise, to question whether there really exist any such principles, or rather whether there exist any principles which are both such that they must never be broken and also such that it is theoretically possible to say with certainty in a given situation that it is this or that action which would constitute a breach of them. Of the moral principles which we most of us accept it seems to be possible to discern roughly two kinds. To the one belong such principles as that one should love one's neighbour, to the other such principles as that one should tell no lies. In the case of the first of these we do not doubt that the principle should always be upheld, but situations arise in which we are uncertain which action best conforms to the principle; in the case of the second we are clear that we would always or almost always be able to say which action would count as telling a lie, less certain that the principle deserves to be upheld in all conceivable sets of circumstances. There seem to be two kinds of rigidity and correspondingly two kinds of elasticity—of interpretation and of application—and it looks as if where we have the one we do not have the other. The principle which is rigid in application (the principle which always applies) is elastic in interpretation in that we do not always know what we must do in order to conform to it; the principle which is rigid in interpretation (the principle whose demands are always more or less unambiguous) seems to be elastic in application in that we are unwilling to say categorically that it ought to be obeyed in all conceivable circumstances. But the principle that we may not do evil that good may come of it seems to require that there exist other moral principles which have both kinds of rigidity. Consider how we should bring home the charge that a man has done an evil action that good may come of it. Let us suppose for example that, in order to prevent the occurrence of a riot which was likely to be costly in lives, he has killed somebody who was in all probability innocent of any riotous intent. (I leave it to the reader to fill in the details of the event; it is idle to try to deny that such situations can occur.) Now if we accuse this man of flouting the always-applicable principle that he should love his neighbour, he will of course deny the charge. He will maintain that what he did saved, in all probability, many innocent lives, and was therefore the action that love required of him in the painful situation in which he was placed. How then was it an evil action that he did? If however we reply that his action was evil[1] because it contravened the principle that one should not take innocent life, he will obviously retort by asking us how we know that this principle is valid in all circumstances. It is not clear that he has failed to do what he certainly ought to have done (namely to love his neighbour); it is clear that he has taken an innocent life, not certain however that this is something that he ought not to have done. How then can we say that he has done evil that good may come of it?

Clearly there is one way of dealing with this problem. This is to say that the Christian revelation contains a set of regulations which are specific enough to guide our conduct, and that what is required of us is that we should keep within these regulations, concerning

---

[1] If we say that a man's action was evil we can still of course allow that it may have been high-minded. Indeed, if we want to say that he did evil that good might come of it, we must allow that it was a high-minded kind of evil; for he did it, *ex hypothesi*, from a laudable motive. It seems to be naïve to deny that there can be high-minded evil actions.

ourselves with the likely consequences of our actions only in those situations in which we have to choose between two or more actions each of which is permitted by the regulations. To help me to choose between innocent actions I may consider which is likely to do most good, but the question whether it is likely on balance to do good is not a question which I may ask in order to determine whether or not an action is innocent. To many Christians a doctrine such as this will doubtless seem excessively legalistic. Whether it is or not is a question which I shall not try to settle, merely observing that if you want to say that there is such a thing as well-intentioned ruth-lessness, and that it is something harmful, you may find it difficult to maintain this if you dismiss this 'legalistic' doctrine out of hand.

So much, then, for the practical issues with which the discussion of moral principles, to which we now turn, is connected. My pur-pose now is to try to separate out the heterogeneous bunch of things that we may have in mind when we speak of moral principles into various rough levels or kinds, and to indicate, roughly once more, the relationship between each of these kinds and the rest of our thought about morals. We shall begin, then, by noticing the exist-ence of what I shall call truistic moral principles. I call them truistic in the sense, approximately, in which the laws of logic are sometimes spoken of as truisms. This does not mean that they are trivial or unimportant, but that they are indispensable and there-fore in one way unhelpful. A man cannot think logically without conforming to the truisms of logic, but this does very little to tell him what to think. One can get no help towards the solution of problems from the laws of logic, simply because all coherent solu-tions must be equally in accordance with them. In a rather similar way one cannot think morally without accepting certain moral truisms, and yet in one sense a truism will never tell one what to do.

The kind of moral truisms that we are concerned with and which are, so to speak, the presuppositions of moral thought, must not be confused with a different and uninteresting kind of truism of which 'A man is under some obligation to try to pay his debts' is or may be an example. For if I am using the word 'debt' in such a way that I should not call something a debt unless I thought that the debtor was under some obligation to try to pay it, then clearly it is logically necessary that a man must try to pay his debts. This however throws no light at all on the question whether he ought to try to pay what the law would call his debts. Again if 'murder' and 'lie' are being used to mean 'morally unjustifiable homicide' and 'morally unjustifiable falsehood' respectively, then plainly it is logically necessary that I must do no murder and tell no lies. It is because this tells us nothing about whether we may take life or tell falsehoods (for any doubt that we had on these heads persists in the form of a doubt about how to apply the terms 'murder' and 'lie'), that this kind of moral truism is uninteresting.

An example (perhaps *the* example) of the kind of truistic moral principles that we are interested in is what is often called the 'golden rule'—'Do as you would be done by', or in Kant's formulation: 'So act that you can at the same time will that the maxim of your act should be a universal law of nature.' In other words it is a truistic moral principle that I may not do to someone else an act which I would not allow to be legitimate if he were in my position and I in his. I cannot, for example, legitimately pursue my own interests in any way in which I am not prepared to allow that others who are circumstanced as I am may legitimately pursue theirs. This is a presupposition of moral thought.

It may be objected by some that the golden rule cannot be a moral truism. For if it were, they will say, the man who does not abide by the golden rule when he is deciding what to do is not thinking morally—is not asking what he ought to do in the moral sense of 'ought'. But the golden rule is altruistic in that it enjoins equal respect for the rights of others; and a principle of altruism cannot be a truistic moral principle, because egoism is a moral outlook, albeit a deplorable one. The man who is thinking egoistically about what to do and the man who is thinking altruistically may both be thinking morally. Any principle therefore which is a presupposition of moral thinking must be neutral between egoistic moral thinking and altruistic. It will be instructive to consider this a little further.

It seems to be essential to the notion of morality that a moral principle must be something in deference to which I sometimes refrain from doing what I would otherwise have been inclined to do. A moral principle must be potentially capable of conflicting with inclination, and reflection about morals is at bottom reflection about what sorts of things can reasonably be preferred above inclination. It follows from this that the principle, 'Always do whatever you are inclined to do' cannot be called a moral principle.[2]

---

[2] There is a certain ambiguity here. 'Always do whatever you are inclined to do' might be a piece of moral advice, for example if it were put forward by a psychiatrist who was

This conclusion seems acceptable. 'Anything goes' does indeed represent an outlook, and an outlook which is alternative to the moral outlook, but it does not represent a moral outlook. Morality is nothing if it is not the preference of one thing over another; and to say that no preferences can be made is not to say something which arises out of the attempt to make such preferences; it is to deny the legitimacy of the enterprise.

'Anything goes' then is not the expression of a moral outlook but a manifesto of the speaker's contempt for morality. Can we also say that egoism is not a moral outlook, as it seemed that we should have to do if we wanted to maintain that the golden rule is a presupposition of morality? It might be argued that we cannot. The egoist, it might be said, can clearly hold principles in deference to which he restrains his impulses; he may for example inhibit his desire to tell a potential benefactor just how ridiculous he finds him. It might be replied that no inhibiting of impulses which is done merely in accordance with the egoistic principle of furthering my own interests counts as moral inhibiting. There are prudential policies as well as moral principles, and it is in deference to his prudential policies, not, if he is consistent, to moral principles, that the egoist refrains from doing what he might otherwise have done. To this it might be retorted that the true theoretical egoist (as opposed to the man who just happens to be selfish) believes that he is entitled to act as he does, and acts with a clear conscience. Therefore, it can be said, his belief that he is entitled to neglect the interests of others counts as a moral belief, and the restraints which he imposes upon himself in the name of the more efficient furthering of his own interests count as moral restraints.

What are we to say? We may begin perhaps by saying this. It would seem that the proposition that a man is entitled to pursue his own interests without regard for those of others may be put forward in either of two very different ways. It may be put forward firstly as a version of 'Anything goes'. That is to say, the man who says that he is entitled to pursue his own interests without regard to those of others may, in effect, be rejecting the whole notion that there are some things that we are entitled to do and other things that we are not entitled to do. He does not believe that there are moral obligations, but that consideration of the interests of others is

---

frightened of the effects of inhibiting our impulses. But in that interpretation there would be something that we might have been inclined to do and that the principle would be telling us not to do, namely to inhibit our inclinations.

not among them; rather he denies that there are any moral obligations. This type of egoism, therefore, is not a moral outlook but a
rejection of morality. But the doctrine that a man is entitled to
pursue his own interests without restraint need not be intended in
this sense. Rather the meaning may be that each man is in fact
morally entitled to pursue his own interests, that there is nothing
in the demands of morality, properly understood, that requires one
man to consider another's interests. It would be difficult to deny
that this is a moral outlook, however deplorable a moral outlook
one may judge it to be.

But the next point to notice is that egoism of this kind does not
conflict with the golden rule. 'Do as you would be done by' does not
enjoin what we would ordinarily recognize as benevolent conduct.
Its altruism is not generosity or kindness, but merely a sort of
impartiality. For it is open to an upholder of the principle also to
believe that no good is done, on balance, by benevolent conduct,
that harsh competition is best for the human race, and that concern
with the welfare of anybody but oneself is an unwarrantable im-
pertinence. So long as such a man is willing to accept tough treatment from others as legitimate, he may use it towards others without infringing the principle that one should do as one would be
done by. The man therefore who does not accept the golden rule is
the man who, when considering how to treat Jones, allows no force
to the question: 'If you were in Jones's position and somebody
treated you as you are proposing to treat Jones, what would you
say about that?'

It is now possible to see how much is involved in treating the
golden rule as a moral truism or a presupposition of morality. For
the man whose reflections upon what to do do not conform to the
golden rule is not reflecting on the questions what men in general
ought to do, how they ought to treat each other, what ends they
ought to pursue. For any process of reflection which does concern
itself with such questions must lead to answers of the form: 'Any
man in circumstances C should always do X.' Since the rights that
I claim are things that I claim that men should allow me, and since
I am myself an example of 'any man' (and Jones is another), I am
forced, if I reflect on what men in general ought to do, to allow
that what I claim ought to be done *to* me ought also (in, of course,
appropriate circumstances) to be done *by* me, and that what may
not be done to *me* may not, if our situation is similar, be done to
Jones. The man therefore who does not conform to the golden rule

in trying to decide what to do does not reflect on what men in general ought to do. Whether his reflections are to be classed as moral reflections can now harmlessly be dismissed as a verbal question. We may observe further that, if we decided that they could not be so classed, we should have the weight of usage on our side. The predominant use of the word 'morality' is one according to which conformity to the golden rule is essential to morality.

We can now see in what sense the golden rule is truistic and also in what sense it is unhelpful. It is truistic because it employs the notion of moral obligation ('one *ought to* do as one would be done by') and employs it in a manner such that to employ it otherwise is to mis-employ it. It is unhelpful because, as we have seen, to subscribe to the golden rule leaves us almost totally uncommitted on the question how to behave.

The golden rule lives in a very exalted and rarefied logical atmosphere, and there are many steps between it and the settling of practical questions. There are perhaps a few other principles (about seriousness of purpose, for example, or the cultivation of talents, or the adaptation of means to ends) which inhabit the same altitude. We shall leave them there and come a little down the mountain to the level at which we meet with principles which are still very 'open' and 'elastic', and therefore very uncertain guides to action, but less open and elastic than the golden rule. Our example of such a principle will be what we will call the principle of benevolence, namely that a man ought always to love his neighbour as himself, where this is taken to mean that he ought always to attach importance to the welfare of those affected by his actions, even as he attaches it to his own. With regard to this principle we will ask the somewhat misleading question how we can get from the golden rule to the principle of benevolence. This is a misleading question if it is taken to mean that we either do or should journey in thought down the mountain from the golden rule to the principle of benevolence. It is a question that is worth asking however because it serves to indicate what are the other issues a decision on which has been (explicitly or implicitly) taken by the man who upholds the principle of benevolence. In order to answer it let us see what alternatives there are to the principle of benevolence which can put forward an equally good claim to the status of moral principles.

An obvious example of an alternative to the principle of benevolence is the attitude of one who believes, in a quasi-Nietzschian manner, in the effectiveness of competition and strife in producing the more valuable human qualities, which he takes to consist in strength, independence and the like. If this man concedes that the excellence of others is of equal importance with his own, and is prepared to allow that others may do to him what he believes he may do to them, then his outlook is a moral outlook, conforms to the golden rule, and is an alternative to the principle of benevolence. For he may well not at all concede that it is his business actively to concern himself either with gratifying the desires or even with furthering the excellence of others. It is open to him to believe, firstly, that it is not good for us to have our desires gratified except when we achieve their gratification in our own strength, and secondly that no man can effectively further the excellence of any one but himself. He will allow that it is right for Jones to do A if the doing of A is likely to strengthen some desirable quality in Jones, but he will not necessarily also allow that it is incumbent upon himself to help, or even to permit, Jones to do A. 'Let Jones', he may well say, 'try to do A, and let me try to stop him. He has every right to try, indeed it would be feeble of him not to; and I have every right to try to stop him. It is from conflicts such as these between men that valuable human qualities are developed.'

We can contrast, then, these two men, the upholder of the principle of benevolence and the believer in jungle law. It is plain that both can be morally serious, that both accept the golden rule; but they interpret it in different ways. What makes them interpret it in different ways, or, if you prefer, what other differences are involved in their differing interpretations? Two come readily to mind. Firstly they probably differ about which human qualities are valuable (or about the order of importance which obtains between the various valuable qualities); and secondly they probably differ, to some extent at any rate, about the methods by which valuable human qualities can be cultivated.[3] So far then we have expressed the contrast between these two men in terms of a conflict of principles, the principle of benevolence and the principle of competition. We see now however that the contrast could equally well be expressed as a contrast between different answers to the questions what human qualities are most worth cultivating and how they can

---

[3] It is likely, for example, that each of them attaches considerable importance to the virtue of courage, and therefore it is likely that they disagree about how in fact this virtue can be produced. For if the upholder of the principle of benevolence came to believe that in a benevolent world there would be no opportunity of acquiring this virtue, that might tend to shake his faith in the principle.

most effectively be cultivated. Principles therefore of this highly general kind could be regarded as concise formulations of answers to questions of the type we have just indicated.

It may be thought that the quasi-Nietzschian upholder of the principle of competition, whom we have contrasted with the upholder of the principle of benevolence, is an uncommon or perhaps even an unreal man. Nevertheless, even if he is in fact an ideal limit, it is obviously possible to devise a whole series of different positions coming in between the two extremes, and some of these positions have certainly been occupied. It seems difficult to determine what precisely was believed by Plato and Aristotle about my duty to my neighbour, but it seems likely that it was something a good deal less than that I should love him as myself. My prime duty is to try to make myself something admirable. Certainly, being a social animal, I need friends, and I must treat them generously. To be too ungenerous is to fail to make myself something admirable, and it is to fail to minister to my own needs. But perhaps no more is required than this. Whether or not this was actually the view of the Greek philosophers, it is clear that it is a possible view and that it does not agree with the principle that one should love one's neighbour as oneself in the interpretation which we have put upon that phrase.

This latter principle, then, is not a presupposition of morality (for there can be moral outlooks alternative to it). Rather it determines one morality among others, and is therefore not completely open. It is however still pretty open, and we can ask now how we can move from this to something less open, to something which is nearer to being a guide to action. Or, to put the same question in a different way, we can ask what is involved in embracing one version of this principle rather than another.

The question at issue is, What is to count as loving one's neighbour? Since we can safely say that to love a man is to be concerned for his welfare we can equally well say that the question is, What is a man's welfare? Is my neighbour's welfare determined by what he wants, by what will make him happy, or by that which he ought to want (i.e. that, contentment with which would be admirable)? Do I love my neighbour if I do all I can to further his wishes, comfort, and aspirations, while remaining indifferent to the question whether their attainment makes him morally laudable? Alternatively do I love him if my zeal is only for his moral character without regard for his happiness? Is the correct compromise that I should care for his happiness just so far as it can be achieved without impairing the happiness of others? Can we indeed say that moral laudability consists in the pursuit of one's own happiness so far as this does not impair that of others, so that to be concerned for my neighbour's happiness and to be concerned for his moral laudability do not conflict?

The fact that questions such as these arise, and can be answered in different ways, means that the course of action which will follow from the principle that a man should love his neighbour is to a large extent undetermined by the principle itself. Once again they can be represented as questions about what ends are worth pursuing, what qualities worth fostering; and these questions in turn provoke questions about what can be effectively pursued and fostered. Consider the following. A man might set a relatively low value on moral excellence. He might hold that certain qualities, courage for example, or chastity, are morally laudable in the sense that it is natural and proper to admire those in whom these qualities are to be found, rather as it is natural and proper to admire Bach's B Minor Mass or Newton's contributions to physics. But he might also hold that, desirable as it is that such excellent qualities should from time to time arise, the cost in happiness of too zealous an attempt at fostering them is not worth paying. Such a man, judging that moral laudability is an end which is worth pursuing only with limited ardour, would hold that the love of my neighbour consists chiefly in concern for his happiness, and in concern for his moral qualities only in so far as they are likely to affect his happiness. To this man one might oppose the man who believes that the pursuit of happiness is unworthy, or self-stultifying, or both, and who judges that love of one's neighbour involves a primary concern for his spiritual welfare, and only a limited interest in his happiness. It is evident, from the comparison of these two men and of the many others whom we might delineate and set beside them, that beliefs about the nature and conditions of human life are going to have a bearing at this stage. This is one of the places, for example, at which a belief in God is likely to make a difference to a man's ethical outlook, because it is likely to affect the manner in which he answers the questions that we have just been considering. It is evident also that the questions which arise at this stage involve a perplexing admixture of factual and evaluative elements. Some questions are fairly straightforwardly factual, for example the question how far it is possible for one man profitably to concern himself with the moral welfare of another. Is it the case that public opinion, moral suasion and legal enactments can have powerful effects for good and evil in human character? This is a fairly straightforwardly factual question. But the question what qualities are to be valued is less straightforward. To set a value on something involves deciding (factually) that it is attainable and that its attainment gives satisfaction, but it also involves deciding (evaluatively) that the satisfaction that it gives is worthy. The whole matter is extremely perplexing. Fortunately however, it is not our purpose to try to answer such questions, but only to indicate the number and variety of those which arise when one is trying to determine what interpretation to put upon the principle that I should love my neighbour as myself.

Clearly we can come a stage further down the mountain by supplying these questions with an answer, and thus arriving at a relatively specific version of the principle of benevolence. For example we might take the man of whom the following things are true. He attaches importance both to moral well-being and to happiness, but holds that there is no gap between them; that is to say, he holds that that which ministers to moral well-being ministers also in the long run to happiness. He believes however that there is a gap between happiness and the gratification of desire, or in other words he holds that it may often be the case that a man cannot attain happiness unless some of his desires are frustrated. With these beliefs, our man will accept one among many specific versions of the principle of benevolence. He will hold that when I am considering whether something ought to be done I must ask myself what effect the action is likely to have on the happiness and on the moral character of those whom it affects but that I need not concern myself with the question whether it will give them what they want. This gives him a relatively precise principle of choice in the sense that it tells him what things he ought to try to determine when he is choosing how to act.

It gives him something relatively precise, but what it gives him is still a *principle* of choice, and not what I shall call a *definite action-rule*. It is clear that moral codes often contain definite action-rules (or it will be clear, when we have said what these are); and we shall want to ask how we arrive at such rules, and into what kinds they may be divided. It will be necessary, shortly, to try to indicate what sort of thing is meant by a definite action-rule. Before we start on this, however, let me observe that in going direct to definite action-rules, we are sliding rapidly down the mountain-side, overlooking in our precipitate descent many layers of principles of choice which are at once more specific than the specific version of the principle of benevolence that we have just been considering and also less specific than definite action-rules. Some of these (for example 'Never ill-treat a stranger') might be thought of as *relatively* definite action-rules. In practice moral codes probably contain not very many definite action-rules as I shall define these, their place being taken by action-rules which are only relatively definite. However this is a complication which for our purposes we can ignore, since much of what I shall say about definite action-rules applies with minor modifications to any rules which are definite enough to act as moderately efficient guides to action. Our problem is approximately this. People hold, for example, principles such as that I should love my neighbour (which is not a definite action-rule) and principles such as that I should not commit adultery (which is). Now what is the relationship between principles of these two kinds? It is possible to argue that members of the second kind are subordinate to those of the first. Thus it could be said that adultery is wrong because it will never or almost never be, overall, an implementation of the principle that one should love one's neighbour. Equally however it could be argued that adultery is to be avoided not for that reason, or not only for that reason, but rather because it is, in itself, wrong. It might indeed further be argued that we could never ascertain how to implement the principle of benevolence unless we knew that certain things were right and certain others wrong, for we could never, for example, tell whether we were doing a man good or evil if we could not know whether the things that we were helping him to do were things that it is right or wrong for a man to do. If I help a man to seduce his friend's wife, am I advancing his welfare? Therefore, it could be said, decisions about the rightness and wrongness of particular kinds of actions are certainly not derivable from general principles such as that of benevolence, and if we are ever to know how to act we need to know about the rightness and wrongness of particular kinds of actions. The question arises therefore how we could know things of this kind. In order to consider this question it will be convenient to oversimplify matters and to suppose that we can (as indeed to *some* extent we can) separate actions into what I shall call definite kinds, and take decisions about the rightness or wrongness of any action of some definite kind.

In order to make it a little clearer what I mean by 'definite action-rules' and 'actions of a definite kind' it will be necessary to rush in upon some very difficult territory. To survey it in a tolerable way would delay us far too long, and I shall beg as many questions as I shall raise. The problems to which we shall fail to do justice are more or less those discussed by Miss Anscombe in her admirable book *Intention*. Very roughly, then, let us say that there exist many phrases which can be used to describe human actions (by which I mean things that men deliberately do), and which have the following characteristic, namely that in order to determine whether what I am doing conforms to one of these descriptions not very much of the remoter significance of my action has to be taken into account, and in particular it is not necessary to settle any questions of a moral kind. We will call such phrases *neutral action-descriptions*.[4] To determine whether Jones is honouring his father it may be necessary to ask whether, in the circumstances, Jones Senior ought to be treated by his son in the way in which he is being treated; and therefore 'honouring his father' is *not* a neutral action-description. To determine whether Jones is working on the Sabbath, however, it is not necessary to settle any moral question (or so it was thought by the scribes at any rate) and therefore 'working on the Sabbath' is a neutral action-description. So are 'writing his name', 'signing a cheque' and 'forging his brother's name'.

The last example deserves some comment. If the question whether a certain neutral action-description fits a certain action cannot depend upon the decision of a moral question, then a neutral action-description cannot imply moral approval or condemnation. It might be thought therefore that 'forging a signature' cannot be a neutral action-description, since forgery is both illegal and also commonly disapproved of. This would be a mistake however. Even a man who believes that one ought never in any circumstances to forge a signature must allow that 'Forgery is sometimes innocent' is not a contradiction in terms, from which it follows that '*wrongful* counterfeiting' cannot be part of the meaning of 'forgery'. We shall perhaps tend to shy away from the word 'forging' as a description of what seem to us to be innocent cases of counterfeiting, but we cannot refuse to admit that the description is ap-

---

[4] If a man sends de Gaulle a box of tennis balls he may be trying to provoke a war; but 'trying to provoke a war' will not be a neutral action-description because it takes too much of remoter significance into account. One cannot try to provoke a war without doing *something* (in this case sending de Gaulle tennis balls) and it is the phrase which answers the question what the man did that provides the neutral action-description.

plicable, in the way in which, for example, we could refuse to admit that the description 'cruelty' is applicable to some punishment which we deemed it morally necessary to impose. 'Cruelty' implies moral condemnation; 'forgery' at most suggests it. We can guess that the speaker disapproves of Jones' action if the speaker says that Jones forged a signature; but he has not told us that he does, and we have no right to complain if he continues with something like: '. . . and I think he was right to do so'. It is perhaps worth adding that 'forging' and 'cruelty' are comparatively clear cases; the one clearly does not, the other clearly does, imply a moral attitude. But there are other words which are less clear, for example 'lying'. Some people seem to prefer to withhold the description 'lie' from a falsehood which they deem to be innocent, thus showing that in their usage 'lie' implies a moral condemnation; others do not seem to follow this practice. There will therefore be words (like 'lying') about which we shall not be able to lay down without qualification either that they can or that they cannot occur in a neutral action-description.

It is clear that we are skating on thin ice, but it is perhaps also sufficiently clear what I mean by 'a neutral action-description'. I shall say next that all those actions which conform to some one neutral action-description constitute a *definite kind* of action. Acts of forgery therefore are actions of a definite kind, acts of cruelty are not. Acts of cruelty must be wrongful, and Smith and Jones may disagree about whether Brown did a cruel act without disagreeing about what he did. When it has been established, therefore, under which neutral action-descriptions Brown's act falls (for example that it was a beating of a dog), it is still not settled[5] whether it was a cruel act; in this sense membership of the class of cruel acts is 'indefinite', and this is why cruel acts do not constitute a definite kind. On the basis of this we can proceed to an informal definition of a *definite action-rule* by saying that a definite action-rule enjoins or forbids any action of some definite kind. (Thus 'it is wrong to forge a signature' is a definite action-rule; 'one should honour one's parents' is not.) And since, if I enjoin A, I forbid the omission of A, and *vice versa*, we can shorten 'enjoin or forbid' to 'forbid'.[6] A

[5] All this needs a great deal of qualification. For our present purposes it will perhaps do to say that a sufficiently lengthy factual description of an act may settle to all intents and purposes that it was a cruel act; but what is *settled to all intents and purposes* is still not *settled*, as I am here using the word, so long as it is logically possible for someone to disagree.

[6] This is to be taken as a mere device for abbreviation. If it were taken otherwise problems would arise which I do not intend to try to deal with.

definite action-rule then forbids the performance of any action of some definite kind.

I observed at the beginning of this chapter that moral principles seemed to fall apart into those which seem always to be valid but which are elastic in interpretation, and those which are not necessarily always valid but which are rigid in interpretation. We can now see more clearly why this is so. Principles which are not always valid but which are rigid in interpretation are definite action-rules. They are rigid in interpretation precisely because it is a definite question whether a certain action is or is not of a certain definite kind. Beating a dog is beating a dog, and if that is what Brown was doing, that is what he was doing. I may be mistaken of course, but Brown will know. They are not necessarily always valid precisely because we do not have to settle whether or not Brown was acting rightly before we can say that he was beating his dog. 'Beating his dog' therefore implies no moral condemnation (though it may suggest it), and for that reason the principle that one should never beat a dog can always be challenged. The point might be put as follows. Where a description is such that we retain freedom of manoeuvre over the question whether to apply it in a particular instance, there we have no qualms over allowing that we shall approve (or condemn) everything to which we decide to apply it. Where however we have no freedom of manoeuvre in the matter of application, there we naturally want to retain freedom to approve or disapprove, as may seem best to us, of some action to which, as we have to concede, the description certainly applies. I have no hesitation in saying that one ought never to do a cruel act, simply because I know that if I come across some case of severity, which I know to be extreme but believe to be necessary, I can and shall withhold the description 'cruelty' from it. I hesitate to say that one ought never to tell a deliberate falsehood because I hesitate to give away in advance my right to approve of doing what would be unquestionably just this in some situation which might conceivably arise. So long as I am allowed to boggle over *whether* the cap fits, I need not hesitate to condemn *whatever* the cap fits. If I am denied the former liberty I may think it prudent to demand the latter.

It is clear that many people are willing to assert definite action-rules; they form a conspicuous part of what are often called 'moral codes'. It is clear also that the man who subscribes to a definite action-rule is apparently willing to forego both the liberties of which we have just spoken. On the other hand it is also clear that

definite action-rules are subscribed to in at least two different ways.
To many people a definite action-rule is acceptable merely as a rule
of thumb. That is to say, they subscribe to the principle that one
should not tell falsehoods because, they think, the right decision
in situations where one might tell a falsehood is usually the decision
not to. 'Tell no falsehoods' is therefore a good rule to give to children and to others who cannot judge, simply because it will usually
be found to lead to the right action. Others however would subscribe to the principle much more energetically than this. They
hold that it is not simply that when a man tells a falsehood it will
usually, as a matter of fact, be the case that he has adopted the wrong
solution to his problem, but rather that always, or almost always, to
tell a falsehood is to do something which is wrong *simply because
it is telling a falsehood*. Both of these ways of subscribing to definite
action-rules give rise to problems. If I treat them merely as rules
of thumb which tend to give the right answer I seem to imply that I
have some independent means of telling which answer is the right
one. If I think it is usually best to put the milk in before the tea, I
presumably think this gives the best results, and determine which
results are best by the independent means of tasting the stuff. But
is it really plausible to say that I have come to learn that truth-
telling usually gives the best results without, in coming to learn
this, making any use of the principle that it is in itself good that the
truth should be told? But the other side of this principle is that it is
in itself wrong, at any rate to some extent, to tell falsehoods. If, on
the other hand, I say that it is in itself wrong to tell falsehoods, then
it seems that I claim to have some means of prejudging what will
be the moral quality of an act of a certain kind no matter what may
be the situation in which the act arises. And this is liable to the
objection that it seems to be unsatisfactory to suppose that we can
determine the moral quality of an action except by considering it
in the light of the situation to which it was a response.

Perhaps we can get a little more light on the question whether it
is adequate to treat such definite action-rules as we may subscribe
to merely as rules of thumb if we notice that there is more than one
kind of definite action-rule. There are, first, those which we may
describe as *factitious*. By a factitious action-rule or principle I mean
a principle which a man thinks it right to uphold without thinking
that it would be (apart from the principle) wrong to do the things
which the principle forbids. An obvious example of such a principle
is: that one should drive on the left. Nobody who, in England,

upholds this principle supposes that there is anything inherently wrong with the act of driving on the right. The point is that there are cogent reasons for standardizing the rule of the road, that this is the standard which prevails among us, and that this is why it should be upheld. A slightly different kind of factitious principle can be illustrated by the rule that doctors must not advertise. If one accepts that doctors may charge for their services, one may wonder why they may not advertise them. No depravity, one feels, would necessarily be at work in the doctor who wished to advertise. The rule is upheld not because it is thought that the activities which it outlaws are in themselves morally deplorable activities, but because it is felt that a better situation is produced if such activities are forbidden. These two examples of factitious principles may seem rather unimportant ones. Reflection suggests however that a substantial part of the moral code of many people is in fact composed of such principles. Many for example would hold that the rules of sexual behaviour are of this kind. They would, perhaps, be unwilling to claim that there is anything intrinsically superior in monogamy over polygamy, though they would be willing to say that one ought to conform to the rule established in one's own society. Monogamy to such a man would be analogous to the rules of the road, and its detailed regulation could develop in a similar way. When, for example, an accepted practice of flashing lights has shown itself to be workable, it becomes a custom to which it is wise to conform; similarly when conventions of divorce have established themselves and shown themselves to be practicable, they can then be adopted as new regulations by which the institution of marriage can be governed and to which the law should be conformed. Others again might hesitate to say that they found anything intrinsically wrong in telling lies (any more than in self-advertisement by doctors), but would assert that they believed that a better situation is created if each man can have confidence in the word of another, and that for that reason lying should be outlawed.

It is clear that, if something is put forward as a factitious principle, then what we must do to decide whether it is a good or bad one is firstly to question whether it does in fact achieve what it is said to achieve, and secondly to assess the moral value of that which it renders possible. Clearly also this value may be of either or both of two roughly distinguishable kinds. What the principle renders possible may simply be something that all or most men want (as they want to travel in safety), or it may be something which the upholder of the principle believes to have a claim upon our allegiance as moral beings. Thus the mutual trust which a ban on lying serves to foster may well be thought not merely to be something convenient, as safety on the roads is convenient, but something which we *ought* to want even if, as it happens, we do not want it.

So much for factitious principles. They are more important than they seem at first sight. Many however would claim to uphold principles which are definite action-rules but which are not factitious, in that the actions which they forbid are actions which are inherently wrong. Before we ask in what ways actions of some definite kind could be inherently wrong it will be convenient to consider an objection to the whole notion that there can be such a thing as inherent wrongness attaching to a definite kind of action. This is the objection that, since evil is always a matter of motivation, it cannot be the case that any definite kind of action is inherently wrong. For wrong actions are all and only those actions which are ill-intentioned, and ill-intentioned actions do not constitute a definite kind.

Now the man who argues thus may seriously intend what he says, along with all its corollaries. Perhaps the most embarrassing of these corollaries is that I am always, surely, wasting my time when I consider what I ought to do, except in so far as I am merely trying to ascertain the facts of my situation. For if we assume that I can, consistently with such a view, choose some action as that which I ought to do (i.e. if we assume that 'what I ought to do' retains a meaning now that whatever is well-intentioned is morally sound), then *whatever* I choose will be right, since its motive will be laudable; for I chose it as that which I ought to do. This makes it difficult to see what a man might be doing when he was trying to decide which action would be right. However, it is possible that an upholder of the view that no actions are wrong but those which are ill-intentioned might be prepared to accept this consequence. It is also possible, though, that such a man is misled by an easy and dangerous confusion. This is the confusion between the point that one cannot entirely think ill of a man's action if he has acted sincerely for what he believes to be the best, and the point that one cannot say that he has made a morally erroneous choice. The first of these points seems obviously sensible, the second seems to be plainly disputable; and it is certainly disputed. It is very widely held that, although action-rules are of course not the whole of the moral story, they are nevertheless a legitimate and necessary part of it. To see the validity of this it may be useful to distinguish between two different kinds of wrongness or evilness which we may find in an action. One of them has no connection with the question to what definite kind the action belongs; the other may well have. There is a certain kind of evilness which can infect even the innocent actions of evil men, just as there is a goodness which is often to be found in the outrageous actions of the saintly. If there have been inquisitors who have persecuted with humility and charity, so there have also been men whose sanctimoniousness and other defects of character have rendered obnoxious their corporal works of mercy. This does not mean that persecution is to be applauded nor works of mercy discouraged. This kind of goodness and evilness has little to do with the nature of what is done, much to do with the character of the man who does it. If my character is such that it takes the bloom off whatever I do, then the fact that my visit to my sick relative had something obnoxious about it does not mean that I ought not to have visited him; for there might surely have been the same obnoxious character about whatever I did instead. And if my character is such that it puts a bloom on whatever I do, this does not mean that I am as well employed robbing banks as visiting the sick. When we are discussing the topic of what we ought to do, we are not discussing the topic of qualities of character, or of virtues and vices; and *vice versa*. This does not mean that the two topics are disconnected—they are not; but neither should be allowed to shout the other down. Even the good man sometimes asks what he ought to do (*ama et fac quod vis* is an epigram), and sometimes, incidentally, gets the wrong answer. The topic of moral rules belongs to the topic of what a man is considering when he is trying to decide what to do. At that point he cannot be directly considering what sort of character to have.

When we say, therefore, that some definite kinds of action can be inherently wrong we are not imputing to every action of those kinds that form of evil quality which may infect, as we saw, even the innocent actions of evil men. We are not denying that actions of those kinds may have been done by the saintliest of men with the highest of motives; we are suggesting that, if they have been, then the agents were guilty of moral error. We can return therefore to the point that many men subscribe to definite action-rules which they do not regard as factitious, because they believe that the actions forbidden by such rules are inherently wrong, inherently not-to-be-done. We can go on to ask in what this inherent wrongness or not-to-be-done-ness might consist.

I do not intend to attempt a full answer to this question. A sketch must suffice, and we may begin by observing that it seems likely that the grounds, on which any action of some definite kind may be thought to be inherently wrong, are likely to be divisible into those which are connected with what such an action is likely to lead to, and those which are connected with what such an action is likely to proceed from—with 'consequences' on the one hand and something which we will for the moment call 'motives' on the other. It may be objected however that there can be no difference between saying that some action-rule is factitious and saying that the actions that it forbids are inherently wrong because of their consequences; for we said that the reason why we uphold a factitious principle is that we think that the consequences of outlawing what it outlaws are bene-ficial; and this is the same as to say that the consequences of the actions that it forbids are undesirable. This, however, is not entirely true. The question is whether the undesirable consequences are to such an extent part of the action that it is impossible for a reason-able man to will the action without willing the consequences. Factitious principles are those which forbid actions to which this does not apply. (The distinction is clearly not hard and fast.) Thus if I deliberately hurt somebody, the pain which I cause is a conse-quence of my action, but hardly one which I could claim not to have foreseen. If a doctor advertises his services he may well fail to see what harm he is doing. This is why a morally enlightened and sensitive man may still have to learn the factitious principles which apply to some sphere with which he is unfamiliar—for instance the 'ethics' of some profession which he is entering. I must know that it is wrong to inflict needless pain (unless of course I hold a general theory which makes me think otherwise); I may well not know that anything objectionable is happening when an employer in an industry which is contracting departs from the principle: 'first in, last out'. This is because this latter principle is factitious.

It is, then, possible to think that any action of some definite kind is inherently wrong on the ground that I dislike the consequences to which any such action directly leads; and an action-rule forbid-ding actions of such a kind need not be called factitious. The grounds on which I dislike the consequences may be various, with the same sort of variation as we have noticed before. The conse-quences may be simply objectionable in the sense that anybody *would* object to them, or they may be morally objectionable in the sense that anybody *ought to* object to them. What causes pain is objectionable in the first sense, what causes envy is objectionable in the second. But it may well be held that when I say that any action of some definite kind would be inherently wrong, I do not usually or primarily mean that its direct consequences are morally unacceptable. When I say that acts of ostentation are deplorable acts I do not primarily mean that envious or resentful feelings are among their direct consequences, and that these are objectionable.

What, then, do I mean? Probably something rather to the effect that no man who thought of his fellow-men as he ought to think of them would wish to indulge in acts of ostentation—or that if, being human, he did so wish, he would also wish to inhibit this wish. In fact I think ill of the motive from which acts of ostentation proceed, in the sense that I think that such acts would seldom or never be done by a man whose moral outlook was entirely sound, whose ends were those which it is morally laudable to pursue, and whose system of priorities between his ends was what it ought to be in order to do justice to their relative importance. This is, I think, an important source of the notion of inherent wrongness, and one which has had too little attention from moral philosophers. The example with which we introduced it—that of acts of ostentation—is not perhaps a very convincing example of acts likely to be thought inherently wrong. But there are other much more important examples that can readily be thought of—for instance the institution of slavery.[7] It is probably a little naïve to think that slave-owning societies will always contain more unhappiness or more wickedness than societies in which all men are free. Men tend to adapt themselves to the institutions that they have, and to make both the best and the worst of them, often at the same time. It is doubtful therefore whether those who object to slavery ought to object to it for what it leads to rather than for what it *is*. For the consequences of emancipation are likely to be roughly six of one and half a dozen of the other in respect both of human misery and of good and bad effects on character. Therefore there is some force in the arguments of those who say that, in a slave-owning society, acts done by slave-owners in accordance with the institution are not at all necessarily acts whose direct consequences are morally unacceptable. Indeed it is easy to imagine that in such a society in some circumstances a man might well think that it was a sound factitious principle that

---

[7] An institution can be thought of as an action-system.

he ought to act in accordance with the institution of slavery which is entrenched in his society. Nevertheless (rather as a man may uphold the principle of driving on the left even though he thinks that it would be better if we conformed to the continental custom) he may also think that the institution is inherently wrong because it distorts the true relationship between human beings, because nobody who saw that a slave is a fellow-human would want to retain the institution if he could get rid of it. Similarly those who condemn any lack of candour, or slackness in the pursuit of truth, tend to do so, surely, not so much because they believe that either the direct or the more remote consequences of pursuing the truth are likely to be of benefit to mankind, but rather because they judge that respect for the truth is something that any right-minded man will have. The notion of what is in accordance with human nature (as respect for truth is in accordance with human nature) is one that has been much blown upon by moral philosophers in the last few centuries, but it is one which remains influential in our thought; and I think that it is time for it to be reinstated. This is not to say that we can use it (as, perhaps, it has sometimes been used) as a sort of philosopher's stone by which we can transmute facts about what is into facts about what ought to be. What is in accordance with human nature is what it is fitting that we, being the kind of creatures that we are, should think and do; and *fitting* is of course an evaluative notion. Nevertheless there is good sense in the idea that if we want to know what sorts of things we ought to value, what business we ought to occupy ourselves with, then we cannot wisely consider these questions without taking note of what sort of creatures we are and what are our passions and our abilities. It is this type of reflection which can conduct us to the conclusion that we cannot justly either abandon respect for truth or treat our fellows as chattels. Often, then, when actions of some definite kind are said to be wrong what is meant is that actions of that kind would seldom or never be done by those who attached value to those things which it is fitting that we should value, and attached to each of these the relative value which belongs to it in reality.

We have been asking how the kind of principles which we called definite action-rules can come to have a place in moral codes. We do not pretend to have given anything like an exhaustive answer to this question, but we have found three roughly distinguishable ways in which they can enter. Firstly they may be factitious principles, rules that we deem it wise to uphold and conform to because we think that the overall consequences of such conformity are morally beneficial. On the other hand they may be rules which we deem it, not wise, but necessary to uphold on the ground that the actions which they forbid are actions which are inherently wrong, and will be felt to be objectionable by any morally sensitive man— which is not to say 'by any morally laudable man'. We saw also that there were two ways at least in which the actions forbidden by some definite action-rule might be inherently wrong; what is morally objectionable about them might be either the direct consequences of such actions, or it might be the frame of mind from which they would normally proceed—or, of course, it might be both.

If this is anything like a correct sketch of how definite action-rules come to be upheld, what is their status? It seems that we shall have to say that it is logically a subordinate one. Ultimately it seems that it is the ends that we ought to pursue, the things that we ought to try to avoid, the relationships between men that we ought to foster, that determine what definite action-rules we ought to uphold. In a word, it is what is *worth while* or what is *valuable* that should dictate our principles. This is not to say that men ought first to decide what is valuable and then go on to consider, in the light of that, what principles to hold. That would be for most of us, perhaps for all of us, an impossible task. Rather it is to say that, if a man *were* to try to work out his moral code explicitly from first principles, it would be the answer to the question, 'What things ought we to value?' that would provide him with his first principles.

This has a corollary that we must notice. If the starting point of morality is what we have said it is, then it seems inconceivable that we could ever derive from that starting point definite action-rules of unqualified universality. To put it differently, if the inherent wrongness of any action of some definite kind is due to the undesirability of the direct consequences of actions of that kind or to the wrongness of the frame of mind from which such an action would normally proceed, then it seems incredible that *every* action of that kind should be one that ought not to be done. Is it possible to find some kind of direct consequence so objectionable that it could *never* be right to choose that consequence? Is there any definite kind of action such that no action of that kind would *ever* be done by a man who valued only that which was truly valuable? How would either of these things be established? One would suppose that the effect which I ought to try to bring about is that which, in the situation in which I act, is the best that I can bring about, where 'the best' means that which is most in accordance with the pursuit of everything that ought to be pursued and with the avoidance of everything that ought to be avoided. Is there any effect which could *never* be the best effect possible in some situation, and which would therefore *never* be chosen by the man whose choices were determined by a right scale of values?

Doubtless the answer is that in practice there will be actions which will never be chosen by such a man. If I asked you to invent a situation in which it might be my duty to torture my wife to death, giving her to believe that I hated her, you might be able to invent such a situation, but it is likely that we will never encounter it. But in theory it seems that any definite action-rules which I may uphold on the basis of rational reflection must be qualified by an *other-things-being-equal* clause.[8] It would seem that if I uphold some definite action-rule as binding in absolutely every situation, then I must do so *factitiously*. That is to say, it seems that I cannot dispute that in principle every definite action-rule may on some occasion enjoin the wrong action, but I can nevertheless decide that I will uphold certain of such rules without qualification on the ground that it is better so. This I may reasonably do if I think that the small number of occasions on which obedience to the rule would lead one to make the wrong choice are far outweighed by the many occasions on which one would be likely to make the wrong choice if one felt that the rule could be set aside. Thus I might decide to uphold quite universally the rule that one must never take an innocent[9] life, knowing that on occasion this will lead to consequences which I must regard as morally undesirable (as, for example, when by refusing to kill a man who has done nothing worthy of death, I cause a riot which is costly in lives). This I might do because I also know that the greater danger is that people should come to think that innocent lives can be taken in situations which in no sense justify such action.

Hackneyed as this result is, there is something a little paradoxical about it. We are saying that if a definite action-rule ought to be upheld universally, this is not because of the inherent wrongness of the actions which it forbids, but because it is morally expedient

---

[8] This can be reinforced by the reflection that definite action-rules can of course conflict, as 'Always give money to beggars' and 'Always pay your debts' might on occasion conflict.

[9] 'Innocent' here must of course be given a 'definite' sense, e.g., 'who has not committed a capital offence'.

that it be so upheld. However that may be, though, we can now
return to where we started from. It seems that the principle that one
must not do evil that good may come does not strictly require, as we
thought it might, unqualified divine commandments having the
form of definite action-rules, the transgression of these being that
which determines what is to count as evil in this context. For it
seems that I can say that Jones is doing evil that good may come of it
if Jones is breaking some definite action-rule which I think it
morally expedient to uphold universally. Clearly however if there
are any definite action-rules whose universally binding force rests
on divine commandments, then this will simplify matters. It will
dispose, for example, of the problem how we are to determine which
definite action-rules we are to uphold universally.

Whether the Christian revelation does contain such definite
action-rules I shall not here consider. I shall conclude by observing
that I do not find the notion that it does contain them so intrinsically unplausible as some writers seem to find it. That the creature
should have been given by his creator rules to walk by does not seem
absurd. There is after all no reason why we should regard such
rules as *arbitrary* impositions. We have already seen that a man
might come to think it morally expedient that some rule should be
upheld universally, and in that case it might presumably *be*
morally expedient that it should be so upheld. This might be the
reason why universal obedience to it was a divine commandment.
We need however to be a little careful how we say, in the context
of definite action-rules, that whatever is commanded by God is
commanded because it is independently right. For to say that
something is independently right might seem to mean that we can
see it to be right out of our own resources. But it is difficult to see
how we could ever come to be sure that in the case of some definite
action-rule universal obedience to it is the only right answer. Our
argument has suggested that a man might, not unreasonably, decide to uphold some definite action-rule universally, but it has not
even tended to suggest that he could *know* that he was right to do
so, in the sense that it would be wrong to do otherwise. At this point
we can no doubt appeal to the divine omniscience and say that,
what man cannot know, God can, namely that in the case of the
action-rule in question universal obedience to it is in fact morally
the best course in that it does most to promote those things which
we ought to try to promote. This will allow us to say, if we wish,
that universal obedience to the rule is in fact right in a sense which

is anyhow fairly close to the ordinary sense of 'right'. For it will allow us to say that the conclusion that the rule ought to be upheld universally is the conclusion that we should come to if we took into account those considerations which we ought to take into account when we are thinking morally, and if we were also omniscient. Probably however we shall not want to go quite as far as this. After all what we were trying to do was to argue that the definite action-rules, which, *ex hypothesi*, we are required to conform to universally, are not arbitrary; and we can do this, surely, if we can show that they are rules which it is normally best to conform to. It does not seem absurd to suppose that the creator might require his fallible creatures always to do that which it is normally best to do.

The conclusion seems to be roughly as follows. If we say that to do an action of some kind, K, is always wrong, part at least of what we mean is that a K action is never to be done. About this part of what we mean there is no difficulty. We have seen that a man may reasonably decide that no K action is ever to be done, if he thinks it better to outlaw K actions altogether rather than allow himself and others to decide when to do them. We have seen also that he may have reason to think that total abstention from K actions is enjoined by God. But if we go on to say that the reason why no K action is ever to be done is that every K action would always be wrong, it is not so clear what we now mean.[10] It is of course plain that we are now using 'wrong' in such a way that it is not simply equivalent to 'not to be done'; for that every K action would be one that is not to be done is not a reason why no K action is ever to be done. In what sense, then, could the wrongness of an action be a *reason* for not doing it? What kind of wrongness could this be? We tried to see what inherent wrongness might be thought to consist in, and it seemed to us that it must consist either in the badness of what the action directly brings about or in the badness of what the action comes from. In fact to say that any action of some kind is wrong, in the sense in which this is a reason for not doing such an action, is to say something which is not primarily about the action considered as a member of some definite kind. For while it is possible to

---

[10] This is not the same point as that made in the previous paragraph. There I was arguing that we could never know for sure (failing divine authority) that some definite action-rule was a good rule to uphold universally; here I am about to argue that no definite action-rule can ever be such that every single infringement of it would be, on its own merits, and apart from its being an infringement of a valuable rule, an independently wrongful act.

generalize about the good or evil which any K action is likely to produce, or about the state of mind from which a K action is likely to result, it hardly seems reasonable to expect such generalizations to hold universally. Since what makes us include an action in the class of K actions is logically independent of the frame of mind in which it is done or of the good or evil to which it directly and foreseeably gives rise, it would have to be an accident if it were the case that every single K action was done from morally undesirable motives or gave rise to morally undesirable direct consequences. Therefore it seems that we can say that every K action is wrong if we mean by this that no K action is ever to be done; but if by 'wrong' we mean something further, something which gives us a reason for avoiding K actions, then by the 'natural light' at any rate we are not entitled to say that every K action must be wrong. Principles then which are such that it is always possible to say what would count as a breach of them (in other words definite action-rules) can indeed be held to be valid universally if we decide that it is best, or that it is our duty, to uphold them universally. But we cannot argue that what makes it best to uphold such a principle universally is that every breach of such a principle would be an inherently wrong act. The notion of inherent wrongness is an intelligible notion which ought not to be jettisoned, but it cannot be used to sustain the view that certain principles ought never to be infringed. There may well be certain principles which ought never to be infringed, but this is not because every such infringement would be the wrong response to the situation in which it was done.

14

MORAL DILEMMAS

John Lemmon

I N this paper, I attempt to characterize different varieties of moral dilemma. An assumption made throughout is that an affirmative answer can be given to the question: does a human being have free will? Without this assumption, in fact, there does not seem to be much for ethics to be about.

There are very many different kinds of moral situation in which a human agent can find himself or put himself. Without making any pretence of defining the distinction between moral and non-moral situations, let us merely list some kinds of situation which it would be generally agreed can safely be called moral. I shall begin with the most straightforward and gradually move into areas which could be described as 'dilemmatic'.

1. The first, and it seems the simplest, class of moral situation is this: we know what we are to do, or have to do, or ought to do, and simply do it. Within this class there are several sub-classes, which it will be worth our while to distinguish, depending on the source of our knowledge of what we are to do. What sources are distinguished may well depend on the society to which the agent in question belongs. Thus, if I may stray, like so many philosophers, into the sociology of ethics for a while, our own society tends to distinguish such sources as duties, obligations, and moral principles. (Classical Greek society, if we may go by its language, does not seem to have made a clear distinction between obligation and duty.) For example, a soldier may receive a battle order, and act on it directly, because he knows that it is his *duty as a soldier* so to do. Or a man

may know he is to attend a certain meeting, and do so, because, having given his word that he will be there, he is *under an obligation* to attend. Or a man may know that he ought to tell the truth, and do so, because he holds as a *moral principle* that one should always tell the truth—a slightly unrealistic example, since moral principles tend to be prohibitive rather than compelling: a better example would be that of a man who knows he is not to commit adultery with a certain woman, and does not do so, because he holds it to be a moral ruling that one should at no time commit adultery.

To summarize these three subcases: first, one may know what one is to do, and do it, because one knows it to be one's duty to do that thing; second, one may know what one is to do, and do it, because one knows oneself to be under an obligation to do that thing; third, one may know what one is to do, and do it, because one holds it to be the right thing to do in view of some moral code.

It follows logically, I would wish to claim, that a man ought to do something, if it is his duty to do that thing. Equally, he ought to do it if he is under an obligation to do it, and he ought to do it if it is right, in view of some moral principle to which he subscribes, that he should do it. But the converse implications do not, I think, hold. It might be true that a man ought to do something, and yet it not be his duty to do it, because rather it is the case that he is under an obligation to do it; or, even though he ought to do it, he is under no obligation to do it, but rather it is his duty to do it; or, even though he ought to do it, it is not that it is right to do it in view of some moral principle which he holds, but rather a case of duty or obligation.

To see that these converse implications fail, it will be necessary to take a closer look at our (rather parochial) concepts of duty and obligation. A man's duties are closely related to his special status or position. It nearly always makes sense to ask of a duty 'duty *as what*?' The most straightforward case is that of duties incurred in virtue of a job: thus one has duties as a policeman, duties as headmaster, duties as prime minister or garbage-collector. In many societies, family relationships are recognized as determining duties: thus there are duties as a father, mother, son, or daughter. Less clearly delineated duties, in our society at least, are those of a host, those of a friend, those of a citizen. I do not think there are such things as one's duties as a human being, unless they be duties toward dogs or other members of the animal kingdom, for being

a human being is not being in any special or distinguishing position, unless it is *vis-à-vis* dogs perhaps. The same point emerges
from the adjective 'dutiful'. A dutiful X is someone who does his
duties *as an* X; a dutiful parent is one who does his duty as a parent.
No clear sense attaches to the phrase 'a dutiful bachelor', at least in
our society, for the status of bachelor is not thought of as bringing
with it certain duties.

If duties are related to a special position or status, which distinguishes the man holding the position or status from others,
obligations on the other hand are typically incurred by previous
committing actions. Of course, again what actions are regarded as
committal will vary from society to society. To us, the most
familiar committing actions are promising or giving one's word
generally, and signing one's signature. If you swear to tell the
truth, from the moment of swearing you are under an obligation to
tell the truth. If you promise to attend a meeting, then from that
moment you are under an obligation to attend a meeting. If you
sign your name to an I.O.U., then from that moment you are
under an obligation to return the borrowed money. Less clearly
delineated cases of obligations, at least in our society, are the obligation to return hospitality having received it and the obligation to
give money to a beggar having been asked for it. This last case
illustrates a concept which has relatively rare application for us—
that of being put under an obligation to someone by their conduct
rather than one's own. In certain societies, I believe, a knock on the
door of one's house by a stranger at once puts one under an obligation of a firm kind to provide hospitality and, if necessary, a bed for
the night.

If this admittedly sketchy analysis of the notions of duty and
obligation is at all correct, it becomes easy to see how a man can
be under an obligation to do something, though it is not his duty
to do it, or how a man's duty may be to do something though he
is under no obligation to do it. For example, it may be true that
I ought to vote against a Communist candidate in some election,
because it is my duty as a citizen to do this, though there is no
clear sense in which I am under an obligation to vote against the
Communist (I have made no promises, accepted no bribes, given
my word in advance to no one). On the other hand, it could
easily be that I am, in a different situation, under an obligation
to vote against the Communist just because I have given my word
that I shall do so, even though it may not in fact be my duty to do

so. This is not, of course, to deny that we may both be under an obligation and have it as a duty to do something. For example, in the witness stand it is my duty as a witness to tell the truth, and I am also under an obligation to tell the truth since I have sworn an oath to do so.

An interesting borderline case between obligation and duty, which when properly understood helps, I think, to mark the watershed between them, is the following. Children are often thought to be under some kind of obligation to help their parents in old age, and it is often thought that it is their duty to do so. Is this more properly to be considered a case of obligation or a case of duty? I suggest that we can consider it both ways, but that thinking of it one way is different from thinking of it the other way. If we regard it as a duty to help our parents, we are thinking rather of our special relationship to them, our status as children. If, on the other hand, we think of ourselves as under an obligation to our parents, it is surely in virtue of what they have done for us in the past, when we were children, that we are under this obligation—that is, it will be a case of our having been put under an obligation in some way by them. This difference in the mode of thought becomes clear if we vary the example slightly. Suppose they turn out to be not parents but foster parents. Then we may well feel that our duty is less because the relationship is less close, but our sense of obligation may be no less great in view of what they have done for us. On the other hand, if our parents have not in point of fact done a great deal for us, we may feel in no sense under any obligation to help them, but our sense of duty may be just as real because of our close relationship with them.

Broadly speaking, then, duty-situations are status-situations while obligation-situations are contractual situations. Both duties and obligations may be sources of 'oughts', but they are logically independent sources. And a third source, independent of the other two, is that it is right to do something in view of a moral principle. I have not discussed this here because it is well discussed in almost all contemporary ethical writing, while the concepts of duty and obligation tend to be neglected.

I shall not in fact be very disturbed to learn that there are aspects of the concept of duty or the concept of obligation which I have omitted, or even that I have missed either concept's most central aspect, as we have it. My main concern is rather that there are generically different ways in which it can come to be true that we ought to do something or ought not to do something. While 'ought' is a very general word of ethical involvement, 'duty' and 'obligation' and 'right', as I am using them at least, are highly specialized words.

Yet another way of putting what I want to say would be the following. It is analytic that one ought to do one's duty and that one ought to fulfil one's obligations. But that it is one's duty to do what one ought to do and that one is under an obligation to do what one ought to do are synthetic and false. In the case of 'right', I think it is analytic that one ought to do what it is right to do, but I am not sure whether it is analytic or synthetic that it is right to do what one ought to do—for special reasons which I will not go into here.

2. A second, slightly more complex, class of ethical situations in which agents find themselves may be described thus: we may know what we are to do, or ought to do, or have to do, and yet in various ways be tempted not to do it, and as a result either do or not do what we are or ought to do, either out of a conscious decision or not. This class includes as a subclass those cases commonly called cases of acrasia, where we know what we ought to do and for various reasons and in various ways fail to do it. There is a clear sense in which all examples in this second class of moral situation are dilemmatic. We are, as we often say, torn between duty and pleasure, or between our obligations and our interests, or between our principles and our desires. None the less, I do not wish to call these cases *moral* dilemmas, because in all these cases our moral situation is perfectly clear. We know where our duties lie or what our obligations are or what our moral principles determine for us here, but for various *non*-moral reasons are tempted not to stick with morality.

It might be as well to say a little here about the so-called problem of acrasia. Some philosophers, notably Aristotle, have found it difficult to explain how someone could know what he ought to do and still not do it. Socrates appears to have adopted the position that acrasia did not occur—that is, if a man acts contrary to what he should do, this can only be because he does not know what he should do, is mistaken or deluded about what he should do, and the like. Even Hare admits that the occurrence of acrasia is paradoxical on his view: for if a man knows what he ought to do in the full sense, that is, sincerely assents to the imperative entailed by the 'ought' statement in question taken as a value-judgment, then he cannot fail to act accordingly. Hare in fact makes this position analytic in view of his definition of a value-judgment.[1] It seems to me that one should rather argue contrapositively here. It is so notorious a fact about human agents that they are often subject to acrasia that any ethical position that makes this seem queer or paradoxical or impossible is automatically suspect for just this reason. Of Socrates we can say that as a plain matter of fact he was just wrong—acrasia does occur, or, in Aristotle's phrase, knowledge just is, however sad this may be, frequently dragged about by desire.[2] The situation with respect to Aristotle is more difficult because of the obscurity of his doctrine of the practical syllogism, but, if I understand this doctrine correctly, he claims that a piece of moral reasoning (practical reasoning) leads immediately to action when the conclusion in full particularity is drawn; and this must be plain incorrect in view of the existence of acrasia, so that it is no use his trying to explain the existence of acrasia by using this model. Similarly with Hare. He should not have defined value-judgments in such a way that sincere assent to them entails an imperative leading to action, since in quite normal senses of the words a man precisely does assent to a value-judgment sincerely and still fails to act accordingly, in the situation of acrasia. I suspect that behind this philosophical amazement that there should be such a phenomenon as acrasia lies the Aristotelian (or Socratic) picture of man as a rational animal. How this definition could survive the millions of counterexamples during the last two millenniums remains mysterious, unless it has simply flattered the race. (It would surely be better to define man as that tragic animal who is sometimes capable of thinking rationally but in general incapable of acting so.) Perhaps acrasia is one of the best examples of a pseudo-problem in philosophical literature: in view of its existence, if you find it a problem you have already made a philosophical mistake.

A more interesting subclass of the second class of moral situation is the following special case of acrasia: an agent knows what he ought to do, fails to do it for various reasons, and then pretends to himself that he has done it. Or more commonly in the negative: an agent knows that he should not do something, nevertheless does it, and yet pretends to himself the he has not done it. It is said, for example, of Queen Elizabeth I that she had certain ministers executed by signing their death warrants and then a few days later asked the whereabout of the ministers; on learning of their execu-

[1] R. M. Hare, *The Language of Morals*, O.U.P. 1952, p. 169.
[2] Aristotle, *Nicomachean Ethics*, 1147 b 16-17.

tion, she blamed others for acting without her consent. This conduct seems to betray the knowledge that the ministers should not have been executed; for various reasons the Queen wished them to be executed; she acted in accordance with these wishes, but later pretended to herself that she had not so acted.

The analysis of this type of pretence belongs rather to the psychologist than to the philosopher. But there are also philosophical problems here, raised in an acute form by Sartre in his discussion of *mauvaise foi*. Queen Elizabeth's action is a good example of bad faith in Sartre's sense. For she was in a way lying to herself about what she had done. In fact many, and most simple, examples of acts in bad faith fall into the subclass we are at present considering or very nearly do so. Consider Sartre's own famous examples: the woman in the restaurant who has gone out with a certain man for the first time; he takes her hand; she knows that she is called on to make a decision, either to remove her hand or to leave it there with all that that would or might imply; but she does not take a decision; by leaving her hand there and yet pretending that it is not there, she pretends to herself that there is no decision to be taken.[3] Or again Sartre describes a homosexual who suffers from acute feelings of guilt at his actions. 'In fact it frequently happens that this man, while recognizing his homosexual inclination, while avowing each and every particular misdeed which he has committed, refuses with all his strength to consider himself "a pederast".'[4] This man does what he thinks he should not do, and then in various ways and by various devices denies to himself that he has really done what he knows that he has done. The ways of self-deception and pretence are legion, but perhaps one more is worth instancing, since it appears to be very common. A man may realize that life with his wife has become intolerable and that he should seek a divorce, but he does not do so either because of the expense or because he fails in social courage or for other reasons or for a combination of these. He may well now say that he could not obtain a divorce, though he knows perfectly well that he could if he tried. Here the self-pretence is, not that one has in fact done what one should have done when one knows that one has not done it, but that one could not do what one knows perfectly well that one could do.

Self-deception, pretending to oneself, *mauvaise foi*—this is a phenomenon which occurs. Hence, as in the case of acrasia, we

---

[3] J. P. Sartre, *Being and Nothingness*, trans. by H. E. Barnes (New York, 1956), pp. 55-56.
[4] *Ibid.*, p. 63.

should be wary of philosophical positions which make its existence paradoxical. None the less, there is a philosophical problem here, namely the problem of how to describe the phenomenon without contradiction. For, as Sartre says, to be in bad faith is in a way to lie to oneself, and yet the concept of lying implies a duality, the duality of the deceiver and the deceived. The liar must apparently know that P is true, and yet say not-P. But now what will be self-deception? The same person must both know that P and yet be persuaded that not-P. Sartre states the paradox thus:

> It follows [in the case of bad faith] that the one to whom the lie is told and the one who lies are one and the same person, which means that I must know in my capacity as deceiver the truth which is hidden from me in my capacity as the one deceived. Better yet I must know the truth very exactly in *order* to conceal it more carefully—and this not at two different moments, which at a pinch would allow us to re-establish a semblance of duality—but in the unitary structure of a single project. How then can the lie subsist if the duality which conditions it is suppressed?[5]

I think the paradox here rests partly on a confusion between knowing and believing. A man cannot logically both know that P and know that not-P; for, if he really knows that P, then P is the case; and if he knows that not-P then not-P is the case; but it cannot be that both P and not-P. On the other hand there is no logical reason why a man should not know that P and yet believe that not-P. For, although people cannot know what is not the case, they may and do believe what is not the case, so that it does not follow from his believing that not-P that in fact not-P, and no contradiction is obtained. If it is argued that knowing that P entails believing that P (which in any case I would doubt), there is still no contradiction: for a man may both believe that P and believe that not-P, though he may not both believe that P and not believe that P. In fact it seems to be a straightforward fact about human beings that they entertain contradictory beliefs, and self-deception is just a special case of this situation. The paradox here, if there is one, arises only from our faulty assessment of human beings: there are no logical difficulties.

Sartre raises, however, a second and graver difficulty in the notion of self-deception. 'That which affects itself with self-deception must be conscious of its self-deception since the being of consciousness is consciousness of being. It appears then that I must

[5] *Ibid.*, p. 49.

be in good faith, at least to the extent that I am conscious of my self-deception.'[6] Admittedly, as it stands, this is not a strong argument. There is no reason to suppose that all the time we are conscious we are also conscious that we are conscious; indeed there are good reasons in the form of a familiar infinite regress to suppose that this is not the case. So that there is no reason why a man should not deceive himself and not be conscious that he is doing so—indeed this seems to be a familiar fact about human beings once again. On the other hand we are sometimes conscious of being conscious, and there do seem to be situations in which we not only deceive ourselves but are aware at the time of doing so. But this description is genuinely contradictory: it is logically impossible to be aware that you are being deceived, for this implies that you are both being deceived and not being deceived at the same time. None the less, though strictly contradictory, there are many things which this phrase 'aware that you are being deceived' might loosely mean: it might mean that you thought you were being deceived; it might mean that you were aware that someone (perhaps yourself) was trying to deceive you; it might even mean that you were aware that someone (perhaps yourself) was trying to deceive you and that later, after your guard was dropped, they succeeded. For example, in buying a car we may be aware that we are being deceived by the dealer and, in the end, actually be deceived. And there is a parallel to this in the case of self-deception.

Self-deception, in any form is, I suppose, a piece of irrational behaviour. It is like hiding something and simultaneously instituting a personal search for that thing. What I have been trying to bring out here is that we must not mistake the irrationality of the behaviour for the contradictoriness of its description. When properly understood, there are no logical barriers to the existence of self-deception.

3. It is well past time to reach the main topic of this paper. My third class of moral situation constitutes what I take to be the simplest variety of moral dilemma in the full sense. The characterization of this class is as follows: a man both ought to do something and ought not to do that thing. Here is a simple example, adapted from Plato. A friend leaves me with his gun, saying that he will be back for it in the evening, and I promise to return it when he calls. He arrives in a distraught condition, demands his gun, and announces that he is going to shoot his wife because she has

[6] *Ibid.*

been unfaithful. I ought to return the gun, since I promised to do so—a case of obligation. And yet I ought not to do so, since to do so would be to be indirectly responsible for a murder, and my moral principles are such that I regard this as wrong. I am in an extremely straightforward moral dilemma, evidently resolved by not return-ing the gun.

The description of this class of cases may perhaps cause alarm; for it may well be thought to be contradictory that a man both ought and ought not to do something. To indicate why I do not think this is so, I will begin by considering the logic of the modal verb 'has to', or 'must', and then contrast this logic with that of the modal 'ought'. If a man has to do something,[7] it does follow that he does that thing, in the sense that if he does not do it it cannot have been true that he must do it. This emerges quite clearly, I think, from the following fact of usage: a man announces that he must do something, but it later emerges that he has not done that thing. Then he will now repeat his earlier claim, not in the form that he *had* to do it, which would suggest falsely that he had done it, but in the form that he *ought* to have done it. Or, if at a party I say that I have to go, this will be taken as a sign heralding my departure. But if I merely say that I ought to go, this is entirely compatible, human weakness being what it is, with my staying for another hour.

It follows from this that 'must' and 'must not' are contraries in the logician's sense. That is, it cannot be both true that I must do something and that I must not do it: for if I must I will, and if I must not I will not, which is a contradiction. On the other hand, it may well be the case that I neither must do something nor must not do that thing. For example, it is neither true that I must light a cigarette nor that I must not light a cigarette. Hence 'must' and 'must not' may well both be false, though they may not be both true.

'Must not' should not be supposed to be the negation of 'must', in the way that 'cannot' is the negation of 'can'. The proper nega-tion of 'I must tell the truth' is, roughly, 'I do not have to tell the truth'. In an entirely similar way, 'ought not' is certainly not the negation of 'ought'. For example, it is true neither that I ought to be playing chess nor that I ought not to be playing chess; hence 'ought' and 'ought not' are not contradictory. But are they even contrary to one another? In the case of 'must' and 'must not' we

---

[7] As opposed, I think, to *having it to do*: for that might mean only that it was on his agenda, i.e., list of things he ought to do.

showed them to be contrary by showing that 'must' implied 'will'
and that consequently 'must not' implied 'will not'. Hence an
explicit contradiction is derivable from the assumption that a man
both must and must not do something. But no similar contradiction
is derivable from the assumption that someone both ought and
ought not to do something; for it certainly does not follow from the
fact that a man ought to do something that he will do it, nor does it
follow from the fact that a man ought not to do something that he
will not do that thing. There seems no reason, therefore, why we
should regard 'ought' and 'ought not' even as contraries, still less
as contradictories. It seems to me that 'ought' and 'ought not' may
well both be true, and that this description in fact characterizes a
certain class of moral dilemma. Indeed, the Platonic example cited
would not be a dilemma at all unless it was true that the man both
ought to return the gun and ought not to return it. It is a nasty fact
about human life that we sometimes both ought and ought not to
do things; but it is not a logical contradiction.[8]

My motive for carefully distinguishing some of the sources for
'ought's' earlier in this paper should now be apparent. For moral
dilemmas of the sort we are at present considering will appear
generally[9] in the cases where these sources conflict. Our duty may
conflict with our obligations, our duty may conflict with our moral
principles, or our obligations may conflict with our moral principles. The Platonic case was an example of a conflict between principle and obligation. A simple variant illustrates a conflict between
obligation and duty: the man with whom the gun is deposited may
regard it as his duty as a friend not to return the gun, even though
he is under an obligation to do so. And duty conflicts with principle
every time that we are called on in our jobs to do things which we
find morally repugnant.

A natural question to ask next is: How are moral dilemmas of
this simple kind to be resolved? There are certain very simple
resolutions, known from the philosophical literature, which we
should discuss first; but I do not think they are in practice very

[8] Professor M. Lazerowitz pointed out to me in discussion the following consequence
of the view above: If X ought to do P and ought to do Q, then X ought to do P and Q,
by a principle of deontic logic which I and others accept; hence, in the cases under
consideration, X ought to do both P and not-P; now, if 'ought' implies 'can,' it follows
that X can do both P and not-P, and yet it is a logical truth that X cannot do both P
and not-P; so a contradiction seems to be obtained. I view this, however, as a refutation
of the principle that 'ought' implies 'can,' to which there are surely clear counterexamples even without the introduction of the present instances.

[9] Though of course by no means always: two duties, or two obligations, may well
conflict with one another.

common. First, we may hold to some very sweeping 'higher-order principle' such as 'Always prefer duty to obligation' or 'Always follow moral principles before duty or obligation'. This last precept, for example, at once resolves the Platonic dilemma mentioned earlier, which, as I described it, was a simple clash between principle and obligation. Secondly, and rather less simply, we may have in advance a complex ordering of our various duties, obligations, and the like—putting, for example, our duties as a citizen before our duties as a friend and our duties as a friend before any obligations we may have incurred—in virtue of which the moral dilemma is resolved. But dilemmas in which we are morally prepared, in which we, as it were, merely have to look up the solution in our private ethical code, are rare, I think, and in any case of little practical interest. Of greater importance are those dilemmas in this class where some decision of a moral character is required. And here it must be remembered that the failure to make a decision in one sense is itself to make a decision in another, broader, sense. For our predicament is here so described that, whatever we do, even if we do nothing at all (whatever that might mean), we are doing something which we ought not to do, and so can be called upon to justify either our activity or our inactivity. The only way we can avoid a decision is by ceasing to be any longer an agent (e.g., if we are arrested, or taken prisoner, or kidnapped, or die). This precise situation leads to another familiar pattern of bad faith, in which we pretend to ourselves either that no decision is called for or that in one way or another the decision has been taken out of our hands by others or that we are simply the victims of our own character in acting in this way or that, that we cannot help doing what we do do and so cannot be reproached for resolving the dilemma in this way or that. If, however, we are to act here in good faith, we shall recognize that the dilemma is what it is and make the best decision we can.

Now what kind of considerations may or should affect the decision? The situation is such that no moral, or at least purely moral, considerations are relevant, in the sense that no appeal to our own given morality can decide the issue. We may of course consult a friend, take moral advice, find out what others have done in similar situations, appeal as it were to precedent. But again none of these appeals will be decisive—we still have to decide to act in accordance with advice or precedent. Or again we may approach our decision by a consideration of ends—which course of action will, so far as we can see, lead to the best result. (I do not think it is an accident, by the way, that the word 'good', or rather its superlative 'best', makes its first appearance at this point in our discussion; for it is typically when we are torn between courses of conduct that the question of comparing different actions arises, and hence the word 'good', a comparative adjective unlike 'right', is at home here; the consequence, admittedly paradoxical, of this view of 'good' is that it is not properly a word of moral appraisal at all, despite the vast attention it receives from ethical philosophers; and I think I accept this conclusion.) Thus a consideration of ends determines a solution to the Platonic dilemma discussed earlier. Although I ought to return the gun and also ought not to return the gun, in fact it is evidently best, when we weigh up the expected outcome, not to return the gun, and so to sacrifice one's obligation to utilitarian considerations. Of course, when I say that this solution is evidently the best, I do not mean that it cannot be questioned. What I do mean is that it can only be seriously questioned by someone whose whole attitude toward human life is basically different from that of a civilized western human being. Someone who thinks that it would really be better to return the gun must either hold the importance of a man's giving his word to be fantastically high or else hold human life to be extremely cheap, and I regard both these attitudes as morally primitive.

4. I shall pass on now to the next, more complex, class of moral situations which might be described as dilemmatic in the full sense. Roughly, the class I now have in mind may be described thus: there is some, but not conclusive, evidence that one ought to do something, and there is some, but not conclusive, evidence, that one ought not to do that thing.[10] All the difficulties that arose in the way of making a decision in the last class of cases arise typically here too, but there are now difficulties of a new kind as well. Moreover, in this class of cases there can be no preassigned moral solution to the dilemma in virtue of higher-order principles or a given ordering of one's duties and obligations and the like, because part of the very dilemma is just one's uncertainty as to one's actual moral situation, one's situation with respect to duties, obligations, and principles. For example, it may be unclear whether it really is one's duty as a citizen to vote against the Communist candidate, and

---

[10] At this point we bid farewell to the deontological mapping of moral concepts on which we have partially relied up to now. The new area is not charted enough for that and perhaps should not be charted in that way at all.

also unclear whether one is under an obligation to vote for the Communist candidate in view, let us say, of financial help received from the Communists in the Resistance during the war. Hence one is in a moral dilemma because there is some evidence that one should vote Communist and some that one should not, though in neither case is the evidence conclusive.

A good illustration of the kind of complexity this type of situation may embrace is again from Sartre:

> I will refer to the case of a pupil of mine who sought me out in the following circumstances. His father was quarrelling with his mother and was also inclined to be a 'collaborator'; his elder brother had been killed in the German offensive of 1940 and this young man, with a sentiment somewhat primitive but generous, burned to avenge him. His mother was living alone with him, deeply afflicted by the semi-treason of his father and by the death of her oldest son, and her one consolation was in this young man. But he, at this moment, had the choice between going to England to join the Free French Forces or of staying near his mother and helping her to live. He fully realized that this woman lived only for him and that his disappearance—or perhaps his death—would plunge her into despair. He also realized that, concretely and in fact, every action he performed on his mother's behalf would be sure of effect in the sense of aiding her to live, whereas anything he did in order to go and fight would be an ambiguous action which might vanish like water into sand and serve no purpose. For instance, to set out for England he would have to wait indefinitely in a Spanish camp on the way through Spain; or, on arriving in England or in Algiers he might be put into an office to fill up forms. Consequently, he found himself confronted by two very different modes of action; the one concrete, immediate, but directed towards only one individual; the other an action addressed to an end infinitely greater, a national collectivity, but for that reason ambiguous—and it might be frustrated on the way. At the same time, he was hesitating between two kinds of morality; on the one side, the morality of sympathy, of personal devotion and, on the other side, a morality of wider scope but of more debatable validity. He had to choose between these two.[11]

A crude oversimplification of this example might depict it thus: the boy is under some obligation to stay with his mother; or, perhaps better, his mother by her own position has put him under some obligation to stay with her, since she is now dependent on him for her own happiness. Consequently, he is conscious in some de-

[11] Sartre, *Existentialism and Humanism*, trans. by P. Mairet (London, 1948), pp. 35-36.

gree that he ought to stay with her. On the other hand he feels some kind of duty to join the Free French in England—a duty perhaps to his country as a citizen. But this duty is far from being clearly given; as Sartre stresses, it is felt only ambiguously. It may be his duty to fight, but can it really be his duty, given his obligation to his mother, to sit in an office filling out forms? He is morally torn, but each limb of the moral dilemma is not itself here clearly delineated.

An interesting feature of this case, and of the class of cases in general which we are considering, is that, in attempting to reach a decision, the arguments which try to establish exactly what one's moral situation is are not distinguishable from those which attempt to resolve the dilemma itself. Thus the boy is unclear where his duty lies partly because he is unclear what exactly would be the outcome of his decision to leave his mother, and this outcome is also relevant to the decision itself, as a utilitarian consideration affecting his choice.

Sartre's example has an important further feature, which marks out a particular subclass of the class of moral dilemmas in general: the dilemma is so grave a one, personally speaking, that either decision in effect marks the adoption on the part of the agent of a changed moral outlook. It does not seem to have been much observed by ethical philosophers that, speaking psychologically, the adoption of a new morality by an agent is frequently associated with the confrontation of a moral dilemma. Indeed, it is hard to see what else would be likely to bring about a change of moral outlook other than the having to make a difficult moral decision. On the nature of such a change there is time here only to say a few things. First, the change frequently and always in serious cases is associated with a change in fundamental attitudes, such as the change from liberalism to conservatism in politics or the change from Christianity to atheism in the field of religion. And the reasons given for the moral change may well be identical with the reasons given for the change in fundamental attitudes. This last kind of change is neither fully rational nor fully irrational. To persuade someone to change his fundamental attitudes is like getting someone to see an aesthetic point—to appreciate classical music or impressionist painting, for example. Arguments can be given, features of music or painting may be drawn to the person's attention, and so on and so forth, but none of these reasons is finally conclusive. None the less, we should not rush to the opposite conclusion that matters of aesthetic taste are purely subjective. In a somewhat similar way we may persuade someone, or he may persuade himself, to change his fundamental attitudes, and so to change his moral outlook, at a time of moral crisis. Roughly speaking, Sartre's boy has to decide whether to be politically engaged or not, and this decision may well affect and be affected by his fundamental attitudes.

I am not at all saying that this kind of serious case is common; indeed, I think it is rare; but it is still of the greatest importance to ethics to investigate it, because it is of the greatest practical importance in a man's life. There may well be people who have never had to face a moral situation of these dimensions. But for Antigones and others who live faced with occasional major crises, the appropriate reasoning for this kind of moral dilemma is of vital importance. On the other hand, it is not at all clear what the role of the philosopher should be here. If we listen to much of contemporary ethical writing, his role is merely to analyse the discourse in which such reasoning is couched; the task of deciding what are good and what are bad ethical arguments belongs to someone else, though it is never quite made clear to whom. It is my own view that, even though it may be part and an important part of the philosopher's job to analyse the terminology of ethical arguments, his job does not stop there. Perhaps no one is properly equipped to give moral advice to anyone else, but if anyone is it is the philosopher, who at least may be supposed to be able to detect bad reasoning from good. It is a corollary of this view that a philosopher is not entitled to a private life—by which I mean that it is his duty to hold political and religious convictions in such a form as to be philosophically defensible or not to hold them at all. He is not entitled to hold such beliefs in the way in which many non-philosophers hold them, as mere articles of faith.

5. After this brief digression, I must return to my classification of moral dilemmas: for there is one more kind that, with some hesitation, I should like to introduce. This is an even more extreme kind of dilemma than the last and probably of even rarer occurrence. I mean the kind of situation in which an agent has to make a decision of a recognizably moral character though he is completely unprepared for the situation by his present moral outlook. This case differs from the last in that there the question was rather of the applicability of his moral outlook to his present situation, while here the question is rather how to create a new moral outlook to meet unprecedented moral needs. This case is in some respects

easier for the agent and in some respects harder to face than the last: easier, if he recognizes the situation for what it is, because he at least knows that for sure he has some basic moral rethinking to do, which is often not clear in the previous case; but harder, because basic moral rethinking is harder work in general than settling the applicability of given moral principles to a particular situation. A typical, but morally wrong, way of escape from this dilemma is again to act in bad faith, by pretending to oneself that the situation is one which one can handle with one's given moral apparatus.

A possible real instance of this kind of moral dilemma is that which faced Chamberlain in his negotiations with Hitler in 1938. He ought to have realized that he was dealing with a kind of person for which his own moral outlook had not prepared him, and that as Prime Minister he was called upon to rethink his moral and political approach in a more realistic way. This he failed to do, either because he was genuinely deceived as to Hitler's real character or, as I suspect, because he deceived himself on this point: if the latter, then he was guilty of the type of bad faith to which I am alluding.

The main point of this variety of moral dilemma is that, at least if correctly resolved, it forces a man to develop a new morality; in the case of the last type of dilemma, this was a possible outcome but by no means a necessary one. So perhaps this is the place at which to say a little about what is involved in such a development. Here the analogy with aesthetics, which Sartre and others have cautiously drawn, may be useful. There may come a point in the development of a painter, say, or a composer, where he is no longer able to go on producing work that conforms to the canons of composition which he has hitherto accepted, where he is compelled by his authenticity as a creator to develop new procedures and new forms. It is difficult to describe what will guide him in the selection of new canons, but one consideration will often be the desire to be (whatever this means) *true to himself*. It may well be that an appropriate consideration in the development of a moral outlook is the desire to be, in the relevant sense whatever that is, true to oneself and to one's own character. But I will not pursue this topic here, because I confess myself to be quite in the dark as to what the sense of these words is.

To conclude, I will not attempt to summarize, but rather I will say what I would like to see done and what I know I have here failed properly to do. I should like to see a detailed breakdown of the different kinds of difficult moral situations in which human beings, living as they do in societies, find themselves, because in my opinion too much attention has been paid in contemporary ethical writing to the easy, rule-guided, moral situation. The five types of ethical situation which I have here tried to distinguish might well be replaced by five hundred types, human life being what it is. Such an analysis will require sympathetic treatment of real moral problems considered in detail, and it will require a proper analysis of the concepts of choice and decision—active moral concepts, rather than the passive, spectator-like, concepts of good and right. Secondly, I should like to see a proper discussion of the arguments that go to resolve moral dilemmas, because I do not believe that this is an area of total irrationality, though I do not believe that a traditional logical approach (the logic of imperatives, deontic logic, and whatnot) will do either. This will entail saying what constitutes a good and a bad moral reason for making a decision, and so will bring the moral philosopher out from his corner, where I think he has been too long, and back into the familiar but forgotten Socratic position of trying to answer the ever-present but ever-changing question: How should a man live?

15

SOCIAL MORALITY AND INDIVIDUAL IDEAL

P. F. Strawson

MEN make for themselves pictures of ideal forms of life. Such pictures are various and may be in sharp opposition to each other; and one and the same individual may be captivated by different and sharply conflicting pictures at different times. At one time it may seem to him that he should live—even that *a man* should live —in such-and-such a way; at another that the only truly satisfactory form of life is something totally different, incompatible with the first. In this way, his outlook may vary radically, not only at different periods of his life, but from day to day, even from one hour to the next. It is a function of so many variables: age, experiences, present environment, current reading, current physical state are some of them. As for the ways of life that may thus present themselves at different times as each uniquely satisfactory, there can be no doubt about their variety and opposition. The ideas of self-obliterating devotion to duty or to the service of others; of personal honour and magnanimity; of asceticism, contemplation, retreat; of action, dominance and power; of the cultivation of 'an exquisite sense of the luxurious'; of simple human solidarity and co-operative endeavour; of a refined complexity of social existence; of a constantly maintained and renewed affinity with natural things —any of these ideas, and a great many others too, may form the core and substance of a personal ideal. At some times such a picture may present itself as merely appealing or attractive; at others it may offer itself in a stronger light, as, perhaps, an image of the only sane or non-ignoble human reaction to the situation in which

we find ourselves. 'The nobleness of life is to do thus' or, sometimes, 'The sanity of life is to do thus': such may be the devices
with which these images present themselves.

Two quite different things may be urged against, or in mitigation
of, this picture of a multiplicity of pictures. First, it might be said
that the many, apparently conflicting pictures are really different
parts or aspects, coming momentarily into misleading prominence,
of a single picture; this latter being the composite ideal image of
our coolest hours, in which every god is given his due and conflict
is avoided by careful arrangement and proper subordination of part
to part. And it may be true of some exceptional individuals that
they entertain ideal images which exhibit just such a harmonious
complexity. I believe this to be rarer than we sometimes pretend;
but in any case to describe this situation is not to redescribe the
situation I have spoken of, but to describe a different situation.
The other mitigating point has more weight. It is that, however
great the variety of images which dominate, at one time or another,
our ethical imaginations, our individual lives do not, as a matter
of fact, exhibit a comparable internal variety. Indeed they scarcely
c⸜uld. Something approaching consistency, some more or less un-
steady balance, is usually detectable in the pattern of an individual
person's decisions and actions. There are, so to speak, empirical
grounds for ordering his ideal images in respect of practical efficacy,
even, perhaps, for declaring one of them to be practically dominant.
This point I shall grant. I think it is easy to exaggerate it; easy to
exaggerate the unity of the personalities of those we say we know,
when we really know them only in one or two particular connections; easy to dismiss as phases or moods whatever lacks conformity
with our only partly empirical pictures of each other. But I shall
not dwell on this. What I shall dwell on is precisely this readiness,
which a great many people have, to identify themselves imaginatively at different times with different and conflicting visions of the
ends of life, even though these visions may receive the scantiest
expression in their actual behaviour and would call for the most
upsetting personal revolutions if they received more.

This fact about many people—a fact which partly explains,
among other things, the enormous charm of reading novels, bio-
graphies, histories—this fact, I say, has important consequences.
One consequence is that when some ideal image of a form of life is
given striking expression in the words or actions of some person,
its expression may evoke a response of the liveliest sympathy from

those whose own patterns of life are as remote as possible from conformity to the image expressed. It is indeed impossible that one life should realize all the ideal pictures which may at one time or another attract or captivate the individual imagination. But the owner of one life may with perfect practical consistency wish that his conflicting images should all be realized in different lives. The steadiest adherence to one image may co-exist with the strongest desire that other and incompatible images should have their steady adherents too. To one who has such a desire, any doctrine that the pattern of the ideal life should be the same for all is intolerable; as it is to me. The way in which I have just expressed the position makes its practical consistency look more simple than it is. One cannot simply escape the conflict between different ideal images by diffusing their realization over different lives. For different lives interact and one's own is one of them; and there may be conflict in the areas of interaction. One is not forced to welcome this, though one may; it is simply something that in fact goes with the fulfilment of the wish for this kind of diversity in the pursuit of ends. Equally one is not precluded from taking one side in a conflict because one has wished that both sides should exist and has some sympathy with both.

I think there can be no doubt that what I have been talking about falls within the region of the ethical. I have been talking about evaluations such as *can* govern choices and decisions which are of the greatest importance to men. Whether it falls within the region of the moral, however, is something that may be doubted. Perhaps the region of the moral falls within it. Or perhaps there are no such simple inclusion-relations between them. The question is one I shall come back to later. I should like first to say something more about this region of the ethical. It could also be characterized as a region in which there are truths which are incompatible with each other. There exist, that is to say, many profound general statements which are capable of capturing the ethical imagination in the same way as it may be captured by those ideal images of which I spoke. They often take the form of general descriptive statements about man and the world. They can be incorporated into a metaphysical system, or dramatized in a religious or historical myth. Or they can exist—their most persuasive form for many—as isolated statements such as, in France, there is a whole literature of, the literature of the maxim. I will not give examples, but I will mention names. One cannot read Pascal or Flaubert, Nietzsche or

Goethe, Shakespeare or Tolstoy, without encountering these profound truths. It is certainly possible, in a coolly analytical frame of mind, to mock at the whole notion of the profound truth; but we are guilty of mildly bad faith if we do. For in most of us the ethical imagination succumbs again and again to *these* pictures of man, and it is precisely as truths that we wish to characterize them while they hold us captive. But these truths have the same kind of relation to each other as those ideal images of which I have already spoken. For pictures of the one kind reflect and are reflected by pictures of the other. They capture our imagination in the same way. Hence it is as wholly futile to think that we could, without destroying their character, systematize these truths into one coherent body of truth as it is to suppose that we could, without destroying their character, form a coherent composite image from these images. This may be expressed by saying that the region of the ethical is the region where there are truths but no truth; or, in other words, that the injunction to see life steadily *and* see it whole is absurd, for one cannot do both. I said I would give no examples, but I will allude to one near-contemporary one. Many will remember the recorded encounter between Russell and Lawrence, the attempt at sympathy and the failure to find it. That failure is recorded in such words as: 'I thought there might be something in what he said, but in the end I saw there was nothing' on the one hand; and 'Get back to mathematics where you can do some good; leave talk about human beings alone' on the other. The clash was a clash of two irreconcilable views of man, two irreconcilable attitudes. The spectator familiar with both may say: Russell is right; he tells the truth; he speaks for civilization. He may also say: Lawrence is right; he tells the truth; he speaks for life. The point is that he may say both things. It would be absurd to hope for a reconciliation of the two conflicting attitudes. It is not absurd to desire that both should exist, in conflict.

The region of the ethical, then, is a region of diverse, certainly incompatible and possibly practically conflicting ideal images or pictures of a human life, or of human life; and it is a region in which many such incompatible pictures may secure at least the imaginative, though doubtless not often the practical, allegiance of a single person. Moreover this statement itself may be seen not merely as a description of what is the case, but as a positive evaluation of evaluative diversity. Any diminution in this variety would impoverish the human scene. The multiplicity of conflicting pictures is itself the essential element in one of one's pictures of man.

Now what are the relations between the region of the ethical and the sphere of morality? One widely accepted account of the latter is in terms of the idea of rules or principles governing human behaviour which apply universally within a community or class. The class may be variously thought of as a definite social group or the human species as a whole or even the entire class of rational beings. It is not obvious how these contrasting conceptions, of diversity of ideal and of community of rule, are related to each other; and in fact, I think, the relationship is complicated. One way of trying to harmonize the ideas would be as follows. This way is extremely crude and inadequate, but it may serve as a starting point. It is obvious that many, if not all, of the ideal images of which I spoke demand for their realization the existence of some form of social organization. The demand is in varying degrees logical or empirical. Some ideals only make sense in a complex social context, and even in a particular kind of complex social context. For others, some complexity of social organization seems, rather, a practically necessary condition of the ideal's being realized in any very full or satisfactory way. Now it is a condition of the existence of any form of social organization, of any human community, that certain expectations of behaviour on the part of its members should be pretty regularly fulfilled: that some duties, one might say, should be performed, some obligations acknowledged, some rules observed. We might begin by locating the sphere of morality here. It is the sphere of the observance of rules, such that the existence of some such set of rules is a condition of the existence of a society. This is a minimal interpretation of morality. It represents it as what might literally be called a kind of public convenience: of the first importance as a condition of everything that matters, but only as a condition of everything that matters, not as something that matters in itself.

I am disposed to see considerable merit in this minimal conception of morality. By this I mean not that it is really, or nearly, an adequate conception—only that it is a useful analytical idea. There would be objections to claiming that it was an adequate conception. One objection might be simply expressed by saying that, after all, being moral is something that does matter in itself, that it is not simply an affair of complying with rules in a situation where the observance of some such rules is an indirect condition of approximating to ideal forms of life. There is a lot in this objection. But it is not an objection to *using* the minimal idea of morality. We might for example argue that there was an intricate interplay between ideal pictures of man on the one hand and the rule-requirements of social organization on the other; and that one's ordinary and vague conception of morality was the product of this interplay. This would be one way—I do not say the right way—of using the minimal idea of morality to try to get clearer about the ordinary idea. I shall come back later to this question too.

Meanwhile there is another objection to be considered. I think there is something in it as well, but that what there is in it is not at all straightforward. It turns on the idea of the universal applicability of moral rules. The idea is that it is a necessary requirement of a *moral* rule that it should at least be regarded as applying to all human beings whatever. Moral behaviour is what is demanded of men as such. But we can easily imagine, and even find, different societies held together by the observance of sets of rules which are very different from each other. Moreover we can find or imagine a single society held together by a set of rules which by no means make the same demands on all its members, but make very different demands on different classes or groups within the society. In so far as the rules which give cohesiveness to a society are acknowledged to have this limited and sectional character, they cannot, in the sense of this objection, be seen as moral rules. But the rules which do give cohesiveness to a society may well have this character, whether acknowledged or not. So the prospect of explaining true morality in terms of what I called the minimal conception of morality is a poor one. Now it is possible to admit the principle of this objection, and then meet it with a formal manoeuvre. Thus a rule which governs the professional behaviour of Samoan witch-doctors can be said to apply to all men under the condition that they are witch-doctor members of a society with the general characteristics of Samoan society. Or again, a rule which might be held to apply to ten-year-old children, namely that they should obey their parents in domestic matters, could be represented as applying to all men without exception, under the condition that they were ten-year-old children. Obviously there is a certain futility about this manoeuvre, and equally obviously there is no compulsion to execute it. We might simply drop the idea of moral rules as universally binding on men as men. Or we might say that though there was something in this idea, it was absurd to try to apply it directly and in detail to the question of what people were required to do in particular situations in particular societies. And here we might be tempted by another manoeuvre, which we should note as a possible one even if we do not think that it, either, is altogether satisfactory. We might be tempted to say that the relevant universally applicable, and hence moral, rule, was that a human being should conform to the rules which apply to him in a particular situation in a particular society. Here universality is achieved by stepping up an order. A man should perform the duties of his station in his society. This allows for an indefinite variety of societies and of stations within them; and would also seem to allow us, in so far as we regarded the universal rule as a truly moral one, to see at least part of true morality as resting upon and presupposing what I called the minimal social interpretation of morality.

Enough, for the moment, of objections to this minimal idea. Let me set out some of its merits. First we must be clearer about what this minimal interpretation is. The fundamental idea is that of a socially sanctioned demand made on an individual in virtue merely of his membership of the society in question, or in virtue of a particular position which he occupies within it or a particular relation in which he stands to other members of it. I spoke of rules in this connection; and the rules I meant would simply be the generalized statements of demands of this type. The formula I employ for the fundamental idea is deliberately flexible, the notions of a society and of social sanctioning deliberately vague. This flexibility is necessary to do justice to the complexities of social organization and social relationships. For instance, we can regard ourselves as members of many different social groups or communities, some of which fall within others; or again, when I speak of the social sanctioning of a demand which is made on an individual member of a group in virtue of his position in the group, we may think of the social sanction of that demand sometimes as arising only within the limited group in question, sometimes as arising also within a wider group which includes that limited group. A position in a society may or may not also be, so to speak, a position in society. Thus a position in a family generally gives rise to certain demands upon the holder of that position which are recognized both within the family and within some wider group or groups within which the family falls. The same may be true of membership of a profession or even of a professional association. On the other hand, some of the demands of certain class or caste moralities receive little or no extraneous reinforcement from the wider social groupings to which the members of the limited class also belong. Or again what one might call the internal morality of an intimate personal relationship may be as private as the relationship itself. One of the merits I should claim for this approach to morality is precisely that it so easily makes room for many concepts which we habitually employ, but which tend to be neglected in moral philosophy. Thus we talk of medical ethics, of the code of honour of a military caste, of bourgeois morality and of working-class morality. Such ideas fit more easily into an account of morality which sees it as essentially, or at any rate fundamentally, a function of social groupings than they do into the more apparently individualistic approaches which are generally current.

Another merit which I shall claim for the present approach is that it makes it relatively easy to understand such notions as those of conscientiousness, duty and obligation in a concrete and realistic way. These notions have been treated almost entirely abstractly in moral philosophy in the recent past, with the result that they have come to some of our contemporaries[1] to seem to be meaningless survivals of discarded ideas about the government of the universe. But as most ordinarily employed I do not think they are that at all. There is nothing in the least mysterious or metaphysical in the fact that duties and obligations go with offices, positions and relationships to others. The demands to be made on somebody in virtue of his occupation of a certain position may indeed be, and often are, quite explicitly listed in considerable detail. And when we call someone conscientious or say that he has a strong sense of his obligations or of duty, we do not ordinarily mean that he is haunted by the ghost of the idea of supernatural ordinances; we mean rather such things as this, that he can be counted on for sustained effort to do what is required of him in definite capacities, to fulfil the demand made on him as student or teacher or parent or soldier or whatever he may be. A certain professor once said, 'For me to be moral is to behave like a professor.'

Suppose we now raise that old philosophical question: What interest has the individual in morality? The question may force us to a more adequate conception of morality than the minimal interpretation offers by itself. It certainly forces us to strike, or to try to strike, some delicate balances. The only answer to the question so far suggested is this: that the individual's ethical imagination may be captured or fired by one or more ideal pictures of life which require for their realization the existence of social groupings and social organizations such as could not exist in the absence of a

[1] Cf. G. E. M. Anscombe, 'Modern Moral Philosophy', *Philosophy*, January 1958.

system of social demands made on individual members of these groups or organizations. I have already hinted that this answer is too crude, that the interplay between ethical ideal and social obligation is more intricate than it suggests. The answer is also not crude enough. The picture of the ideal form of life and the associated ethical vision of the world tend to be the products of the refined mind and relatively comfortable circumstances. But when we ask what the interest of the individual is in morality, we mean to ask about all those individuals on whom socially sanctioned demands are made; not just about the imaginatively restless and materially cosy. We need not, perhaps, insist upon just the same answer for all; but, if we take the question seriously, we must insist on *some* answer for all. There may seem to be a broader answer which does not altogether depart from the form of the over-refined answer. For who could exist at all, or pursue any aim, except in some form of society? And there is no form of society without rules, without some system of socially sanctioned demands on its members. Here at least is a common interest in morality as minimally conceived, an interest which can be attributed to all those about whom the question can be raised. Still we may feel that it is not enough. And in this feeling is the germ of the reason why the minimal conception of morality is inadequate to the ordinary notion, at least in its contemporary form; and perhaps, in uncovering the reason for this inadequacy, we may discover too what there is in the notion of the universal applicability of moral rules.

We have arrived at the fact that everyone on whom some form of socially sanctioned demand is made has an interest in the existence of some system of socially sanctioned demands. But this fact seems inadequate to answer the question what the individual's interest in morality is. We can begin to understand this inadequacy by thinking of the different things that might be meant by the social sanctioning of a demand. 'Sanction' is related to 'permission' and 'approval'; and also to 'power' and to 'penalty'. A socially sanctioned demand is doubtless a demand made with the permission and approval of a society; and backed, in some form and degree, with its power. But the idea of a society as the totality of individuals subject to demands may here come apart from the idea of society as the source of sanction of those demands. The sanctioning society may simply be a sub-group of the total society, the dominant sub-group, the group in which power resides. Mere membership of the total society does not guarantee membership of the sanctioning part of the society. Nor does a mere interest in the existence of some system of socially sanctioned demands guarantee an interest in the particular system of socially sanctioned demands to which one is subjected. But unless at least one, and perhaps both, of these nonguaranteed conditions is satisfied, it does not seem that the fulfilment of a socially sanctioned demand comes anywhere near being what we should regard as the fulfilment of a moral obligation. That is to say, if I have no foothold at all in the sanctioning part of society, and if no interest of mine is safeguarded by the system of demands to which I am subject, then, in fulfilling a demand made upon me, I may indeed, in one sense, be doing what I am obliged to do; but scarcely what I am *morally* obliged to do. No wonder, then, that the question 'What is the individual's interest in morality?' is not answered by mentioning the general interest in the existence of some system of socially sanctioned demands. The answer now scarcely appears to touch the question.

Suppose, then, that we consider the idea of a society such that all its members have *some* interest, not merely in there being a system of socially sanctioned demands, but in the actual system of demands which obtains in that society. It seems that we can ensure such an interest even to the powerless and enslaved by stipulating that the system includes not only demands made on them in the interest of their masters, but also demands made on their masters in their interests. We might be tempted to say that by thus securing to them an interest in the system of demands, we secure to them also some sort of position or foothold in the sanctioning part of society. Certainly, when the master recognizes moral obligations to his slave, we shall be at least one step nearer to allowing that the slave is not merely subject to the demands of his master, but may recognize a moral obligation to fulfil them. Even in this extreme case, then, we can approach the situation which everyone would agree to regard as characteristically moral, the situation in which there is reciprocal acknowledgment of rights and duties.

Still I think we must admit a distinction of two stages in this approach to the characteristically moral situation. Interest in claims on others and acknowledgment of claims on oneself are connected but not identical. It is a tautology, though not an easy one, that everyone subject to moral demands has some interest in morality. For a demand made on an individual is to be regarded as a moral demand only if it belongs to a system of demands which includes demands made on others in his interest. It would be agreeable, as

I just now suggested, to be able to argue strictly that this fact carries with it the conclusion that mere self-conscious membership of a moral community implies at least in some degree extending one's sanction to its system of demands, to the extent of genuinely acknowledging as obligations at least some of the claims which others have on one, even if only provisionally and with the strongest desire that the system should be different. But to argue so would be to equivocate with the phrase 'membership of a moral community'. There would be nothing self-contradictory about the idea of one who recognized his interest in the system of moral demands and resolved merely to profit by it as much as he could, fulfilling its demands on himself only in so far as his interest calculably required it. He might get away with it successfully if he were subtle enough in his practice of the hypocrisy which this policy would necessarily involve. But it is an important fact that hypocrisy would be necessary. It is connected with the further fact, a fact of human nature which can probably be explained in a number of ways, that quite thoroughgoing egotism of this kind is rare. But for this fact there could be no such thing as a system of moral demands. We cannot argue that it is a tautology that *anyone* subject to moral demands who recognizes his interest in the system of demands must also genuinely acknowledge some obligations under the system. But we can argue that it is a tautology that the *generality* of those subject to moral demands must genuinely recognize some obligations under the system of demands. For if this were not so, there would be no such thing as a system of moral demands and hence no such thing as being subject to a moral demand.

These steps from a minimal to a more adequate conception of morality (i.e. to a conception which at least begins to square with what we nowadays vaguely understand by the word) may easily encourage abstract exaggerations and distortions in moral philosophy. For instance, the necessary truth that the members of a moral community in general acknowledge some moral claims upon them may be exaggerated into the idea of a self-conscious choice or adoption of the principle of those claims—so everyone appears, grandly but unplausibly, as a moral self-legislator. This is an exaggeration which has appealed, in different forms, to more than one philosopher. Again these steps reveal something genuinely universal in morality: the necessary acceptance of reciprocity of claim. And *one* way in which a demand made on one individual in the interest of others can be balanced by a demand made on others in his interest is

through the operation of a general rule or principle having application to all alike. But it does not follow from this that *all* moral
claims have, or are seen by those who acknowledge them as having,
the character of applications of universal principles holding for all
men. There is no reason why a system of moral demands characteristic of one community should, or even could, be found in every
other. And even within a single system of reciprocal claims, the
moral demand may essentially *not* relate to a situation in which
any member of the system could find himself *vis-à-vis* any other.
Here are two reasons why it is misleading to say that moral behaviour is what is demanded of men as men. It might, in some cases,
be essentially what is demanded of Spartans by other Spartans, or of
a king by his subjects. What is universally demanded of the members of a moral community is something like the abstract virtue of
justice; a man should not insist on a particular claim while refusing
to acknowledge any reciprocal claim. But from this formally universal feature of morality no consequences follow as to the universality of application of the particular rules in the observance of
which, in particular situations and societies, justice consists.

One must beware, however, of meeting exaggeration with coun-
ter-exaggeration. It is important to recognize the diversity of possible
systems of moral demands, and the diversity of demands which
may be made within any system. But it is also important to recognize that certain human interests are so fundamental and so general
that they must be universally acknowledged in some form and to
some degree in any conceivable moral community. Of some interests, one might say: a system could scarcely command *sufficient*
interest in those subject to its demands for these demands to be
acknowledged as obligations, unless it secured to them *this* interest.
Thus some claim on human succour, some obligation to abstain
from the infliction of physical injury, seem to be necessary features
of almost any system of moral demands. Here at least we have types
of moral behaviour which are demanded *of* men as men because
they are demanded *for* and *by* men as men. Another interest which
is fundamental to many types of social relation and social grouping
is the interest in not being deceived. In most kinds of social grouping for which there obtains any system of moral demand and claim
at all this interest is acknowledged as a claim which any member of
the group has on any other; and perhaps most such groupings could
scarcely exist without this acknowledgment. When all allowance
has been made, then, for the possible diversity of moral systems and

the possible diversity of demands within a system, it remains true
that the recognition of certain general virtues and obligations will
be a logically or humanly necessary feature of almost any conceivable moral system: these will include the abstract virtue of justice,
some form of obligation to mutual aid and to mutual abstention
from injury and, in some form and in some degree, the virtue of
honesty. This guarded recognition of the necessary universal applicability of some relatively vague and abstract moral principles is
itself a corrective to the idea of unbounded freedom of choice of
such principles on the part of the individual.

I spoke earlier of the need for striking some delicate balances,
and I hope that the nature of some of these is now apparent. Constant checks are required if these balances are not to be lost. We
have seen in what sense it is true that everyone on whom a moral
demand is made must have an interest in morality. But we have also
seen that the existence of a system of moral demands (at least as we
now understand this concept) requires some degree of general readiness to recognize claims made upon one even when this recognition
cannot plausibly be said to be in one's own interest. The existence
of some such readiness needs no more to be argued for than the
existence of morality in general. But it is necessary to emphasize
it in order to correct another exaggeration, the exaggeration which
would represent all morality as prudential.[2] To say that this readiness to acknowledge the claims of others does not need to be argued
for is not to say that it does not need to be explained. We may discuss its natural sources; and the terms in which we do so will change
with the state of our psychological knowledge: the appeal to the
concept of sympathy, for example, will scarcely now seem adequate.
But, however we explain it, there is no need to sophisticate ourselves
into denying altogether the existence or fundamental importance
of this recognition of others' claims. Again, we have seen that the
fact of acknowledgement of claims may be blown up into the picture
of the self-legislating moral agent; and here we should do well to
scale down our pretensions to freedom by remembering, if nothing
else, the importance of the training we receive and the limited
choice we exercise of the moral communities to which we belong.
Finally, we have acknowledged some force in the idea of universally
applicable principles of moral demand and claim. But to keep
within bounds the pretensions of this idea, we must insist again on
the flexibility of the concept of a social group, upon the diversity of

[2] Cf. P. R. Foot, 'Moral Beliefs', *Proceedings of the Aristotelian Society*, 1958-59.

groups and upon the absurdity of the idea that detailed demands could be shifted indifferently from group to group or apply to all members alike within a group.

There are further important moral phenomena of which the account I have given makes little or no explicit mention. Some of these it might even seem, at first sight, to exclude. Is there not such a thing as moral criticism, from within a society, of the existing moral forms of that society? Cannot different systems of socially sanctioned demand, under which those subject to demands genuinely acknowledge obligations, be the subject of relative moral evaluation? Cannot there be situations in which men may or should recognize moral obligations to each other, although there is no common society of which they are members and there is no concept of a 'social' relationship which can be at all plausibly represented as applying to their situation? Any acceptable account of morality must certainly allow an affirmative answer to these questions; and there are others which will suggest themselves. But they no more yield a reason for mistrusting the approach I have adopted than the inadequacy of what I called the minimal interpretation of morality gave a reason for wholly discarding that idea. By enriching the minimal interpretation with certain applications of the notions of interest, and of acknowledgment of obligation, we obtained what was recognizably a concept of social morality. It is necessary only to draw out the significance of certain elements in *this* conception in order to make room for the ideas of moral criticism, and of a morality which transcends standard forms of social relationship. I have remarked already that, because certain human needs and interests are as fundamental and as general as they are, we shall find correspondingly general types of virtue and obligation acknowledged in some form and in some degree in almost any conceivable moral system. Now it is characteristically by analogy with, and extension of, acknowledged forms of these, that moral development proceeds, and that these ideas themselves assume more refined and generous shapes. And moral criticism at its most self-conscious proceeds characteristically by appeal to, and interpretation of, such general moral ideas as those of justice, integrity and humanity: existing institutions, systems of demand and claim, are criticized as unjust, inhumane or corrupt. We may say that so far from excluding the idea of moral criticism, the concept of social morality, as I have outlined it, makes fully intelligible the nature and possibility of such criticism. For we can perceive how the seeds of criticism lie in the morality itself; and we may even hope, on this basis, to achieve some understanding of the complex interrelationships between social and economic change, the critical insights of individual moralists, and the actual course of moral evolution. (It is, for instance, an easy consequence of our principles that moral *formalism*—i.e. a rigid adherence to the letter, with no appeal to the spirit, of the rules—will tend to be at a maximum in a static and isolated society, and that moral *disorientation* will tend to be at a maximum when such a morality is suddenly exposed to radical change.) Just as a social morality contains the seeds of moral criticism, so the two together contain the seeds of a morality transcending standard social relationships. It is easy to see how the tendency of at least one type of self-conscious and critical morality is generalizing and anti-parochial, as it is anti-formalist. Some moralists would maintain that a true concept of morality emerges only at the limit of this generalizing process. This is a judgment in which, as it seems to me, the sense of reality has become quite subordinated to zeal. But wherever we choose to say that 'true morality' begins, I have no doubt whatever that our understanding of the concept of morality in general is best served by the kind of approach that I have sketched. Where what we are dealing with is a developing human institution, it is no reproach to an explanation that it may be described as at least partially genetic.

But now it is time to return to the question of the relation between social moralities and those ideal pictures of forms of life which I spoke of at the outset. All I have so far explicitly said about this is that the realization of any such ideal requires the existence of forms of social grouping or organization which in turn require the existence of a system of socially sanctioned demands on their members. We have since remarked that a system of socially sanctioned demands would fall short of being a system of moral demands unless those demands were not merely enforced as demands, but also at least in some degree generally acknowledged as claims by those subject to them; and it follows from this that to be a member of a moral community cannot merely be a matter of convenience, except perhaps for those who can practise a sustained hypocrisy of which few are in fact capable. Yet it may still be true in general to say that the possibility of the pursuit of an ideal form of life quite pragmatically requires membership of a moral community or of moral communities; for it is extremely unlikely in fact that the minimal social conditions for the pursuit of any ethical ideal which anyone is likely to entertain could in practice be fulfilled except through membership of such communities. But of course the relations between these two things are much more intricate and various than this formulation by itself suggests. The possibilities of collision, absorption and interplay are many. The way I have just expressed the matter perhaps makes most obvious the possibility of collision; and this possibility is worth stressing. It is worth stressing that what one acknowledges or half-acknowledges as obligation may conflict not only, crudely, with interest and, weakly, with inclination but also with ideal aspiration, with the vision that captures the ethical imagination. On the other hand, it may be that a picture of the ideal life is precisely one in which the interests of morality are dominant, are given an ideal, overriding value. To one dominated temporarily or permanently by such a picture the 'consciousness of duty faithfully performed' will appear as the supremely satisfactory state, and being moral not merely as something that matters but as the thing that supremely matters. Or again the ideal picture may be, not that in which the interests of morality in general are dominant, but rather one in which the dominating idea operates powerfully to reinforce some, but not perhaps others, of a system of moral demands. So it is with that ideal picture in which obedience to the command to love one another appears as the supreme value.

This is still to draw too simple a picture. Let us remember the diversity of communities to which we may be said to belong, and the diversity of systems of moral demand which belong to them. To a certain extent, though to an extent which we must not exaggerate, the systems of moral relationships into which we enter are a matter of choice—or at least a matter in which there are alternative possibilities; and different systems of moral demand are variously well or ill adapted to different ideal pictures of life. The ideal picture, moreover, may call for membership not merely of communities in which certain interests are safeguarded by a system of moral demands, but for membership of a community or of a system of relationships in which the system of demands reflects in a positive way the nature of the ideal. For one crude instance of this, we may think again of the morality of a military caste in connection with the ideal of personal honour. In general, in a society as complex as ours, it is obvious that there are different moral environments, different sub-communities within the community, different systems of moral relationships, interlocking indeed and overlapping with one another, but offering some possibilities of choice, some possibilities of adjustment of moral demand and individual aspiration. But here again, at least in our time and place, it is the limits of the direct relevance of each to the other that must finally be stressed. Inside a single political human society one may indeed find different, and perhaps widely different, moral environments, social groupings in which different systems of moral demand are recognized. But if the one grouping is to form part of the wider society, its members must be subject too to a wider system of reciprocal demand, a wider common morality; and the relative significance of the wider common morality will grow in proportion as the sub-groups of the society are closely interlocked, in proportion as each individual is a member of a plurality of sub-groups and in proportion as the society is not rigidly stratified, but allows of relatively free access to, and withdrawal from, its sub-groups. In a political society which thus combines a wide variety of social groupings with complex interlocking and freedom of movement between them the dissociation of idiosyncratic ideal and common moral demand will doubtless tend to be at its maximum. On the other hand an ideal picture of man *may* tend, in fact or in fancy, to demand the status of a comprehensive common morality. Thus Coleridgean or Tolstoyan dreamers may play with the thought of self-enclosed ideal communities in which the system of moral demands shall answer exactly, or as exactly as possible, to an ideal picture of life held in common by all their members. Such fancies are bound to strike many as weak and futile; for the price of preserving the purity of such communities is that of severance from the world at large. More seriously, there may be some attempt to make the whole moral climate of an existing national state reflect some ideal image of human solidarity or religious devotion or military honour. In view of the natural diversity of human ideals—to mention only that—such a state (or its members) will evidently be subject to at least some stresses from which a liberal society is free.

To conclude. I have spoken of those ideal images of life of which one individual may sympathize with many, and desire to see many realized in some degree. I have spoken also of those systems—though the word is too strong—of recognized reciprocal claim that we have on one another as members of human communities, or as terms of human relationships, many of which could scarcely exist or have the character they have but for the existence of such systems of reciprocal claim. I have said something, though too little, of the complex and various relations which may hold between these two things, viz. our conflicting visions of the ends of life and the systems of moral demand which make social living possible. Finally I have glanced at the relations of both to the political societies in which we necessarily live. The field of phenomena over which I have thus loosely ranged is, I think, very much more complex and many-sided than I have been able to suggest; but I have been concerned to suggest something of its complexity. Some implications for moral philosophy I have hinted at in passing, mainly by way of an attempt to correct some typical exaggerations of contemporary theory. But the main practical implications for moral and political philosophy are, I think, that more attention should be concentrated on types of social structure and social relation, and on those complex inter-relationships which I have mentioned as well as others which I have not. For instance, it is hard not to believe that understanding of our secular morality would be enhanced by considering the historical role that religion has played in relation to morality. Or again, I doubt if the nature of morality can be properly understood without some consideration of its relationship to law. It is not merely that the spheres of morality and law are largely overlapping, or that their demands often coincide. It is also that in the way law functions to give cohesiveness to the most important of all social groupings we may find a coarse model of the way in which systems of moral demand function to give cohesiveness to social groupings in general. Similarly, in the complexity of our attitudes towards existing law we may find a model of the complexity of our attitude towards the systems of moral demand which impinge upon us in our social relations at large—or upon others, in theirs.

Finally, I do not think there is any very definite invitation to moral or political commitment implicit in what I have said. But perhaps one question can be raised, and in part answered. What will be the attitude of one who experiences sympathy with a variety of conflicting ideals of life? It seems that he will be most at home in a liberal society, in a society in which there are variant moral environments but in which no ideal endeavours to engross, and determine the character of, the common morality. He will not argue in favour of such a society that it gives the best chance for the truth about life to prevail, for he will not consistently believe that there is such a thing as the truth about life. Nor will he argue in its favour that it has the best chance of producing a harmonious kingdom of ends, for he will not think of ends as necessarily capable of being harmonized. He will simply welcome the ethical diversity which the society makes possible, and in proportion as he values that diversity he will note that he is the natural, though perhaps the sympathetic, enemy of all those whose single vision of the ends of life drives them to try to make the requirements of the ideal co-extensive with those of common social morality.

16

MORALITY AND THE TWO WORLDS CONCEPT

R. F. Holland

THE idea of an antithesis between two worlds, the outer world and the inner, between the realm of objects and occurrences which physicists, chemists or zoologists study and the realm of the mind in which are to be sought the processes (and perhaps the *immediate* objects) of thought and reflection, knowledge and remembrance, feeling and desire—this idea is the thread out of which a large part of the history of philosophy has been woven, and it is only recently that investigations into its composition have led to some reluctance to spin more of it. Moral philosophy has been in a different situation *vis-à-vis* the two worlds concept from that of some other branches of philosophical enquiry, for instance the philosophy of perception, which as traditionally conceived could scarcely have existed without it. Without it, no *philosophical* theories of perception—as distinct from scientific theories embodying laws about the behaviour of light, the functioning of the eye and so on—could ever have come to be formulated. Theories of morals, on the other hand, invite a division into those in which the inner-outer distinction plays a role of vital importance, and those in which it is present only as an incidental feature. This division is, I believe, the most deeply rooted of all the divisions it is possible to make between moral philosophies, and it puts into the same hemisphere two luminaries who might otherwise[1] be regarded as standing at opposite poles from one another—Kierkegaard and Kant. These two, together with Socrates and Plato, are the outstanding exponents of the two worlds

[1] Cf. E. A. Gellner's paper in *Proceedings of the Aristotelian Society*, 1954.

thesis in moral philosophy, and of the point of view which connects
morality with inwardness. I shall try, in what follows, to compare
and put into some sort of perspective the behaviour of the inner-
outer dichotomy in a selection of their writings.

In Kierkegaard's *Stages on Life's Way* there is a treatment of the
question: What is the difference between being married to a
woman and simply living with her, however happy and successful
and fraught with love one's life with her may be? Kierkegaard is in
no doubt that there is a crucial distinction to be drawn between
these two conditions, although to judge from appearances, to judge
from any external or outward standpoint, no difference whatever
may be discernible. A couple whose relationship is of the second
kind might be pillars of respectability; the woman might wear a
ring on her finger, both of them might have sworn an oath and
signed a book, have gone through some ritual in a register office or
in a church. These are the commonly accepted criteria of marriage;
they make a relationship a marriage in the legal, the civic, the
aesthetic sense, but they do not turn it into a marriage of the kind
about which Kierkegaard wishes to speak. And if this be lacking he
holds that the couple, for all their conformity with convention, for
all their success and their happiness, will be living thoughtlessly,
their relationship founded upon what he calls a world-minded
deification of existence; which, he says, is perdition. Marriage, in
the sense in which he wishes to use the term, is a τέλος, a supreme
work of freedom. It is not something immediate, but implies a resolution. Love, though it can prompt, does not resolve. Hence there is
a gap between love's immediacy and marriage. This gap is bridge-
able only by a resolution. Kierkegaard insists moreover that the resolution must be on hand from the beginning and that a marriage
cannot be regarded as something capable of growing up by degrees
after a couple have lived together for some time. If the resolution be
not there from the start then something has come amiss and in his
view something irredeemable. A seduction has taken place instead
of a marriage.

The resolution about which Kierkegaard is speaking must be one
of a special kind. He cannot be speaking of a decision simply to
terminate a situation in which a number of different courses of
action have presented themselves for consideration; not of a proposal, howsoever firmly made and far-seeing, to take a plunge in one
direction rather than another—for how could *that* produce a marriage as distinct from an indefinitely prolonged association? It looks

as if the resolution must be in some sense a generalized one, not a resolution to do just this or just that in this or another situation and subject to these or other conditions. It must be an unconditional resolution. Kierkegaard says of it that it has nothing to do with probability, nothing to do with the upshot. It is not, in other words, a resolution whose actuality or effectiveness is judgeable in terms of what it accomplishes: it is not concerned at all with what is outward, with one's success or progress in the world. It is an *eternal* resolution as well as one that is made at a time. In it, so Kierkegaard says, a bond of union is forged between the pagan and the spiritual, between love and reality. To be capable of making it one needs reflection and also faith.

To be capable of making it—but what is this? To be capable of doing what? If there is nothing specific, no one deed rather than another to be performed, what difference can remain between the person who makes the resolution and the person who does not? There surely has to be something which the former does or achieves and which the latter does not. But to the question, *What does the resolution achieve?* only two answers are allowed to be given. First, the resolution puts the maker of it into a relationship with eternity. Second, it achieves nothing: there is nothing in the world that it achieves, that it enables one to grasp. In the world—the external world—one ventures all; one suffers; one's attitude is to be that of resignation. All the ends that are here to be achieved one dismisses from view, for they are only relative ends. As far as the eternal is concerned, and that is the only absolute end, the whole of time and existence is a period of striving.[2]

What the existing individual must do in making his eternal resolution, therefore, is to strive or will, and to will absolutely, while renouncing all acquisition for himself. What he wills is in fact this renunciation. But the question we still wish to be answered is: In just what way does he will it, in what does his willing of it consist? This is indeed the great question for Kierkegaard also. But whereas our problem here, in asking this question, is that of investigating the sense, if any, that can be attached to the idea of an eternal resolution, the problem for Kierkegaard is that of how to live—of how an individual may put himself, in his temporal existence, into a relationship with eternity. There is one solution which could be offered and which he appears to rebut with peculiar force by using, as an example of an eternal resolution, the resolution to

[2] *Unscientific Postscript* ch. IV, § IIA.

marry. This is the suggestion that the individual may solve his problem by sitting motionless in a monastery, though that is one possible way of construing inwardness and seemingly the most radical form of renunciation of the relative ends of the world. The rejection of relative ends must be encompassed, Kierkegaard believes, in action, not through inactivity. Now although he does not actually say this, it seems to me that a directive that might be given, and indeed the only practical directive that could be given to anyone who should ask how he is to will in action an eternal resolution, be it willed in connection with marriage or in any other connection, is the directive that he should do whatever thing he does entirely for its own sake. In other words (somewhat Irish-sounding words perhaps), to reject relative ends, to eschew the doing of anything for the sake of a worldly end, is to treat the doing of everything in life[3] as an end in itself. In this way alone would it be possible in one's doings in the world to achieve the requisite freedom from the world and hence a relationship with the eternal. In so far as one's doings cease to be doings for the sake of some end then the less, in a sense, do they amount to doing and the more they approximate to suffering: and it is in suffering that the freedom is said to be greatest and the world and the eternal come closest together.

Let me return to Kierkegaard's point that the resolution is the outcome of reflection. He also speaks, like Socrates, of the necessity for recollection. What reflection and recollection amount to in this context is self-knowledge, the understanding of one's inner nature: the first precept for one who would attain to inwardness is γνῶθι σεαυτόν, naturally. It would be a radical misunderstanding to suppose that self-knowledge could consist, on the one hand of any kind of intuitive awareness or self-authenticating experience of what is going on in one, or on the other hand that it could result from any coldly experimental enquiry. It is not attainable in a scientifically diagnostic way, has nothing to do with psychological investigation for instance. There is not here, as in many other contexts, the identification of knowledge with certainty; for it is (so Kierkegaard affirms) a searching, not a conclusion, and it is carried on with fear and trembling. Undoubtedly self-knowledge can be identified to some extent with insight into the motives from which one acts, though Kierkegaard characteristically declines to sanction this

[3] In *life*, i.e., in connection with others. A purely aesthetic inwardness is possible also— the artist creates for creation's sake when he does not do so for fame or money or the gratification of his public—but this has to do rather with imagination than with reality, the reality of suffering (*Training in Christianity*, O.U.P. 1941, p. 186).

identification explicitly. But awareness of what one is (of one's motives as they are) would be impossible without a conception of what one might have been or might become (a conception of one's motives as they ought to be—the conception of the ethical reality in accordance with which the maker of an eternal resolution strives and wills). Accordingly the search, in so far as it establishes anything, is said by Kierkegaard to establish that one is guilty and a sinner; and this result was foreshadowed from the start. As to the validity of the result, one's guarantee is the quality of the search. The quality of one's relationship to a τέλος is the guarantee of the absoluteness of that τέλος. It is one's relationship to eternity that defines it as eternity (*Unscientific Postscript*).

I have tried to indicate in the foregoing remarks concerning Kierkegaard, something of the relationship between the conceptual dichotomy of Inner and Outer and the notions of Striving or Willing, End or Result, the need to do something specific, Eternity, Freedom, Knowledge and Motive (I shall want to consider later the way in which the notion of Happiness fits into this scheme of relationships). I do not suppose that Kant exercised much influence upon Kierkegaard directly, or in the direction which this comparison might seem to suggest, but there is nevertheless to be found in Kant's *Groundwork of the Metaphysic of Morals* a set of conceptual relationships which corresponds quite closely to the one I have so far outlined.

The contrast between the inner and the outer is drawn at once in Kant's famous opening remark that the only thing that can conceivably be called good without qualification is a good will. This will is contrasted with talents, with gifts of nature and of fortune, with power, riches, honour, health and general well-being. A good will is not good, says Kant, because of what it effects or accomplishes, not through its aptness for the attainment of some proposed end (its existence has nothing to do with the upshot, to use Kierkegaard's expression). As the bearer of unconditional value the will is thus, for Kant, a denizen of the inner world; but it is also conceived as an agent whose activity impinges on the outer world, where it can suffer hindrance at the hand of nature and inclination. Kant might well have said of the good will what Kierkegaard said of a resolution such as the resolution to marry, namely that it unites the temporal with the eternal. He says in fact that the will stands at the parting of the ways, where it is subject to two distinct and opposing influences—an internal influence, for which another name is the motive of duty, and the external influence of inclination. In so far however as it is at the beck of inclination, determined by alien causes, it is unfree: and this amounts to saying that it is unfree in so far as its activity is geared to the production of any end or result. To be an entirely free will the will must be an entirely inward will. Freedom is not to be found in the realm of phenomena (the outer world) where everything is determined, but belongs to the noumenal (which is the same as eternal and is also to be equated with the inner world) where too there is determination, but of a different kind—the will's determination to be a good will, the determination to legislate in accordance with the moral law.

The question which one may now be tempted to ask of Kant is: What does the moral law enjoin us to do? Some of his critics have grumbled on the ground that he fails to tell us. He provides a formulation of the moral law in imperative terms, but all that the imperative seems to say is: Obey the moral law!—or to put this in the form which Kant reached *via* an analysis of what he took to be involved in the notion of a law, namely universality: Act only on that maxim through which you can at the same time will that it should become a universal law.

The idea that it is a defect of Kant's position that he should be unable to deduce as a consequence of his premises any specific type of action that we must always do or avoid rests on a misunderstanding. To make any such stipulation as a condition of morality would be tantamount to assessing the goodness of the will from an external standpoint, judging it from the point of view of its achievements or results. For Kant to do this would be for him to contradict himself; and in so far as he tries to do this then he actually does contradict himself. To know that your will is good is not to know that this in particular is to be done or that in particular avoided: [4] to search in this direction is to search in the outer world, which is the wrong direction. Instead you are required to look inward; to know yourself; to ensure that your motive is not one of inclination, i.e. that you are not doing whatever you do for its own sake. Kant's practical

---

[4] This is by no means to assert that the morally good man can be indifferent to, and under no necessity to discharge, any actual obligations that may be placed upon him—which would be an absurd thesis to maintain. The point is rather that the nature of moral goodness is such that it cannot be grasped piecemeal. The task is not like that of learning the dates of the kings of England for instance, a matter of having one's attention drawn to an increasing number of 'moral facts', or the gradual cataloguing of more and more prohibitions and licences, with the idea that one would understand all there was to know about morality after every conceivable example had been enumerated. ('Nothing could be more fatal to morality than that we should wish to derive it from examples.')

imperative—So act as to treat humanity, whether in your own person or in any other, always as an end and never simply as a means—is thus a consequence of his premises in a way that the categorical imperative, i.e. the imperative about universalization, is not. The latter is really a gigantic kink in the argument, a distraction that gets introduced because *inter alia* Kant, not being content to regard moral determination (the manner in which the good will is determined to will) simply as the negation of a determination to obtain some sort of advantage for oneself (which is what the subjection of the will to inclination and the forces of nature amounts to), insists on conceiving it as a kind of parallel shadow of this—a conformability to a non-natural counterpart of the law or laws of phenomena.

The use of the contrast between the inner and the outer for the purpose of saying something about the difference between a moral man and a man of no morality cannot be separated and regarded as something distinct from its use in pointing to the difference between a man and a machine. For one of the effects of the double use of the same dichotomy is precisely to secure that these two distinctions merge conceptually into a single contrast. Hence the two important equations which are to be found in Kant, first between the will that is not good and the will that is not free—which is one way of assimilating the non-moral man to the robot; secondly, the equation of the good will with rationality, the thesis that moral defect is somehow a deficiency of knowledge or understanding—again the defect of the robot. An appearance of these two equations has been noticed already in Kierkegaard. With regard to the second, since obviously the idea that being moral is a matter of reason or understanding is not confined to those moral theories in which the contrast between the inner and the outer is prominent, I want here to direct attention towards the difference in the sort of connection that is made between morality and understanding, or else in the sort of reason with which morality is connected, when a moral theory centres itself upon this conceptual dichotomy.

In the late Professor G. C. Field's book *Moral Theory* a chapter entitled 'The Kantian Fallacy in Other Forms' begins with the following words:

> No one, except his immediate disciples, has attempted to take over and defend Kant's system in all its details. No later writer of any importance has accepted the proposition that goodness simply means universality, in Kant's sense. But, as we have seen, that theory is only the result of a more fundamental error. And this fundamental error,

as we shall find, reappears in many different forms in later writers. The fundamental objection to the theory is that it fails to fulfil one of the fundamental conditions of any correct account of the moral fact. Whatever goodness is, it is at least in some way a reason for action, a reason for pursuing those things where it is present and avoiding those where it is absent. And any account of it which fails to show why it should be a reason for action, still more an account which describes it in such a way that it could not possibly be a reason for action, stands condemned.

In his suggestion that goodness according to Kant 'simply means universality' I believe that Field was diverting the attention of his students from what is of greatest importance in Kant's moral philosophy; however, his 'fatal objection to the theory' happens not to be contingent upon pre-eminence being given to the categorical imperative and it is with this objection that we are concerned. Goodness is certainly not, in Kant's opinion, *a reason* (for action, for the pursuit of anything); it is—*reason*. The indefinite article, the absence of which Field condemned, constitutes the dividing line between the standpoint of Socrates, Plato and Kant on the one hand and the standpoint of Aristotle and the Utilitarians on the other. To Kant the problem: How can reason be practical? meant something quite different from what it meant to Aristotle. It was not for Kant the problem: How can reason be or become practical reason? (How is φρόνησις attainable by a rational animal?), but rather: What is the connection between pure reason and morality? Hence Kant's persistent use of that odd-sounding juxtaposition 'pure practical reason'. His answer to the question was, in brief, that reason and morality are connected internally—the connection is not to be sought in the outer world but in the inner. The nature of the reason here determines and is determined by the nature of the connection.

As a synonym for 'pure reason' Kant used the term 'a priori reason' and the significance of these terms is to be found primarily in what they deny. Pure reason is that which contains no admixture of the empirical. It has nothing to do with one's ability to manage a household for example. It is no sort of capacity to cope in a discriminating fashion with matters that are variable and contingent; is no sort of skill in fact. It is not *savoire-faire* which one might acquire by experience, by knocking about the world. It is not something that is exercised about the means of securing any end.[5] It is, in short, the

---

[5] Contrast *Nic. Eth.* II 6, 9; III 3; VI 5-11.

very antithesis of prudence, as φρόνησις may be rendered, accurately enough, into English. The prudent man takes out insurance policies: the man who is seriously concerned with the ethical, Kierkegaard said, must risk all. So far from having to do with insight into the circumstances of this or that time and place, pure reason focuses itself upon the timeless, the eternal. The knowledge with which Socrates equated virtue, when he rejected the mention of particular instances of things to be done or not done as irrelevant to an understanding of the nature of virtue, is thus akin to Kant's pure reason. It is not, as Plato expressed it, knowledge of the world (of many particulars) but knowledge of one thing only—the Form of the Good.

Field's criticism of Kant is reminiscent of the ultimate objection brought by Aristotle against the belief that the way to an understanding of morality lay through the Theory of Forms: 'Even granting that the good which is predicated of different things were somehow a unity or that it somehow stood by itself, still it clearly would not be something that man can practise or possess.'[6] Aristotle, as H. W. B. Joseph remarked, 'was more interested in the multiplicity of virtues than in the unity of virtue', and Plato's peculiar reformulation of the Socratic thesis seemed to him only to throw into relief its inherent absurdity. Supposing the Form of the Good to signify a remote and gaseous super-entity, he decided that Plato had portrayed goodness as something that could have no bearing on life. But it is not entirely evident that this was Plato's own supposition (the idea that he was not all the time concerned most seriously with life were an absurdity indeed); nor does the eternal seem to have signified for Kierkegaard any kind of gaseous realm.

The conception of goodness as an eternal Form, with the attendant conception of life's wisdom as other-worldly wisdom, is the expression of an attitude to life which Aristotle failed to 'get inside' in the way a person whose outlook is non-religious is apt to make no sense of religion. In fact the Platonic, the Kantian and the Kierkegaardian conception of morality, with its reference to Forms, to Noumena and to the Eternal, may as well be called outright the religious[7] conception of morality. It is characteristic of religious utterances that they should require to express an attitude to the

---

[6] *Nic. Eth.* I 6.
[7] That Kierkegaard distinguishes between the ethical and the religious has not been forgotten here or previously. This distinction does not imply a separation let alone a conflict: it is essentially a hermeneutic device. Kierkegaard presents only one great anti-

world by talking about something that seems to be beyond the world. So we are tempted perhaps to put it. Yet with this way of stating the matter we are in trouble immediately. For in speaking of an attitude to the world we surely mean an attitude to the entire universe, to the world as a whole. But it is logically impermissible to speak of something beyond the world as a whole. How then, we must ask, could a language even *seem* to refer to something beyond the world in this sense, except to someone who had misunderstood it? However, the terms 'world' or 'universe' could have been employed equivocally in our statement, being used on their second appearance in the way an astronomer for instance might habitually use them (there would be a great deal for language to refer to beyond that). Such an equivation would permit sense to emerge from the statement; but only, it seems, by forcing us straight back upon the distinction between the inner and the outer. For the world *qua* subject of astronomical and other scientific investigations is the outer world as opposed to the inner world. If it be only the outer world that Forms, Noumena, Eternity—or God—can be said properly to be beyond, then how can the reference to Forms and the rest be anything more than a reduplication of the already existent reference to the inner?

That the Kingdom of God, which is eternal, is also within you is a well known Christian dictum. Somewhat similarly, Plato equates the Formal unity of virtue with an inward unity—δικαιοσύνη is a state of the soul. But suppose one were to say to a Christian that the Kingdom of God is *only* within you. How might he be expected to react to this? The acceptability of the assertion that the Kingdom of God is within you depends upon the context in which this assertion is made and upon what else is said alongside it. It could hardly be other than an offence to a Christian to say that the Kingdom of God is *only* within you, because he would naturally construe this as a way of saying that his belief in God were a fantasy (as if he had created God, instead of God having created him). It might seem as if it were a question of God being agreed to exist but being excluded from other places that were properly his; but to suppose this to be the source of the offence would, I think, be a misunderstanding. The saying that the Kingdom of God is within you could, I suppose, be uttered as an epitome of the entire truth by a Christian who was

thesis, one *either/or*—the choice between the aesthetic mode of life and the ethico-religious. The ethical requires the religious for its full expression and in isolation from it would represent a transitional stage only.

sure how to construe it. But it is a statement which might with the greatest of ease be misconstrued, a statement the Devil himself could use. If Plato's assertion that δικαιοσύνη is a state of the soul had stood by itself, unaided by any reference to the Forms, it might readily have been taken over by a Protagoras and perverted into what is virtually the antithesis of Plato's intention μέτρον δικαιοσύνης ἔστιν ἄνθρωπος. Kierkegaard likewise, when he advocates the cultivation of inwardness, is always sensible of the fact that there is more than one possible form of inwardness. The genuine has to be distinguished from the spurious: it is only one kind of inwardness that puts one into a relationship with the eternal. Truth is to be identified with subjectivity, but the Kierkegaardian species of subjectivity is vastly different from Hume's kind wherein 'a thousand different sentiments, excited by the same object, are all right'. The references by Plato, Kant and Kierkegaard to Forms, Noumena and the Eternal, whatever else they may involve, are thus a cardinal qualification as well as a reinforcement of the distinction between the inner and the outer in its relation to morality. In one way they add greatly to the difficulty of understanding the connection between morality and the inner, but in another way they are the safeguard against its being misunderstood.

Plato went to great pains in insisting that the man in whom knowledge of the good was dominant—i.e. the just man—was the happiest; and Aristotle, in condemning Plato's good as a thing which had become somehow separated from human desire and satisfaction, may seem to have ignored this. I say he *may seem* to, because I think that in fact he did not ignore it but made his objection notwithstanding. An error of H. A. Prichard provides the clue. Prichard thought that Plato wanted to justify morality by showing it to be profitable: he thought that Plato thus provided 'perhaps the most significant instance' of the mistake on which moral philosophy rested.[8] Prichard rightly regarded a confusion between morality and expediency as the most radical mistake a moral philosopher could make and he was perceptive enough in his contention that if the task of moral philosophy be taken to be that of supplying *a reason* why we should act in the ways we think we ought to act then there can be no such thing as moral philosophy. But in the case of Plato he jammed the cap down over the wrong head. Socrates was not made to answer Thrasymachus by saying that justice paid in

[8] *Mind* 1912, p. 22; reprinted in *Moral Obligation*, O.U.P. 1949, p. 2.

the sense that Thrasymachus had maintained that injustice paid. It is because Plato was concerned to avoid and was largely successful in avoiding the mistake attributed to him by Prichard that his standpoint seemed unsatisfactory to Aristotle.

It appeared impossible to Prichard that if one were deeply concerned about morality one could at the same time be deeply concerned about oneself. He did not therefore pause to consider very closely what happiness meant for Plato and in just what way it was connected with virtue. The connection was made and that was enough. The just man was supposed by Plato to be concerned for himself; justice was *of interest* to him; so Plato's moral philosophy was tainted with utility. But if this taint was to be found in Plato's moral philosophy, it was also to be found in—of all people—Kant's. In his lecture on *Duty and Interest*[9] we find Prichard observing in a shocked tone that even Kant insisted that duty and interest were intimately connected—the connection in question being not, of course, that between my duty and other people's interest but that between my duty and my personal interest. Kant says, towards the end of *Groundwork*, that to make the nature of the interest we have in morality comprehensible is an impossibility identical with the 'subjective impossibility of *explaining* freedom of will'.[10] Autonomy and personal interest thus go together: it is *self-interest* that is equated with heteronomy. He affirms in another passage that the interest which morality has for us is indeed the highest possible interest, though it 'carries with it no interest in mere states', by which he means, as Paton notes, agreeable states of affairs and states of feeling.[11]

Where Kant thus speaks of our interest in morality he could equally, had he wished, have spoken of our happiness. He only refrained from this, I believe, because he recognized that the latter term was most commonly used and understood in the sense of well-being, the Aristotelian εὖ ζῆν καὶ πράττειν; that it was used to signify something in the world whose nature can be pointed out—some 'mere state', as he put it.[12] Using the term himself therefore in conformity with the prevailing notion, he asserted that happiness, as something which our inclinations are designed to further, is connected with morality only through the existence of an indirect duty: one has a duty to assure one's own happiness because un-

---

[9] P. 4. [10] H. J. Paton's translation, *The Moral Law* (1948), p. 128.
[11] Pages 117 and 144 of Paton's translation.
[12] Cf. his reference in ch. I of the *Groundwork* to 'health and that complete well-being and contentment with one's state that goes by the name of happiness'.

satisfied wants are a temptation to transgression. When however he affirms that in striving to be moral one is concerned with one's interest and with one's highest possible interest, though without being selfishly concerned, Kant is in close agreement with Plato and Kierkegaard. The just man, the man who is concerned about morality, is concerned about his own happiness according to Plato—infinitely concerned, says Kierkegaard; but he is not feathering his nest or seeking a benefit. Since this crucial distinction eluded Prichard it is no wonder that he was hard put to it to find any moral philosophy that did not rest on a mistake.

The battle against utilitarian and aesthetic misconceptions of morality had reduced Prichard to a state of siege. All he could advocate was a sort of scorched earth policy; moral philosophy had better be given up, he was inclined to say. Kant however (though this is not always sufficiently recognized) was fundamentally on the offensive, even if in deploying his forces he got into cramped positions. Plato and Kierkegaard wielded an unrestrictive armoury. The pre-eminent position of happiness as well as reason, in relation to the problem of living in the way one ought to live, was not in the least to be played down. Instead, the inner-outer dichotomy was employed in order to split each of these concepts into two, so that with the one part jettisoned and the other magnified their connection with morality might be reinforced. Discrete and variable reasoning was supplanted by a rationality perilously hard of attainment but of an infrangible kind: the happiness of the most superior type of worldly existence imaginable was dismissed for the sake of a τέλος of a different order—a happiness which would be inward and eternal. The pragmatic conception of ethics whose attractiveness over its rivals seemed to reside in its teleological outlook was thus represented as having failed to be teleological enough.

This same process of splitting and partial jettisoning was already in operation upon the notion of goodness at the beginning of the *Groundwork* where Kant, contrasting the goodness of the will with other goods, allowed only the good will to be called good *unconditionally*. Particularly instructive in this connection is the passage in the *Gorgias*[13] where Socrates defines the standpoint of morality with extraordinary conciseness by means of a distinction between two kinds of badness, asserting that it is worse to do harm than to suffer it—a contention which is received with incredulity by Polus for whom 'better' and 'worse' have no other significance than 'more

[13] 469B.

expedient' and 'less expedient'. It should be observed that there is
no question here of measurement. If I were faced with the alternative between injuring another and suffering injury myself, it would
not become less wrong for me to injure him in so far as the injury I
might avoid became commensurate with the injury he might suffer,
nor would it cease to be wrong at the point at which the injury I
might avoid become greater than the injury he might suffer, even if
such an assessment were possible. Those who said that everybody
was to count as one might just as well have said, from Socrates' point
of view, that nobody was to count as anything (for if each of us is to
count as one then nobody can count for more than I do, nobody's
pains can be more important than mine). The transition from
egoism to morality is not to be accomplished by converting 'expedient for me' into 'expedient for the aggregate'. What Socrates
does is to replace 'good for me' in the sense of 'expedient for me' by
another kind of good (the soul's goodness) which is not merely still
my good, but is more personally mine than before since nothing
whatever can deprive me of it.

In the *Nicomachean Ethics* the contrast between goods of the
soul and bodily goods, also between goods of the soul and external
goods, is prominent enough,[14] but it has now been altered in force.
This is mainly the consequence of Aristotle's insistence that happiness should be something *ostensive*—a definite and palpable objective which could be aimed at and secured and which could be
located in some describable pattern of activity, some public and
non-subjective state of affairs. In Aristotle's moral philosophy therefore the scope of the distinction between the inner and the outer is
restricted to differentiating between various types of desirable situations. Its sphere of operation lies *within* the bounds of the aesthetic
plane (for Mill somewhat similarly the difference between Socrates
and a fool or a pig is an aesthetic difference only): ψύχης ἐνέργεια
or no, happiness must remain identical with τὸ εὖ ζῆν καὶ πράττειν.

Aristotle's conception of happiness was not indeed so whole-
heartedly naturalistic as that of Bentham, who more than anybody
else tried to treat it as a commodity of plainly measurable dimensions and seemed to dream of himself running a kind of social
power-station from which he could generate huge amounts of this
commodity to huge numbers at small cost. Still, Aristotle's good
was commercial enough for him to share in some degree the remarkable capacity of the Utilitarians and their modern successors

[14] 1098 b 13.

for knowing what was good for other people. What I mean is this: Aristotle, who had been more interested in the multiplicity of virtues than in the unity of virtue, ended up—paradoxically enough —by wanting to put everyone into the strait-jacket of a single happy life. For θεωρία (whether it fulfilled all his earlier stipulations or not) was put forward as his candidate for *the* happy life. No matter who you were, this was the life for you; this was your ultimate end, the place where your happiness lay. On the other hand Plato, who believed that virtue was a unity, did not recommend everyone to live the same kind of life. Quite the reverse, for in Plato's view happiness cannot be defined as a life whose activity conforms to this or that indicable pattern; happiness is something inward. Hence if you ask Plato what you are actually to do, the response (the only possible response) is τὰ ἑαυτοῦ πραττεῖν; each is to live his own life and nobody else's.

17

THE CHRISTIAN CONCEPT OF LOVE

Dewi Z. Phillips

THIS paper is selective, and to that extent, arbitrary. There are many concepts of love (despite the Freudian view) and I do not touch on most of them. There is the love involved in lust, romantic love, the love of average respectable marriages, love of friendship, love of beauty, love of God, and so on. I make no attempt to prove the reality of these ideas of love. I take that for granted. What I want to do is to set out certain problems which arise from *one* idea of love, namely, that found in the Christian commandment to love our fellow men. Certain interpretations of this idea are open to serious moral objections. There is one interpretation of the commandment which avoids these objections, but even this has little, if anything, to say about problems which arise from the nature of human love in certain contexts.

It would be a misunderstanding to look for *the* answer to the problems which I mention in this paper, since people's answers will be as different as their loves.

Can I be commanded to love? Can I have a duty to love? Kant seemed to think that acting from a sense of duty is acting from the highest motive. But does it make sense to say that I can love a woman out of a sense of duty? Is not this the same as saying that I do not love her at all? True, we often have occasion to point out a husband's obligation to his wife, the parents' obligations to their children, the friend's obligations to his friend. But the occasions on which these reminders are given are those where the relationships referred to have broken down in some way or other: 'You have a duty to your wife. You can't leave her.'—'Yes, I see that. But I can't love her.'

It is one thing to say that these relationships entail obligations, but quite another thing to say that a sense of duty can be the motive for the love which in ideal cases makes these relationships what they are. Again, duties arise and can be met within these relationships ('No, I'd better not stay. I've promised to take my wife out tonight.'), but this is not to say that the relationships can be participated in out of a sense of duty.

In what sense then do Christians say that we are commanded to love our fellow men? How can we regard love as a duty? Clearly, I am not called upon to love all women as I love my wife, to love all children as I love my own, to love everyone as I love my friends. But if not, what am I called upon to do when told to love my fellow men?

One cannot understand the Christian love of others unless one understands its connection with love of God. The Christian concept of love is very different from the love found in the relationships we have mentioned, where the love depends on the particularity of the relationship. What does this particularity refer to? Consider marriage: 'Wilt thou have *this* woman . . .?' Am I saying that there is only one girl for you in the world? No! It is not that *this* woman *is* different from all others, but that she *becomes* different from all others in becoming *your wife*. Similarly, my friends are different from other people because they are my friends. But according to Christian teaching, I must love all men because *all men are the same*. They are children of God. But what kind of love is this?

'. . . "Thou shalt love." It consists first and foremost in the fact that you must not love in such a way that the loss of the beloved would reveal the fact that you were desperate, that is, that you simply must not love despairingly.'[1]

When the person I love is *this* person rather than another, the death of the beloved is the worst that can happen. This is not so in Christian love of others, since they are loved, not because of their being *these* persons rather than others, but simply because of their *being*.

'The neighbour is your equal. The neighbour is not your beloved for whom you have a passionate partiality. . . . The neighbour is every man. . . . He is your neighbour through equality with you before God. . . .'[2]

---

[1] Kierkegaard, *Works of Love*, Princeton Univ. Press 1946, p. 34.   [2] *Ibid.*, p. 50.

And again, 'Belief in the existence of other human beings as such is *love*.'[3]

Christian love of fellow men seems to have little in common with the love that exists between husband and wife, parents and children, friend and friend. In many outstanding examples of Christian love, say, St Peter Claver or St Vincent de Paul, charity is shown to those whom the charitable person did not know.

What conclusions can be drawn from these differences between the way the concept of love is used in the Christian commandment and the way it is used elsewhere? What I want to do now is to show how certain possible, if not necessary, implications of the Christian concept of love are open to moral and religious objections, and at the same time try to point to an alternative interpretation of the concept which is free from such censure.

Christianity seeks that which is essential in all men. There are inessential things, but in the last analysis, these can be ignored. But what is this essential thing which all men have in common? Their identity as children of God.

'The difference is the confusion of the temporal existence which marks every man differently, but the neighbour is the mark of the eternal—on every man. Take a number of sheets of paper, write something different on each of them so that they do not resemble each other, but then take again each individual sheet, do not be confused by the different inscriptions, hold it up to the light, and then you can see a common mark in them all. And so the neighbour is the common mark, but you see it only by the light of the eternal, when it shines through the differences.'[4]

But what is the mark of the eternal? That is the difficult problem. Christians hold that 'the eternal' has been captured in certain specific propositions about God, for example, that God became incarnate in Jesus of Nazareth. It follows, according to them, that what is of eternal importance is that they should try to get all men to give assent to this special revelation of God. As a matter of fact, this conclusion does not follow at all. Even if you believe that you have eternal truth, it does not follow that you ought to proselytize. One may say that something is the eternal truth, but at the same time stress the importance of each man's coming to it for himself. Many Christians seem to think that men have a duty to follow *this*

<hr>

[3] Simone Weil, *Gravity and Grace*, Routledge 1952, p. 56.
[4] *Works of Love*, p. 73.

way of life rather than another. This is difficult to understand from a moral point of view. Certainly, we often condemn those who hold moral opinions which are different from our own. We say they are wrong in holding such views. But when the views and actions in question are tied up with a culture different from our own, the position is altered. If I hear that one of my neighbours has killed another neighbour's child, given that he is sane, my condemnation is immediate. (There are exceptions. See Faulkner's *Requiem for a Nun*.) But if I hear that some remote tribe practises child sacrifice, what then? I do not know what sacrifice means for the tribe in question. What would it mean to say I condemned it when the 'it' refers to something I know nothing about? If I did condemn it I would be condemning murder. But murder is not child sacrifice.

'The ethical expression of Abraham's action is that he wished to murder Isaac: the religious expression is that he wished to sacrifice him.'[5]

My moral opinions are bound up with the way of life I lead. Various influences have helped to shape my morality. This does not mean that when I make moral judgments I say anything about the way of life I lead or that the meaning of the moral judgments can be expressed in terms of the influences which, in part, account for them. For example, a person brought up in the Welsh Nonconformist tradition is likely to have strong views on what activities should be allowed on a Sunday, views either in sympathy with or in reaction against the tradition. When he makes his moral judgment on this matter, however, he is not saying anything about the tradition, but about what activities ought to be allowed on a Sunday. I must, on the other hand, understand the significance of actions before I can judge them.[6] My understanding is not limited by one tradition, I understand something of the other traditions within the same culture, however vague my grasp of them may be. For example, in belonging to one tradition of Christian worship one usually has some idea of the other traditions as well. When we consider different cultures however, the position is altered radically. What should Buddhists do on Sunday? When I do not understand ways of life and worship different from my own, I had better refrain from judging.

---

[5] Kierkegaard, *Fear and Trembling*, O.U.P. 1939, p. 34.
[6] The concept of 'understanding' actions is of central importance for moral philosophy, and requires far more attention than the passing reference I give it above. To pursue the concept, however, would take the argument too far from the track I want to follow.

But do Christians need to understand? Sometimes they speak as if even within the same culture there were only one morality; as if all one has to determine is whether what one judges is the same as or different from what one believes. If what one judges is the same, it is true; if different, it is false. The question is whether Christianity allows a *serious* consideration of competing moralities and religions. Must it not say that these are part of the inessential in man, the confusing inscriptions which hide from us the common mark in all men—their identity as children of God? But can one speak of competing moralities as incidental and peripheral? Are they not rooted and grounded in the actual ways of life that men pursue?

> The first point to be made is just that there are different moralities, opposing sets of rules of human behaviour. This is because there are different ways of life, different 'movements', each with its own rules of procedure for its members. Such rules, it may be noted, need not have been formulated; but the more important point is that formulated or unformulated, they are not to be regarded as preceptual or mandatory . . . the moral question is of how people do behave and not of their 'obeying the moral law'; obedience, or the treating of something as an authority, is just one particular way of behaving, the moral characterization of which has still to be given. The phrase 'how people do behave' may be misleading here. It is not a question of taking any type of activity in isolation; we do not have a morality until we have a way of life, a number of ways of behaving that hang together, that constitute a system—and it is in the conflict of such systems that rules come to be formulated. From this point of view it might be best to say that a morality *is* a way of life or a movement; and in that case the person who spoke in the name of 'morality' would be neglecting to specify the movement he represented.[7]

But am I mistaken in thinking that Christianity does speak in the name of 'morality', *the* way, *the* truth, and *the* life? These other beliefs and ways of life must consist of what is inessential. But how far is one justified in ridding men of the essential in order that they gain the essential truth? How high a price can be put on truth? If you say that no price is too high, the logic of persecution is complete. The end justifies the means. To torture or to kill (the means) is justified by the resultant confession (the end). On the other hand, you may say that some prices are too high. Christians say that only free confession is worth while. But it is notoriously difficult to know

---

[7] John Anderson, 'Art and Morality', *Australasian Journal of Psychology and Philosophy* Dec. 1941, pp. 255-6.

where to draw the line. Persecutors are obsessed by the idea that a free confession is just out of reach: 'A little more . . . a little longer . . . and then perhaps . . .'[8] and so on. Because of the supposition that most men confess belief at the hour of death ('Who is to know what a man says to his God at such a time?'), one can never tell whether the end justified the means. Camus notes that Scheler sees Christian neighbour-love and humanitarianism as two sides of the same coin. Such love is an excuse for oppression, and Scheler claims that it is always accompanied by misanthropy. 'Humanity is loved in general in order to avoid loving anybody in particular.'[9]

But as Camus points out, there is another kind of love of humanity. It does not involve elevating 'the essential' above all else. It is the love of humanity of which Ivan Karamazov speaks. Each individual is accepted as he is. The death of *one* child is too high price for *harmony*. If anything is essential, it is 'the individual good' as opposed to 'the common good', 'eternal truth', etc. As Kant expressed the matter, human beings should be treated *'never merely as means, but in every case at the same time as ends in themselves'*.[10]

Is there an interpretation of the Christian concept of love which is not open to the moral objections we have mentioned? I think there is. To show this, it is necessary, of course, to deny that what we have considered hitherto is the Christian concept of love. Think of Kierkegaard's remark concerning the concept, 'The neighbour is every man. . . . He is your neighbour through equality with you before God.' The kind of relationship between believer and unbeliever which we have considered is not a relationship of equality, but of inequality: one had the truth while the other had nothing. The 'truth' is considered to be so important that any treatment of the unbeliever is justified if it leads to assent to the truth. For Simone Weil, this is a distortion of the Christian concept of love. The special revelation is loved more than the neighbour; love of dogma replaces love of man. It is in this way that atrocities are committed in the name of love. The kind of religion one supports depends on whether one loves dogma or whether one loves man. The way towards love of God cannot begin with the former.

[8] I owe this observation on the psychology of persecution to Professor G. P. Henderson.
[9] *The Rebel*, Peregrine ed., p. 24.
[10] *Fundamental Principles of the Metaphysic of Ethics*, trans. Abbott, 1959 ed., p. 52.

Simone Weil calls love of man a 'form of the implicit love of God'. She contrasts this with the moral distinction between justice and charity. Simone Weil considers the account of Thucydides of the ultimatum the Athenians gave to the people of Melos when they asked them to join them in their war against Sparta. The men of Melos invoked justice 'imploring pity for the antiquity of their town'. The Athenians brush aside this reference to justice, saying,

> 'Let us treat rather of what is possible. . . . You know it as well as we do; the human spirit is so constituted that what is just is only examined if there is equal necessity on both sides. But if one is strong and the other weak, that which is possible is imposed by the first and accepted by the second.'
>
> The men of Melos said that in the case of a battle they would have the gods with them on account of the justice of their cause. The Athenians replied that they saw no reason to suppose so.
>
> 'As touching the gods we have the belief, and as touching men the certainty, that always by a necessity of nature, each one commands wherever he has the power. We did not establish this law, we are not the first to apply it; we found it already established, we abide by it as something likely to endure for ever; and that is why we apply it. We know quite well that you also, like all the others, once you reached the same degree of power, would act in the same way.'[11]

According to Simone Weil, most people have gone a step further than the Athenians, who at least recognized that they were brushing aside considerations of justice, in accepting as justice what one can be reasonably expected to do or what one can reasonably expect to receive in a given situation. If one's conception of justice varies with the circumstances, then it is likely that whenever one has the power to command, one will do so. When such a concept of justice is found in religion, it tends to be located in the so-called justice of a cause—the cause of a particular religion. No atrocity can be an injustice if it can be shown to further the cause. Simone Weil accuses the Hebrew religion of this distortion: confusing love of man with love of the cause. 'The religions which represent divinity as commanding wherever it has the power to do so are false. Even though they are monotheistic they are idolatrous' (p. 102).

True religion, for Simone Weil, is the religion which manifests true love. But what is this idea of love? If we hold the relativistic concept of justice, we shall regard charity as a supererogatory act: as something we need not have done. According to Simone Weil, the

---

[11] *Waiting on God*, Fontana ed., pp. 98-99.

Christian concept of love does not recognize this distinction. It equates justice and charity. How does this come about?

To answer the above question one must distinguish between two important concepts in Simone Weil's thought: 'attachment' and 'detachment'. 'Attachment' belongs to all relationships of inequality: the strong and the weak, the conqueror and the conquered, employer and employee, and so on. Justice in these relationships is what the strong, for instance, can reasonably be expected to give, and what the weak can reasonably expect to receive. Charity would then be giving more than one is expected to give as an employer, let us say.

> Beyond a certain degree of inequality in the relations of men of unequal strength, the weaker passes into a state of matter and loses his personality. The men of old used to say: 'A man loses half his soul the day he becomes a slave' (p. 100).

On rare occasions, however, we find a person not using his power, but instead, having compassion on the person to whom he stands in a relationship of inequality. Simone Weil calls this 'the supernatural virtue of justice', and says that it 'consists of behaving exactly as though there were equality when one is the stronger in an unequal relationship' (*ibid.*). This is where 'detachment' is important. It is the possibility of acting in a way which is not determined by the relative criteria of reasonableness which function in unequal relationships. It is the possibility of detaching oneself from one's special status, and seeing the other as an equal. Simone Weil says that, 'He who treats as equals those who are far below him in strength really makes them a gift of the quality of human beings, of which fate had deprived them' (p. 101). We recall her other remark, 'Belief in the existence of other human beings as such is *love.*'[12]

Compassion is not easy to achieve. It is easy enough to give bread to the starving, money to the needy or clothes to the naked. It is not surprising that a person does these things. 'What is surprising', as Simone Weil says, 'is that he should be capable of doing so with so different a gesture from that with which we buy an object. Almsgiving when it is not supernatural is like a sort of purchase. It buys the sufferer' (p. 104).

It is difficult to act from compassion partly because it involves a contemplation of other people as one's equal. This contemplation

[12] See p. 316.

is akin to another form of the implicit love of God which Simone Weil talks about, namely, the love of the beauty of the world. In some ways, this is easier to understand because it is a more common experience. For example, when ambition threatens to destroy us, and we have come to regard everyone and everything as instruments for our own use, what Simone Weil calls 'The love we feel for the splendour of the heavens, the plains, the sea and the mountains, for the silence of nature' can give us is something which cannot be used, namely, the beauty of the world. One cannot use beauty, one can only contemplate it, since as Simone Weil says, 'it only gives itself, it never gives anything else' (p. 122). By this kind of contemplation one's self-centredness is destroyed. One is able 'to see the true centre outside the world'. This contemplation of the beauty of the world—cf. Wittgenstein: 'Not *how* the world is, is the mystical, but *that* it is' (Tractatus 6.44)—has a parallel in the love of one's neighbour. People can be seen not in relation to my needs and uses, but as human beings—not *how* they are (rich, poor, educated, ignorant, useful, useless, etc.) but *that* they are. Simone Weil says that this act of contemplation 'places the Good outside this world, where are all the sources of power' (*Waiting on God*, p. 105). Her own life illustrates the kind of powers of courage and endurance given to those who possess this love.

It is important to note that Simone Weil did not think it necessary that those who possessed this love should attribute it to God. She did think, however, that such love is religious and the result of divine activity. This was partly due to her insistence that this love could not be achieved by an effort of will; it only comes by contemplation. That is why she calls it a gift; for her, a gift from God. One has a duty to wait on God, but one cannot have a duty to receive. Simone Weil also thought that this form of implicit love of God leads to a more explicit love of God. It is outside my present task to discuss the difficult question of how this is brought about. All I have been concerned to show is that there is one interpretation of the Christian concept of love which is free from the moral objections we have considered hitherto.

Why do I call Simone Weil's treatment of the concept of love an *interpretation* of the Christian concept? I do so because some of the implications of her standpoint are contrary to orthodox Christian teaching. One of the most important implications of her analysis is that it leaves no place of priority for any one religion. The third form of implicit love of God Simone Weil considers is the love of religious practices. She holds the view that the kind of contemplation she has been considering takes place most naturally within the religion of one's own land and culture. 'All religions pronounce the name of God in their particular language' (p. 136).

A man can call on God best in his own language and idiom. There should be no searching for words in such worship. Simone Weil cannot give assent to the Christian desire and policy to change men's religious allegiances. Can Christianity take other religions seriously? It is not a case of Christianity being a *better* religion. This would assume the existence of an objective religious norm. But is the norm any more than what we believe in? If any part of the beliefs of other religions is true, it is regarded as *an approximation to Christian truth*. Christians then say that it follows that a love of men involves the desire to bring them from approximate to complete truth. Hence missionaries. It is the identification of complete truth with Christian truth which has inspired religious protests like that of Simone Weil.

> Personally, I should never give as much as a sixpence towards any missionary enterprise. I think that for any man a change of religion is as dangerous a thing as a change of language is for a writer. It may turn out a success, but it may have disastrous consequences. . . .
>
> The various authentic religious traditions are different reflections of the same truth, and perhaps equally precious. But we do not realize this, because each of us lives only one of these traditions and sees the others from the outside.[13]

The claim of any religion to have the whole truth distorts love of man into love of dogma. Simone Weil recognizes the difficulty of comparative religion as a study, since each religion must be understood from the inside. Understanding can only come, if at all, through a sympathetic bond with the religion in question. But as Simone Weil says.

> This scarcely ever happens, for some have no faith, and the others have faith exclusively in one religion and bestow upon the others the sort of attention we give to strangely shaped shells.[14]

Simone Weil is not, of course, advocating a rejection of allegiance to particular religions. She sees too clearly how so-called impartiality can lead to a vague and empty religiosity. What she is

---

[13] *Letter to a Priest*, Routledge 1953, (10) and (11).
[14] *Waiting on God*, p. 137.

saying is that such allegiance need not lead one to make claims to possess the entire truth. Sympathetic understanding of other religions is the necessary condition for retracting such a claim.

On the other hand, *all* religions are not suited for what Simone Weil calls, 'calling on the name of the Lord'. We have seen already how love of dogma, and belief in the infallibility of a cause can lead to a religion very different from the kind she advocates. Dostoevsky called such religion the religion of the devil. His Grand Inquisitor says to Christ who has re-visited the earth,

> We are not working with Thee, but with *him*—that is our mystery. It's long—eight centuries—since we have been on *his* side and not on Thine. Just eight centuries ago, we took from him what Thou didst reject with scorn, that last gift he offered Thee, showing Thee all the kingdoms of the earth. We took from him Rome and the sword of Caesar, and proclaimed ourselves sole rulers of the earth, though hitherto we have not been able to complete our work. But whose fault is that? Oh, the work is only beginning, but it has begun. It has long to await completion and the earth has yet much to suffer, but we shall triumph and shall be Caesars, and then we shall plan the universal happiness of man.[15]

By what criterion does Simone Weil call such religion false? How is she able to judge that 'The true God is the God we think of as almighty, but as not exercising his power everywhere'?[16] She says that 'Those of the Athenians who massacred the inhabitants of Melos had no longer any idea of such a God' (p. 101). All right, but they did have an idea of God. How can one prove that this idea of God is wrong? Simone Weil answers as follows,

'The first proof that they were in the wrong lies in the fact that, contrary to their assertion, it happens, though extremely rarely, that a man will forbear out of pure generosity to command where he has the power to do so. That which is possible for man is possible also for God' (p. 101).

In this answer, Simone Weil is profoundly right. What other proof of the truth of a religion could one ever ask for or hope to possess?

Before ending, I want to consider another major difficulty. I said at the outset that even the interpretation of the Christian concept of love which avoids many moral objections has little to say about

---

[15] *The Brothers Karamazov* Bk V., ch. V.   [16] *Waiting on God*, p. 101.

problems which arise from human love in certain contexts. Examples of these problems must now be considered.

Love found in intimate human relationships often gives rise to moral perplexity. When such situations occur, what has Christianity to say? In a moral perplexity the question I ask myself is, 'What ought I to do?' I have no clear-cut choice between right and wrong. I have conflicting obligations. No reference to a categorical law or immoveable principles seems to help. But is not this what Christianity does? Does it not take a strange view of such problems by ignoring their complexity and by treating them as problems of casuistry? Is Christianity any more than 'thou shalt' and 'thou shalt not'?

But of course it is. There is a distinction between the general will of God and the special will of God. The general will of God refers to anything it makes sense to call the will of God. The special will of God is what God wants me to do here and now in this situation. But not only moral principles clash, divine precepts clash too, leaving the believer praying to know the will of God. There is religious perplexity as well as moral perplexity.

But there is a difference. Even when I do not know the will of God for me, I can rule out certain answers because *they could not* be the will of God. The known will of God is 'the given' in terms of which the problem must be solved. If I believe, I must start 'here' and bring all else into relation with 'the here'. In moral perplexity I do not start anywhere in that sense. Certain difficulties arise which call for some kind of an answer. My answer need not conform to any pre-established code however. The question is, 'What can I do?' (This is not a question about logical possibilities!) 'What can I do and still live with myself as a person?' No one outside the dilemma can answer the question.

What does Christianity say in face of such situations? Simone Weil herself has some strange things to say. She is suspicious of most forms of human attachment. She claims that this attachment can arise from two motives, namely, from a recognition of good in the loved one or from a need for the loved one. Simone Weil holds the view that there is evil involved in love which arises solely from need. She even compares it with drunkenness and avarice: 'that which was at first a search for some desired good is transformed into a need by the mere passage of time' (p. 155). When this happens between persons, 'When the attachment of one being to another is made up of need and nothing else', then, according to

Simone Weil, 'it is a fearful thing. Few things in this world can reach such a degree of ugliness and horror' (p. 155).

But if we think of examples of human love where the need for the loved one has destroyed the people involved, would we feel happy about talking in this way? Consider Tolstoy's *Anna Karenina* or Hardy's *Jude the Obscure*. We might call what happened to Anna and Vronsky or to Sue and Jude tragic, but surely not ugly or horrible! Simone Weil seems far too concerned with the preservation of the autonomy of the people involved in such relationships. In order to preserve this autonomy she advocates what she calls, 'transforming affection into friendship'.[17] 'Do not allow yourself to be imprisoned by any affection. Keep your solitude.'[18] This may have some point where friendship is concerned, but it seems out of place in relationships such as those between husband and wife, lover and loved one or parents and children. Here, one is often involved through mutual need in precisely the kind of way which Simone Weil deplores. Apart from advocating detachment she has nothing positive to say about the problems which arise from the nature of such love. We are still faced with problems such as those portrayed by Tolstoy and Hardy.

Consider the situation in *Jude the Obscure*. Sue and Jude are both unhappily married. They love each other and want to live with each other. They regard marriage as sacred, but on the other hand, Jude was tricked into marriage, while Sue married out of a 'love of being loved'. Eventually, Sue goes to live with Jude, but her conflict is not resolved, indeed, it is just beginning. She has a choice: she can either stay with Jude or return to the husband she does not love. She knows that if she leaves Jude it will break him, and yet, in the end, this is what she does. We may feel uneasy about her choice. We might have chosen differently, but then it would have been our problem and not Sue's. In dilemmas such as this, if one asks the person involved who is to decide what he ought to do, the appropriate answer is, 'I am.'

Tolstoy's Anna decides differently. She stays with her lover, though she realizes that the social death to which the relationship has condemned her is slowly destroying her as a person. She ends it all in suicide. What would Christians say about these decisions? That Sue did the will of God, I suppose. But did she have obligations to Jude? What is one to say to Anna? Repent and return to God?

[17] *Waiting on God;* see p. 158.   [18] *Gravity and Grace,* p. 60.

I am not denying that prayer and the kind of contemplation Simone Weil advocates can help in the case of some problems. For example, a marriage may look like breaking up. The husband and wife think at first that parting is the only answer. On the other hand, if the husband and wife pray about their difficulties, they may, through prayer, find a way of going on which preserves some integrity in their relationship. It may not be the life they dreamed of when they started their married life, but it is something, nevertheless, which gives their marriage a meaning. In the very act of praying, and the kind of reflection on one's life this involves, the possibility of a new way through difficulty is seen.

On the other hand, prayer and reflection seem out of place in other situations such as those described by Tolstoy and Hardy. This is partly because although waiting on God may bring new insight to a perplexity, the insight must be in accordance with the known will of God. Any answer is not permissible. Most Christians, I take it, would say that it cannot be the will of God for Anna to stay with Vronsky or for Sue to remain with Jude. This is the difficulty. What morality allows to be considered as a serious possibility, religion dismisses. Such dismissal ignores the complexity of such situations. It will not do simply to call these tragedies horrible or ugly. Neither will it do to say, as many Christians tend to, that had it not been for sin these situations would not have occurred. In the novels mentioned, Christians might say, But for the sin of adultery the tragedies would not have occurred. Even so, now that sin *has* occurred, what does Christianity say about obligations created in sinning? Or can there be no obligation as the result of sin?

In any case, sin will not explain all tragedies. In Faulkner's *Pantaloon in Black* the negro, whose young wife dies, gets drunk and kills a workmate who had made a habit of tormenting him. The story illustrates what Simone Weil says about such relationships, 'When the degree of necessity is extreme, deprivation leads to death. This is the case when all the vital energy of one being is bound up with another by some attachment.'[19]

What ought he not to have done in order to avoid ending his life in tragedy? The answer, I presume, is: loved his wife so much. But how odd to say, as Simone Weil does, that what such people ought to do is 'to transform affection into friendship' or to say with Kierkegaard, 'you must not love in such a way that the loss of the beloved would reveal the fact that you were desperate. . . .'[20] In

[19] *Waiting on God*, p. 155.   [20] See p. 315.

the relationships we have considered, how could the death or deprivation of the loved one reveal anything else?

As I said at the outset, there is no one answer to the jungle of
problems arising from the Christian concept of love. This paper
simply tries to show that these problems are more complex than we
often suppose, and that there are more problems than we care to
think, to which God alone has the answers.

18

SITUATIONAL ETHICS

George Woods

WE are living in an age which is calling for a review and reformulation of both Christian doctrine and Christian ethics. But the call is curiously confused and muffled. It is rather an expression of dissatisfaction with the traditional formulations than a call to reform on the basis of an agreed method or an agreed metaphysic. The basic issues have not yet become explicit. Our present theological situation may in years to come be compared with the amorphous Deistic controversy in the eighteenth century when traditional theology was coming under the pressure of the methods of natural science and history before these methods had been fully developed and expertly applied to the Christian tradition. It was a premature crisis. But in the contemporary field of Christian ethics, there has been a more positive and explicit movement. Situational ethics have become widely known and there has been a clear difference of opinion within the Christian tradition as to whether this type of ethics is a rejection of Christian morality or its fulfilment in contemporary terms. In this essay, I wish to give a critical appreciation of the contribution of situational ethics to the progress of the Christian moral tradition.

In an address to the members of the international congress of the World Federation of Catholic Young Women delivered by Pope Pius XII in 1952,[1] the Pope referred to a message which he gave over the radio a few days earlier in which he described the new ethical movement as a new conception of the moral law. He described it as 'ethical existentialism', 'ethical actualism', 'ethical in-

---

[1] 18th April, 1952. *Acta Apostolicae Sedis* 44 (1952), pp. 413-419. Cf. *Nouvelle Revue Théologique* 1952, pp. 643-647.

dividualism' elsewhere called '*Situationsethik*' or '*morale de situation*'. It could also be described as contextual or circumstantial ethics. The various descriptions emphasize that it is an ethic of moral situations in which the individual accepts the responsibility of making free moral decisions. I think the movement owes its popularity to a number of causes which are not easily consistent with one another. It appeals both to those who reject and to those who accept Christian theism. It is congenial to the atheistic existentialists. They study the human situation and conclude that man is not bound by an essential nature which he cannot discard or to which he ought to conform. Man is free to make moral decisions and it is in the making of his moral decisions that he creates his moral standards. He is not tied to the past and he is open to the future. He loses his life in making inauthentic decisions and he finds his life in making decisions which are genuinely his own. He achieves his existence in making existential decisions in the situations in which he finds himself. His ethics are in a sense situational. The secular humanists also find the conception attractive. They have no faith in God or in individual survival after death but they emphasize the value of human personality. In any situation, the truly moral decision is one which gives the primacy to personal values. The responsibility of the moral agent is to study the facts of the situation and to select what are known from experience to be the most appropriate means of promoting mature personal life. And many who are more interested in practical affairs than in debating whether they might be described as atheistic existentialists or secular humanists are attracted by a conception of ethics which seems to lay an emphasis upon the actual facts of the case. Those who are trained in the empirical methods of science and history are also very likely to prefer an interpretation of making moral decisions which makes full use of the personal and the impersonal sciences in ascertaining the facts of the situation. For rather different reasons, situational ethics have been sympathetically regarded by some Christian theologians, usually by those standing in the Protestant tradition. They interpret the act of making a Christian moral decision as a response to the call of God to the individual in the actual situation in which he has been placed. It is an ethic of vocation or calling to the individual believer in his individuality in his situation in its full particularity. He answers a unique situation. No one can deputize for him and no one can occupy precisely his situation in human history.

If there is great variety in the grounds which dispose people to look with favour upon situational ethics, there is greater unanimity in what the situationalists distrust or reject. Desiring to treat each case on its merits, they are naturally opposed to any uninformed or unimaginative application of a biblical precept to a complex contemporary situation. But their main opposition is to the conception of a universal moral law which is authoritative in all situations without exception. They reject the view that the proper procedure in making moral decisions is to recognize the relevant universal moral law and to apply it to the particular case. In their view, this method of reaching a decision is more likely to be misleading than trusting to immediate moral insight given in a study of the actual situation. They are equally distrustful of any enumeration of acts which are absolutely good or absolutely bad in all circumstances. Their attention is concentrated upon the infinite diversity of the concrete situations in which the individual has to make his moral decisions.

The public controversy about the attitude which Christian moralists ought to take towards situational ethics has disclosed sharply opposed views. Pius XII in the speech already mentioned said that even a child who knows its catechism would realize that this new morality was incompatible with Catholic faith and practice. The fundamental obligations of the moral law were based upon the nature of man as such and those of the Christian moral law were based upon the being and acts of God. Situational ethics emphasized the importance of right intention but they did not emphasize sufficiently the necessity of right acts. Encouragement was given to the false principle that the end justifies the means. And the Christian martyrs had been willing to sacrifice their lives in situations where their sacrifice appeared useless. Moreover, in the Catholic moral tradition proper attention had always been given to the independence of the individual conscience and to the need to consider carefully the circumstances of each particular case. Catholic morality left a vast field open to the initiative and personal responsibility of the Christian.

On 2nd February, 1956, the New Morality was analysed and condemned as contrary to traditional Catholic doctrine in an instruction of the Holy Office.[2] In a further illuminating article[3] by J. Fuchs, S.J., it is made plain that what is condemned is not the

---

[2] *A.A.S.* 48 (1956), p. 144. Cf. *N.R.Th.* 1956, pp. 649-650.
[3] 'Morale théologique et morale de situation', *N.R.Th.* 1954, pp. 1073-1085.

exercise of a proper prudence in the application of Natural Law to particular cases but a tendency to subordinate the objective moral law to some kind of subjective judgment which the individual claims to be immediate and decisive.

In what is a valuable criticism of situational ethics this article examines (i) The situation as the call of God, (ii) The call of God in the situation, and (iii) Recognizing the call of God. It contains a sympathetic understanding of the real difficulties which arise in applying universal moral laws, while claiming that they must not be rejected. A compact and forceful defence of situational ethics was given by Professor Joseph Fletcher in the *Harvard Divinity Bulletin* for October 1959 in an article on 'The New Look in Christian Ethics'. He characterizes the Christian conscience in six propositions. (i) Only one thing is intrinsically good, namely, love: nothing else; (ii) The ultimate norm of Christian decisions is love: nothing else; (iii) Love and justice are the same, for justice is love distributed; (iv) Love wills the neighbour's good whether we like him or not; (v) Only the end justifies the means: nothing else; and finally, (vi) Decisions ought to be made situationally, not prescriptively. He comments (p. 16):

> Many people prefer to fit reality to rules rather than *vice-versa*. Legalism always emphasizes order and conformity, while 'situation ethics' puts its premium on freedom and responsibility. Situation ethics always suspects prescriptive law of falsifying whether it is the *scripture* legalism of biblicist Protestantism or the *nature* legalism ('Natural Law') of Catholic philosophy.

The debate has continued in the chapter on 'The New Morality' in the Bishop of Woolwich's book, *Honest to God*.[4] He cites with approval the words of Paul Tillich, 'Love alone can transform itself according to the concrete demands of every individual and social situation without losing its eternity and dignity and unconditional validity' (*The Protestant Era*, p. 173).

We therefore face the question, Are wholly situational ethics incompatible with Christian ethics? or Should Christian ethics become wholly situational? This question admits of no clear answer because the terms are not clear. An essential preliminary step towards any adequate answer must be an examination of the variety of way in which the word 'situation' may be understood. Without a

---

[4] J. A. T. Robinson, *Honest to God* (SCM Press 1963), ch. 6.

clearer understanding of the various uses of this word, there can be no clarity in the phrase 'situational ethics', or in the phrase 'Christian situational ethics'.

When we think of a moral situation, what do we have in mind? I believe we tend to think of ourselves as morally free persons who are on the point of making a moral decision in a moral situation. This may offer a useful starting point to a study of various conceptions of a moral situation but it is no more than a starting point. In reality, a moral situation is a more complex matter. A moral agent does not occupy a situation as an impersonal entity occupies a position in space. Even the only pebble on the beach has not chosen to occupy a particular situation which it may later forsake at will. We can make such a pebble the object of our central attention but it does not consciously possess an environment. Situations are more significantly occupied by persons. The personal occupants are aware of their circumstances through the interest which they take in their environments. In the nursery rhyme, the cat which went to see the queen found greater interest in the saucer of milk. The fact that the occupation of a situation by a person is largely a matter of his conscious interests is shown by our unwillingness to say that someone who loses consciousness continues to occupy his situation in the same sense as before he became unconscious. All reports of personal situations have to be given by those who are or were in some way involved in them. The accounts are given by the agents who acted or by the patients who were affected or by spectators who saw what happened. As the accounts given by the agents have a certain primacy, it was not surprising that the first description of a moral situation which occurred to our minds was in the form of an account offered by the moral agent observing himself in action. In fact, the moral situation is one which may be viewed from various standpoints and very probably no exhaustive account is ever given even when all the available accounts are presented. Moreover, each possible observer may look at the situation in his private or in his official capacity. What he notices is affected by the type of interest which he is displaying. And the interest which is being taken may be taken in a great variety of matters within the moral situation. It may, for example, be concentrated upon the moral agent who is on the point of making a moral decision or upon the action which is taken on the basis of the decision. Even the reference to the situation suggests quite improperly that the boundaries of each moral situation are clearly visible. This is not so. What we call the present situation is the situation as it presents itself to us at the time when we are observing it. This is not a timeless moment but a period during which the situation suffers no significant change. It may be quite transient but it must have sufficient stability to be recognizable as a situation. Our fuller or wider appreciation of any historical situation must stretch out towards the past and the future. We may expand its boundaries indefinitely. Many of the facts from the past which we have chosen to include in the situation are irrecoverable for a variety of reasons. Many of the later anticipated facts which we are taking into consideration are unforeseeable. Our knowledge of the past and of the future facts which we have chosen to admit as constituting the moral situation which is under observation may also be affected by a deliberate suppression or distortion of the truth. In the absence of a thorough exploration of what is to count as a constituent of a moral situation, little is said in speaking of 'situational ethics'.

There are still deeper problems in deciding what shall be taken as constituting a moral situation. Our interest may be primarily in a state of things which might have been otherwise or in some unchanging state of things which makes possible the series of changing states. We may be interested in either the course or the constitution of the world. We may be concerned about the cycle of the seasons or about the order of nature. We may study the events of human history or the character of human nature which makes historical events possible. When we speak of a moral situation, it is important to know whether we are giving our main attention to the current state of things or to the basic conditions which permit a succession of situations to take place. Our interest may be in moral situations or in the total situation in which they may arise. At this point, the Christian situationalist finds himself in disagreement with the atheist. The Christian sees the world as created and sustained and redeemed by God in Christ. He is bound to attach some meaning to belief in divine providence and will not view a moral situation as wholly accidental. He will also view the persons concerned as people capable of eternal life in Christ. These Christian convictions about the total situation are not taken by the Christian as considerations which may possibly be introduced after the real discussion is completed. They are essential constituents of the moral situation as understood by the Christian. No system of situational ethics is clear which is not explicit about the view which is held about the total situation in which moral situations occur.

We must also face the fact that we have daily experience of finding that what we believe to be the case fails to correspond with what proves to be the case. Our recollections of the past are disproved and our anticipations of the future are disappointed. What we take to be true often turns out to be untrue. This is so both of our views of the total situation and of the particular situations which we observe. By care and diligence we may reduce the margin of error but it remains a possibility when we are dealing with matters of fact. We are bound to act in a moral situation, in the sense that we act in the situation as it is known to us, but we are bound to admit that the real situation may be partly or largely different. This possible difference between the true situation and the situation as known to us may account for a tendency in situational ethics for the emphasis to fall upon the conscientiousness of moral decisions rather than upon the rightness of the action which is taken. The major concern can be for the blamelessness or blameworthiness of the moral agent rather for the moral rightness of the action which he took or failed to take. When we are despondent about the practicability of foreseeing the results of our actions, we can find some consolation in affirming that we must always act according to the best of our knowledge and belief, that is, we must make the best decision we can in the light of the circumstances known at the time. This is unexceptionable advice but a system of ethics which has no more to say about the manner of distinguishing between actions which are right or wrong is of little practical help. To be told to do our best does not help us very much in deciding what to do.

But the advocates of Christian situational ethics do not limit themselves to advising moral agents to study the situation carefully and to act conscientiously. Their advice is that people should act as Christians. Their actions should always be an expression of Christian love. This is not merely a sentimental liking for those whom we find psychologically congenial. It is a steady and sustained good will which wills the true good of our neighbour. His true good is interpreted as the enjoyment of eternal life here and hereafter. All our actions are to promote his true life. Guided by Christian love the individual Christian will see what any situation requires. He will see the necessity of doing acts which those who lack Christian insight thought to be unnecessary. The ability to possess and express this Christian goodwill raises the whole problem of grace and freewill but my present concern is to examine whether Christian love is in itself a sufficient guide to Christian action. We may

think of goodwill in general without troubling to think of it in its
particular expressions, but a new situation is created when we contemplate taking some particular action. To take responsible moral
action, we require a reasonable knowledge of the situation, a reasonable knowledge of our methods and powers of affecting the situation
and some kind of notion of the new situation which we desire to
create. We make our moral decision and act upon a confused awareness of all these. I doubt whether a simple account can be given of
the actual process by which we make our moral judgments. But in
making these judgments, we are assisted by all kinds of traditional
expressions of the moral standard. Amongst these are bodies of
maxims, principles and laws. The Christian situationalist may
rightly emphasize the need to study the particular situation and
the character of the world in which the situation occurs and the
value of general principles of laws which economically embody the
lessons of past experience. But he is unwilling to believe that
Christian love can ever be identified with any absolutely universal
moral laws or any acts judged in themselves to be absolutely good.
He believes that there are no laws or deeds which are absolutely
good in all circumstances. He claims that there will always be
justifiable exceptions, exceptional situations in which Christian
love will be a better guide than any law.

This rejection of universal moral laws is less surprising than it
appears at first sight. There is no wholesale rejection of all moral
laws. They are acknowledged to be of great value in many ways.
What is rejected is the conception of any universal moral law to
which there are no exceptions but the number of exceptions is taken
to be very small indeed. The exceptions are wholly exceptional.
The matter for discussion, therefore, is the moral justification of
rare exceptions which are made not through moral irresponsibility
but in obedience to what is believed to be the Christian obligation
of love towards God and neighbour. An adequate consideration of
this problem would require an analysis of the whole operation of
making exceptions. Probably the most useful procedure would be
to examine a whole series of actual instances where the facts of the
exceptional situation are well known and where the precise formulation of the relevant moral law is also known. A study of actual
hard cases might disclose the various ways in which the application
of a universal moral law is found to be morally unsatisfying. But I
confine my attention here to a more general and rather tentative
study of the problem of normality and exceptionality in regard to

the expression and application of the Christian moral standard. I think a distinction has to be drawn between those expressions of the standard which enjoin and those which do not enjoin some particular course of action. Those which prescribe some course of action are distinguishable into those which specify an action with some particularity and those which specify some very general action. The injunctions cover very few or very many situations. The consequence is that the more particular injunctions tend to require many exceptions to be made in the large number of situations to which the injunction fails to apply. And the more general injunctions cover more situations but tend to be deficient in the more particular and practical advice which the moral agent is demanding. I see no way of prescribing a course of action which can combine the advantages of both particular and general injunctions.

It may be asked whether the generality of laws of moral action can attain absolute universality without becoming meaningless. Any direction to act in a certain way cannot be absolute in the sense of being unrelated to anything which is the case about the moral agent and the world in which he acts. Any act is an action in a world. Activity in no situation whatever is meaningless.

The difficulty of finding universal moral laws of action which require no exceptions in their application to exceptional cases is somewhat reduced if the moral standard is expressed in forms which do not suggest any particular course of action. Expressions of the moral standard as a quality of living, a spiritual disposition, a general outlook of attitude do not call for exceptions to be made in exceptional situations. The duty of Christian love remains in all cases. There are quite a number of ways in which the moral standard can be so expressed as not to include any direction about any particular action to be taken. This is a useful practice but the moral agent is left with the responsibility of deciding what he ought to do in a particular situation. Despite the possible defects of what are claimed to be universal moral laws, he may welcome their assistance as embodying many lessons drawn from centuries of practical experience.

There are undeniably difficulties in the expression of the Christian moral standard in terms of universal moral laws which are to be applied in all situations. Circumstances alter cases because cases largely consist of circumstances. But there are also difficulties in moving to the other extreme and envisaging every situation as unique. If every situation is taken to be unique, it would appear that it ought to be treated as an exception. But is any kind of rational conduct possible in a series of situations which lack even sufficient comparability to be called situations without exception? If we seek guidance from the history of thought, we face the fact that the problem of the universal and the particular has never been solved by the denial of one or the other. I suspect that a Christian who believes in a moral standard, though he will gratefully acknowledge the insights of situational ethics, is bound to believe that the exceptions are made within some kind of stable context. When the moral standard is expressed in some kind of law of action, it is hard to conceive that the whole body of such laws can consist of exceptions. It looks like an attempt to fill a wage packet with nothing but deductions. It is doubtful whether absolute exceptions or a totality of exceptions have any meaning. Moreover, if the Christian is under an obligation to love his neighbour in all situations, it is hard to conceive what this obligation may mean if no regard is given to the characteristics of human nature and the world in which men live. It is difficult to comprehend the meaning of Christian love in a world very unlike the one of which we have experience. This suggests that a full understanding of Christian love must include a full understanding of man in his human situation. An appreciation of a universal moral obligation involves an understanding of the world in which the obligation is experienced. I think that any deepening analysis if situational ethics will always tend towards a search for consistency in the moral standard and for consistency in the basis of morality.

In an age when the study of Christian ethics is somewhat retarded and when a great deal of ethical discussion is not constructive, careful attention should be given to any movement of ethical thought which appeals to a large number of seriously minded people. Situational ethics certainly deserves sympathetic investigation. It rightly emphasizes the necessity of a proper study of the facts of each moral situation. And it rightly indicates some of the defects and dangers of formalism in the expression and application of the moral standard. These two points are, in fact, a recovery of emphases which have been characteristic of a sound Christian moral tradition. The error in some situational ethics has been an inadequate analysis of the manifold forms of the moral standard and of the fundamental structure of the human situation to which the standard applies. Christian situational ethics must be worked out in the human situation as understood in the traditional Christian understanding of the world, the soul and God, but this does not mean that this tradition never requires reformulation. Situational ethics are a natural response to the modern situation but as the study of Christian ethics advances, it is likely that they will be seen to have been the ethics of a transitory situation, an interim ethic.

19

THE FAMILY IN CONTEMPORARY SOCIETY

from an Anglican Report

Christian ethics obviously demands the relating of theology to life. It is not always realized how much contemporary developments have changed this task. On this point, the group which prepared this report at the behest of the Archbishop of Canterbury and in connection with the Lambeth Conference of 1958 remarked:

In so far as theology is meant to afford guidance for living, it has to be kept relevant to the actual circumstances of life. In a stable society this can be done fairly easily. But when the circumstances of life are changing rapidly, it is much more difficult to make relevant and useful theological assertions. A greater mental effort is needed both to grasp the nature of new situations and to ensure that the theological principles brought to bear are not contaminated with out-of-date sociological assumptions.

Theologians can now draw on much more detailed information about the circumstances which are relevant to practical theology. This is great gain; but it also complicates the theologian's task. He has to assimilate a great deal more than his predecessors had to assimilate before he can say anything worth while; and he has to do it more quickly, if he is to keep abreast of change. Sustained co-operative effort is demanded in order that practical theology may produce something better than irrelevant generalities.

The information with which practical theology has to grapple includes the analysis of trends and predictions concerning their future outcome. Such predictions may not be ignored. For instance, it would be absurd to consider the Indian population problem while excluding statistical forecasts from the material considered. Indeed in this instance it is mainly predicted developments that pose moral problems. On the other hand predictions are not certainties. For instance, the recent discovery that disease-bearing insects are becoming immune to the insecticides in use reminds us that forecasts of population increases can only be founded on a balance of probabilities. All this complicates the theologian's task considerably.

It is thus evident that, in matters which are treated by the social sciences, the kind of preparation that used to be thought adequate to justify theological pronouncements is no longer adequate. The bearing of the Christian faith on many matters can only be worked out by sustained co-operation between experts in various fields of study.

This group then considered four issues: the theology of marriage and the family; contraception; the Christian attitude to material development; and religion as a social bond.

1. THE THEOLOGY OF MARRIAGE AND THE FAMILY

During the past thirty years theological thought about marriage has developed considerably.

1. Full weight has been given to New Testament teaching about the union of man and woman in 'one flesh' and the analogy it bears to the union of Christ and his Church. It is now fairly generally recognized that the union of man and wife ought not to be regarded mainly as a means to bringing children into existence, but as a 'two-in-oneship' which has value in itself and glorifies God. It has become common to think of children as the 'fruit', rather than as the 'end' of the marriage union; and monogamy is more often defended by reference to the demands of love and of the gift of self which is made in marriage than by reference to the needs of offspring.

2. In keeping with this development a new value is ascribed to *coitus*, which, as the specific and consummating act of marriage, is seen to be no mere means to generation, but an act of positive importance for the marriage union and for the perfecting of husband and wife. This intrinsic value is affirmed as against the old opinion that *coitus* always needed the 'good' of generation to justify

it. Since the unitive virtue of the act depends partly on the manner in which it is performed, value is attributed to love-making also.

3. Lest the new orientation of thought about marriage should cause procreation to be regarded as merely subsidiary to the personal relationship of husband and wife, there is renewed insistence in some quarters on the dignity of parenthood as participation in the creativity of God and on the fact that the procreative purpose is part and parcel of marriage, not an optional *addendum* to it.

4. Increased understanding of the cycle of fertility in woman has made deliberately non-generative *coitus* a practical possibility even for those who reject contraception. In consequence new moral questions are posed. On the one hand, to what extent may man and wife rightly use *coitus* with sole reference to their own relationship? On the other hand, how are man and wife to determine the extent of their procreative responsibility? Is there a discoverable 'duty' to have children, or should procreation be regarded as a matter of vocation rather than of duty? In addition there is still the vexed question whether contraception is admissible or, if it is admissible, in what circumstances it may rightly be used. On these matters which are relevant to population problems, debate continues.

5. The importance of the family as the basis of a wider society continues to be underlined. The family-community is a model situation in which the meaning of human relationship is learnt. In particular, it is one of the few groupings in the modern world in which human persons have status and are respected simply because they are human persons, and not because they are useful. This is what makes the family the principal school of charity. Wherever, on the contrary, children are either valued for the potential contribution to the family's wealth or, in different circumstances, regarded as economic liabilities, family life is bound to be corrupted.

6. Eucharistic doctrine has been used to illuminate the meaning of Christian marriage, and this is to be welcomed. We can usefully develop, as far as it will go, a parallel of which we are reminded by the last general rubric attached to the form of Solemnization of Matrimony in the English Prayer Book of 1662: 'It is convenient that the new-married persons should receive the holy Communion at the time of their Marriage or at the first opportunity after their Marriage.' For marriage, like the Service of Holy Communion, is set in a social context—there is the need to be in love and charity with our family as with our neighbours—and it has a social outcome. Each is an offering of a human fellowship for a divine em-

powering. Further, just as in the Service of the Holy Communion, the natural elements of bread and wine are those means by which the grace of God is received, so we may think of the most intimate relationships of marriage as being elements in space and time whereby God's grace is given to enable a man and wife to continue in such a fellowship together as enables them to 'do all such good works as [God has] prepared for [them] to walk in'. We need not argue that every theme of Eucharistic doctrine can be developed to give direct teaching about Christian marriage. But if we begin to understand Christian marriage in terms of the Eucharist, we are all the more likely to give Christian marriage the significance it deserves, rather than to understand it in terms which make a travesty of its character.

7. Besides all these considerations, there is also the question, partly theological, partly canonical, of how a genuine marriage is made, involving questions of consent, consummation, and so on. The search for this understanding is relevant to situations where the Church finds marriage customs which differ from those of the older Christendom, and is important for the formulation of Christian law.

The Theology of Marriage and Rapid Social Change

Theology points to certain analogies—for instance, between the marriage union and the union of Christ with his Church, and between the parent-child relationship and the divine Fatherhood and Sonship; it throws light on the nature of 'two-in-oneship' and of the family community; it teaches about love and the gift of self; and it speaks of the ends of procreation and of mutual society, help, and comfort. But it does not supply a single unalterable pattern for married and family life. This life has found expression in different patterns in different places at different times. Therefore the scope for generalization about the form it should take in situations of rapid social change is very limited indeed. The pattern appropriate to any situation can only be discovered by actual experiment on the part of actual Christian spouses and families. The role of the Church is not so much to make pronouncements as to supply the help of wise priests and counsellors and the support of Christian community to those who are making the experiments.

The situation in parts of Africa will illustrate this. For instance, it is easy to condemn the system of migrant labour, pointing out that repeated absences of husbands are plainly inimical to marriage and family life. But, since equally plainly the system cannot be altered quickly, such judgment is not very helpful. The need is rather to find ways of creating Christian marriage and families in the inescapable circumstances. Again, it is of little avail to lament the fact that town-life is destroying what was good and stable in tribal marriage. The task of creating a pattern of African married life that can be lived in towns cannot be evaded. This is not at all to deny that the Church should use other means to promote situations more favourable to family life; but the immediate practical need is for Christians to show how Christian marriage can be achieved even in hostile circumstances.

In order to provide the help and support that is needed, the Church has, on the one hand, to grasp the nature of each situation and, on the other, to keep clear the distinction between what is essential in Christian marriage and what are accidental patterns of married behaviour. Here missionary experience should prove very valuable; for the problems set by rapid social change are similar in many respects to those which confront the missionary when he seeks to promote Christian marriage among people of a culture quite different from his own.

It should perhaps be remarked that there is a problem of social change in England as well as overseas, and these observations may be offered. The first is that the conception of marriage has tended to become increasingly 'individualistic', in that those who marry may think of their relationship as a purely private affair which has little or no relation to the families from which they come. This is in sharp contrast with (for instance) tribal notions of marriage in Africa. Obviously there are dangers in carrying either conception to extremes.

The second observation is that a pattern of married life seems to be establishing itself which has two stages. First comes 'marriage', during which stage man and wife both work outside the home. Thus the break between unmarried and married existence is less marked than commonly it used to be. It is the beginning of the second stage, when the couple 'start a family', that involves the revolutionary change in their manner of life. Often this is the more critical point of personal adjustment.

Population Problems

In this field there is more scope for useful generalization. On the other hand, some of the questions posed impinge upon matters of theological debate. The lack of a common mind necessarily causes some indefiniteness; but the temptation must be avoided to take refuge in vague pronouncements which evade the difficult issues.

The situation in India exemplifies the new type of problem. Largely as a result of improved and improving medical services, the population is multiplying at a rate which cannot be matched by increases in the production of food and other necessities. Disaster is predicted unless the growth of population can be checked; and since to withdraw medical attention is unthinkable, the only remedy seems to be to restrict the number of births. Thus several difficult questions are posed.

1. We are naturally suspicious of State intervention in a matter so personal as the procreation of children; but it is difficult to see how any government, confronted by the kind of prospect that has been mentioned, could be justified in refusing to do anything to reduce the number of births. It is true that in the event predictions may be falsified—for instance, if disease were unexpectedly to escape from control; but a government can only act on the best information obtainable. It has to be recognized that birth rates have already been influenced by State action. It will be generally allowed that justification for such action could hardly be stronger than it is in the Indian situation.

2. But what are the limits of justifiable intervention? We have become accustomed to financial inducements being offered to parents to encourage procreation. Where it is discouragement that is aimed at, it would seem to be unjust positively to penalize parents who think it right to have more children than seems good to the government. As for propaganda, there can be no reasonable objection to a government's publicizing the need for fewer births and using its resources to persuade people to act accordingly. Moral difficulties emerge only when a government actively encourages methods of birth-prevention of which the moral lawfulness is disputed. The Church cannot acquiesce, for instance, in policies of abortion or sterilization for limiting births.[1] What about contraception? The morality of this means will be discussed further below.

3. A question that needs further consideration is whether a situation of the Indian kind imposes a definite obligation on parents to limit their family in accordance with State recommendations. As has been remarked, man and wife now have it in their power to

---

[1] The matter was discussed further, leading to rather a different conclusion on sterilization, in the later report on *Sterilization: an Ethical Enquiry* (Church Information Office, 1962).

choose generative or non-generative intercourse. Consequently, quite apart from situations like the Indian, it has to be considered on what principle the extent of procreative possibility is to be determined. This is a comparatively new question which has not so far received any very clear answer. It may be that it should be answered in terms of 'vocation' rather than of 'duty'. As a rule the vocation to seek to have a family large enough to be a school of human relationships is implicit in the vocation to marriage; but it has usually been allowed that there may be exceptional vocations to childless marriage although husband and wife are, as far as they know, capable of procreating. In the past such a vocation was assumed to involve abstinence from intercourse. Whether there can be vocations to have intercourse only on occasions when conception is impossible or very improbable is a new question to which the answer is not immediately apparent.

If procreation is rightly regarded as a vocation, then it seems that it is not within the competence of a third party to determine that a couple have not that vocation, however undesirable the birth of a child may appear to be in the particular circumstances. In other words, if in a situation like the Indian a government were to declare against families of more than a certain number, the question for parents would not be one of obedience or disobedience, but rather one of discerning vocation in the light of all the circumstances, including the governmental declaration. The predicted consequences of more births, to society as well as to the children themselves and to the families concerned, may not be disregarded; but parents are entitled to reflect that predictions may be falsified and that in any case unfavourable circumstances do not destroy the value of existence.

4. Alike in situations that seem to demand a reduction of the birth-rate and in situations which seem to demand an increase the chief concern of the Church will be to foster the sense of responsibility and vocation in its married members. Whether it is proper for the Church to help to promote morally legitimate measures which States may take on the basis of predictions is a difficult and delicate question which can only be answered by those who know all the circumstances. Where the future of a nation seems to be in danger it may seem intolerable that it should 'sit on the fence'. But as a rule it is undesirable that it should tie itself to any general policy, whether of 'many children' or of 'few children'; for the impression must not be given that the family exists for the sake of society; and

this matter of procreation must be kept personal—whatever the circumstances.

EXTENDED NOTE: MARRIAGE IN BIBLICAL TEACHING

It cannot be doubted that the Bible for the most part[2] would emphasize the high significance of marriage. This emphasis arises in at least three ways:

(*a*) *By talking of God in terms of words and phrases and incidents that have to do with marriage*; for example, the marriage covenant between the Israelites is associated with Yahweh's covenant with his people (Mal. 2.10-16); there are the familiar similes of the woman in travail (Isa. 13.8; Rom. 8.22; Gal. 4.19) and of birth (Isa. 37.3; 66.9; Hos. 13.13); and use is often made of the pictures of bride and bridegroom (Isa. 61.10; Jer. 2.32; Matt. 25.1; John 3.29; Rev. 21.2; 22.17). Further, God is 'known' as a husband 'knows' his wife.

(*b*) *By the actions of our Lord himself*, for example at the marriage in Cana of Galilee.

(*c*) *By our Lord's teaching*, which emphasizes above all the significance of the one-flesh unity which marriage brings (Matt. 19.6).

But these positive themes which would emphasize the high calling of marriage, in which the most physical and fleshly of relations can be hallowed and informed by God, were, until recently, often neglected because of a different emphasis which is to be found in St Paul.

[2] The most obvious exceptions occur in the Old Testament where polygamy is not only recognized, but generally practised. We may recall the large harems of David and Solomon. We have, further, divers examples of a matriarchal type of marriage, when the husband resides in the wife's clan and the children are counted as her family. Such a concept of marriage lies behind the story of Jacob and his marriage to the daughter of Laban (Gen. 31) and behind the story of Shechem and Dinah (Gen. 34); and it is not unrelated to the *mot'a* or *sadiga* marriage such as Samson contrived to contract (Judges 14), a marriage in which the wife remained with her people, being visited from time to time by her husband.

On the other hand, the levirate marriage (Deut. 25.5) is sometimes traced to polyandry; and a depressed concept of womanhood lies behind the association of a wife with a man's chattels (Ex. 20.17) and behind the provision that a son could inherit his father's concubines. (Cf. the resentment of Ishbosheth when Abner took Rizpah, one of Saul's concubines.)

That some of these examples from the Old Testament find ready parallels in certain countries today should make us all the more cautious in our appeal to the Bible, whose authority must necessarily reckon with some doctrine of 'progressive revelation'. The authority of the Bible as a whole is not something which belongs mechanically to any and all of its parts.

For St Paul, marriage is undoubtedly a second best, with celibacy
and virginity as ideal courses (see I Cor. 7—especially vv. 1, 5, and
9). But it has to be emphasized that, equally for St Paul, marriage is
not in any way sinful. The reference we have just given does not of
course by itself in isolation represent St Paul's total view, which in
fact stems from presuppositions with which it is integrally related.
For St Paul, when he wrote this epistle, considered that the end of
the world was at hand and a time of great tribulation was imminent.
In these circumstances he commended celibacy and virginity on
prudential grounds. At such a critical period people without little
children to care for would be fortunate indeed. At the same time
Paul's views on marriage are not at all ascetic in character. He never
considers that marriage is an evil thing which the Christian should
utterly renounce. It is true that he chose celibacy for himself, and as
we have said, advised it for others, though he had no wish to
restrict people's freedom or to 'throw a halter on them' (I Cor.
7.35). Above all, his high view of marriage is clear from his exhortation in Eph. 5.25: 'Husbands love your wives, as Christ also
loved the Church and gave himself for it.' We could hardly imagine
a greater significance being given to married life than this. Further,
we can recall that in Ephesians 5, St Paul echoes the gospel teaching
and takes the one-flesh mystery of husband and wife as an apt model
for the relation between Christ and his Church.

II. CONTRACEPTION

To consider the family in contemporary society, whether, for
example, in Great Britain, or India, or the West Indies or Japan, is
to raise for various reasons the question of family planning and
consequently the question of using contraceptives to that end. In
Great Britain contraception is widely advocated and used not only
where there are grave objections to the birth of children, but also
for spacing births without interrupting intercourse and for facilita-
ting earlier marriage of the two-stage pattern which has already
been mentioned. In India and Japan it seems to many to be the only
practical solution of economic and demographic problems, unless
abortion (already legalized in Japan) or sterilization are to be
countenanced. There is therefore urgent need to establish, if possible, an Anglican attitude to this practice.

There follow three separate treatments of the moral problem, in which contraception is considered as a relatively isolated matter and the question of intrinsic moral quality is raised.

The first treatment sets out a more traditional standpoint; the second discusses contraception with special reference to the 'ends' and 'object' of coitus, *categories which, it believes, have been wrongly construed in traditional moral theology; the third example displays a much less* a priori *view altogether.*[3]

EXAMPLE I

It is necessary to distinguish two opinions in favour of contraception:

A. That contraception is a positive good—a discovery which enables human beings to realize more fully the potentialities of the relationship between man and woman, and which therefore deserves to be a normal feature of married life.

B. That contraception is an evil to be avoided if possible, but one that can be transformed into a relative good in circumstances where there is a greater evil to be avoided.

A. *The opinion that contraception is a positive good.*

There is here no question of some evil in the situation (poor health, economic circumstances, etc.) that needs to be offset. On this view it is quite simply better—more appropriate to a rational nature—that man and wife should be enabled to dispose at discretion of two types of *coitus*: one which has to do exclusively with their relationship to each other; and another of which the primary meaning consists in participation in creation. For thus, on the one hand, procreation becomes rational and voluntary: there is no danger of being lured into it by overpowering desires or of having to accept it as an unwilled consequence of serving the marriage relationship; and on the other hand *coitus* for the sake of the personal relationship can be regulated in accordance with the requirements of that relationship, instead of being largely controlled by decisions about the desirability of conception. Each type of *coitus*

[3] [This sentence of summary was not in the original Report. *Editor.*]

can then be regulated according to the particular moral considerations which apply to it.

It is maintained that this pattern of sexual life is not contrary to what is found in nature, but rather a rational development of it. Nature itself provides, by recurring sterile periods, for *coitus* which has no intrinsic end beyond the personal relationship of man and wife. Quite apart from contraception there are two types of *coitus* and two moral questions, viz., the question of obligation to procreate and the question of how 'relational' *coitus* ought to be regulated. The advantage of contraception is that it permits reproduction of a sterile period at will, and so enables man and wife to make the occasions of 'relational' *coitus* fit their personal needs, instead of their having to submit to a physiological time-table which may not suit their needs at all. There is also the point that a woman's periods may be too variable to allow using the sterile times.

Before examining this opinion we had better decide what we mean by 'contraception'. It is only a source of confusion to identify contraception, considered as an act of having moral quality, with some contemporary technique which will probably be superseded. Thus, if we identify contraception with the prevalent method of keeping spermatozoa out of the uterus and killing them, it is possible to object that this procedure changes the physical structure of the sexual act; for even if it is granted that closing the uterus is merely reproducing what happens in pregnancy, spermicide is open to challenge on the ground that it makes nonsense of the giving and receiving of seed which (whether the woman is sterile or not) seems to be an integral part of that structure. But such an objection would not lie if temporary sterilization were to be achieved by some preparation taken orally; for then the physical structure of the act would not be modified at all. It may in other circumstances be necessary to scrutinize the morality of particular methods of contraception; but what we are concerned with here is temporary sterilization itself, not particular ways of bringing it about.

It may be remarked that this cuts most of the ground from under the so-called 'aesthetic' objection; for as a rule that objection rests upon a mental image of a particular technique. In any case it is in the highest degree subjective. In the matter of the *usus matrimonii* no reliance can be placed on the emotional reactions of individuals, since such reactions are so much governed by a person's sexual experience—or lack of it.

We now come to the main question at issue, viz., whether the advocates of contraception are right in saying:

1. that it is in the true line of human development (i.e. 'natural' in the moral theologian's sense of the word) that man and wife should be free to determine for themselves when they will have 'relational' *coitus*, without reference to the cycle of fertility and sterility that is found in the unmodified biological process; and

2. that there is no inherent difference, ontological or moral, between *coitus* during the temporary sterility that belongs to the biological process and *coitus* during temporary sterility artificially induced.

1. The question whether biological processes may be manipulated to subserve personal relationships has some affinity with the question how far the marital union itself is within man's dominion. In both matters conflicting judgments are found among Christians. Thus there are those who think that the marriage bond is subject to man, so that, if it no longer subserves personal relationship, it can be dissolved by human authority and be replaced by another marriage. On the other hand there are those who believe that those who marry thereby submit themselves to a metaphysical union which, once made, is beyond human control. Similarly in this matter of the *usus matrimonii* some, as we have seen, think that man has such dominion over his biological processes that he may modify them, at any rate to the extent involved in contraception; but others see the biological pattern as something 'given', which has metaphysical implications, and to which man and wife must submit themselves in order to achieve the purposes and receive the blessings of marital union. The kind of submission meant here is not to be confused with an unreasoning and fatalistic 'Let nature take its course'. The rational nature of man shows itself in seeking to understand the biological processes better and in making use of the knowledge gained, not to supersede the processes by human inventions, but to fulfil the implicit pattern more completely. So, for instance, study of the processes reveals that there is a place in marriage for 'relational' *coitus*; but it does not support the notion that it is proper to man to enjoy such *coitus* at will: the pattern disclosed is one that imposes definite limitations. (It should be noted, by the way, that this view of the matter does not involve any *universal* proposition about man's dominion over his body. *Coitus*, like marriage to which it pertains, is a special case.)

2. If we see *coitus* simply as a spatio-temporal event, which can be fully described in physiological and psychological terms, then it may be possible (though some may question this) to regard *coitus* during sterility artificially induced as ontologically and morally equivalent to *coitus* during the sterility which is found in the biological process. But if we believe that *coitus* has metaphysical implications, then the equivalence disappears. It is only to the act which is 'given', and not to any human counterfeit, that the metaphysical union in one flesh is attached. Here again we see the analogy with marriage. In order that union in one flesh may be *initiated*, man and woman must submit themselves to the divine ordinance concerning the gift of self: if some other form of consent is substituted, their union may possibly be valid in a purely legal sense, but there can be no assurance that it is metaphysically valid. Similarly, in order that the same union in one flesh may be *consummated*, man and woman must submit themselves to the specific act as 'given'; if some modification is substituted, there can be no assurance that anything is achieved in the metaphysical realm.

It therefore seems that those who advocate contraception are either denying, or at least ignoring, these metaphysical implications of *coitus*, and treating the act simply as a spatio-temporal event. They seem to be content with the outward aspect of the act—penetration, orgasm, and the physical and psychological consequences of orgasm. That is not equivalent, as opponents of contraception have sometimes unfairly suggested, to saying that the *pleasure* of the act may be sought while the *end* of the act is frustrated; for even on the spatio-temporal level the act has 'relational' value. But it is certainly to ignore the analogy between *coitus* and sacraments. In a sacrament the promise of a supernatural gift depends on due performance of the rite according to the divine ordinance; in *coitus* the metaphysical union in one flesh depends on submission to the act as 'given'. In brief, there is no assurance that *coitus* during contraception can constitute consummation in more than a merely legal sense.

As a rule those who approve of *coitus* with contraceptives condemn *coitus interruptus*. But once the notion of 'givenness' is jettisoned, it becomes difficult to find adequate grounds for this condemnation. It is indeed maintained that *coitus interruptus* is bad for health, while *coitus* during contraception is not; but although ill consequences may suggest that the act they follow is contrary to human nature, they are not by themselves sufficient to settle the question. Perhaps the main ground of distinction that is alleged is that *coitus interruptus* lacks 'relational' value. But so does *coitus* during contraception, if we include under 'relational' the consummation of metaphysical union. If on the other hand only the spatio-temporal is to be considered, more careful research would be needed before a worth-while conclusion could be come to. 'Relational' value seems to attach itself to the oddest sexual activities. It is well known that many people cannot find any satisfaction at all in the normal act of *coitus*, but find it in variations that most would condemn. On what grounds are we to say that these are not pioneers in the development of the sexual life?

It is in this connection that the spread of contraception gives rise to a fear that may or may not be justified, but which at least suggests caution. It is, to say the least, suspicious that the age in which contraception has won its way is not one which has been conspicuously successful in managing its sexual life. Is it possible that, by claiming the right to manipulate his physical processes in this matter, man may, without knowing or intending it, be stepping over the boundary between the world of Christian marriage and what one might call the world of Aphrodite—the world of sterile eroticism against which the Church reacted so strongly (perhaps too strongly) in its early days? For one of the characteristics of the latter world was (and is) the exercise of unlimited self-determination in sexual activity. Once submission to the 'given' pattern is abandoned, all kinds of variations on the sexual theme which heighten satisfaction can appear to be enrichments of the sexual life. Admittedly this is a very difficult subject to handle; for in sexual matters the usual Christian counsel of 'indifference' to pleasure simply does not apply. The sexual act as 'given' seems to demand, for its due performance, deliberate heightening of, and abandonment to, sensation. But that is all the more reason why the definite limitations imposed by the 'given' pattern are necessary.

Is any scientific research possible in this field? It could only deal with the spatio-temporal effects of various types of sexual activity; but that would be something. It would certainly be a help to have some factual material to work on. For instance, are the effects of *coitus* during normal periods of sterility and *coitus* during induced sterility the same or different? It has been suggested here that the two acts are ontologically different; they are apt to be psychologically different: are the consequences also different? Is *coitus* during contraception a *sedatio concupiscentiae*? or does it perhaps stimulate appetite? One receives an impression that the answers which have so far been given to this sort of question have owed too much to prejudice and too little to evidence.

The upshot of all this, it may be suggested, is that it would be very unwise at this juncture for the Church to endorse in any way the opinion that contraception is a positive good needing no special circumstances to justify it.

B. *The opinion that contraception, though normally to be avoided, can be justified by circumstances.*

In 1930 the Lambeth Conference gave majority support to this opinion, but the background of the committee's discussion and of the resolution which was then passed was very different from the circumstances of today.

1. The theological revaluation of *coitus* as a symbol of and means to the union of man and wife in one flesh was then only in its early stages. Today few would commend prolonged abstinence from intercourse as 'the primary and obvious' method of preventing conception; for if *coitus* is the characteristic act of marriage, which differentiates it from other relationships, and the seal of marriage union, then prolonged abstinence is contrary to the nature of marriage and requires either special vocation or strong circumstantial justification.

2. In 1930 the scientific basis of what has come to be called 'the rhythm method' of controlling conception was only just being established; and so the Conference spoke as if choice was confined to abstinence and contraception alone, and as if intentionally non-generative intercourse stood or fell with contraception. Today it is recognized that nature itself provides for purely 'relational' intercourse; it is generally allowed that such intercourse is permissible during natural infertility; and the question at issue is whether such infertility may be reproduced artificially and, if it may, in what circumstances.

3. The background of the 1930 discussion was concern about 'the decline of the birth-rate throughout the civilized world'. Today, on the contrary, minds are chiefly exercised by the overpopulation of certain territories.

A contemporary argument for the occasional justification of contraception starts from a belief that it is desirable that such limitation or spacing of families as vocation or circumstances require should be achieved without enforced abstinence over long periods. It is held that often the rhythm method affords the means to this end, but that in circumstances where it is not eligible, and the choice lies between abstinence and contraception alone, contraception may be chosen.

Is this judgment reconcilable with the view of *coitus* given above (in 1A)? Some would say not. They would argue that no circumstances can have the effect of changing a counterfeit into the genuine 'given' act of *coitus*. On the other hand, others would say that, although circumstances cannot alter the ontological status of *coitus* with contraceptives, they can and do alter its moral status; that the modified act, though ontologically different from *coitus* during natural infertility, may on occasion be morally equivalent, being the best symbol of love and union that is eligible in the circumstances.

It is remarkable that hardly any attempt seems to have been made to indicate the kind of situation in which this latter judgment would hold good. Perhaps the reason is that, if procreation is to be treated in terms of vocation rather than of duty, no brief and simple guidance can be given. For the same reason, and also because more co-operative work on the question is badly needed, the casuistry of the matter cannot be discussed here.

The implications of this type of judgment on contraception for people living in Indian or similar conditions call for special consideration. The existence of such conditions does not immediately justify contraception in any particular case, since rhythm *may* still be eligible. It may be that there are many whose education or intelligence does not enable them to use rhythm, but who can yet be taught to use contraception. Again, it may be argued that the Indian house is on fire, and that the only fire-brigade action that has the slightest chance of being effective is a State campaign in favour of contraception. But these considerations do not suffice to show that contraception is permissible for all.

EXAMPLE II

Notes on the Morality of Contraception considered with reference to the 'Ends' and 'Object' of Coitus

I. In moral theology the traditional determinants of the morality of an act are its object, its circumstances, and the agent's intention;

and of these, the object is regarded as primary. It has been described as 'that natural tendency or result which, when adequately qualified or defined, specifies the action as being one of a particular class'.[4] In practice it is difficult to consider the object of an act without making reference to its end (*finis operis*); and this is particularly so in the matter now under discussion—the morality of *coitus* with the use of contraception. Consequently moralists have usually been inclined to treat this problem in terms of the *finis operis* of *coitus*, rather than in terms of its object; and we shall follow their practice here.

II. *Coitus*, considered in itself, comes within the category of indifferent acts, such as walking and eating, and is therefore morally neutral. Regard, therefore, must be paid to circumstances, and to the agents' intentions, when attempting to decide whether any concrete act of *coitus* is good or bad. In general, we may say that the good act of *coitus* must be (1) free, that is, it must be an act to which both parties consent, knowing to what they consent, and there must be no constraint due to force or fear; (2) conformable to reason and to the divine will, as they are seen to relate to sexual and coital behaviour; (3) adequately related to the end or ends of the act. This means, in effect, that *coitus* must occur within the context of a certain kind of responsible sexual relationship, which may be defined theologically as the common life of one-flesh, and institutionally as 'marriage' (recognizing that more than one form of institutional relationship between the sexes may conform to reason, and that different institutional forms may co-exist—e.g., the ecclesiastical and the civil).

Consideration of circumstances leads to the conclusion that the morally neutral act of *coitus* becomes bad when it occurs in conditions which contravene the above requirements, such as fornication and adultery. But is it true, on the other hand, that every act of marital *coitus* is good? And in particular, is marital *coitus* with the use of contraception morally good?

III. Before considering the question, What is the end (*finis operis*) of *coitus*? it is well to bear in mind the kind of human act with which we are dealing. No treatment of *coitus* is adequate or realistic which fails to recognize the profoundly mysterious nature of this particular mode of human intercourse. Even the Bible regards it as a distinctive means by which one person attains a certain 'knowledge' of another which cannot be mediated otherwise, but the full

---

[4] R. C. Mortimer, *The Elements of Moral Theology*, 1947, p. 66.

content and significance of this unique relational experience can neither be apprehended nor expressed by the individual, for its character and meaning are as infinitely variable as is the structure of sexual relationship itself.

Appreciation of the mystery of *coitus* and a deeper understanding of the relationship between man and woman make it difficult for the modern theologian to speak with the same confidence as his predecessors about the proper ends of *coitus*, or to regard it merely as one among many comparable human acts. Traditionally, the principal end of *coitus* has been defined as generation—though other subsidiary ends, such as the relief of incontinence and mutual endearment, were also recognized; but such a classification hardly does justice either to the complexity of the act or the realities of experience. If the true ends of *coitus*, as determined by God's purpose, are to be apprehended by means of the exercise of an informed reason, then it would seem that some redefinition is necessary.

IV. *Coitus* may be said to have a two-fold end (or, if it be preferred, two separate ends).

1. Biologically, its purpose is *generative*—that is, the fertilization of the ovum by a spermatozoon.

2. On the personal plane, its purpose is *relational*. Husband and wife become one-flesh in principle at the physical consummation of their union, and their *coitus* plays an important part in the progressive realization of all that one-flesh implies. It serves to direct creatively the powerful (and potentially disruptive) sexual impulses, so that they are expended in acts which develop and enrich the relationship; it is a means for the expression of love; and it is also an important aspect of the 'mutual society, help, and comfort' of married life. Finally, it is in a very real sense 'sacramental' of the whole meaning of wedlock.

One very important aspect of this relational purpose deserves special mention, and suggests a legitimate extension of the meaning of 'procreation'. It would now be generally agreed that procreation implies co-operation with God in his creative work—that it is really creation on behalf of God. It would also be agreed that such co-operation in the divine work of creation involves the education of the child to maturity, and not merely its begetting and birth. Consequently the procreative task of parenthood is not completed until the last child is fully adult.

To this task, the parents' *coitus* makes a valuable contribution.

Once conception has occurred, it plays an important part in the maintenance of harmonious relationship between the couple, and thus promotes the well-being of the child, first before birth, and then during the whole period (some seventeen or more years) of growth towards maturity. Especially in the vital formative years (up to the age of five or six) it can thus help to ensure the stability and security of the child.

V. It will immediately be apparent that this two-fold end is not, and cannot be, attained with every act of *coitus*.

1. Generation is so controlled by biological and other factors that its achievement is uncertain and, relative to the total incidence of *coitus*, comparatively rare. Conception cannot occur during the infertile period of the menstrual cycle, nor after the menopause, yet *coitus* can take place satisfactorily at those times. Furthermore, male sterility or physiological defect in the female may prevent *coitus* from resulting in conception.

2. The relational end of *coitus* is always attained, either (*a*) constructively, in the expression of love, the building up of the one-flesh union, and the fulfilment of the 'procreative' task of parent-hood (in the sense explained above—see IV. 2) or (*b*) destructively, in the expression of lust, and in exploitation of another person, whether in or outside marriage (cf. I Cor. 6.16). *Coitus* is a personal act of such a kind that it is seldom without its effect upon the characters of the participants, either for good or for ill.

VI. The two-fold nature of the end (*finis operis*) of *coitus* is not denied by traditional systems of morality, but it is always assumed that the generative end, though least certain of attainment, is never-theless primary and determinative. Accordingly, it has been held that every act of *coitus* must at least (to use the customary phrase) be *aptus ad generationem*—'suitable for generation'. This require-ment is not interpreted to exclude *coitus* during times of infertility; it is sufficient that nothing be done which would prevent concep-tion, were conception possible. It is not necessary that the act be performed always in circumstances which ensure or favour concep-tion; but no artificial contraceptive measure is permissible.

It has yet to be shown, however, on what grounds (other than *a priori* ones) generation is determinative among the ends of *coitus*. Such an assumption was doubtless natural and inevitable at a time when the relational significance and the intrinsic mystery of *coitus* were not recognized; then it was easy to regard the act principally as a generative mechanism to which, in consequence of the Fall, a certain remedial function is now annexed in marriage. But it is difficult any longer to maintain such a view, and it is at least arguable to the extent of probability that any attempt to classify the ends of *coitus* in order of supposed importance or priority is misconceived. On the other hand, every consideration of coital morality must take account of two things. (1) Human *coitus* is an act of unique quality and significance involving to a greater degree than any other the whole person as a psychosomatic unity. (2) Human *coitus* cannot be treated as an isolated and self-subsistent act. Being an act of the whole person, it is in some sense expressive of an attitude to life and to God. Each act of *coitus* between husband and wife must be seen, therefore, as part of a total pattern of relationship.

With this caution against attaching greater importance to the individual act of *coitus* than to the general pattern of coital relationship which is one aspect of the common life of husband and wife, two alternative approaches to the problem of contraception may be proposed.

VII. According to certain moral theologians, the good act of *coitus* must be *aptus ad generationem*; but generation is only one end of *coitus*, and that the least certain of attainment. Moreover, an act which, while *aptus ad generationem*, is an exploitation of one spouse by the other, can hardly be regarded as other than morally bad. The good act of *coitus*, therefore, might better be defined as that which conduces to fulfilment of the act's proper two-fold end (or, if it be preferred, the act's proper ends).

Such a re-classification, however, does not take us very far. It avoids any isolation of the generative end, but it does not escape the error of treating the individual act of *coitus* as a self-subsistent entity, rather than as a single element in a complex relational pattern, the morality of which must be assessed as a whole. In the latter connection the following facts need consideration.

1. The 'proper two-fold end' (or the 'proper ends') of *coitus* are impossible of fulfilment in every act, because generation and procreation (using these terms in the sense already defined) depend upon favourable biological conditions, and upon the existence of parental responsibility.

2. Fulfilment of the relational end of *coitus* is possible independently of the attainment or the non-attainment of the other end.

It is arguable, then, that the morally good act of *coitus* is really that which forms part of a pattern of relational acts of consistent with the 'proper two-fold end' (or the 'proper ends') of sexual intercourse in marriage. In the normal marriage, husband and wife will desire certain coital acts to be both relational and generative, and others to be only relational; in selecting against generation, are they to be morally restricted to periods of natural infertility, or may they extend such periods artificially by the use of contraceptive appliances—provided always that this is done in such a way that it does not render the general pattern of coital relationship inconsistent with the 'proper two-fold end' of *coitus* within marriage? The answer made to this question will depend upon two further considerations—the extent of human freedom, and the nature of the 'given' structure of the coital act; and to these we shall return later.

VIII. Alternatively, it is arguable that moralists have over-simplified the problem of contraception by treating *coitus* as if it were simply one species of physical act—whence (partly) their preference for discussing this problem in terms rather of the act's end than of its 'object'.

On the contrary, it would seem that there are actually two species of *coitus*, or two kinds of coital act. These have sometimes been described as 'relational' and 'generative'—but the distinction is hardly accurate, since it suggests that the act is either relational or generative, whereas all *coitus* is necessarily in some sense relational. It is preferable to say that there are two species of *coitus*, or two kinds of coital act: (1) the 'generative', performed under conditions which are biologically favourable to conception, and (2) the 'non-generative', performed when conception is biologically impossible.

This abstract distinction takes no account of the agents' intention. By observing the biological processes of the human body, however, man can determine what conditions are favourable or unfavourable to conception; consequently he can decide, within the limits set by those conditions, whether any particular act shall (at any rate, in intention) be generative or non-generative. This capacity for selecting between the two kinds of coital act represents in itself an advance also in man's understanding of his nature. A further advance is marked by realization that non-generative *coitus* has a positive value of its own, as a relational act—that it is not merely a 'safe' form of sexual indulgence.

Growing appreciation of the relational value of *coitus* has been accompanied by greater understanding of human biological processes, and of the means whereby these processes can be subjected to rational control. Not only has more accurate observation of the bodily functions made selection between generative and non-generative *coitus* easier, but contraception now enables man to decide more or less at will, by the employment of artificial methods, whether or not *coitus* shall be generative; and there is good ground for believing that scientific research will eventually place in his hands even simpler and more reliable means, such as preparations designed to produce temporary sterility. Even now, therefore, the question of selection hardly arises; rather, we have to ask whether it is morally permissible to render a particular act of *coitus* non-generative artificially by creating conditions which make conception impossible.

Many would hold that such a revision of the natural coital pattern, in the interests of the marital relationship, the family, and the community, is a rational development by means of which biological processes can be controlled and directed in order to serve personal and social ends. The distinction between generative and non-generative *coitus* still holds good, but both kinds of *coitus* derive a new and enhanced significance from the fact that each becomes a responsible act chosen with reference to a specific situation. This choice, however, must be justified as a legitimate exercise of human freedom, and as consistent with the intrinsic nature of coital acts.

IX. Discussion of the morality of contraception is often confused by the different senses in which the words 'nature' and 'natural' can be used. Dr Kirk draws attention to this when he asks what is meant by describing the contraceptive appliance as unnatural:

> Is 'unnatural' the same as 'artificial'; and if so, is all 'artificial' interference with the processes of nature—all control of those processes by the methods of science—to be adjudged immoral? Or is it only this process [i.e., generation] which may not be so controlled or modified? And if so, why is 'artificial' (i.e., scientific) control debarred from coming to the aid of natural control (i.e., complete abstinence) in this matter alone?[5]

Clearly it is incorrect to treat 'unnatural' and 'artificial' as synonymous, for human artifice may serve to assist nature; and it is not simply because contraception involves the use of artificial means that certain moralists regard it as unnatural. It is important, therefore, to clarify the customary terminology.

[5] *Conscience and its Problems*, 1933, p. 295.

M*

In the traditional usage of moral theology, 'natural' means consonant with the true nature of a person or thing, as that nature has
been given by God and is perceived by the exercise of an informed
reason. That is natural to man which is consistent with human
nature as designed by the Creator—and 'nature', in this sense,
cannot be controlled or manipulated; man can only either conform
to his nature, or violate it. If, therefore, the structure of *coitus* as
determined by biological and physiological factors is seen to be
given to man as part of his 'nature', then any interference with that
structure (such as by contraceptive methods) will appear 'unnatural'; but selection between generative and non-generative
coital acts by the use of the 'safe period' will be accepted as 'natural'.

On the other hand, to theologians or philosophers who think in
other than traditional moral-theological terms, 'nature' will generally denote the realm of impersonal creative and regulative forces
or processes, including the functions of the human body. On this
view, it will seem entirely consistent with man's 'nature' (in the
moral-theological sense) as a rational being invested with dominion
over the sub-human orders and, *a fortiori*, over his own physiological and biological processes, that he should exercise responsible
control and direction over 'nature', or the physical realm. This
conception of man will see him as at once part of nature, and transcendent over nature by virtue of the spirit which makes him distinctively human.

X. It is in the second of these two senses that Dr Niebuhr uses the
terms 'nature' and 'natural' in an illuminating section of his
Gifford Lectures where he considers man's paradoxical situation—
at once a child of nature, and a spirit standing outside nature. Set
at the meeting-place of two realms, he cannot reduce himself to the
proportions of nature or destroy his innate freedom over natural
processes; nor, on the other hand, can he use that freedom to achieve
complete independence of nature. Nevertheless, because of his freedom of spirit he can use natural forces creatively—he can direct
and re-direct the vitalities of the natural order. Within the limits of
finitude, his spiritual freedom allows him to break the harmonies of
nature, to transcend natural forms, to revise natural unities, and to
create new realms of cohesion and order.

In the light of this understanding of man and his nature we must
consider the argument that contraception is prohibited by the
natural law. Such a prohibition, says Dr Niebuhr,[6]

[6] *The Nature and Destiny of Man*, 1941-3, I, p. 298.

assumes that the sexual function in human life must be limited to its function in nature, that of procreation. But it is the very character of human life that all animal functions are touched by freedom and released into more complex relationships.

And he goes on to maintain that

It is not possible to escape the natural fact that the primary purpose of bisexuality in nature is that of procreation. But it is not easy to establish a universally valid 'law of reason' which will eternally set the bounds for the function of sex in the historic development of human personality.[7]

It is important to recognize that sexuality in man is not, and indeed cannot be, simply a 'natural' sexuality, though it retains its natural character and purpose. No longer does it find expression only or chiefly in an instinctive urge to reproduce; by incorporation into the human psyche it is transformed and raised to a new level of significance—one that is personal, and not merely biological. Because of its deep involvement with man's personality and its instrumentality in the expression of relational values, *coitus* transcends the simple functionalism of natural copulation. Moreover, God himself has radically differentiated human *coitus* from that of the animals by constituting it to be the means by which the one-flesh *henosis* is established and consolidated.

Because human sexuality is thus demonstrably supra-natural as well as natural, the distinction already made between generative and non-generative *coitus* is valid. Yet it is a distinction which does not reside in the nature of the respective acts themselves since, considered simply as acts, generative and non-generative *coitus* are identical. We are thus reminded that although human sexuality is caught up into the realms of personality and is thereby transformed, it remains none the less firmly rooted in nature and subject to certain natural physiological unities. Yet man is not under bondage to these unities, for his freedom allows him to transcend them in order to control sexuality for ends which lie beyond nature as such.

The fact that man in his freedom stands above nature, and is therefore at liberty to interpret sex in terms of personality and relation and to use it for the achievement of personal and relational ends, leads to the conclusion that contraception is morally right in certain circumstances. Thus man may legitimately extend the range of non-generative *coitus* as it exists in nature, by the use of contraceptive devices, but only so long as this is done in obedience to

[7] *Ibid.*, I, pp. 298-9.

relational or social needs. In other words, contraception must always represent a responsible use of human freedom in the interests of personal relationship or of the community. The relational needs of man and woman in marriage may demand that *coitus* shall be independent of natural cycles of fertility and infertility; yet man's liberty of spirit allows him only to modify and adjust, and not to abolish the natural unities of physical sexuality.

XI. According to the traditional moral-theological conception of 'nature' and the 'natural', on the other hand, human freedom is even more limited in its scope, since it only permits a right of selection between generative and non-generative *coitus* based upon observation of the biological cycle of fertility and infertility. Further, it would be argued that man is not free to modify in any way the 'given' structure of *coitus*, observance of which is essential if the relational benefits annexed to the act are to be obtained. Because, according to Scripture, *coitus* makes man and woman 'one flesh', it necessarily has metaphysical implications; but these implications are nullified by any interference with the act such as to destroy its 'natural' character. In other words, the introduction of a contraceptive appliance has an ontological effect; it changes true *coitus* into a specious imitation from which the appointed relational benefits are withdrawn. Hence contraception is both morally wrong because it is contrary to human 'nature', and powerless to secure the benefits at which it aims because it immediately converts the act of *coitus* into a transaction void of metaphysical significance, and therefore void of positive value.

Impressive though these arguments are, it is by no means easy to sustain them on other than *a priori* grounds. It is by no means certain that if human *coitus* has a 'given' structure, that structure is disclosed or determined exclusively or even principally by physiological or biological factors. *Coitus* is only 'natural', or consonant with man's true nature, when it exhibits all the characteristics of a responsible personal act expressive of a certain integral relationship between the man and woman concerned. But any attempt to define abstractly the empirical features which guarantee that *coitus* is 'natural' must be regarded as misconceived and doomed to failure, for by its very 'nature' *coitus* between human beings is not an act of such a kind that it can be so defined. It cannot be considered as 'given' apart from the relational context within which it is 'given'. And it is arguable that it is fully consistent with the 'nature' of human *coitus* as 'given' that man, by the responsible exercise of his freedom, should modify certain of its 'mechanical' details in order to increase its relational potentialities.

So, too, with the second argument. *Coitus* certainly has a metaphysical significance, but since this is derived from its personal character, it can never be nullified; this has been expressed in another way by the statement made earlier that *coitus* is always relational, even though its effect may be destructive. Likewise, it is evident that certain benefits are annexed to *coitus*—but it is impossible to define the precise empirical conditions which must be fulfilled in order to secure such benefits. Again, all that can be said is that the relational blessings conveyed by the act depend upon the quality of the personal relationship of the pair in question, who will receive from their intercourse proportionately to what they bring to it.

The difficulty about both arguments (that from the 'natural' or 'given' structure of *coitus*, and that from the conditions supposedly prerequisite in order to ensure the benefits of the act) is that they are so easily countered on empirical grounds—and this is deliberately stated as a difficulty in the way of accepting the arguments, rather than a proof that they are wrong, since in this matter especially the empirical approach is apt to be regarded as suspect. There is abundant evidence to show that *coitus* can be both 'natural' and relationally immoral (as when man and woman exploit each other), and that contraception appears to promote the highest personal ends of sexual union. These facts cannot be ignored or dismissed as insignificant; they suggest that the allegedly 'natural' performance of the act cannot *per se* guarantee the benefits attributed to it, and that those benefits can follow in impressive measure from acts which are alleged to be morally 'unnatural'. It is pertinent, therefore, to ask whether 'natural' *coitus* (in the traditional moral-theological sense) is not simply an arbitrary *a priori* concept to which there is no correspondence in reality.

Is there, then, no objective criterion by which the morality of physical sexual acts between man and woman can be assessed? Surely we may say that for human *coitus* to be 'natural' it must above all have integrity as a responsible personal act—although (because of its unique and mysterious quality [see §§ III and VI]) it is manifestly impossible to define in advance the precise general conditions which ensure integrity, since many factors are involved which elude or defy definition. A valid conception of the 'given' structure of *coitus*, therefore, must take fully into account the fact that personal and relational factors are 'given' no less than the physiological and biological factors—and that the former must not be separated artificially from the latter.

XII. Thus, whether we consider the unique and mysterious character of human *coitus* (§§ III and VI), its relational significance (§§ III; IV, 2; V, 2), its proper ends (§§ IV, V, VI, and VII), its species (§ VIII), and its 'nature' and 'given' structure (§§ IX, X, and XI); or whether we consider the range of man's legitimate freedom consequent upon his paradoxical situation as a being at once involved in, and transcendent over the natural order (§§ X and XI); we reach the conclusion that there are very strong moral-theological grounds for regarding the responsible use of contraception by married persons as morally right.

Appendix

Dr Niebuhr's treatment of contraception in the context of his discussion of human freedom has already been mentioned. It may be useful, as an Appendix to these notes, to summarize the teaching of another eminent modern theologian, Dr Karl Barth, who deals with family limitation in *Die Kirchliche Dogmatik*.[8] His argument is outlined as an interesting contribution to the subject under discussion, not as though it were all necessarily endorsed.

Barth observes that there is general unanimity among moralists and theologians upon the duty of responsible family planning, but that they differ upon the question of the means to that end. There are four choices open to husband and wife:

(1) Complete abstinence. This is a 'heroic' course, and not impossible, but it may have psychological consequences which would prove calamitous for the marriage. (2) The safe period. Relatively, this may appear the ideal method; but how far in fact do all the statistical calculations and calendrical observations necessary for its use affect the *natura intrinseca* of *coitus*? Is *coitus* really natural (in the sense described in § X, above), when its spontaneity is checked by the rule of the 'Conception-Calendar'? And how much remains of its relational value, if *coitus* is attended by constant anxiety as to its 'safety'—as is often the case with something so uncertain as the safe period? (3) *Coitus interruptus*. This is the simplest and probably the most ancient method, but it is a 'wretched' one, and one shown by clinical experience to be attended by special psychological dangers. Only 'insensitive couples' can contemplate it, and those

[8] English: *Church Dogmatics* III/4, pp. 269-77.

who practise it imperil their union. Nevertheless, some seem to find it satisfactory. (4) Contraception. The contraceptive appliance is not evil because it is 'technical', though it may, in some forms, be aesthetically uncongenial, and can be positively evil if used with unworthy motives.

Concerning all these methods there are two things to be said:

(*a*) Each one is in some sense 'unnatural' in that, by comparison with the course of nature, it involves human arrangement, direction and regulation. If, therefore, human interference with the 'natural' character of *coitus* is rejected on principle, then all four possibilities would have to be rejected. But if human interference is not rejected on principle, then no selection can be made on principle in favour of one method as against the others.

(*b*) About all the methods there is something embarrassing, strained and artificial. But equally, unrestrained copulation and unlimited generation is 'unnatural' in that it is not consistent with man's true nature. If, therefore, family limitation is accepted as the responsible, truly human course, a price must be paid, no matter what the positive or negative (abstinent) decision may be—and it will never be small. This is the inevitable cost of man's mastery over nature, especially when it involves the cause of human existence itself.

If, then, family limitation is determined upon, a choice must be made between four courses, each of which is in its own way unnatural and embarrassing. What considerations should govern the choice?

(*a*) The choice must be made in faith, not in fear or doubt; and it must be made with a free conscience, in the conviction that in the concrete situation in question the decision must be thus, and not otherwise. Moreover, because the choice is made in faith, it is also made with the confidence that should it prove to have been mistaken, there is foregiveness for sin and the gift of enabling grace. The decision must never be made with a bad conscience.

(*b*) The choice must follow from the common deliberation and resolution of husband and wife. The course they follow must be consistent with the whole meaning of their marriage, and an expression of the significance of their life-long union. It must unite them in a solidarity of decision, the carrying out of which must be part of the common enterprise of marriage.

Thus Barth does not express any special reference for or against contraception, but sees man caught in a situation where, if he would act responsibly in marriage, he cannot avoid taking a decision which will be embarrassing and 'unnatural'. In effect, therefore, the matter is left to the informed conscience of the individual —or rather (if the phrase may be allowed) to the common conscience of the one-flesh *henosis*; the honest and conscientious choice of husband and wife is the right choice for them at the time and in the situation when it is made. Yet considering the four alternatives as Barth defines them, it is clear that contraception is on the whole perhaps the least unsatisfactory of the different 'unnatural' courses open to the married.

EXAMPLE III

A less a priori approach

The third view begins with the assumption that what is involved in Christian marriage is necessarily subject to development. It is assumed that there is no easy translation of a Christian metaphysics into the empirical features of specific situations. The basic question is then: Can the use of contraceptives in such and such particular circumstances constitute a legitimate development of the Christian concept of marriage?

The claim would be that the use of contraceptives can enable a man and wife together to offer to God a one-flesh unity in a worship which can be not only reasonable—because it has paid due heed to the framing and fashioning of themselves and their family—but holy as well. It may for instance, be held, as by many in the West, that responsible parenthood in general demands some family limitation. Again, it may happen, as in India, Japan and the West Indies, that economic circumstances compel births to be severely restricted. In such circumstances, the use of contraceptives enables planning to occur without a man and wife having to exclude altogether some realization of the one-flesh unity which, as we have seen, is a distinctive feature of Christian marriage.

When family limitation is a grave necessity, contraception may provide the only possible means by which there can be some realization of that one-flesh unity without which marriage can become no more than an external bond—or at best a companionship of friends; at worst, a progressive isolation of man and wife.

1. Against this view, and while agreeing on the importance of the unitary aspect of marriage, it would be argued that the use of contraceptives mars the act and detracts from the one-flesh unity. Now this may be an empirical assertion. In this case we can agree that something of the spontaneous unity is lost by the use of contraceptives, however much certain contraceptives may in this respect be less unsatisfactory than others. At the same time, three observations must be made:

(i) That all 'safe period' calculations likewise mar and tamper with the act. Indeed, the only occasion when an act could not be said to be 'tampered with' or to be 'marred' would be when it was utterly spontaneous. But then, of course, it might have other characteristics not at all morally praiseworthy.

(ii) Further, is there every *any* intercourse which is *not* as *a matter of empirical fact* 'defective' and 'marred' in some way? Is there ever any complete and perfect self-giving? Again is sexual intercourse to be considered in any case as an act *complete in itself*? Supposing that children are likely to originate from the act and that such children are then condemned to malnutrition, famine, and so on, the situation is not merely the simple one of choosing the one symbol which is better than another. The question now becomes, which life—one with contraceptives, the other without, and all those in the setting of famine and malnutrition—which life is best offered to the glory of God? In short, in such a case the problem is not one of contraceptives as such, but of the procreation of children in a certain economic situation. It might be said that here we have background considerations somewhat comparable with St Paul's presupposition, and it is plainly a situation which we could answer in St Paul's way. The difference is, however, that the contemporary presupposition does not anticipate direct intervention of God. What it emphasizes is that in defending contraception, we ought positively at the same time to be working out a theology of rapid social change and betterment. It is in the working out of such a theology that the moralist must 'enter into the genuine anguish of mind' which besets so many of his contemporaries. Meanwhile, the leading question will always be: Is it better to have no intercourse at any time so as to avoid children altogether, or, on occasion, to use contraceptives? Which of these makes the better offering to the glory of God?

(iii) Finally, let it be noted that in no circumstances can sexual intercourse with contraceptives be rightly called an act of 'self-love'. As an empirical description this plainly fails.

If the argument that contraceptives mar the act and make it defective is, however, an *a priori* assertion, it would follow from the claim that *coitus* without contraceptives completely pictures and re-produces an element in Christian doctrine. Such a supposition surely brings with it the most profound epistemological difficulties; nor in any case need we take such a view of the structure of Christian doctrine in itself. Nor can it be seriously supposed that there are any 'biological laws' which somehow picture irrevocably God's will, unless 'biological laws' are being used in a sense which makes them incapable of any empirical modification, in which case the assertion might be true without being particularly informative. Otherwise it sponsors a view of the laws of nature that could hardly at this time be substantiated and a view that carries with it a meta-physical picture which is hardly an essential part of the Christian tradition.

2. The second argument is based on the premise that the use of contraceptives is 'unnatural' or 'against nature', and that its being so makes it necessarily wrong.[9]

Once again, this assertion could either be metaphysical or empiri-cal. If it is metaphysical it would be a claim that the use of contra-ceptives conflicts with 'natural law' or with a 'given' metaphysical pattern. But we should then have to ask the grounds on which such claims are made, and we can anticipate great problems arising both in regard to the concept of natural law and in the epistemology which lies behind the metaphysical claim. If, however, the claim is empirical, it amounts to very little. To say that the use of contra-ceptives interferes with what 'nature' would do if left alone is no answer to the question, unless we identify God with the physical order after the manner of those who see more of God in earthquakes than in the devoted labours of those who toil to rescue their victims. But for the Christian the physical world, as it is given to us, is the raw material out of which by God's grace he is to fashion a world more in accordance with God's will than it is when he finds it. The only sense in which the 'unnatural' is wrong is that according to which the 'natural' is the perfection of creation towards which we aspire, and the knowledge whereby we are enabled to control the actual and mould it after the image of the ideal comes to us by the grace of God working through the devotion of scientific investiga-

[9] The following paragraphs are closely based on a discussion of contraception in Dr L. Hodgson's book, *Eugenics* (1933), in the Standpoint series, edited by the late Dr K. E. Kirk.

tors. If it enables us to deflect the course of gametes into channels through which they will contribute to the making of a better civilization than would result from their being left alone, it is showing us the way to use actual 'nature' for the creation of the ideally 'natural'. To confuse the two senses of 'natural' is nothing but confusion of thought, and the resulting position belongs to pantheism, not to Christian theism. To prove that contraception is wrong because 'unnatural', it would be necessary to show that it is inimical to the best development of human life. This is a question we shall have to face in section 5, below.

3. The third argument is based on an appeal to the sacredness of life. Here it is important to distinguish between Christian and non-Christian views of life, for there are some kinds of reverence for life which are distinctly not Christian, e.g. the reverence for life which underlies the child-marriage of India and also favours the unchecked spread of vermin. The same non-Christian attitude to life can be seen in the view that the birth of children is somehow an inexorable working out of a 'natural force' within us: as well as in the view that children like chattels are the expression of a parent's property and material wealth, and so the more, the better. Such attitudes to children can be found today in, e.g., the West Indies.

For the Christian, however, life is not God but God's. Our duty is to ask what God wills it to become, and to reverence physical life as the raw material of spiritual life. Now life, as we have seen, exists in countless living creatures, and its existence is maintained by the processes of reproduction in their many forms. The whole system culminates in mankind, where there appear creatures capable of development *as individuals* into citizens of Heaven. According to the Christian view of the world, its purpose is to produce human beings and train them for their eternal life of communion with God.

Now we see the full importance of the difference of status between gametes and zygotes. If it is true that the *individual* human life begins with the formation of the zygote, then it follows that reverence for the sacredness of life requires of us that we should so control the behaviour of gametes as to make of them the best zygotes that we know how to. If we can enlist in this endeavour the discoveries of medical science, and the ingenuities of modern manufacturing methods, this will not necessarily involve any failure in reverence. On the contrary, the refusal to make use of them might well be held to argue irreverence both towards the Spirit of God in his guidance of doctors and machine-makers, and towards the true sacredness of life. Any other view seems to imply that superstitious reverence for life which reveres it not as the instrument of God's creative purpose, but as itself, in all its manifestations, God.

4. The fourth argument is an appeal to authority. It is stated, and stated truly, that to many saintly people the thought of contraception is so repugnant as to argue a radical incompatibility between those practices and the development of holiness of character. 'When in doubt on such matters,' it has been said, 'I think it is wisest to trust to the instincts of the holiest men and women I know, and they are against them.'

This argument deserves serious attention. If the testimony of those most advanced in that life is against any practice, that is a very weighty argument against its morality.

But, in the case before us, this testimony is far from being unanimous enough to provide a simple solution of our problem. One knows other Christians, not less advanced in holiness (so far as one can judge in these matters), who have no such 'instincts'. How is one to judge between them? Only if there are independent arguments which convince us in favour of the one or the other.

5. The fifth argument we need to consider would stress the virtues of self-control and would argue that the use of contraceptives is likely to weaken moral fibre. Now, without doubt, an invaluable contribution has been made to moral progress by the necessity to wrestle for the mastery of sexual desire. Further, we can be suspicious of any popular demand for contraceptives in an age when moral calibre is on the decline.

At the same time it must be pointed out that even with the use of contraceptives, marriage quite obviously leaves much room for the exercise and learning of self-control. In every marriage there are occasions when one partner desires intercourse and the other does not. Contraceptives are no use here; self-control is the only alternative to cruelty. We thus return to our original point that contraceptives are not to be seen as substitutes for self-control where self-control is called for, but as instruments to make possible a joint life of the quality which a Christian marriage demands.

6. Finally, the case of death seems not without its parallels. Death might be said to have a Christian significance; yet we do not hesitate to bring 'human tamperings' to bear on it. The empirical approach would see this situation as in principle parallel to the question of birth control. For in the use of contraceptives we begin to be 'scien-

tific' about the most precious and responsible of all activities, namely procreation, as we have for years been 'scientific' about death.

Admittedly, the greater our lordship over nature, the stronger our moral calibre needs to be, and the greater we need to realize our dependence on God. It is not without significance that the greatest moral problems of our age arise from scientific developments in relation to birth and death: contraception on the one hand; atomic warfare on the other.

Along with any justification of the use of contraceptives then, there needs to go an emphatic effort to increase a sense of moral responsibility generally. But we conclude that there are no satisfactory arguments against the position set out at the start which claims that a Christian marriage may justifiably include the use of contraceptives.

CONTRACEPTION: A COMMENT ON THESE ATTITUDES

(1) In the first (Example I) *coitus*, like marriage itself, is said to have a 'given' pattern to which metaphysical significance attaches, and to be a sign of union which effects what it signifies; and it is argued that if certain essentials of the 'given' pattern are not preserved there can be no assurance that the metaphysical blessing will be received. In short, the metaphysical apparatus which belongs to the *ex opere operato* view of the Christian sacraments is here extended to *coitus*. The conclusion is that contraception makes an act of intercourse a misleading counterfeit of the *coitus* to which the promise of union in one flesh is annexed, and that therefore it cannot rightly be regarded as a positive good, capable of enriching the marriage relationship. The paper then goes on (IB) to inquire whether intercourse modified by contraception can be justified in certain situations which morally exclude the 'given' act, and suggests that it can.

Some will think that this treatment of the question founders on the difficulty of demonstrating that something in the metaphysical realm is bound up with an empirical event of which the essential features can be unalterably specified. In this instance (it may be asked) can we specify exactly those empirical features which are

needed to safeguard union? Can we be absolutely sure that any
different features necessarily exclude that union? Moreover no one
would maintain that each and every detail of *coitus* is 'given' and
unalterable. There is thus the added difficulty of distinguishing
'inventions' which destroy the metaphysical significance from legitimate developments of sexual behaviour which preserve it. Again,
if we combine IA and IB, we have to make room for the possibility
that approximations to the 'given' act may be permissible on occasion. Some will see here an ultimate appeal to insight; and if such
an appeal has to be made, the hope of establishing something incor-
rigible and guaranteed beyond question remains unfulfilled.

The philosophical difficulty is that of conceiving a metaphysical
language which is translatable into unmistakable empirical terms.
While every Christian must agree that God's revelation in Christ is
'given', not every Christian will thereby conclude that in the same
sense the particular empirical features of every Christian situation
are likewise 'given' or that a comprehensive deductive metaphysical
pattern is also 'given'.

(2) The second treatment (Example II) takes the customary categories of moral theology and seeks to show that they have been
wrongly used in this matter as a result of imperfect appreciation of
the function of *coitus* in marriage. It is argued that, in view of
certain empirical considerations which are discussed, it is misleading to speak of procreation as 'the primary end' of *coitus*; that
coitus inevitably serves different ends on different occasions; and
that contraception can represent a responsible use of human freedom in the interests of a joint development of personality and,
through that, of the family as a whole. Thus a justification for contraception is found, not in any special circumstances, but in the
nature of the marriage relationship itself.

A weakness of this treatment, some will think, is that it does not
provide a firm basis for making a moral distinction between *coitus*
modified by contraception alone and other sexual actions for which
a certain relational value may be claimed, but which are generally
condemned by Christian moralists.

(3) The third treatment (Example III) exemplifies a quite different approach. Eschewing any kind of *a priori* starting-point, except
the broadest background of Christian doctrine, it begins by postu-
lating a case in which man and wife have conscientiously decided
that in their particular circumstances the use of contraceptives can
be made part of the offering of their marriage to the glory of God.

Here is a claim to valid insight. The paper then proceeds to discuss, by way of point and counter-point, certain objections to their decision that the couple might be called upon to face; and it concludes that none of these is sufficient to invalidate the claim to insight.

This approach to the matter is that of the spiritual adviser rather than that of the ordinary moralist. Those who adopt it do not claim to enunciate incontrovertible Christian principles of universal validity which could stand as axioms for the development of a deductive ethic. The appeal to insight is, in their opinion, fundamental and their concern is to teach those who have decisions to make to bring their particular situations, in all their empirical complexity, alongside other situations in which the Christian response is recognizable through their understanding of the Christian faith.

Some may see a difficulty here. If the discussion of objections in this paper bears only upon the particular case postulated at the outset, and if the refusal to formulate general principles is absolute, no guidance at all can be offered for the future. All we can say, on the basis of actual insights known to us, is that contraception has sometimes been justified in the past: we cannot predict that it will ever be justified in the future, still less adumbrate the sort of situation in which it might be justified. If on the other hand it is only a certain kind of general principles that is repudiated, viz. a kind which purports to be 'incontrovertible' and 'of universal validity', then it seems that the position here adopted is not after all so very different from the position of the ordinary moral theologian, who would say that, at the most, only a few primary principles can be of this kind. However that may be, if this second interpretation is correct, it can then be asked what guidance for the future emerges from this paper; and the answer seems to be that the refutation of objections to contraception, if held to be adequate, establishes human liberty by the negative method of showing that there is no certain evidence that contraception must always be wrong. On the general question whether contraception should be regarded as a normal element in the relations of husband and wife, or only as a permissible response to particular emergencies, this method can of course give no guidance.

In spite of the manifest divergencies between these three treatments of the question, there is a meeting-point of practical importance in the judgment that a conscientious decision to use contraceptives would in certain circumstances be justified. Even the kind of argument found in Example IA does not necessarily conflict with such a conclusion; for although some who endorse that argument would say that contraception so alters the nature of intercourse that no conceivable circumstances could make it permissible, others would argue as in IB that there are circumstances of such urgency as to make contraception relatively the lesser evil and morally eligible.

III. The Christian Attitude to Material Development

A. In this matter it is important to do justice to the full Christian tradition, not least because it incorporates two different if only superficially incompatible themes.

1. The importance of the material world is implicit in any doctrine of the Incarnation. It was human flesh that our Lord took upon himself and which he glorified. It was the Gnostic and Manichean heresies which belittled the significance of the material world and even denied its 'reality'. Moreover the Christian belief is that man has been given a certain dominion over God's creatures. It is proper to him to learn to realize the potentialities of the material world; and as a rule human persons need to possess and administer at least some material things in order to develop fully the capacities of human nature.

2. Along with this, however, goes an emphasis on the supremacy of the eternal, so that the material world gains all the significance it has in virtue of being taken into the creative and redemptive purposes of God. Apart from God, the world must be viewed as no more than a Cosmos (*Κόσμος*). 'The world' in this sense is something apart from God, supposedly self-sufficient, and in this way misdirected in its character. Cf. John 1.10; I John 2.15; James 4.4; II Peter 2.20.

Sometimes material prosperity, sometimes sheer poverty, can blind people to the significance of the eternal. Both can prevent us from seeing 'the world' in relation to the purpose of God.

B. With that background we can now take up one or two particular questions.

1. What of the 'holy poor'? Has the Christian never to pursue a better standard of living?

Let it be said at once that for some people, and in certain ages, asceticism will be a Christian duty. For this may be the only way in which the supremacy of the eternal can be emphasized. Now it is true that in our own age, when material resources are being so greatly developed, when there is, as never before, the chance of a high standard of living for humanity generally, the importance of the eternal calls for emphasis. It can and has been only too easily asserted that progress is entirely to be measured by a 'high and rising standard of living' (Paley report). But the importance, nay supremacy, of the eternal can be emphasized not by denouncing material development but by showing how these increased resources can be made part of a Christian offering.

In this matter it is relevant to remember that many in Europe think of North America as materialistic because of its higher standard of living, and of themselves by contrast—and since they are conscious of economic difficulties—as avoiding a materialistic emphasis; but spiritual insight does not necessarily increase with economic difficulties. Europeans need to remember that they appear to Africa and the East as the Americans do to them.

Do we accept the current division of wealth between countries and continents as part of the divine purpose? Plainly not. Material development will therefore be welcomed and made part of a Christian offering in so far as at every point there is an endeavour to share it on a world scale. The Christian who fixes on material welfare alone will surely be self-condemned—'he who would save his life shall lose it'. But the Christian who sees material welfare as something which in his own life might be made part of a Christian offering ('for my sake and the Gospel's') will be fulfilling a Christian duty. Nor must the Christian despise pleasure or see it as in essential conflict with virtue. Pleasure need not be excluded from the Good Life.

2. This brings us close to the next question: Can we resolve the tension in Christian morality between mortification and self-realization?

Without doubt every Christian is called to mortification. But material development does not exclude mortification: it simply offers different possibilities of exercising the same virtue. No matter how far material development extends, the Christian welcomes it not for its own sake, and not only for the material comfort and pleasure it may bring to him, but as something which brings with it many opportunities for moral decision as well. These we see at all times of rapid social change. In short, welcoming a material development which we must not as such denounce, let us see it as creative of more occasions of moral decision, and of more occasions when we may recognize our own relative powerlessness. In this way it can then all the more deepen our vision of what abides, and our awareness of that power not our own, which is the heart of the Christian Gospel.

3. In so far as the Christian welcomes material development, he will also welcome the work of all those who search out, develop, and use the gifts of God to meet human needs—and scientists, economists, social scientists, and so on among them. But he will see all the greater need for a constant interchange between those who are concerned with the creation of material welfare, and the clergy and others who are—or should be—guardians of man's spiritual life. For there will be times when a situation seen as a basis for scientific and economic enquiry brings also with it moral demands and the discernment of obligations which, together with man's response to them, are essentially religious activities. This is not to say of course that the more 'religious' a man is the more 'moral' he will also be. So it is that statistics, which are often given nowadays to show that there are as many believers as unbelievers annually convicted in the courts, do not show anything more than that Christians need to be more faithful stewards of their manifold gifts of grace. They do not show that Christian faith has little moral significance; they show all the greater need for matching material development with increased faith and conviction.

Material development is not to be denounced but seen as a challenge which needs to be made part of a Christian offering. To do this will need co-operative thought and action on the part of many Christians united in an adventure of faith and content to follow where that faith may lead.

4. In particular, at a time when the most staggering differences of wealth are no longer between persons and persons, but between nations and nations, problems raised by material development are problems which for a Christian solution will need a far greater emphasis on the concept of the Church Universal. Contrariwise, as these problems are solved, the difficulties which are overcome and the sacrifices which are made will in their own way lead us to an increased awareness of the significance of the world-wide Church.

Material development, therefore,

(i) needs to be matched by an increasing spiritual insight such as the Christian faith can give; and we need not suppose that there are any absolute priorities as between economic development and the development of social welfare services, for both these developments would for the Christian be tested with regard to the 'spiritual development' of which each can and ought to be a part;

(ii) has to be welcomed not only for the new material comforts and pleasures it brings but for the new moral decision it provokes;

(iii) suggests an increasing co-operation between those concerned with its production; and

(iv) at the present time brings problems that for their solution will need a much greater awareness of a concern for the Church Universal.

IV. RELIGION AS A SOCIAL BOND

It is a commonplace to say that there are countless definitions of religion. But among all those definitions two broad and fundamental themes may be discerned.

(a) The religious man is one who appeals to certain *situations*, to situations which are 'what's seen' and more; and the Christian in particular appeals to situations in which he discerns that power of God which is the Gospel.

(b) But besides 'religion' relating to certain situations as these, it is also plainly expressed in *institutions, doctrine, and so on*. In other words, with every religion goes some kind of established culture. Christopher Dawson in *Religion and the Rise of Western Culture* notices that for something like three centuries there was once a spiritual tide steadily making for unity. This found, he would say, a climax in the philosophical systems of the thirteenth century, what Gilson has called the great 'cathedrals of ideas'. Here there seemed to be the possibility of a magnificently planned culture of a religious kind. But what happened? Dawson says: 'On the contrary, it inaugurated a period of intellectual criticism and cultural change which is of the utmost importance for the history of Western culture, but proved fatal to the synthesis of religion and culture that seemed to have been achieved in the previous centuries.'[10] Later he remarks: 'It is as though the spiritual tide which

[10] *Op. cit.*, p. 238.

had been steadily making for unity for three centuries had suddenly turned, so that everywhere in every aspect of life the forces
that made for division and dissolution were predominant.'[11] What
was the mistake? The great mistake was to suppose that a unitary
culture could be translated into an unambiguous intellectual pattern. The mistake was to suppose that a religious situation could be
translated without reduction into politico-scientific terms, into a
metaphysics which was neither more nor less than a super-science.
The medieval mistake was to fail to distinguish between that fellowship and unity which a religion can give to its believers, and the
unity which a political system or a strong administration can create
between people.

So it is that the Christian religion will always supply to the
culture of a people two influences which are to react permanently
on each other:

(a) the influence of a fixed tradition, which will look for uni-
     formity, for firm plans and settled administration, and
(b) a drive for prophetic novelty.

Religion, therefore, will on the one hand be creative of a unity
which a political system can neither copy nor do justice to; it will
also supply prophetic insight which leads to permanent dissatisfaction with things as they are. It will always sponsor institutions
and doctrines that can give stability to society; it will also provide
the source of inspiration to ensure that the society which is stable
is also flexible and adaptable.

Practical Corollaries

1. When a society is disintegrating under rapid social change,
religion can be relevant in three ways.

(a) It will hesitate to sponsor any particular political administra-
    tive pattern, but, if anything, will encourage diversity; no
    pattern of society will be sponsored for its own sake.
(b) In its worship it will seek to provide a unifying bond which
    can be found nowhere else; nor will this fellowship, once
    known in worship, be restricted to the worshipping com-
    munity in the narrow sense. It will more and more leaven the
    whole society.

[11] *Ibid.*, p. 239.

(c) It will also teach that Christian contentment is no synonym for utter placidity and inactivity: it is one which comes from bringing to suffering and change the power of the Gospel.

It has been pointed out that on the face of it science today often provides a harmony and coherence where religion fails. Further, the bonds by which science links both its workers and beneficiaries seem so much the more evident and real than the intangible and shadowy bonds which religion (it might be said) at best would supply. But we have to recognize that developments in science itself are making us all the more aware that scientific procedures and techniques will never supply us with bonds that satisfy the whole man. If scientific development over the last two decades has shown us anything, it is, as the scientists themselves would be first to recognize, that scientific method and techniques alone are not adequate for any fellowship which embodies the whole man. This is not to deny the need and importance of scientific and technological developments: they can, in principle, be welcomed and encouraged. The Christian must denounce none of them, nor the material development they bring, but must emphasize what *more* is needed.

2. When the Christian faith meets an ancient non-Christian civilization, there are, besides these earlier considerations, some important points. To what extent must it be, in relation to this ancient civilization, nothing but a disintegrating force?

The extent to which it can be more depends in large measure on our theological views as to the relation between natural and revealed religion. Distinctive and unique though Christianity be, we need not deny all significance to other religions nor need we condemn *in toto* the institutional, doctrinal, cultural pattern to which they have given rise. Further, the possibility of regarding missionary work as with, rather than for, non-Christian people can come from recognizing that God's grace is given in some measure to all—even the 'heathen' have some kind of moral insight (Rom. 1 and 2).

20

TOWARDS A REHABILITATION
OF NATURAL LAW

Ian T. Ramsey

NO COLLECTION of essays on Christian ethics and contemporary philosophy can afford to neglect the theme of Natural Law, and the present essay is an endeavour to sketch the changing attitude of Christians and philosophers to the concept of Natural Law, to see what there is of the concept that can be legitimately preserved in our own day, what interpretation can be given of it, and what significance it has for Christian morality.

Professor H. L. A. Hart reminds us that Natural Law is normally contrasted with Legal Positivism, though he also reminds us that such are the ambiguities about each term that it is often 'difficult to see precisely what issue is at stake when Natural Law is opposed to Legal Positivism'.[1] But the issue which is important for our purpose arises from the view of legal positivism that 'there is no necessary connexion between law and morals'.[2] Further, since and in so far as morality for an advocate of Natural Law is considered to be definitely characteristic of the reasonable man, we can see why the expression 'legal positivism' is often used, as Hart tells us, in continental literature 'for the general repudiation of the claim that some principles or rules of human conduct are discoverable by reason alone'.[2] So we may express the issue which is of interest to us, and one of the issues on which Natural Law is opposed to Legal Positivism, as being whether there is some necessary connection between law and morality, and in particular whether or not there are moral laws or principles which all reasonable men must accept.

[1] *The Concept of Law*, O.U.P. 1961, p. 253.   [2] *Ibid.*

Expressed alternatively, Natural Law in this context claims that everyone who deserves to be called a person acknowledges some basic moral obligation, which gives rise to moral principles on which there can be general agreement. Further, since moral obligation has been traditionally interpreted in terms of God's will,[3] natural law readily lent itself in days past to a supplementation by Christian principles which were related to that particular 'mystery of his will'[4] which was made known in Jesus Christ.

Here is the traditional concept of Natural Law as it is relevant for our purpose. H. L. A. Hart speaks of the Thomist tradition of Natural Law being 'the clearest, perhaps, because it is the most extreme form of expression of this point of view'—the point of view that there is a necessary connection between law and morality, and he summarizes it as follows: 'This comprises a twofold contention: first, that there are certain principles of true morality or justice, discoverable by human reason without the aid of revelation even though they have a divine origin; secondly that man-made laws which conflict with these principles are not valid law. *Lex iniusta non est lex.*'[5]

In this way, then, Natural Law was expressed in terms of 'principles' which were a common basis for law and morality alike, and principles which, as having 'a divine origin', could be properly incorporated into a moral theology.

What has led to the erosion of this concept of 'natural law'? First, it has been argued that there are no 'principles' which all reasonable men feel bound to accept. Human society the world over is pluralistic, consisting of diverse groups, sponsoring a variety of ideals, and anthropology only adds to the diversity of 'moral principles' that even holiday travel can demonstrate. The comparative study of religions only serves to cast further doubt on the claims that there are universal principles which have their origin in God, and are therefore unconditionally binding on all men as God's creatures.

Secondly, it has been argued, fixed principles arise within, as they evidently characterize a certain type of society. They assume that man and society are in some kind of stable equilibrium, possessing virtually constant features. But how can there be 'fixed principles', if these principles are to have any clear practical relevance, in a time of vast and rapid social change? Developments in the natural and social sciences, and the technological developments which have resulted therefrom mean that man possesses virtually

---

[3] See ch. 9 above.   [4] Eph. 1.9.   [5] *Op. cit.*, p. 152.

unlimited powers of modifying himself and the society in which he lives. Why should we assume that there are fixed principles for social behaviour when the society in which, if at all, they will be used is changing beyond recognition?

Thirdly, many psychologists claim to have shown that some of the apparently most compelling principles are anything but 'reasonable'. They may originate, it is said, from social 'conditioning': even worse, many 'moral prohibitions', especially those concerned with sex, are no more than unhealthy repressions, and the 'good' man is all too often the inhibited neurotic.

Fourthly, philosophers, as we have seen in earlier essays (e.g. chs 5, 8 and 9), have subjected to severe criticism the idea of moral principles such as are essential to traditional Natural Law theory having a 'divine origin'. In any case, talk of axiomatic moral principles confuses law and morals with pure mathematics. Others argue that it is a logical howler to suppose that prescriptive assertions are derivable from descriptions. Yet again, others, impressed by ideas of logical diversity associated with Wittgenstein, argue that a legal system has its own logical character and has to be altogether distinguished from the language of morals. On this view the idea of 'natural law' would be nothing more than a logical confusion.

As Hart reminds us, there have also been historically other confusions alleged by philosophers, and he cites Bentham and Mill by way of example. Mill believed that the theory of Natural Law 'revealed the perennial confusion between laws which formulate the course of regularities of nature, and laws which require men to behave in certain ways'.[6] It was, as Hart expresses it, 'as if the believer had failed to perceive the very different meaning of such words [as "bound"] in "You are bound to report for military service" and "It is bound to freeze if the wind goes round to the north".'

Hart continues:

> Critics like Bentham and Mill, who most fiercely attacked Natural Law, often attributed their opponents' confusion between these distinct sense of law, to the survival of the belief that the observed regularities of nature were prescribed or decreed by a Divine Governor of the Universe. On such a theocratic view, the only difference between the law of gravity and the Ten Commandments—God's law for Man —was, as Blackstone asserted, the relatively minor one that men, alone of created things, were endowed with reason and free will; and

[6] *Op. cit.*, p. 182.

so unlike things, could discover and disobey the divine prescriptions. Natural Law has, however, not always been associated with belief in a Divine Governor or Lawgiver of the universe, and even where it has been, its characteristic tenets have not been logically dependent on that belief. Both the relevant sense of the 'natural', which enters into Natural Law, and its general outlook minimizing the difference, so obvious and so important to modern minds, between prescriptive and descriptive laws, have their roots in Greek thought which was, for this purpose, quite secular. Indeed, the continued reassertion of some form of Natural Law doctrine is due in part to the fact that its appeal is independent of both divine and human authority, and to the fact that despite a terminology, and much metaphysics, which few could now accept, it contains certain elementary truths of importance for the understanding of both morality and law.[7]

It is these 'elementary truths of importance' which (as we shall see) he endeavours 'to disentangle from their metaphysical setting' and to re-state in simpler terms. We shall presently examine Hart's proposals, but before so doing we will mention two other difficulties for Natural Law theory which arise from a Christian context.

The first objection arises from that assimilation of law and morality which is at the heart of Natural Law theory. It is said by some Christians that such an assimilation leads to a 'legalism' which is as foreign to Christian morality as is the Jewish Torah; that Christian ethics must not be developed in a legalistic context, but in a context dominated by the theme of 'unconditional love'.

The second objection which is sometimes heard is that in any case Christianity can provide no firm unalterable principles to take their place alongside those on which Natural Law theory rests. Such an objection is made by those who would stress the unique 'existentialist' character of Christian moral decision, and amongst these who take this view are some who take it because of historical scepticism about the Bible and the gospel narratives in particular. Granting the results of historical criticism, it is said, can we any longer claim to have firm, guaranteed copy-book principles given to us by God in the Bible?

From these five directions then the concept of natural law has come under severe criticism. Can it in any sense be rehabilitated? Hart, as we have seen, believes that in a much chastened sense it may, and I shall start my positive exposition from his view. Hart's interpretation begins from something which he calls 'entirely

[7] *Ibid.*, pp. 183-4.

obvious'. It is that 'ordinary thought about human action', ordinary ways of talking about man's behaviour in the world, what he does and the events that happen to him, alike reveal at least one common assumption. Presumably they might reveal more, but Hart is content to take one. It is the 'tacit assumption that the proper end of human activity is survival', an assumption which 'rests on the simple contingent fact that most men most of the time wish to continue in existence'.[8] He grants that this is 'only a very attenuated version of Natural Law' and that

> the classical exponents of this outlook conceived of survival (*perseverare in esse suo*) as merely the lowest stratum in a much more complex and far more debatable concept of the human end or good for man. Aristotle included in it the disinterested cultivation of the human intellect, and Aquinas the knowledge of God, and both these represent values which may be and have been challenged. Yet other thinkers, Hobbes and Hume among them, have been willing to lower their sights: they have seen in the modest aim of survival the central indisputable element which gives empirical good sense to the terminology of Natural Law.[9]

He sees it as meritorious that this 'minimum purpose of survival' which, he considers, demands the association of men with each other,[10] 'can be disentangled from more disputable parts of the general teleological outlook in which the end or good for man appears as a specific way of life about which, in fact, men may profoundly disagree'.[11] 'Moreover', he continues,

> we can, in referring to survival, discard, as too metaphysical for modern minds, the notion that this is something antecedently fixed which men necessarily desire because it is their proper goal or end. Instead we may hold it to be a mere contingent fact which could be otherwise, that in general men do desire to live, and that we may mean nothing more by calling survival a human goal or end than that men do desire it. Yet even if we think of it in this commonsense way, survival has still a special status in relation to human conduct and in our thought about it, which parallels the prominence and the necessity ascribed to it in the orthodox formulations of Natural Law. For it is not merely that an overwhelming majority of men do wish to live,

---

[8] *Op. cit.*, p. 187.   [9] *Ibid.*

[10] He quotes from Hume, *Treatise of Human Nature*, III ii, 'Of Justice and Injustice': 'Human nature cannot by any means subsist without the association of individuals'. This means, however, that Hart's 'tacit assumption' about 'the proper end of activity' which he calls 'survival' is rather 'continued existence in relation to others'—nothing as simple, or from some points of view so ambiguous, as 'survival'.

[11] p. 187.

even at the cost of hideous misery, but that this is reflected in whole structures of our thought and language, in terms of which we describe the world and each other. We could not subtract the general wish to live and leave intact concepts like danger and safety, harm and benefit, need and function, disease and cure; for these are ways of simultaneously describing and appraising things by reference to the contribution they make to survival which is accepted as an aim.[12]

Whether in fact we can escape metaphysics altogether remains to be seen, but we can at least accept as common ground with Hart this 'minimum purpose of survival', especially when this presupposes relationships with others. Hart then shows that this leads to five 'simple truisms' which 'not only disclose the core of good sense in the doctrine of Natural Law' but 'are of vital importance for the understanding of law and morals, and they explain why the definition of the basic forms of these in purely formal terms, without reference to any specific content or social needs, has proved so inadequate.'[13] Here are what he calls 'natural necessities'—'the truth of which is contingent on human beings and the world they live in retaining the salient characteristics which they have'. We may summarize the five truisms as follows:

(i) Because, and as long as men are vulnerable, law and morality will have to 'restrict the use of violence in killing or inflicting bodily harm'.[14]

(ii) Because men are approximately equal, there must be 'a system of mutual forbearance and compromise'[15] which is the base of both legal and moral obligation.

(iii) Because men are neither devils nor angels, there must be a measure of human altruism. 'With angels, never tempted to harm others, rules requiring forbearances would not be necessary. With devils prepared to destroy, reckless of the cost to themselves, they would be impossible.'[16]
[It might seem that (ii) and (iii) provide us with the same rule introduced from two directions, but (iv) and (v) which follow are certainly quite different.]

(iv) Because the earth provides limited resources, that fact makes 'indispensable some minimal form of the institution of property (though not necessarily individual property), and the distinctive kind of rule which requires respect for it'.[17]

[12] pp. 187-188   [13] p. 194.   [14] p. 190.
[15] p. 191.   [16] p. 192.   [17] p. 192.

(v) Because of the darker side of man's nature, ' "Sanctions"
are . . . required not as the normal motive for obedience,
but as a *guarantee* that those who would voluntarily obey
shall not be sacrificed to those who would not . . . Given
this standing danger, what reason demands is *voluntary*
co-operation in a *coercive* system.'[18]

Here are 'basic rules of law and morals' which are 'necessities',
given 'only the modest aim of survival'.[19] Here is a minimum content for Natural Law. But has Hart given us a full account of it?
Can he escape altogether from metaphysical implications? What is
involved in accepting Hart's 'natural necessities'? There are I
think three logically distinguishable moves in this acceptance.

First, there is the recognition of certain facts about human
beings, viz. that we speak of them having certain specifiable 'needs',
we speak of certain events and circumstances as 'harmful', we speak
in a certain way of the 'function' of bodily organs or changes, e.g. as
Hart remarks, 'We say it is the function of the heart to circulate the
blood, but not that it is the function of a cancerous growth to cause
death.'[20] To speak like this is to make 'the tacit assumption that the
proper end of human activity is survival'. Now undoubtedly all the
facts which Hart mentions are consistent with, and could be said to
follow from, the fact that men aim at survival. But as Hart recognizes, it is not enough that survival should be a 'particular objective, which at a given time one man may happen to have and
another may not'.[21] Nor must this aiming at survival only 'reflect
mere conventions or human prescriptions'.[22] It must not be only
something 'which men regularly do or just happen to desire',[23]
though curiously Hart says on p. 188 'that we may mean nothing
more by calling survival a human goal or end than that men do
desire it'. But his anxiety to distinguish his view from other views
of 'ends' which have for him too many theological overtones leads
Hart to falter in the analysis here. If survival is to be basic to a new
Natural Law, there must be a *moral necessity* about survival,
granted that men and the world and society are what they are
today. Hart never expresses this positive contention in so many
words, but I think this is what lies behind his remark that 'Food
and rest are human needs, even if some refuse them when they are
needed. Hence we say not only that it is natural for all men to eat

[18] p. 193   [19] p. 191.   [20] p. 187.
[21] p. 186.   [22] p. 186.   [23] p. 186.

and sleep, but that all men *ought* to eat and rest sometimes, or that it is *naturally good* to do these things.'[24]

Secondly, how does this *moral* necessity arise? What happens to the 'facts' when they become the occasion of a value-claim? My suggestion is that our talk of eating and resting not only points to a desire for survival, but creates a moral necessity about survival, when the facts which are surveyed take on 'depth' and become the occasion of a disclosure occurring around and through them—just as something may strike us about what is otherwise no more than a cluster of lines, when we recognize those lines as what is called an 'envelope', disclosing an ellipse. It seems to me that Hart's use of the phrase 'entirely obvious'[25] suggests a disclosure basis for the obligation which is thus apprehended intuitively. Unless there were in this way an emergent obligation, there would be nothing about the facts, and nothing about 'survival', to create the crucial moral significance that survival must possess to be the basis of a chastened Natural Law theory. Further, in so far as the obligation is not restricted to the observables around which it arises, it is in that sense metaphysical. It transcends while it includes the facts around which it arises and in terms of which it gains expression. Further, in acknowledging this moral significance in survival, in thus being 'committed' to survival, we come to ourselves as persons which transcend the eating and resting we undoubtedly do, as much as, and in the same sense, the obligation in whose recognition we realize ourselves as most characteristically persons, transcends its constituent facts. We have already seen in an earlier paper how this obligation might bear a legitimate theological interpretation[26] which can be distinguished from a cruder illegitimate version, which might speak altogether unguardedly for example of law, and picture God as an originating lawgiver. This means that we, like Hart, may discard the notion that survival 'is something antecedently fixed [i.e. by God] which men necessarily desire because it is their proper goal or end'. This is being rather too articulate about God. But on the other side Hart's view of 'survival' may be much more like older metaphysical views of man's 'end' than Hart wishes to think, and further, may not at all exclude some further theological contextualization.

On the view I put forward it is in recognizing a dominant moral claim about 'survival' that we recognize ourselves as distinctively persons. It is not surprising then that not only is Hart's minimum

[24] *Ibid.* (italics mine).   [25] *Ibid.*, p. 187 quoted above.   [26] See pp. 160ff. above.

content for natural law expressed in various rules for personal relationships; but that traditionally the recognition of Natural Law has been supposed to be somehow definitive of human personality. For this is in effect none other than the old point that we become persons in discovering a moral obligation.[27] Indeed, though I have not used the word before, and will not use it again, this 'natural' moral insight, definitive of persons, has sometimes been given the name of 'conscience'. So it is not at all surprising that around 'conscience' and the 'deliveries of conscience' there have clustered similar problems to those which surround Natural Law; and there has been an alleged erosion of both by developments in anthropology, sociology and so forth. But, to return to our main theme, what Natural Law theory claims as a 'minimum content' is that so long as man and society and the Universe largely continue to be what they are today, survival will be an obligation agreed by all.

Thirdly, such a basic moral insight gives rise to 'natural necessities' when we judge that certain rules accord with, or match with what the idea of survival portrays as obligatory. These are the more positive 'natural necessities'. But there are also negative necessities, e.g. the prohibition of certain kinds of killing or violence. Indeed, in some ways it is much easier to formulate contrasting negative rules than to formulate stable positive rules which will match the original insight. But it is important to recognize, and not for the first or the last time, that a negative rule—a prohibition—is of little moral value without the original positive obligation with which it contrasts, and in contrasting, illuminates.

Hart, as we have seen, gave us five such 'natural necessities', and all I need say is that I see no logical reason to restrict 'natural necessities' to five or any other number. Nor perhaps does Hart. Ideally, or so it seems to me, we would become morally more and more mature as we developed moral principles and built up a framework of such principles as the fruit of our moral thinking and experience.

Indeed, we can now see that this view of Natural Law—which makes some basic moral claim for the significance of persons, and develops this claim in terms of elementary principles called 'natural necessities'—does not differ in principle from an account of moral principles in general which R. M. Hare might give, and which we have discussed in the earlier essay of which mention has already been made. On this view, we contemplate a certain course of action

[27] See my *Freedom and Immortality*, esp. Chapter II.

as a possibility, and then bring its pattern alongside those principles, with their associated patterns, which depend on and express the degree to which we have articulated our moral insights to date. Whatever we decide will either confirm the set of principles we hold to date, or modify some, or provide us with a supplement for them. Moral thinking will always be characterized by this feature of exploration, though for many reasons[28] we shall be wise to be cautiously conservative towards the principles we already hold at any given time. But my general point is that Hare's account of moral principles neatly interlocks with Hart's view of 'natural necessities' and their derivation from the key-idea of 'survival', given as a basic obligation which is 'entirely obvious'.

I have shown, then, how we might develop Hart's account of 'natural law' so as to suggest a basis for Natural Law in some obligation recognized by all, which would be associated with an idea like 'survival', from which first 'natural necessities' and then principles could be developed as behaviour progressed and became more problematical in more complex situations. At the same time, principles would be less stable as the situations in which they arose became more and more particularized.

Let me try in conclusion to relate this account of Natural Law theory to Christian ethics. It seems to me that in its logical structure the Christian case is identical with that of Natural Law.

If we examine the talk of Christians, and in particular that Christian moral discourse to be found in the Bible, and occurring in the Church (and for our purpose we need not go into details as to what Church or Churches or how much of this discourse is to be regarded as authoritative for moral behaviour), we shall undoubtedly find that it reveals certain key-ideas or primitives. There would however seem to be no universal agreement as to what these key-ideas are, or at least different Christians have often chosen different key-ideas. It is not easy in the Christian case to produce any agreed key-idea as basic as 'survival' was for Hart. For some Christians the key-idea is the Resurrection, for others Salvation by faith, for others unconditional love, and so on.

But in one sense the diversity does not matter. For if the key-idea is to afford anyone a reliable base for moral discourse and action, any one of these key-ideas must be positioned by reference

---

[28] On the one hand there is, for example, the ease of self-deception in matters appertaining to our own interests and happiness, e.g., in matters concerning money or sex or property; and on the other hand the practical wisdom which is bound to be enshrined in the moral inheritance, whether 'secular' or Christian or both, which is ours.

to the whole pattern of Christian discourse, so that a particular key-idea for a particular Christian will represent and express his total commitment. For instance, 'unconditional love' will be empty and useless as a key-phrase unless it arises as the presupposition of parables like that of the Good Samaritan, and the Father and the Two Sons, *logia* like that of 'Forgiveness till seventy times seven': and of the doctrines of Grace and Atonement and so on. Now in arising in this way as a presupposition, the key-phrase will already be associated with certain principles of behaviour implicit in the discourse. It will also be grounded in the kind of disclosure which e.g. the Gospel narratives and Christian doctrines were expressly designed to evoke and perpetuate, a disclosure to which the Christian responds with a characteristic commitment. What the Christian must then do in order to work out a Christian morality in some problematical situation is to set various possible behaviour patterns alongside this Christian perspective of behaviour patterns and principles and see which is the best match. If from such an exercise often repeated the emergent moral principles give rise to a code, let us notice that such a code will not be 'external', for it will have arisen from principles which themselves originated from behaviour patterns which were expressive of a commitment. If the code contains negative prohibitions, these will only be justified on this view in so far as they illuminate and are illuminated by the positive moral obligation which they presuppose and with which they contrast.

In this way Christian ethics has a logic which accords with that of Natural Law as we have interpreted it. But what now of their relationship? The character of this relationship will all depend on the key-ideas which are expressive of each insight. There are obviously at least three practical possibilities. The key-ideas of Christian morality might be identical with those of Natural Law; they might be other and conflicting or at least skew; or they might be other and supplementary.

Now I cannot see any Christian granting absolute identity between the key-ideas of Natural Law and Christian ethics. There have of course been deists in days past who could think of Christianity as a republication of the religion of Nature; but it is notorious that such an attitude failed miserably to do justice to the distinctive claims which Christians make for their faith.

Are the key-ideas to be regarded as other and conflicting? This is sometimes urged to be the case when antitheses are drawn between, for example, justice and love: and there are other views, some of

which are represented elsewhere in this book, which would suggest
a relation that was skew if not exactly crossing in conflict. But I
should have thought that the whole Catholic tradition at any rate
would seek for supplementation.

Let it not be supposed however that supplementation is going
to be an easy matter. Take, for example, Hart's 'survival'. Undoubtedly, this has echoes with the Christian 'principle' which
regards life as being a gift from God which has to be treasured,
just as in an earlier day 'justice' was taken as the Natural Law
concept which straddled across both 'natural' and 'revealed' morality. But how far is Hart's key-idea able to be accommodated to
doctrines of a future life,[29] and indeed to the significance which
Christians give to death—a topic which deserves far more Christian
discussion than it has yet had? Alternatively it has been suggested[30]
that 'Forgiveness' might possibly be taken as the key-idea of Natural
Law when a Christian supplementation might be more obviously
feasible.

But at least there is a possibility of moral principles having roots
both in that moral obligation and those key-ideas which are called
'Natural Law', and in that Christian commitment and discourse
from which characteristic moral obligations and principles can be
likewise derived. What is needed before any significant progress
is made, however, is (a) some elucidation of that basic obligation
and associated key-idea which we would call Natural Law—and
Hart has shown us how to reach this, and one version of the key-
idea which might be found; (b) such a thorough biblical and pat-
ristic study, including a study of Christian moral theology down
the ages, as enables us both to formulate the most reliable Christian principles and the moral obligations they express, relating this
understanding to some key-phrase in terms of which the full
Christian commitment is given.

This is the kind of exploratory task to which the Christian is
called; but it is the less daunting because it will never be completed. All we have to be careful about meanwhile, when faced
with some particularly stubborn moral problem, is that we are alert
to the demands of Natural Law on the one hand, and on the other
hand never enunciate any Christian principle without realizing
that, on the whole, it is more a mnemonic than anything else, whose

[29] Whether this is conceived as everlasting in time or in some other sense 'eternal'.
[30] By the Rev. G. R. Dunstan in a private discussion, and it is clear that in so far as
'survival' for Hart implies a social relatedness, it might be more closely linked with such
a concept as forgiveness.

merit is that it can give us such a catena of associated parables and *logia* as makes evident the moral claim of which it would remind us. For Christian principles are only authoritative and influential for behaviour as and when they proceed from parables and *logia* which themselves disclose that 'love of God, grace of the Lord Jesus Christ, and fellowship of the Holy Spirit' to which, when a man responds, he becomes a Christian. Christian principles will only be authoritative as and when they carry with them, through their associated discourse, that which a Christian would say 'demands my soul, my life, my all'.

If the morality of Natural Law and Christian morality are alike exploratory, if their principles point to as they arise from a moral obligation and commitment which they presuppose and must preserve, the edge is immediately taken off most of the several objections which we listed at the start. For instance, whatever diversification of moral principles we find in different societies, and however difficult it may be to elucidate principles suited to complex decisions in a time of rapid social change, there will nevertheless be some principles which are so stable as to be virtually sacrosanct as long as human beings remain broadly what they now are. Further, as for the criticisms of some psychologists, we must first recall the old point that how the principles may have arisen is logically irrelevant to their present character, and their present claims will be justified or not according as to whether they are grounded in a moral obligation and accord with other moral principles which prove themselves over the most extensive behaviour patterns. Again, far from being neurotic, men are only genuinely 'persons' when they respond freely to moral obligations. The charge of 'legalism' vanishes when it is realized that our whole array of moral 'principles' arises from exploring moral obligations on countless occasions, each of them reminding us of decisions taken in situations of the widest empirical variety and diversity, so that together they provide us with the best map and moral guide-book which we have to date. We need moral principles, and there are moral principles. But they are not copy-book principles, any more than morality is a slavish following of rules. They each point back to an obligation revealed through and around the empirical facts of countless situations, an obligation matched only by a decision in which we realize ourselves characteristically as persons. This is the core of truth, I would suggest, in the claims of those who sponsor 'situational ethics' and talk of an 'existentialist' approach.

There remain only two points to make about the objections we considered above. The difficulty about biblical criticism I hope to take up in the concluding paragraphs of the essay. The remaining philosophical objections have been the concern of the whole paper, and I hope I have shown how in relation to Natural Law the distinctive claims of Christian morality can be justly made.

Our problem today is not that there are no principles, but that such principles as are enunciated have so often lost their moorings, whether as derived from 'natural necessities' and a basic moral obligation, or as needing to be integrated with Christian discourse and the challenge and commitment which that discourse expresses.

So any new explication of 'natural law', and principles to be derived therefrom, needs to be constantly alert to the empirical complexities of every teasing situation, constantly alert to what different academic disciplines are saying about it. Any Christian principles and key-ideas need to square with what biblical scholars and church historians and theologians generally are saying.

In this connection, it is important and relevant to recall what Professor D. E. Nineham said, concluding a series of articles in the *Journal of Theological Studies*.[31]

If the thesis put forward in these articles is sound, the conclusion must be that, though certain passages in our gospels may still be formulated exactly as they were by eye-witnesses of the events concerned, we have no compelling *a priori* reasons for thinking that it is so, and, even if it is, no absolutely watertight criteria for establishing where it is. Accordingly, the gospels must be treated in the first instance as so many formulations of the early Church's growing tradition about the ministry of Jesus; the only thing for which they certainly provide direct evidence is the beliefs about, and understanding of, that ministry in various parts of the early Church between the middle of the first and the early part of the second centuries.

Conclusions of this sort about the gospels have been frequently stated and defended, but, rather strangely, thorough discussions of their implications have been much less frequent.[32] To what extent,

---

[31] 'Eye-witness testimony and the Gospel Tradition', *JTS* 11, October 1960, pp. 254-6.

[32] Professor Nineham remarks in a footnote as this point that: 'A partial exception to this must be made in favour of some discussions which have originated in America, the most recent being chap. iii of Professor W. N. Pittenger's *The Word Incarnate*. Even this, however, is very brief and general, so far as our particular question is concerned.' He also refers the reader to a footnote at the end of his article where he says: 'Since completing this article I have carefully re-read the three short works by Professor John Knox now published in the single volume, *Jesus: Lord and Christ* (Harper 1958). Had I the chance to elaborate the point of view adumbrated in these articles, I should want to a large extent to follow the lines he has laid down.'

and for what purposes, do we need direct eye-witness testimony about the ministry of Jesus? What difference does it make if the gospels do not provide such testimony?

To this question Professor Nineham replies that

It is idle to deny that some real loss is involved in our conclusions. If they are right, it is illegitimate to press the details, and many of the personal traits, in the stories; yet it is precisely through dwelling on such 'human touches' that many Christians have felt themselves brought most vividly into contact with their Lord. And not only is it illegitimate to press these details in an historical interest, it is surely hazardous to press them for devotional purposes, or at any rate for devotional purposes not directly envisaged by the Evangelists. A question-mark is clearly set against some forms at least of *imitatio Christi* devotion and also against the practice, which still largely governs the life of the Churches, of quoting individual sayings and incidents from the gospels as precedents. In general it may be said that if our conclusions were to prove justified, they would have significant implications for devotional and homiletic practice and for moral and ascetic theology, which the Churches for the most part have by no means thought through.

There can certainly be no easy arguments from gospel texts to conclusions about war, poverty, affluence, marriage or anything else. Yet those who should know better often speak as though this were not the case. Because there is no place for extreme historical scepticism, it does not follow that an appeal to (say) the New Testament will provide us with authoritative single principles giving us moral counsel by a simple deductive derivation.

It is plainly no easy matter to rehabilitate Natural Law or to supplement it reliably with Christian principles. But to see what needs to be done and to be struggling to do it, meanwhile holding firm to positions we have already reached, seems to be no less positively wise and profitable for being the only possibility. And no one need doubt that, even today, there is a stable residue of moral principles, and some obligation implicitly recognized as basic—if not, there would presumably be no basis for an ordered society. At the same time the novel problems of a rapidly changing social order and culture keep us for the most part exercised in regions where new moral principles, when they come, come with all the difficulty—and yet with the thrill—of new discoveries.

INDEX

Italic figures refer to contributions

Abner, 347
Abraham, 33, 104, 119, 130, 317
Anderson, J., 318
Anscombe, G. E. M., 140, 149f., 247, 287
Anselm, 57
Antigones, 277
Aphrodite, 353
Aquinas, Thomas, 95, 121, 126, 386
Aristotle, 64, 90, 93, 99, 107, 115, *243*, 266f., 306f., 309f., 312f., 386
Arnold, M., 67ff., 76, 79ff., 84, 87
Autonomy (see also Heteronomy), 128, 144, 153, 156ff., 167ff.

Bach, J. S., 244
Baier, K. M., 32
Baillie, J., 48f., 172ff., 180
Barth, K., 82, 141, 144, 366ff.
Belloc, H., 216
Bentham, J., 312, 384
Berdyaev, N., 183, 195
Berkeley, G., 53
Blackstone, W., 384
Blake, W., 91
Boyle, R., 53
Bradley, F. H., 85, 208
Braithwaite, R. B., 9, 35f., *53-73*, 74ff., *88-94*, 145, 162, 165, 172f., 193f.
Brooks, C., 187
Brown, Patterson, 157ff., 170f.
Browne, Sir Thomas, 104, 118
Brunner, E., 141, 144
Bryson, L., 140
Buddhism, 27ff., 31, 66
Bunyan, J., 68, 79, 106

Burke, E., 198
Butler, J., 9, 82

Caesar, J., 80
Cajetan, 82
Camus, A., 139, 319
Claver, St Peter, 316
Churchill, W. S., 33, 130
Clemenceau, 116
Commands, 32ff., 39, 48f., 97, 99, 140ff., 150, 152f., 168ff.
Commitment, 46, 60ff., 158, 162, 392ff.
Confucius, 41
Conscience, 34, ch. 10, 173, 176, 287, 335, 390
Contraception, 348ff.
Copleston, F. C., 144f., 148
Crombie, I. M., *234-61*

David, 347
Dawson, C., 379f.
Deists, 9, 119, 329
Dennes, W. R., 140
Devil, 175, 324
Dinah, 347
Dostoevsky, F., 68, 76, 79, 123, 324
Dunstan, G. R., 393
Duty, 10, 166f., 228ff., 232, 262ff., 272ff.

Eddington, A. S., 53f.
Einstein, A., 53, 90
Elijah, 56, 75, 90
Eliot, G., 192
Eliot, T. S., 188
Elizabeth, Queen, 267f.
Elton, W., 185, 208, 224

Emmet, D., 226
Empiricism, 9, ch. 3, 74, 77, 89, 140, 176, 197
Ewing, A. C., 156f., 160f., 165ff., 169f.
Existentialists, 138f., 185, 209ff., 268ff., 275ff., 300ff., 319ff., 330, 385, 394

Falk, W. D., 140
Faulkner, W., 317, 327
Field, G. C., 305ff.
Findlay, J. N., 148, 151
Flaubert, 282
Fletcher, J., 332
Flew, A., 90
Foot, P. R., 203, 292
Forster, E. M., 111
Francis, St, 223
Freud, S., 103
Fromm, E., 189
Fuchs, J., 331

Galileo, 89
Gandhi, M., 36
Gellner, E. A., 209f., 299
Gibson, A. Boyce, 36f., *113-26*
Gilson, E., 379
Goethe, 283
Graaff, G. de, 10, *31-52*, 152
Grace, 105f., 120, 177
Gregory the Great, 29

Hägerström, A., 146
Hampshire, S., 185, 207f., 224
Hardy, T., 326f.
Hare, R. M., 9f., 72, 156, 160ff., 168, 184, 201, 204, 206ff., 227, 266f., 390f.
Hart, H. L. A., 382ff., 393
Henderson, G. P., 319
Hepburn, R. W., *181-95*, 196ff., 203, 205, 207, 211, 216f., 222, 224, 226
Heteronomy (see also Autonomy), 103ff., 116, 118f., 167, 284
Hobbes, T., 97, 99, 109, 386
Hodgson, L., 370
Holland, R. F., *299-313*
Holloway, J., 183, 190
Hume, D., 53, 57f., 81, 197f., 309, 386

Ignatius Loyola, 70
Incarnation, 17, 25ff., 119, 123
Isaac, 34, 104, 130, 317
Isaiah, 33
Ishbosheth, 347

Jack, L. P., 173
Jacob, 347
James, W., 184
Jephthah, 119
Jesus (Christ), 17, 25ff., 36, 40f., 52, 64, 68f., 75ff., 79f., 83, 87, 91, 93, 119, 121, 127, 131f., 148, 179, 191, 194, 211, 219, 223, 232, 316, 324, 334, 341, 343, 347f., 374, 376, 383, 395f.
John of the Cross, St, 70, 81
Joseph, H. W. B., 196, 307
Jung, C., 212

Kant, I., 38ff., 43, 48ff., 57, 81, 89, 95, 116, 126, 153, 156, 164, 167, 197f., 211, 225, 238, 299, 303ff., 314, 319
Keats, J., 190
Kierkegaard, S., 138, 190, 208, 299ff., 305, 307ff., 315ff., 319, 327
Kirk, K. E., 361, 370
Knight, M., 51
Knox, J., 395
Koestler, A., 183

Laban, 347
Laird, J., 193
Law and laws, moral, 12, 34, 41f., 45ff., 51, 166, 336ff.
Law, W., 9
Lawrence, D. H., 109, 283
Lazerowitz, M., 272
Lemmon, J., *262-79*
Lewis, C. S., 64
Lewis, H. D., *172-80*
Lindsay, A. D., 118, 185, 191f.
Locke, J., 53
Love, 25, 35ff., 42, 52, 63ff., 76, 81, 83, 85ff., 92ff., 118, 123ff., 145, 233, 300, 314ff., 332, 335
Lucas, J. R., *126-32*

MacDonald, G., 64
MacIntyre, A., 90
Mackinnon, D. M., *77-84*, 90ff.
Maclagan, W. G., 10f., 36, 152ff., 157, 160, 169, 171
McTaggart, J. M. E., 61, 143
Mairet, P., 275
Mahler, G., 43
Mann, T., 105, 111
Marcel, G., 185, 190, 208
Marriage, 110ff., 123ff., 129, 300, 341ff.
Mary, Virgin, 91
Mascall, E. L., 145

Melden, A. I., 134ff., 139, 228
Mill, J. S., 53, 64, 93, 143, 189f., 197f., 312, 384
Mitchell, B., 40
Moral education, 37, 51f., 96, 100ff., 105ff., 115
Moore, G. E., 156, 196, 204
Mortimer, R. C., 12f., 356
Muir, E., 182f., 186, 190, 194f.
Murdoch, I., *195-218*, 226f.
Mystical, 17, 27ff., 42

Napoleon, 206
Nédoncelle, M., 208
Needham, J., 54
Newton, I., 90, 244
Nielsen, K., 133, *140-51*, 158f., 170
Nietzsche, 126, 282
Nineham, D. E., 395f.
Nobakov, V., 206
Nowell-Smith, P. H., 10, 73, *95-112*, 113ff., 133, 153, 155, 159, 170, 184
Numinous, 17, 19, 21, 173, 177

Obligation, 5of., 139, 149f., 159, 174, 263ff., 272ff., 287, 289, 389ff.
Oppenheimer, H., *219-33*

Pascal, B., 282
Passmore, J. A., 146
Paton, H. J., 310
Paul, St, 33, 75, 114f., 127ff., 132, 194, 347f., 369
Penelhum, T., 145
Phillips, D. Z., *133-39, 314-28*
Piaget, J., 100ff., 109, 111, 113, 116
Pilate, Pontius, 80
Pittenger, W. N., 395
Pius XII, Pope, 329, 331
Plato, 95, 109, 140f., 148, 243, 270, 299, 306ff.
Polus, 311
Prichard, H. A., 196, 309ff.

Ramsey, I. T., *9-13, 84-8*, 9off., *152-71, 382-96*
Raphael, 223
Rees, D. A., 140, 143, 148
Rees, R., 135
Rizpah, 347
Robinson, J. A. T., 12, 332
Robinson, R., 11, 170
Roosevelt, F. D., 130
Ross, W. D., 196

Rousselot, P., 208
Rule, golden, 238-41
Rules, 12, 15, 98ff., 108ff., 113ff., 123ff., 127, 131, 178, 181, 191ff., 205ff., 209, 222, 229, 232, 245ff., 279, 284ff., 332
Russell, B., 53, 140f., 143, 158, 197, 283
Ryle, G., 200

Samson, 347
Sartre, J.-P., 126, 190, 268f., 275ff.
Saul, 347
Scheler, M., 319
Schofield, J. N., *74-7*, 89f.
Schopenhauer, A., 147
Shaftesbury, Lord, 67, 69ff., 81, 87, 153
Shakespeare, 283
Shechem, 347
Smart, Ninian, 10, *15-30*, 140
Socrates, 266f., 299, 302, 306f., 309, 311f.
Solomon, 347
Spender, S., 183
Stories (parables, fables), 66ff., 76, 79ff., 86f., 91, 165, ch. 11
Strawson, P. F., *280-98*

Taylor, A. E., 196
Thrasymachus, 95, 309f.
Thucydides, 320
Tillich, P., 172, 332
Tindal, M., 9
Toland, J., 9
Tolstoy, 111, 283, 326f.
Trethowan, I., 159f., 166

Universalizability, 161ff., 208, 227
Urmson, J. O., 228

Variegation of discourse, 10, 16, 384
Verification principle, 54-9, 76
Vincent de Paul, St, 316

Waismann, F., 54
Webb, C. C. J., 232
Weil, S., 316, 319ff.
Weldon, T. D., 204
Welsh, P., 189
Wilde, O., 190
Wisdom, J. T., 226
Wittgenstein, L., 57f., 217, 322, 384
Worship, 19ff., 148ff., 151, 174

Yeats, W. B., 183, 193, 195